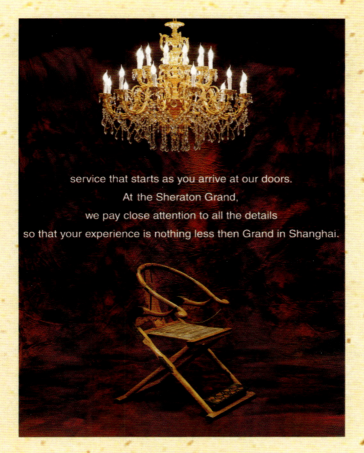

WHO'S WHO IN CHINA

Editorial Team

Published by Inspire Publishing Private Limited
Copyright © 2004 by Inspire Publishing Private Limited

Editor-in-Chief	Gerald Leong
Managing Editors	Li Xuan Xuan (Lauren), Chuan Yeh Chiang (Sheldon)
Senior Editorial Consultant	Holger Grimme
Research Editors	Wanyan Shaohua, Mao Feng (Marc), Ruth Saw
Copy Editors	Yeo Siew Chya (Noelle), CK Chong
Art Consultant	MCN Creatives
Designer	Lee Ai Li (Racheal)
Marketing	Koh Jia Yen (Pearlyn), Ruth Saw, Ng Su-lin

Please direct any comments, questions, or suggestions regarding this publication to:

Editorial Department
Inspire Publishing Pte Ltd
39 Jalan Pemimpin
#04-03 Tai Lee Building
Singapore 577182
T (65) 6358 2289
F (65) 6353 2542
info@inspire-publishing.com

All rights reserved. No part of this publication may be reproduced or used in any form or by any means, electronic or mechanical, including photocopy, recording or any other information storage and retrieval system, without the prior written permission of the publisher. Product or company names and brands mentioned herein are the trademarks or registered trademarks of their respective owners.

Inspire Publishing Private Limited including its employees, shareholders, advisers, information providers, agents and the editorial team cannot accept any responsibilitiy for any loss, injury or inconvenience caused to or suffered whatsoever arising from any errors, representations, opinions, profiles, inaccuracies, omissions, corporate structures, shareholdings, analyses or information of any kind whatsoever that is contained in or arising from this publication. All such informatiion contained herein are based on sources believed to be reliable but has not been independently verified and there is no warranty on the veracity or accuracy of any of the information contained herein. Information contained in this book is not intended to be investment advice of any kind whatsoever and no responsibility shall be accepted whatsoever for any loss, injury or inconvenience caused to or suffered.

Inspire Publishing Private Limited cannot and do not advocate any commercial dealings with any individuals or organisations or corporates represented in this publication nor does the reference or inclusion of a link to any web site(s), email addresses or resources imply any form of endorsement by Inspire Publishing Private Limited.

ISBN 981-05-0509-4

Foreword

China's transformation from a planned to a market economy is beyond the point of no return. Since reforms began in 1978, the state's share of China's economic activity has dropped from 80 percent to less than 30 percent in 2000. Enterprises large and small are forming, restructuring and equipping themselves for market competition.

Already, enterprises such as PetroChina and Ping An are vying to become national champions. Still others, such as Haier, Legend, and Hua Wei, have taken bold steps to conquer international markets. Which of these companies will become global champions? Will they surpass incumbent MNCs to be leaders in their respective industries? If so, when?

Although difficult to bet on specific answers, we can be a lot more certain in predicting that a generation of global champions will emerge from the Chinese economy in the next decade or two. Far more impressive than the growth rate of their revenues and their ambitious plans are the vigour and rigour with which these enterprises and scores of others like them are systematically reforming their business processes, expanding their product lines and building the capabilities needed to win in the global marketplace.

Behind this driving energy is a new generation of business and business-related leaders who are dedicated to the task of transforming their enterprises into global champions with the zeal of missionaries.

This book is about introducing the leading men and women behind these enterprises and describing their already impressive accomplishments so that readers can follow their careers more easily going forward. Whether you are a potential partner, a competitor, or just an interested observer, it pays to know who you are dealing with in China.

Hsieh Tsun-yan
McKinsey & Co

Hsieh Tsun-yan *is a Director and Chairman of Asia for McKinsey & Co, an international consulting firm. He has close to 25 years of consulting experience with global MNCs and Asian enterprises and is a counsel to top business leaders.*

Preface

Research, analyses and rankings were carried out by the editorial team of Gerald Leong, Li Xuan Xuan (Lauren), Wanyan Shaohua, Yeo Siew Chya (Noelle), Chuan Yeh Chiang (Sheldon), Ruth Saw, Mao Feng (Marc) and Chong CK.

Personalities featured in this publication are all Mainland Chinese. The definition of a Mainland Chinese for the purpose of this book is someone born in China or a citizen of China whose main business or work is in China. China-born individuals who are no longer citizens and who spent a significant amount of time outside China are excluded.

In putting the profiles and analyses together, the team met with companies, entrepreneurs, journalists, government bureaus and numerous other sources to build up an extensive database and profile of China's influential. The team also relied on Chinese and English publications including newspapers, magazines, stock market information, statistics, expert opinions, articles and books for their analyses and research materials.

Rankings and assessment of net worth were based on Inspire Publishing's analyses of publicly available information and selected business publications including *Forbes* magazine, *Asiamoney* and other sources. Where net worth of those featured were estimated from their shareholdings of publicly listed companies, the most recent market value of the company up to the editorial cut-off date was used. For non-listed companies, the valuations of these companies were based on an average of comparable listed companies.

Photographs were provided by either Phototex or Photocom. Currency conversions were made at the rate of US$1 : RMB 8.28. The *pinyin* spelling is used for Chinese names. English names are included where applicable.

The research and analyses of this edition of Who's Who in China are based on available information that is current as at 1 May, 2004. Most China companies have not published their financial results for 2003 and as such, 2002 figures represent the latest available at the time of the editorial cut-off date.

Whilst all possible efforts have been made to make the book comprehensive and complete, the team may not have access to all available information relating to the private wealth and relationships of certain individuals who may otherwise qualify as influential for the purpose of this book. The team will however endeavor to add these "yet-to-be discovered influential people" in future analyses.

We welcome feedback from readers on any of the individuals or companies for our next edition. Please forward your comments and suggestions to info@inspire-publishing.com

We trust our readers will find this publication useful in providing information and insights into the backgrounds of those featured and the people and organisations they are associated with.

Gerald Leong
Editor-in-Chief

Table of Contents

The Richest People in China — 1
- Ranking of the Richest People in China — 2
- Geographic Breakdown of the Richest People in China — 5
- Stock markets where China's richest people's companies are listed — 6

Manufacturing — 7
- LU Guanqiu (Wanxiang Group) — 8
- ZHANG Yin (America Chung Nam Inc) — 13
- LI Zhaohui (Shanxi Haixin Iron and Steel Group) — 15
- TAO Xinkang (Xin Gao Chao Group) — 17
- SHEN Wen (Zijiang Group) — 19
- ZHANG Yue (Broad Air Conditioning) Co Ltd — 22
- REN Yunliang (Huafeng Group) — 25
- KUANG Huizhen (Asia Aluminum Holdings) — 27
- WU Ying (UTStarcom) — 29
- ZHU Baoguo (Joincare Pharmaceutical Group) — 32
- WU Liangding (Zhongbao Group) — 34
- HUANG Hongsheng, Stephen (Skyworth Digital Holdings) — 37
- GU Chujun (Greencool Group) — 40
- DUAN Yongping (BBK Electronics Corp) — 44
- ZHANG Yang (Interchina Holdings) — 46
- YIN Mingshan (Lifan Group) — 49
- REN Zhengfei (Huawei Technologies) — 51

Real Estate — 53
- XU Rongmao (Shimao Group) — 54
- YE Lipei, Eddie (Super Ocean Group) — 56
- CHEN Lihua (Fu Hua International HK Group) — 58
- ZHU Mengyi (Hopson Development Holdings) — 60
- ZHOU Jianhe (Junefield Group) — 63
- TONG Jinquan (Changfeng Group) — 65
- ZHOU Zerong (Kingold Group) — 66
- CHEN Jinfei (Tongchan Investment Group) — 69
- CHEN Zhuoxian (Agile Holdings) — 71
- HAN Guolong (Citichamp Holdings) — 72
- HUANG Guangyu (Pengrun Group) — 74
- MIAO Shouliang (Shenzhen Fuyuan Group) — 78
- SONG Weiping (Greentown Group) — 81

Agriculture — 82
- LIU Yonghao (New Hope Group) — 84
- LIU Yongxing (East Hope Group) — 87
- LIU Hanyuan (Tongwei Group) — 89
- GUO Hao (Chaoda Modern Agriculture Holdings) — 92

Information Technology — 94
- DING Lei, William (Netease.com) — 95
- CHEN Tianqiao (Shanda Networking Development) — 98
- ZHANG Chaoyang, Charles (Sohu.com) — 100

INSPIRE PUBLISHING WHO'S WHO IN CHINA

Investment Management — 104
    ANG Wanli, TANG Wanxin brothers (D'Long International Strategic Investment) — 105
    LV Xiangyang (Youngy Investment & Management Group) — 107
    DAI Zhikang (Zendai Investment Group) — 109

Food & Beverage — 112
    MING Jinxing (People's Food Holdings) — 113
    ZHU Yicai (Jiangsu Yurun Food Group) — 115
    ZONG Qinghou (Wahaha Group) — 117

General industries — 119
    RONG Zhijian, Larry (CITIC Pacific) — 120
    SUN Guangxin (Guanghui Enterprise Group) — 124
    GUO Guangchang (Shanghai Fosun High-Tech Group) — 127
    XU Ming (Shide Group) — 130
    ZHANG Yong (Linfeng Group) — 134
    WANG Yusuo (XinAo Group) — 136
    JIAN Yinghai (Jian Enterprise Group) — 138

Leaders of China's Largest Companies — 141
    Top 100 Companies in China — 142
    Geographic Breakdown of China's Largest Companies — 144
    Where China's Largest Companies are Listed — 145

Electronics — 146
    ZHANG Ruimin (Haier Group) — 147
    LIU Chuanzhi (Legend Group) — 151
    YANG Yuanqing (Legend Group) — 154
    LI Dongsheng (TCL Group) — 156
    ZHOU Houjian (Hisense Group) — 158
    TAO Jianxin (Chunlan Group) — 161
    OUYANG Zhongmou (China Putian Corporation) — 163

Financial Services — 166
    JIANG Jianqing (Industrial and Commercial Bank of China) — 167
    WANG Xianzhang (China Life Insurance Company) — 170
    XIAO Gang (Bank of China) — 172
    ZHANG Enzhao (China Construction Bank) — 175
    YANG Mingsheng (Agricultural Bank of China) — 177
    MA Mingzhe (China Ping An Insurance Co Ltd) — 179
    FANG Chengguo (Bank of Communications) — 181

Power and Natural Resources — 182
    CHEN Geng (China National Petroleum Corporation) — 183
    CHEN Tonghai (Sinopec Group) — 185
    LIU Deshu (SinoChem Corporation) — 187
    ZHOU Mingchen (China National Cereals, Oils and Foodstuffs Import & Export Corporation) — 191
    XIE Qihua (Shanghai Baosteel Group) — 195
    LI Xiaopeng (China Huaneng Group) — 198

Telecommunications and Postal Services — 200
    ZHANG Ligui (China Mobile Communication Corporation) — 201
    ZHOU Deqiang (China Telecommunications Corporation) — 204

ZHANG Chunjiang (China Network Communications Group Corporation)	207
LIU Andong (State Post Bureau)	209
YANG Xianzu (China United Communications Corporation)	211
Automotive	213
ZHU Yanfeng (China First Automobile Works Group Corporation)	214
HU Maoyuan (Shanghai Automotive Industry Corporation)	217
JIANG Mianheng (Shanghai Automotive Industry Corporation)	219
MIAO Wei (Dong Feng Automobile Co)	220
Transportation and Logistics	224
WEI Jiafu (China Ocean Shipping (Group) Company)	225
YAN Zhiqing (China Southern Airlines Co Ltd)	229
YE Yigan (China Eastern Airlines Co Ltd)	231
LI Jiaxiang (Air China Group Corporation)	235
Others	237
LIU Wandong (Hongta Group)	238
WANG Shi (China Vanke Co Ltd)	240
JIN Zhiguo (Tsingtao Brewery)	242

Political People — 245

State organs of the People's Republic of China (PRC)	246
Structure of the Communist Party of China (CPC) Leadership	257
Standing Committee of the Political Bureau	259
HU Jintao (President of People's Republic of China)	260
WU Bangguo (Chairman of National People's Congress)	264
WEN Jiabao (Premier of the State Council)	267
JIA Qinglin (Chairman of the Chinese People's Political Consultative Conference)	270
ZENG Qinghong (Vice President of People's Republic of China)	273
HUANG Ju (Vice Premier of the State Council)	276
WU Guanzheng (Secretary of the Central Commission for Discipline Inspection)	278
LI Changchun (Member of the Standing Committee of the Political Bureau)	282
LUO Gan (State Councillor)	285
Vice Premiers and State Councilors	289
WU Yi (Vice Premier of the State Council & Minister of Health)	290
HUI Liangyu (Vice Premier of the State Council)	293
ZENG Peiyan (Vice Premier of the State Council)	296
ZHOU Yongkang (State Councillor & Minister of Public Security)	299
TANG Jiaxuan (State Councillor)	302
HUA Jianmin (State Councillor & General Secretary of the State Council)	304
CHEN Zhili (State Councillor)	306
Military Leaders	309
JIANG Zemin (Chairman of the Central Military Commission of the PRC)	310
CAO Gangchuan (Minister of National Defence)	313
GUO Boxiong (Vice Chairman of the Central Military Commission of the PRC)	315
Ministers	317
LI Zhaoxing (Minister of Foreign Affairs)	318
MA Kai (Minister in charge of the State Development and Reform Commission)	321
ZHOU Ji (Minister of Education)	324

XU Guanhua (Minister of Science and Technology)	327
JIN Renqing (Minister of Finance)	330
WANG Guangtao (Minister of Construction)	333
LIU Zhijun (Minister of Railways)	335
ZHANG Chunxian (Minister of Communications)	336
WANG Xudong (Minister of Information Industry)	337
LV Fuyuan (Minister of Commerce)	340
ZHOU Xiaochuan (Governor of the People's Bank of China)	343
LI Jinhua (Auditor-General of the National Audit Office)	345
WU Dingfu (Chairman of China Insurance Regulatory Commission)	347
SHANG Fulin (Chairman of China Securities Regulatory Commission)	349

Local Leaders — 351

LIU Qi (Mayor of Beijing)	352
ZHANG Lichang (Mayor of Tianjin)	355
CHEN Liangyu (Mayor of Shanghai)	358
ZHANG Dejiang (Secretary of Guangdong Provincial Party Committee)	361

Other Influential People — 363

Economists — 364

LI Yining (Peking University)	365
LIN Yifu, Justin (Director of China Centre for Economic Research, Peking University)	368
WU Jinglian (Development Research Centre of the State Council)	371
ZHANG Weiying (Peking University)	373
HU Angang (Tsinghua University)	376

Educators — 379

Ranking of China's top universities	380
XU Zhihong (President of Peking University)	381
GU Binglin (President of Tsinghua University)	384
WANG Shenghong (President of Fudan University)	386
XIE Shengwu (President of Shanghai Jiaotong University)	388
JIANG Shusheng (President of Nanjing University)	390
PAN Yunhe (President of Zhejiang University)	392
ZHU Qingshi (President of University of Science and Technology of China)	394

Professionals — 396

CHEN Luming (Partner of King & Wood)	397
WANG Zilong (Founding partner of Jun He Law Offices)	398

Culture, Media and National Heroes — 401

ZHAO Huayong (President of China Central Television)	402
CHEN Kaige (Film director)	404
CUI Jian (Rock musician)	407
GONG Li (Movie actress)	409
LIU Xiaoqing (Movie actress)	412
NA Ying (Musician)	415
YANG Liping (Dance artist)	417
ZHANG Yimou (Film director)	419
ZHANG Ziyi (Movie actress)	421
YAO Ming (NBA basketball player)	424
YANG Liwei (Astronaut)	427

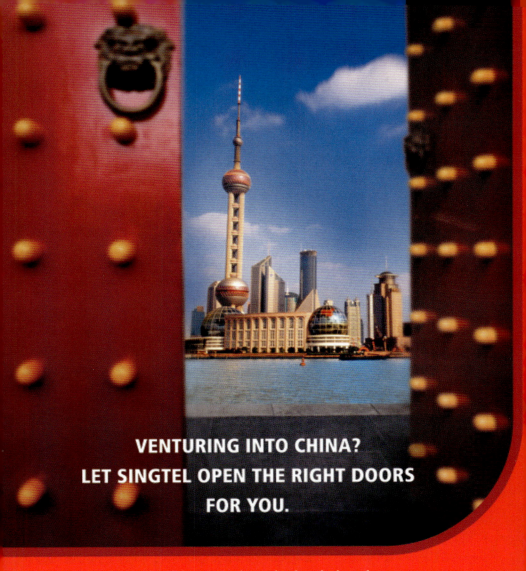

VENTURING INTO CHINA?
LET SINGTEL OPEN THE RIGHT DOORS FOR YOU.

If you are planning to venture into China, you need more than just a business plan. You need a communications partner who understands the complexities and intricacies of the Chinese market and who can tailor specialised solutions for your business.

SingTel is a one-stop communications provider with diverse, comprehensive networks and strong connectivity into China. With its strong relationships with all the local service providers and understanding of the local telecommunications environment, regulations and procedures, SingTel is more than able to provide professional and cost-efficient solutions for your business.

LET ASIA'S NO. 1 TELECOM COMPANY* HELP YOU BECOME NO.1 IN CHINA.

For more information, please contact us at:
Tel: (65)6738 3838 • Email: businessco@singtel.com • Website: www.singtel.com

* Voted "Best Asian Telecom Carrier" by Telecom Asia magazine for 6 consecutive years since 1998.

Australia • China • Hong Kong • India • Indonesia • Japan • Korea • Malaysia • Philippines • Singapore • Taiwan • Thailand • UK • USA • Vietnam

INTRODUCTION WHO'S WHO IN CHINA

Introduction

 "China returns to centre stage 145 years later"

In 1861 the Qing court established the Office for the General Management of Affairs and Trade[1] as Imperial China tried reaching out to the world.

145 years later, China joined the World Trade Organisation (WTO) in 2001 and the world's most populous nation once again reached out to trade with the rest of the world.

China's stated goal is to quadruple its GDP by 2020. If it succeeds, it will become the largest trading nation in the world. And few doubt that China will achieve this economic goal.

The enormous business potential to trade with China has drawn some RMB 4.2 trillion (US$500 billion) of foreign direct investments into the country by 2003. Many foreign companies who took the plunge in China are now profitable.

And China today is transformed. It has some of the largest companies in the world. It is a major force in world affairs. Its cultural influence is on the rise. And its sportsmen are world champions.

In this new China, who are the movers and shakers? Who are the richest people? Who controls China's most powerful companies? Who runs the country? Who are its national heroes? Who are the people shaping China's society today?

Who's Who in China has identified four groups of 148 of the most influential people in China today. These people, the companies they run, the organisations they control and the influence they wield will hold the key to how decisions in a modernising China will be made as well as provide clues to how China will change. The profiles of these small but influential group of people are arranged and presented under four sections in this book:

Section A	China's Richest People	China's richest people who made their money building private companies
Section B	Leaders of China's Largest companies	The powerful senior managers of large state-owned enterprises which have been privatised or floated
Section C	China's Political Figures	The politically powerful within the Communist Party of China (CPC), People's Republic of China (PRC) and the military
Section D	Other Influential People	Influential economists, educators, lawyers, artists, sportsmen, and national heroes who are shaping China's society

Section A and B which covers business personalities are arranged into sub-sections of relevant industry sectors. Section C is presented as sub-sections of various state organs in order of political

---

[1] This is equivalent to the establishment of a ministry of foreign affairs and diplomatic embassies around the world in today's terms.

influence. Section D is organised into the four sub-sections of economists, educators, professionals and the culture, media and national heroes.

Within each of these sections and sub-sections, the various personalities are profiled and ranked by various measures if applicable. Where relevant and possible, the corporate structures of the companies associated with those featured are included.

The richest people's profiles have been selected based on their importance and standing within their respective sectors. As such, only 50 of the top 120 richest people are profiled. The leaders of China's largest companies are also selected based on their importance and standing within their respective industries. 36 of such personalities were profiled in this publication.

We have ranked Section A's richest people by their net worth, Section B's powerful senior managers of China's largest companies by their size (sales).

We have ranked Section C's top nine political members of the Standing Committee of the CPC and the top four most influential people in the People's Liberation Army (PLA) according to what is commonly perceived as relative seniority.

No ranking is assigned to PRC governors or other CPC members outside the Standing Committee[1]. In addition, no ranking can meaningfully be assigned to Section D's other influential people which consists of economists, educators, lawyers, artists, sportsmen and national heroes and as such these personalities are not ranked.

According to *Who's Who in China* rankings and analyses:

Mr Hu Jintao, as the President of People's Republic of China, is the most powerful and influential person in China today.

The richest man in China is CITIC Pacific's Mr Rong Zhijian a.k.a. Larry Yung from Shanghai.

The most powerful man running China's largest company, China National Petroleum Corporation (CNPC), is Mr Chen Geng.

China's national treasure is basketball player, Mr Yao Ming.

Rankings will be placed inside the following colour-coded medals:

Sections	Ranked by	Medals
China's Richest People	Net worth	🟢
Leaders of China's Largest Companies	Sales of companies they manage	🔵
Political Figures	Standing Committee seniority	🔴
Military Leaders	Military rank / seniority	🟡

[1] Governors include vice premiers, state councillors, ministers and local leaders.

INTRODUCTION WHO'S WHO IN CHINA

China's richest people are not the senior executives who run the powerful state-owned enterprises (China's largest companies) but the self-made millionaires who made their money building private companies in sectors such as property, IT, agriculture and manufacturing.

The aggregate net worth of China's wealthiest 120 citizens is estimated to be RMB 225 billion (US$27 billion) or 3% of the estimated RMB 9.1 trillion (US$1.1 trillion) net worth of the top 120 richest people in the world.

China's richest man, Mr Rong Zhijian's net worth of US$975 million is about 2% of the world's richest man, Mr William Gates[1] or 8% of Mr Li Ka-Shing's[2]. Mr Rong Zhijian is ranked 514th richest man in the world compared to Hong Kong's richest man, Mr Li Ka-Shing, who is ranked 19th richest man in the world[3].

The giant state-owned enterprises contributing the most to China's economic charge comes mostly from six sectors: consumer electronics, financial services, oil and gas, telecommunications, automotive manufacturing and transportation.

Behind the successes of these state-owned and private enterprises is the powerful government as well the people who are shaping the country's culture, arts and the sports. 37 political and 25 of such other influential people are featured in this publication.

Out of all these, Chinese leaders are gaining global influence and China's companies have already become world-beaters such as TCL - the largest TV maker in the world, Haier - the largest referigator manufacturer in the world and China Mobile - the largest GSM player in the world.

China, has indeed returned to centre stage.

[1] Net worth of US$46.6 billion, Forbes magazine, February 2004.
[2] 19th richest man in the world with net worth of US$12.4 billion, Forbes magazine, February 2004.
[3] Forbes magazine, February 2004.

The Richest People in China

China's rapid economic growth has created numerous entrepreneurs who have gone on to become some of the richest people in China.

While a few of these have political ties, most had their lives and education interrupted for close to a decade during the Cultural Revolution. But they all bounced back when China's late leader Deng Xiaoping launched market reforms over two decades ago.

By 2001, Jiang Zemin acknowledged the growing role of entrepreneurs in China's economic growth and paved the way for them to become party members in China's Communist Party.

Unlike the powerful senior management of large state-owned enterprises or influential government officials, these millionaires come from all walks of life. And every one of them created their own opportunities whether in the agri-business feeding China's population or the booming property market.

The stories behind this new class of the influential provide the perfect entree into the exciting world of China's Who's Who.

CHINA'S RICHEST PEOPLE   WHO'S WHO IN CHINA

Ranking of the Richest People in China

Rank	Name	Company	Estimated Net Worth[1]		No. of mentions (2001-2003)[2]
			RMB billion	US$ million	
1	Rong Zhijian, Larry*	CITIC Pacific	8.07	975	3
2	Ding Lei, William*	Netease.com	7.60	918	1
3	Xu Rongmao*	Shimao Group	6.71	810	3
4	Lu Guanqiu*	Wanxiang Group	5.54	669	3
5	Liu Yonghao*	New Hope Group	4.68	565	3
6	Ye Lipei, Eddie*	Super Ocean Group	4.15	501	2
7	Liu Yongxing*	East Hope Group	4.06	490	3
8	Chen Tianqiao*	Shanda Networking Development	4.02	485	1
9	Chen Lihua*	Fu Wah International HK Group	3.90	471	3
10	Zhou Jianhe*	Junefield Group	3.48	420	1
11	Zhu Mengyi*	Hopson Development Holdings	3.29	397	2
12	Guo Guangchang*	Shanghai Fosun High-Tech Group	3.15	380	3
13	Sun Guangxin*	Guanghui Enterprise Group	3.14	379	3
14	Xu Ming*	Shide Group	2.80	338	3
15	Liu Hanyuan*	Tongwei Group	2.73	330	3
16	Ming Jinxing*	People's Food Holdings	2.54	307	3
17	Zhang Yong*	Linfeng Group	2.49	301	2
18	Yang Zhuoshu	Zhuoda Group	2.48	300	3
18	Zhang Yin*	America Chung Nam Inc	2.48	300	1
20	Li Zhaohui*	Shanxi Haixin Iron and Steel Group	2.40	290	2
21	Tong Jinquan*	Changfeng Property	2.28	275	1
22	Zhang Chaoyang, Charles*	Sohu	2.22	268	1
23	Liu Genshan	Maosheng International Group	2.17	262	2
24	Wang Chuanfu[3]	BYD Co Ltd	2.17	262	2
25	Tao Xinkang*	Xin Gao Chao Group	2.09	253	3
26	Shen Wen*	Zijiang Group	2.00	242	3
27	Zhou Zerong*	Kingold Group	1.99	240	1
28	Ye Weichen, David	United Food Holdings	1.96	237	3
29	Wang Yusuo*	XinAo Group	1.90	230	3
30	Guan Lingxiang	Full Apex Holdings	1.90	230	1
31	Zhang Fu'en	Lungchuan International	1.90	229	1
32	Guo Hao*	Chaoda Modern Agriculture Holdings	1.86	225	3
33	Zhu Yicai*	Jiangsu Yurun Food Group	1.84	222	3
34	Huo Dongling	Comba Telecom Systems	1.84	222	1
35	Zhang Yue*	Broad Air Conditioning Co Ltd	1.79	216	3
36	Chen Jinfei*	Tongchan Investment Group	1.78	215	3
37	Miao Shouliang*	Shenzhen Fuyuan Group	1.78	215	3
38	Chen Zhuoxian*	Agile Holdings	1.78	215	1
39	Tang Wangli/Tang Wangxin*	D'Long International Strategic Investment	1.76	212	3
40	Huang Guangyu*	Pengrun Group	1.69	204	3
41	Liu Changle	Phoenix Satellite TV	1.60	193	1
42	Ren Yunliang*	Huafeng Group	1.60	193	3

[1] *Forbes, Asiamoney / Inspire Publishing* analysis.
[2] Based on annual appearances on selected net worth rankings. This is an indication of net worth consistency over 2001-2003.
[3] See Mr Lv Xiangyang of Youngy Investment and Management Group
* Featured in **Who's Who in China**

CHINA'S RICHEST PEOPLE WHO'S WHO IN CHINA

Rank	Name	Company	Estimated Net Worth		No. of mentions (2001-2003)
			RMB billion	US$ million	
43	Liang Liansheng	C-Bons Group	1.59	192	2
43	Kuang Huizhen*	Asia Aluminium Holdings	1.59	192	1
43	Mi Enhua	Xinjiang Hualing Group	1.59	192	3
46	Xu Jiayin	Hengda Group	1.57	190	1
47	Huang Junqin	Beijing Towercrest Real Estate	1.55	187	1
48	Han Guolong*	Citichamp Holdings	1.54	186	2
49	Wu Ying*	UTStarcom	1.52	183	3
50	Lv Xiangyang*	Youngy Investment & Management Group	1.50	181	2
50	Zhu Baoguo*	Joincare Pharmaceutical Group	1.50	181	3
50	Lu Zhiqiang	China Oceanwide Group	1.50	181	3
50	Wu Bingxin	Sanzhu Group	1.50	181	1
50	Li Yongjun	Strong Group	1.50	181	1
55	Liu Shaoxi	Yihua Group	1.49	180	3
55	Zhou Qingzhi	Narada Group	1.49	180	3
55	Dai Zhikang*	Zendai Investment Group	1.49	180	1
58	Zhang Rongkun	Fuxi Investment & Feidian Investment	1.47	178	2
59	Jian Yinghai*	Jian Enterprise Group	1.45	175	3
59	Xia Chaojia	Hejia Group	1.45	175	3
61	Wu Liangding*	Zhongbao Group	1.44	174	3
62	Zhang Simin	Neptunus Group	1.37	165	3
63	Zhang Zhiting	Guizhou Shenqi Group	1.35	163	1
63	Ou Yaping	Sinolink Worldwide Holdings	1.35	163	2
65	Huang Hongsheng, Stephen*	Skyworth Digital Holdings	1.34	162	2
65	Hu Chengzhong	Delixi Group	1.34	162	3
67	Dou Zhenggang	Hangzhou Jinjiang Group	1.33	161	1
68	Wu Yijian	Ginwa Group	1.32	159	3
69	Han Zhenfa	Zhengye Group	1.31	158	3
69	Shen Wenrong	Jiangsu Shangang Group	1.31	158	1
71	Li Jinyuan	Tiens Group	1.30	157	2
72	Zhang Guoxi	Guoxi Group	1.29	156	3
73	Li Xinyan	China Longgong Group	1.28	155	1
73	Song Weiping*	Greentown Group	1.28	155	2
75	Gu Chujun*	Greencool Group	1.26	152	2
76	Zhang Lei	Modern Group	1.25	151	2
76	Zong Qinghou*	Wahaha Group	1.25	151	1
78	Gao Yuankun	Linuo Group	1.24	150	2
78	Zhu Jun	The 9	1.24	150	1
78	Liu Xiaoming	Global Bio-Chem Technology	1.24	150	1
81	Liang Xinjun	Shanghai Fosun High-Tech Group	1.23	148	1
82	Huo Chichang	New Zhongyuan Group	1.20	145	1
83	Liu Han and Liu Canglong	Hanlong Group and Hongda Group	1.20	145	1
83	Liu Zhongtian	Liaoning Zhongwang Group	1.20	145	1
83	Shi Jinxiu	Jinxiu Group	1.20	145	1

CHINA'S RICHEST PEOPLE WHO'S WHO IN CHINA

Rank	Name	Company	Estimated Net worth RMB billion	Estimated Net worth US$ million	No. of mentions (2001-2003)
83	Su Zhigang	Chime-Long Group	1.20	145	1
83	Yang Shuping	City Key Group	1.20	145	1
83	Zhang Li	R&F Properties Group	1.20	145	1
83	Zhang Liangbin/Zhang Bin	Sichuan Lixin Investment	1.20	145	1
90	Lou Zhongfu	Guangsha Holdings	1.19	144	3
91	Lily Huang	Norstar Group	1.14	138	1
92	Lan Weiguang	Sinomem Technology	1.13	137	1
93	Zhang Zhixiang	Jianlong Steel	1.11	134	2
94	Liang Wengen	Sany Group	1.10	133	1
94	Zuo Zongshen	Zongshen Group	1.10	133	3
94	Du Sha	Home World Group	1.10	133	2
94	Chen Wwedong	Wanji Group	1.10	133	1
98	Duan Yongping*	BBK Electronics Corp	1.09	132	1
99	Chen Jian	Unionfriend Group	1.08	130	1
99	Shi Shanlin	Changning Group	1.08	130	1
101	Zhou Liankui / Zhou Lianliang	People's Food Holdings	1.06	128	3
102	Shi Wenbo	Hengan International Group	1.04	126	1
103	Shi Yuewu	Zhenxing Group	1.03	124	1
104	Ou Junfa	Global Bio-Chem Technology	1.01	122	1
105	Sun Hongbin	Sunco Investment	1.00	121	3
106	Zan Shengda	Zongyi Group	0.99	120	3
106	Rong Hai	Seastar Group	0.99	120	3
106	Guo Jiaxue	Topsun Group	0.99	120	2
106	Wei Jianjun	Great Wall Automobile Holding	0.99	120	1
106	Xu Maogen	Zhejiang Yuandong Chemical Fibers	0.99	120	1
106	Zhou Yiming	Minglun Group	0.99	120	1
106	Cao Mingfang	Plastic Mould Group	0.99	120	1
106	Zhang Yang*	Interchina Holdings	0.99	120	1
114	Song Dianquan	Coslight Tech International	0.99	119	1
115	Xu Zilian	Hengan International Group	0.96	116	1
116	Han Wenchen	Baoye Group	0.95	115	1
116	Lin Weixiong	Welsun Group	0.95	115	1
116	Wang Yang	Xinyu Group	0.95	115	1
116	Zhang Guofang	Guofang Group	0.95	115	1
120	Shen Jiasang	Wah Sang Gas Holdings	0.94	113	2
120	Yin Mingshan*	Lifan Group	0.94	113	3
122	Li Xinghao	China Chigo Air	0.93	112	2
122	Feng Guangcheng	Guangyu Group	0.93	112	1
124	Nan Cunhui	Chint Group	0.91	110	3
124	Zhang Hongwei	Orient Group	0.91	110	3
126	Wang Chunming	Guodong Group	0.86	104	1
127	Ma Huateng	Tencent	0.83	100	1
127	Zhang Kaiyong	Zhongkezhi Group	0.83	100	1

Note: Ren Zhengfei of Huawei Technologies is featured although unranked

CHINA'S RICHEST PEOPLE WHO'S WHO IN CHINA

Geographic Breakdown of the Richest People's Companies in China [1]

Province/Country	Number of Companies	Province/Country	Number of Companies
Guangdong	27	Shaanxi	3
Hong Kong	16	Tianjin	3
Shanghai	13	Xinjiang	3
Zhejiang	12	Chongqing	2
Beijing	11	Hunan	2
Sichuan	6	Shanxi	2
Hebei	5	U.S.A.	2
Jiangsu	4	Gansu	1
Shandong	4	Guizhou	1
Fujian	3	Hubei	1
Heilongjiang	3	Jilin	1
Liaoning	3	Singapore	1

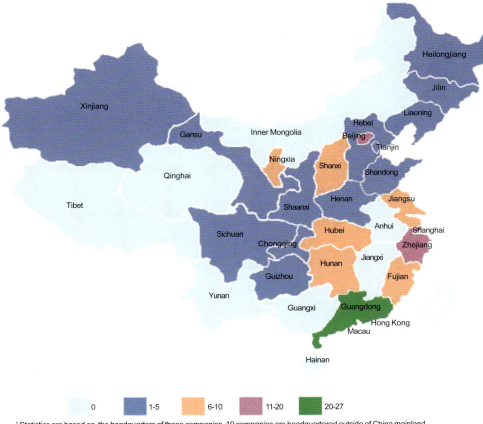

Legend: 0 | 1-5 | 6-10 | 11-20 | 20-27

[1] Statistics are based on the headquarters of these companies. 19 companies are headquartered outside of China mainland (i.e. in Hong Kong, USA, and Singapore).

CHINA'S RICHEST PEOPLE WHO'S WHO IN CHINA

Stock markets where China's richest people's companies are listed

Name	Shanghai	Shenzhen	Hong Kong	Singapore	NASDAQ
Wanxiang Group LU Guanqiu	✓	✓			✓
America Chung Nam Inc ZHANG Yin					
Shanxi Haixin Iron and Steel Group LI Zhaohui					
Xin Gao Chao Group TAO Xinkang					
Zijiang Group SHEN Wen	✓				
Broad Air Conditioning Co Ltd ZHANG Yue					
Huafeng Group REN Yunliang					
Asia Aluminium Holdings KUANG Huizhen			✓		
UTStarcom WU Ying					✓
Joincare Pharmaceutical Group ZHU Baoguo	✓	✓			
Zhongbao Group WU Liangding					
Skyworth Digital Holdings HUANG Hongsheng, Stephen			✓		
Greencool Group GU Chujun		✓✓	✓		
BBK Electronics Corp DUAN Yongping					
Interchina Holdings ZHANG Yang			✓✓		
Lifan Group YIN Mingshan					
Huawei Technologies REN Zhengfei					
Shimao Group XU Rongmao	✓		✓		
Fu Hua International HK Group CHEN Lihua					
Super Ocean Group YE Lipei, Eddie					
Hopson Development ZHU Mengyi			✓		
Junefield Group ZHOU Jianhe					
Changfeng Group TONG Jinquan					
Kingold Group ZHOU Zerong					
Tongchan Investment Group CHENG Jinfei					
Agile Holdings Chen Zhuoxian					
Citichamp Holdings HAN Guolong	✓				
Pengrun Group HUANG Guangyu					
Shenzhen Fuyuan Group MIAO Shouliang					
Greentown Group SONG Weiping					
New Hope Group LIU Yonghao	✓	✓			
East Hope Group LIU Yongxing					
Tongwei Group LIU Hanyuan					
Chaoda Modern Agriculture Holdings GUO Hao			✓		
Netease.com DING Lei, William					✓
Shanda Networking Development CHEN Tianqiao					
Sohu.com ZHANG Chaoyang, Charles					✓
D'Long International Strategic Investment TANG Wanli, TANG Wanxin	✓✓	✓✓✓			
Youngy Investment & Management Group LV Xiangyang					
Zendai Investment Group DAI Zhikang			✓		
People's Food Holdings MING Kamxing			✓	✓	
Jiangsu Yurun Food Group ZHU Yicai			✓		
Wahaha Group ZONG Qinghou					
CITIC Pacific Group RONG Zhijian, Larry			✓		
Guanghui Enterprise Group SUN Guangxin					
Shanghai Fosun High-Tech Group GUO Guangchang	✓				
Shide Group XU Ming	✓✓				
Linfeng Group ZHANG Yong	✓				
XinAo Group WANG Yusuo	✓				
Jian Enterprise Group JIAN Yinghai	✓				

✓ denotes the number of listings including subsidiaries

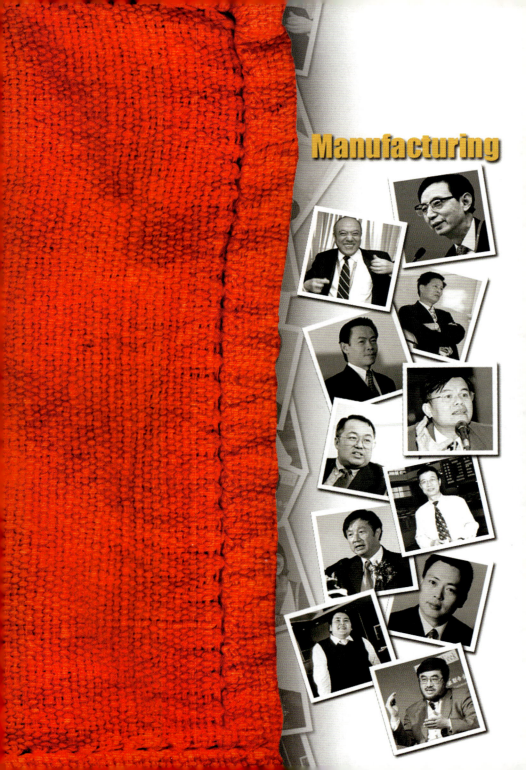

Manufacturing

"Knowing how to make money in China is not real ability; the truly capable individual should head for the overseas market and make money there."

Mr Lu Guanqiu

CHINA'S RICHEST PEOPLE WHO'S WHO IN CHINA

Lu Guanqiu Wanxiang Group
"Manufacturer extraordinaire"

#4

Corporate position   Chairman of Wanxiang Group

Net worth   RMB 5.5 billion (US$669 million)

Having braved numerous uncertainties in the past, Mr Lu Guanqiu's luminary accomplishments in his 30-year career is nothing short of extraordinary.

A Zhejiang farmer's son, Mr Lu managed to build a small bicycle repair shop into a top 500 China enterprise and automotive parts giant. Today, he is ranked No. 4 among China's richest people and is estimated to possess a net worth of RMB 5.5 billion (US$669 million).

Mr Lu started his own business shortly after completing his secondary school studies. His first venture involved setting up a rice and flour-processing factory. This nearly bankrupted him when it was alleged that he operated an underground black market factory.[1] Not one to be embittered in setbacks, Mr Lu merely took this hiccup in stride. In 1969 he took over a machinery repair factory. This pivotal period paved the way for his future involvement in the automotive parts industry.

In 1980 Mr Lu got his lucky break when he was asked by the local government to run what was previously the Ningwei Machinery Repair Factory. He spent the next few years restructuring the company which he re-named Wanxiang Universal Joint Factory. The company was successful and soon developed into a major domestic automotive parts player. The company was subsequently listed on the Shenzhen Stock Exchange.

Ever ready for competition, Mr Lu has been preparing the Wanxiang Group since China entered the WTO. He commented, "The challenge will always be there. We cannot avoid it. In the past it used to be long distance competition, now it is zero distance competition. Domestic market competition has turned into international competition and international competition has been brought into China. We must be ready to deal with this competition."

While Mr Lu is a familiar face in China's manufacturing world, he has also been successful in his political endeavours. As a delegate to the National People's Congress, he has been actively lobbying the government for a broader private sector prerogative that would help create more jobs. The Wanxiang Group today has 26 companies overseas and Mr Lu is set on building his company into a major automotive parts manufacturer in the future.

---

[1] Ma Hongtao, *Half An Hour About Economics*, CCTV, 27th December 2001

Sheraton Grand Tai Ping Yang Hotel Shanghai, an Int'l 5-star hotel sits strategically between downtown and Hongqiao Int'l Airport (12mins), and the new citywide freeway which provides easy access to Pudong Int'l Airport (45mins) and SNIEC Pudong (35mins). Shanghai Intex, Shanghai Int'l Trade Center, Shanghaimart, and nearby shopping centers are all within walking distance. The Sheraton Grand offers 496 elegant and comfortable guestrooms including suites with 9 restaurant & lounge/bar. It also boasts a Grand Ballroom and 13 meeting rooms with total space area of 1,452sqm.

A GREAT HOTEL BECAME GRAND
(Formerly The Westin Tai Ping Yang)

5 Zunyi Nan Road
Shanghai 200336 P.R. China
Tel: 86 21 6275 8888
Fax: 86 21 6275 5420
EMAIL: sheratongrand@uninet.com.cn
WEB: www.sheratongrand-shanghai.com

CHINA'S RICHEST PEOPLE WHO'S WHO IN CHINA

Birth date	January 1945
Hometown	Hangzhou city, Zhejiang Province
Education	Junior High School
	Honorary Ph.D., Hong Kong University of Science and Technology

Background

1965-1969	General manager of a small rice & flour-processing factory
1969-1979	General manager, Ningwei Machinery Repair Factory
1980-1989	Contracted by the China government to operate Ningwei Machinery Repair Factory (later renamed to Wanxiang Universal Joint Factory)
1988-	Took over Wanxiang Universal Joint Factory from the local government
1990-	Founded Wanxiang Group

Political affiliation

Member of the National People's Congress

Honours and awards

China's Best Entrepreneur

National Labour Model

Corporate structure of Wanxiang Group

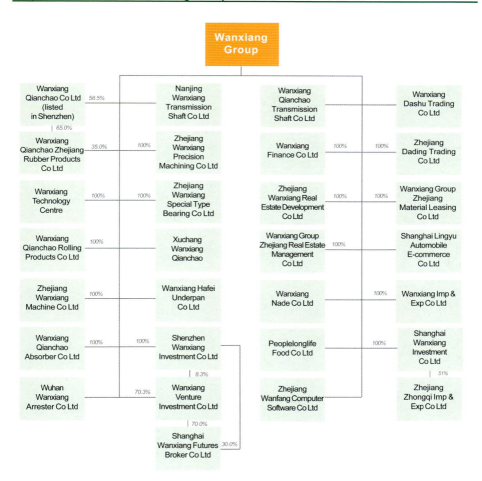

Corporate structure of Wanxiang Qianchao Co Ltd (listed in Shenzhen)

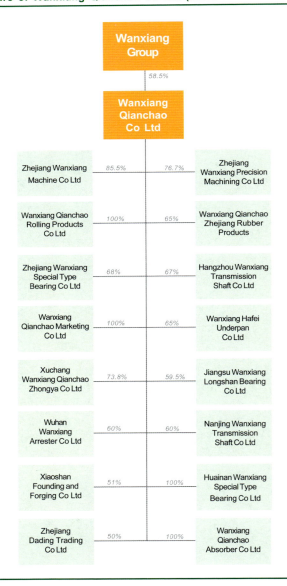

Contact information
Address Wanxiang Road, Ningwei Town, Xiaoshan City, Zhejiang, China
Telephone 86-571-8283 2999   Facsimile 86-571-8283 3999   Website www.wanxiang.com.cn

CHINA'S RICHEST PEOPLE WHO'S WHO IN CHINA

Zhang Yin America Chung Nam Inc
"The lady pulp magnate"

Corporate position	Founder and President, America Chung Nam Inc
Net worth	RMB 2.5 billion (US$300 million)

Ms Zhang Yin, the founder and president of America Chung Nam Inc, is not only one of the richest women in China, but also someone with a remarkable foresight. At a time when environmental concerns elude many, it was Ms Zhang's vision that helped build her paper recycling empire into what it is today. Ms Zhang's qualities such as her sense of self-discipline were probably instilled into her when she was a child. Born into a military family, Ms Zhang is the eldest among eight brothers and sisters[1].

She majored in finance during her university days before starting her career in Shenzhen. In 1985, Ms Zhang emigrated to Hong Kong and set up a scrap paper trading business while she was still in her twenties. Under her leadership, business flourished and the company began running paper mills in the Guangdong province.

In 1990, opportunities and prospects beckoned from America and Ms Zhang emigrated again from Hong Kong to the United States. Together with her husband, Mr Liu Mingzhong, the pair founded America Chung Nam Inc in 1990 to serve as a United States based broker securing and supplying recycled paper to mills in China. Ms Zhang noted that the United States has the largest paper manufacturing industry due to the tremendous demand for paper, which creates a unique supply of high quality waste paper for recycling. She explained that her decision to shift her supply base from Hong Kong to United States was due to the insufficient supply of recycled paper. Business thrived and the company soon became the leading United States exporter of recycled paper.

The America Chung Nam Inc operates state-of-the-art production capacity mills in Jiangsu and Dongguan today and is set to continue to prosper under Ms Zhang.

Birth date	1957
Hometown	Guangdong Province
Education	Bachelor degree, majoring in Finance

Background

1985-1990	Immigrated to Hong Kong and established a scrap paper trading business
1990-	Immigrated to United States and founded America Chung Nam Inc, acting as president

---

[1] *Hua Sheng Newspaper,* 21st May 2003

Political affiliation

Member of the Chinese People's Political Consultative Conference

Main industries of America Chung Nam Inc

Paperboard and paper-based packaging products

Other information

Married to Mr Liu Mingzhong, general manager of America Chung Nam Inc

Contact information
Address Xin Sha Gang Industrial Zone, Mayong Town, Dongguan City, Guangdong, China, 523147
Telephone 86-769-8826 888   Facsimile 86-769-8824 198   Website www.ndpaper.com / www.acni.net

Li Zhaohui — Shanxi Haixin Iron and Steel Group
"Man of iron determination, mind of steel"

Corporate position	Chairman, Shanxi Haixin Iron and Steel Group
Net worth	RMB 2.4 billion (US$290 million)

Born in 1981, Mr Li Zhaohui may be the youngest person on the list of China's richest, but his fortune is certainly staggering. Mr Li was pursuing his university degree in Monash University in Australia in 2002 when he abruptly inherited his family's business, following his father's untimely death[1].

His father, Mr Li Haicang, then already one of China's richest people, was founder of Shanxi Haixin Iron and Steel Group. The corporation prospered during Deng Xiaoping's era in the early 1980s. The late Mr Li ranked 27th on the list of China's richest people by *Forbes* magazine at that time.

In January 2003, his father, Mr Li Haicang, was fatally shot in his office by a failed businessman who then killed himself. With no other successor in the organisation, Mr Li had to drop his university studies and return to China. Despite his youth and lack of experience, Mr Li is known to be surprisingly mature in business dealings. He swiftly took the reins of the iron and steel business his father had painstakingly built up in coal-rich Shanxi province.

In 2002, the Haixin Group reported revenues of RMB 2.7 billion (US$325 million), resulting in taxes of RMB 115.9 million (US$14 million) in 2002. This alone accounted for one third of all taxes in the relatively poor Haixin County[2]. Mr Li Zhaohui continues to lead the Group into profitability.

Birth date	1981
Hometown	Wenxi County, Shanxi Province
Education	University education, majoring in Business Studies, Monash University, Australia

Background

2003-   Began managing the Shanxi Haixin Iron and Steel Group, acting as chairman

Main industries of Shanxi Haixin Iron and Steel Group

Steel products

Other information

Son of Mr Li Haicang, the founder and former chairman of Shanxi Haixin Iron and Steel Group, who was murdered in January 2003 as a result of a business dispute. He has a sister.

---

[1] *Economic Observer*, 27th January 2003
[2] *Beijing Modern Business News*, 25th August 2003

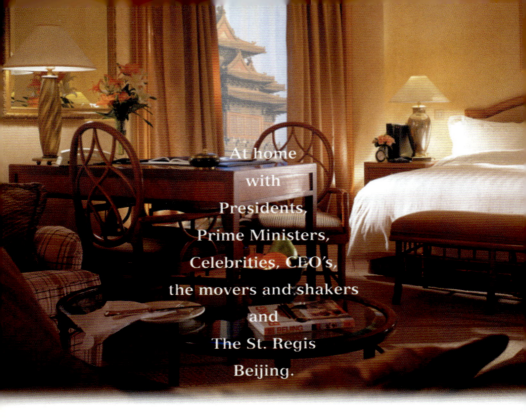

Tao Xinkang Xin Gao Chao Group
"Planting the roots for success"

#25

Corporate position	President, Xin Gao Chao Group
Net worth	RMB 2.1 billion (US$253 million)

Mr Tao Xinkang's ingenuity serves as an inspiration to many. His business started as a small furniture workshop in 1979 with savings of only RMB 10,000 (US$1,207). His desire to develop his business led him to North east China in 1986 to secure a steady supply of timber. He spent the next eight years in North east China developing his business.

He only returned to Shanghai in 1994 and founded the Xin Gao Chao Group. The company grew to become the largest private enterprise in Shanghai.

In 1999, he began the toilsome affair of planting his own forest on a large-scale to maintain a steady supply of timber for his business. The reforestation efforts will begin to bear fruit and be ready for logging as early as 2005.

Given his business acumen, the company's sales of furniture soared and his business prospered. He is now ranked No. 25 among China's richest people and is estimated to possess a net worth of RMB 2.1 billion (US$253 million).

Mr Tao once said, "My factories are my home, and my business is my dearest lover." He attributed his success to a few factors - specialisation in the timber industry, passion for his line of business, a controlled expansion without over-reliance on debt, emphasis on sales, being cautious, sincere and always keeping to one's word.

Today, he still stresses on the importance of a good supply of resources whether timber or otherwise. In 2000, Mr Tao invested in a power plant to generate his own electricity.

The Xin Gao Chao Group is one of the biggest private companies in China, employing more than 20,000 staff with sales peaking over RMB 6.0 billion (US$720 million)[1].

Birth date	1953
Hometown	Fengxian County, Shanghai
Education	High School

[1] Duan Wei, *New Youth – Fortune*, 8th October 2002

CHINA'S RICHEST PEOPLE WHO'S WHO IN CHINA

Background

1979	Set up a small furniture workshop
1986	Expanded the furniture workshop into a factory
1986-1994	Moved to Northeast China to develop the timber business
1994	Moved back to Shanghai and founded Xin Gao Chao Group
1997	Invested in forest plantation
2000	Finished construction of a power station owned by the Group

Subsidiaries of Xin Gao Chao Group

Sino-America Joint Venture Shanghai Xin Fu Wood Co Ltd
Sino-America Joint Venture Shanghai Xin Mei Paint Co Ltd
Sino-Canada Joint Venture Shanghai Xin Hong Wood Co Ltd
Sino-UK Shanghai Joint Venture Xin Ying Wood Co Ltd
Joint Venture Shanghai Xin Mei Wood Co Ltd
Shanghai Xin Meige Wood Villa Co Ltd
Shanghai Xin Lin Wood Co Ltd
Shanghai Xin Sen Biotechnology Co Ltd
Shanghai Xin Du Building and Decorating Project Co Ltd
Shanghai Xin Chen Fireproof Board Co Ltd
Shanghai Xin Gaochao Group Co Ltd
Shanghai Xin Mei Real Estate Co Ltd
Shanghai Touqiao Building Material Co Ltd
Shanghai Xin Jin Wood Co Ltd
Shanghai Xin Jia Wood Co Ltd
Shanghai Xin Yue Wood Co Ltd
Shanghai Yaer Co Ltd
Shanghai Gao Chao Furniture Centre
Shanghai Xin Gao Chao Furniture factory
Shanghai Gao Chao Hotel

Other information

Mr Tao has a wife and son in Canada.

Contact information
Address No. 787, Kang Qiao Rd., Kang Qiao Industrial Development Area, Shanghai, China, 201315
Telephone 86-21-5812 0789   Facsimile 86-21-5812 1558   Email director@xingaochao.com.cn   Website www.xingaochao.com.cn

Shen Wen Zijiang Group
"Shanghai's instrumental figure"

Corporate position	Chairman, Zijiang Group
Net worth	RMB 2.0 billion (US$242 million)

As chairman of Shanghai Zijiang Group, Mr Shen Wen commands the gargantuan task of overseeing 12,000 employees and more than 50 different businesses.

In 2002, the Zijiang Group reported revenues of over RMB 8.3 billion (US$1 billion) and paid taxes of RMB 828 million (US$100 million). The Group includes Shanghai Zijiang Enterprise (code: 600210, listed since from August 1999), listed on the Shanghai Stock Exchange.

Mr Shen started his own plastics manufacturing business in 1983, branching into trading and printing. Five years later, he imported a US$1 million printing and packaging machine expanding his business further. Soon after, he began diversifying into the property business and became one of the pioneers in the Shanghai real estate business. Mr Shen and his Zijiang Group today own a ritzy five-star hotel and his businesses have extended to Hong Kong and the United States.

Plastic packaging, bottling and precision instruments continue to be the principal businesses for Zijiang Group. Almost one-third of the foreign soft drink manufacturers, such as Coca Cola and Pepsi, use bottles manufactured by Zijiang Group. Mr Shen is currently developing a RMB 4.1 billion (US$500 million) science park in Shanghai.

Mr Shen is the second highest tax-paying enterpreneur in Shanghai. He is also a member of the Chinese People's Political Consultative Conference.

Birth date	1958
Hometown	Shanghai

Political affiliation
Member of the Chinese People's Political Consultative Conference

Main industries of Zijiang Group
Printing and packaging, precision instruments and Shanghai real estate

CHINA'S RICHEST PEOPLE WHO'S WHO IN CHINA

Corporate structure of Zijiang Enterprise Group Co Ltd (Listed in Shanghai)

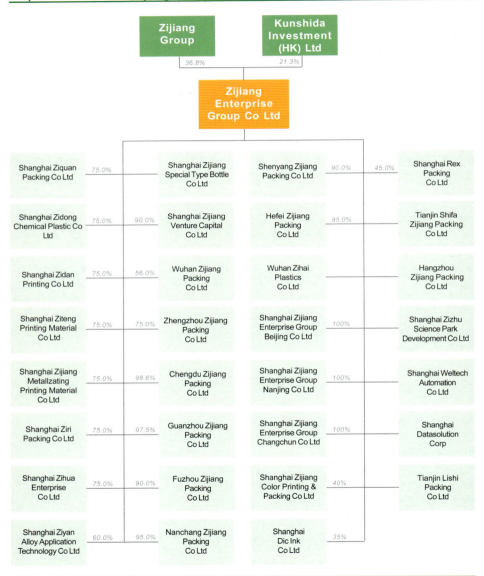

Contact information

Address F9, Zhongsheng Building, No. 8 Xianxia Road, Shanghai, China
Telephone 86-21-6278 9119   Facsimile 86-21-6278 5020   Website www.zijianggroup.com

China Compass Series 2004/2005

Jointly produced by China Council for Promotion of International Trade (CCPIT) and Inspire Publishing Private Limited

Inspire Publishing's China Compass Series is a collection of trade directories for China's most important industries. The series is the first ever English language collection of trade directories of the top industries in China.

China Exhibition & Trade Fair Almanac
Directory of China's Foreign Service Companies
China Food and Beverage Industry Guide
China Construction, Building Materials and Real Estate Industry Guide
China Automobile & Automotive Parts Industry Guide
China Communication and IT Industry Guide
China Electronic Industry Guide
China Fashion, Textiles & Garment Industry Guide
China Transportation and Logistics Industry Guide
China Petroleum and Chemical Industry Guide
China Pharmacy & Traditional Chinese Medicine Industry Guide

39 Jalan Pemimpin
#04-03 Tai Lee Building
Singapore 577182
Tel: (65) 6358 2289
Fax: (65) 6353 2542
www.inspire-publishing.com
info@inspire-pubishing.com

CHINA COMPASS SERIES

"It would be more true to say that I like the notion of adventures and challenges than to say that I simply like jets."

Mr Zhang Yue

CHINA'S RICHEST PEOPLE WHO'S WHO IN CHINA

Zhang Yue Broad Air Conditioning Co Ltd
"Conditioned for fame"

Corporate position	Co-founder and CEO, Broad Air Conditioning Co Ltd
Net worth	RMB 1.8 billion (US$216 million)

Until 1992, Mr Zhang Yue taught art in a public school. Few would imagine that his enthusiasm for science and technology would one day see this art teacher invent a revolutionary air-conditioning technology in 1988 with his brother, Mr Zhang Jian. China's first direct-fired absorption (DFA) chiller/heater was conceived and the result was groundbreaking. Based on this new product, the Zhang brothers founded the Broad Air Conditioning Co Ltd in 1992 with just RMB 30,000 (US$3,623) start-up capital.

The company expanded rapidly and the Zhang brothers' endless strive to innovate was again rewarded by another invention in 2001, the world's first central system air conditioner using gas power. Today, Broad Air Conditioning continues to champion the use of environmentally friendly products.

According to Mr Zhang, a company's greatest strength is "not its technology, but its management system." He explains that a company is doomed to fail without a proper system in place, and therefore a leader should always focus on building a system that prevents unnecessary errors[1].

With about 1,600 employees, the company reported sales of RMB 1.2 billion (US$145 million). Today, Mr Zhang's company has set up branches in over 20 major cities in China. It has also opened subsidiaries in New York and Paris. The company's air-conditioning units dominate 60% of the Chinese central air-conditioning market and are distributed to over 10 countries in the United States, Europe, Middle East and Southeast Asia.

Mr Zhang strongly believes in keeping his company private and has no plans to take his company public. He is also proud to declare that his company has a zero debt record.

A flying enthusiast, Mr Zhang is also the first Chinese to own and pilot his own private jet.

Birth date	1960
Hometown	Changsha City, Hunan Province
Education	Bachelor of Engineering, Harbin University of Technology

[1] Mr Zhang's speech at the 10th anniversary of Broad Air Conditioning

CHINA'S RICHEST PEOPLE WHO'S WHO IN CHINA

Background
Before 1992	Public school teacher
1992-	Co-founded Broad Air Conditioning and acted as CEO

Main industries of Broad Air Conditioning
Central air conditioners

Contact information

Address Cyber Tower, Haidian District, Beijing, China, 100086
Telephone 86-10-8251 4688   Facsimile 86-10-8251 5208   Website www.broad.com

Ren Yunliang Huafeng Group
"Teeing towards the riches"

Corporate position	Chairman, Huafeng Group
Net worth	RMB 1.6 billion (US$193 million)

"I am lucky. In the 20 years since I started my business, I am indeed fortunate to have travelled the most glorious 13 years with the communist government."
Mr Ren Yunliang, interviewed by Guangming Daily (March 2003)

As a well-heeled member during the period of Cultural Revolution, Mr Ren Yunliang was labelled a member of the *bourgeois* and was sent to do hard labour in the countryside.

In 1983, Mr Ren and his wife, Ms Liu Shulan, dabbled in the fur trade starting with a sum of RMB 58,000 (US$7,000), money paid to them from the local government as compensation for their forced labour during the Cultural Revolution[1]. They then spent a short stint in Shenzhen in 1986, before moving to Dalian where the couple's big break came with the setting up of a transportation and retail business. They started with three trucks in Dandong, a city at the Liaodong Peninsula in Northeast China. Thereafter, Mr Ren's foray into the real estate business reaped him more than RMB 66.2 million (US$8 million).

In 1993, Mr Ren developed the 36-hole Golden Pebble Golf Course, one of China's top golf courses, at the cost of a phenomenal RMB 2.1 billion (US$250 million)[2]. And ever since then, golf has become one of Mr Ren's deepest passion. In 2000, Mr Ren invested RMB 12.4 million (US$1.5 million) to build a ceramic manufacturing plant. Mr Ren's diversified pursuits are manifested in the Huafeng Group which holds a hybrid of 19 different business interests ranging from special equipments, high-technology plastic water pipes, north east China real estate, golf courses, tourism, shipping ports and international trade. Huafeng Group reported revenues of around RMB 8.3 billion (US$1 billion) in 2002 and paid taxes of around RMB 165.6 million (US$20 million) for the past two years.

Mr Ren is a habitual traveller. His philanthropic efforts for many charities have earned him several awards. Mr Ren was quoted as saying, "As a private enterprise under the socialist regime, Huafeng's expansion objective is not aimed at making profit, but to contribute to building a prosperous society."

Birth date	1953
Hometown	Dandong City, Liaoning Province
Education	Bachelor in Economics, North East University of Finance and Economics

[1] *New Fortune*, Vol. 4, 2003
[2] Li Zhiwei, *Guang Ming Daily*, 4 March 2003

CHINA'S RICHEST PEOPLE WHO'S WHO IN CHINA

Background

1982-1985	Manager, Friendship Shopping Mall, Dandong City
1985-1990	General manager, New Friendship Shopping Mall, Dandong City
1990-1993	Chairman, Friendship (Group) Co Ltd, Dandong City
1991-1992	Chairman, Dalian Huafeng High-tech Development Co Ltd
1993-	Chairman, Dalian Huafeng Group

Political affiliation

Member of the Chinese People's Political Consultative Conference

Honours and awards

Director of Ren Yunliang Education Foundation, Dandong City, 1989

Parliament Medal by the Parliament of United States, 1994

One of the Ten Outstanding Private Entrepreneurs in China, 1995

Outstanding Entrepreneur of Dalian, 2000

Main industries of Huafeng Group

Special equipments, plastic pipes, Liaoning and Changchun real estate

Other information

Married to Ms Liu Shulan, vice chairman of Huafeng Group.

Contact information
Address 20th floor, Hongfu Building, No. 45 Shanghai Road, Zhongshan District, Dalian, Liaoning, China, 116001
Telephone 86-411-2821 612   Facsimile 86-411-2821 680   Website www.dalianhf.com

Kuang Huizhen Asia Aluminium Holdings
"Steeling oneself against all odds"

Corporate position	Founder and Chairman, Asia Aluminium Holdings
Net worth	RMB 1.6 billion (US$192 million)

With more than two decades of experience, Mr Kuang Huizhen cuts an illustrious figure in the non-ferrous metal trading and manufacturing industry.

He moved to Hong Kong at the age of 17 and started out in the waste metal business. His devotion to this business led him to the United States, Middle East and Japan in 1981 to expand his market reach. In September 1992, he established Asia Aluminium Holdings and stayed as its chairman ever since.

Riding on the back of China's building and construction boom and growing demand for aluminium and stainless steel products, Asia Aluminium Holdings developed rapidly in the last 10 years. The company also managed a listing in 1998 in Hong Kong (Asia Aluminium Holdings, code: 0930). Asia Aluminium also attracted a strategic partner in the form of Indalex Aluminium Solutions from the United States, the world's third largest aluminium extractor.

Asia Aluminium reported revenues of RMB 2.1 billion (US$250 million) in 2002 and paid taxes of RMB 74.5 million (US$9 million) for the last two years. The company has not only grown into Asia's largest aluminium extractor, but has also attained recognition internationally for its superior standards of quality and business accomplishments. In 2002, Asia Aluminium was named as one of the ' World's 200 Best Small Companies', by *Forbes Global* and ranked 302nd among the 'Top 500 International Chinese Enterprises' by *AsiaWeek*.

In 2003, Asia Aluminium announced a major decision to establish the "Asia Aluminium Industrial City" in the high-tech development zone of Zhaoqing city, Guangdong province in South China. The group also disclosed another agreement to partake in a HK$3 billion (US$385 million) project for the production of aluminium panels and plates, the first facility to be established in the industrial city. It is expected that the plant will become operational in 2005, with full capacity reaching 400,000 tonnes in 2007.

Since Mr Kuang noticed that China is heavily reliant on imports for the supply of premium flat rolled products, he has positioned his company to tap this market opportunity. The panel/plate project is the first facility in the industrial city.

"We have reserved sufficient space for the establishment of other manufacturing and processing facilities in the future," assured Mr Kuang.

Mr Kuang oversees the Group's operations and steers its overall corporate and business development. He is active in the industry and public services, and is currently the chairman of the Guangdong Nanhai Non-ferrous Metals Association.

CHINA'S RICHEST PEOPLE WHO'S WHO IN CHINA

Birth date	1955
Hometown	Nanhai City, Guangdong Province
Education	Middle school

Background

1972-1982	Moved to Hong Kong and started a waste metal business
1981-1992	Headed to the United States, Middle East and Japan to expand his business
1992-	Established Asia Aluminium Holdings and acted as chairman

Other titles and positions

Chairman, Guangdong Nanhai Non-ferrous Metals Association

Main industries of Asia Aluminium Holdings

Aluminium extrusions

Corporate structure of Asia Aluminium Holdings

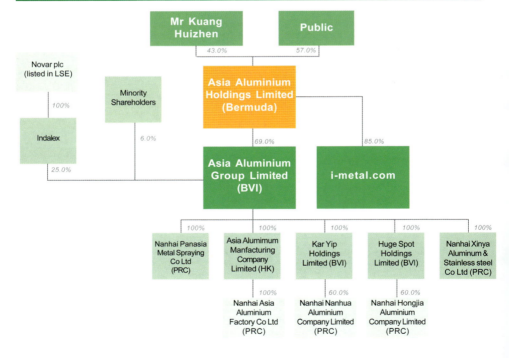

Contact information

Address 12th Floor, Railway Plaza, 39 Chatham Road South, Tsimshatsui, Kowloon, Hong Kong
Telephone 852-2789 0200   Facsimile 852-2398 1808   Website www.asiaalum.com

Wu Ying UTStarcom
"Reaching for the highest star"

Corporate position	Co-founder and Vice chairman, UTStarcom President, UTStarcom (China)
Net worth	RMB 1.5 billion (US$183 million)

 "Bring back talent, technology, management and capital from the United States"
Mr Wu Ying's motto

The chronicle of Mr Wu Ying's career path has been a source of inspiration to Chinese students studying abroad. In 1987, Mr Wu went to the United States with only US$30 in hand. He became the vice chairman of NASDAQ-listed UTStarcom and president of UTStarcom (China) 15 years later. His estimated net worth is about US$183 million.

After graduating from New Jersey Institute of Technology in 1987, Mr Wu began working as a researcher in Bell Labs and Bellcore Lab. Soon after, he founded Starcom Co Ltd with some partners. He returned to China in 1992, making him amongst the first group of overseas-educated students to return to China. In 1995, when Starcom and Unitech merged to become UTStarcom (Nasdaq – UTSI UTStarcom Inc), Mr Wu was appointed president of UTStarcom (China).

To the new generation of entrepreneurs, Mr Wu stands as the epitome of power and capability.

UTStarcom (China) is today the leading telecommunication equipment supplier to China's two leading fixed line operators. UTStarcom (China) is also the market leader for the 'PAS Wireless Cityphone', with more than 30 million users in Mainland China in almost all key cities apart from Shanghai.

In 2002, Taiwanese wireless-service provider First International Telecom Corp inked deals with UTStarcom and DDI Pocket of Japan to jointly tap the Mainland Chinese and Japanese markets for low-tier wireless services. In the same year, Mr Wu estimated that China Telecom would nearly double its PAS subscriber base to 15 million by the end of 2002, with the figure expected to top 50 million in 2004.

Today, UTStarcom's clientele consists of the largest, most well established global telecommunications service providers in China. In addition, the company also targets smaller, emerging carriers, such as Yahoo!BB in Japan and Reliance Infocomm in India, which focus on providing IP-based voice, video and data services.

In May 2003, UTStarcom acquired the CommWorks division of US-based 3Com Corporation to reinforce its sales presence outside of China. By the end of December 2003, UTStarcom reported revenues of more than RMB 15.7 billion (US$1.9 billion), of which 86% was generated from China, 10% from Japan and earned a gross profit of more than RMB 5.3 billion (US$636 million). By the end of 2003, UTStarcom employed a total of approximately 5,500 full-time employees worldwide.

CHINA'S RICHEST PEOPLE WHO'S WHO IN CHINA

Birth date	1961
Hometown	Beijing
Education	Bachelor of Engineering, majoring in Radio Technology, Beijing Industrial University, 1982
	Master's degree, New Jersey Institute of Technology, United States, 1987

Background

1978-1982	Student at Beijing Industrial University
1982-1985	Working in China
1985-1987	Student, New Jersey Institute of Technology, United States
1987-1991	Worked at Bell Labs and Bellcore Lab, United States
1991-	Founded Starcom Co Ltd with other partners
1992-	Returned to China
1995-	Starcom and Unitech merged into UTStarcom, President, UTStarcom (China)

Main industries of UTStarcom

Telecoms infrastructure and equipments

Subsidiaries of UTstarcom

Name	Place of Incorporation or Organisation
UTStarcom China Co Ltd	China
UTStarcom (Chongqing) Co Ltd	China
UTStarcom Telecom Co Ltd	China
Hangzhou Starcom Telecom Co Ltd	China
Advanced Communications Devices Inc	U.S.A.
UTStarcom S.A. de C.V.	Mexico
UTStarcom GmbH	Germany
UTStarcom Japan KK	Japan
UTStarcom Hong Kong Ltd	Hong Kong
UTStarcom Ltd (Thailand)	Thailand
UTStarcom Cayman Inc	Cayman Islands
UTStarcom International Service Inc	U.S.A.
UTStarcom International Product Inc	U.S.A.
UTStarcom Communication Technology (Hangzhou) Company Limited	China
Issanni Communications Inc	U.S.A.
RollingStreams Systems Ltd	Cayman Islands
UTStarcom (Shenzhen) Technical Co Ltd	China
UTStarcom Canada Company	Canada
UTStarcom Ireland Limited	Ireland
UTStarcom Singapore Pte Ltd	Singapore
UTS Taiwan Ltd	Taiwan
UTStarcom Networks Solutions (Brazil)	Brazil
UTStarcom Australia Pty Ltd	Australia

Contact information

Address 10th Floor, The 2nd Building, Oriental Trading City, Oriental Square,
No. 1 East Chang An Street, Dong Cheng District, Beijing, China, 100738
Telephone 86-10-85205588 Facsimile 6-10-85205599 Website www.utstar.com.cn

CHINA'S RICHEST PEOPLE WHO'S WHO IN CHINA

Zhu Baoguo Joincare Pharmaceutical Group
"Concocting the formula to riches"

Corporate position	Founder and Chairman, Joincare Pharmaceutical Group
Net worth	RMB 1.5 billion (US$181 million)

"Shenzhen is a city of migrants. There is a dynamism from this new generation of people who overrides localism and traditional ways of thinking."

Mr Zhu Baoguo, on the city of Shenzhen

Mr Zhu Baoguo graduated from Henan Normal University and was trained as a technician. He spent the first year of his career in a chemical factory in Henan Province as a technician. He later spent six years working for another local company, Feilong Fine Chemical Product Co Ltd. Recognising the immense potential in the healthcare line, he started his own business, founding the Shenzhen Amier Food Co Ltd (later renamed Shenzhen Taitai Pharmaceutical) in 1992.

Within 10 years, Mr Zhu has transformed Shenzhen Taitai Pharmaceutical[1] into an all-encompassing business with a wide range of healthcare products, including its signature Taitai beauty essence. Mr Zhu has said of his success, "Because our products cannot be easily duplicated, many of our consumers in other provinces have found no close substitute."

The presence of the Taitai brand has also surged with the acquisition of a Zhuhai-based Hong Kong health pharmaceutical company that manufactures its own brand of western medicine. The company now control two listed companies, Taitai Pharmaceutical Co Ltd, which was listed in Shanghai in June 2001 (code: 600380) and Livzon Pharmaceutical Co Ltd, which was listed in Shenzhen in June 2002 (code: 000513).

With about 3,600 employees, Shenzhen Taitai Pharmaceutical reported revenues of RMB 7 billion (US$850 million) and paid taxes of RMB 99.4 million (US$12 million).

Birth date	1961
Hometown	Xinxiang City, Henan Province
Education	Bachelor's degree, majoring in Chemistry, Henan Normal University, 1985

Background

1985-1986	Technician, Xinxiang 5th Chemical Factory, Henan Province
1986-1992	General Manager, Feilong Fine Chemical Product Co Ltd
1992-2003	Founded Shenzhen Amier Food Co Ltd (the former name of Shenzhen Taitai Pharmaceutical), acting as chairman and president
2003-	Chairman, Joincare Pharmaceutical Group[1]

[1] Shenzhen Taitai Pharmaceutical was renamed to Joincare Pharmaceutical Group in August 2003.

Main industries of Joincare Pharmaceutical Group

Health products and pharmaceuticals

Corporate structure of Joincare Pharmaceutical Group

Contact information

Address 23/F, Office Tower, Xin Xing Square Di Wang Commercial Centre,
5002 Shen Nan Dong Road, Shenzhen, China, 518008
Telephone 86-755-8246 3888   Facsimile 86-755-8246 1436   Website www.taitai.com

CHINA'S RICHEST PEOPLE WHO'S WHO IN CHINA

Wu Liangding Zhongbao Group
"At the wheel of power"

Corporate position	Chairman, Zhongbao Group
Net worth	RMB 1.4 billion (US$174 million)

Mr Wu Liangding started his career in a small factory in Shaoxing County in the 1960s, first working as an accountant then later as a sales manager. His propensity for revamping organisations was apparent when he was appointed by the government of Shaoxing to establish Xinchang Spinning Equipment Factory in 1982.

After 10 years of operation, the company was restructured, along with two other companies, to form the Zhongbao Group. Mr Wu has been the chairman and CEO of Zhongbao Group ever since.

A series of reforms, spearheaded by Mr Wu, spurred the growth of the Zhongbao Group. He has often been extolled by many for his efficacy in restructurings and acquisitions. In 1993, Mr Wu restructured and founded Zhejiang Rifa Holding Group Co Ltd, which is now headed by his eldest son, Mr Wu Jie, as the president. In 1998, he again restructured and founded Zhejiang Wanfeng Auto Holding Group Co Ltd, this time with his wife Ms Chen Ailian as the president. Subsequently, these two companies became two holding companies with more than 21 subsidiaries. From 2001, he decided to focus less on operational affairs and concentrate more on financing requirements of his companies.

To date, Mr Wu has been working for Zhongbao Group for more than 40 years. The Zhongbao Group is now the leading aluminium alloy wheel manufacturer for motorcycles and cars in China.

In recognition of his distinguished efforts on technological innovation and corporation management, Mr Wu has also received numerous awards.

CHINA'S RICHEST PEOPLE WHO'S WHO IN CHINA

Birth date	September 1946
Hometown	Shaoxing City, Zhejiang Province
Education	University level
Professional qualifications	Senior economist

Background

1961-1982	Accountant and sales manager at the 2nd Light Machine Factory of Xinchang County, Zhejiang Province
1982-1992	Deputy director and director, Xinchang Spinning Equipment Factory
1992-2001	Founded the Zhongbao Group, acting as chairman and the CEO
2001-	Retired as CEO, remaining as chairman of Zhongbao Group

Honours and awards

Labour Model in China's Light Industrial Sectors

Outstanding Entrepreneur in China's Light Industrial Sectors

Outstanding Entrepreneur of Zhejiang Province

One of the 10 Innovative Entrepreneurs of Zhejiang Province

One of the 10 Outstanding Entrepreneurs in the Light Industrial Sectors of Zhejiang Province

Main industries of Zhongbao Group

Aluminium wheels and machinery

Other information

Mr Wu is re-married and has four sons and a daughter. His eldest son heads Zhejiang Rifa Holding Group Co Ltd as president. His eldest daughter is the general manager of the international trading department of Zhejiang Zhongbao Industry Co Ltd. His second son specialised in aerospace design and works at China Southern Airlines. His third son studied in Peking University before going to the UK for his MBA. His youngest son is still schooling.

CHINA'S RICHEST PEOPLE WHO'S WHO IN CHINA

Corporate structure of Zhongbao Group

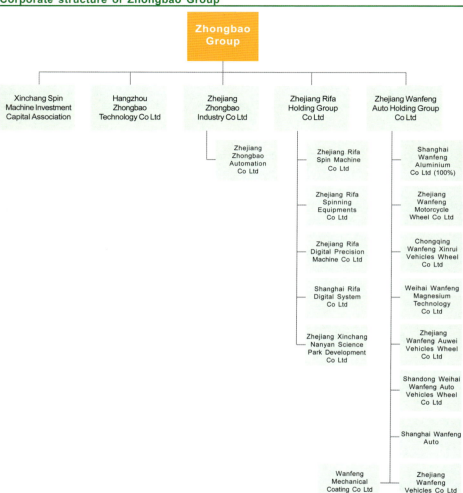

Contact information
Address Nanyan High-tech Industrial Park, Xinchang, Zhejiang, China, 312500
Telephone 86-575-6299 666, 6299 200   Facsimile 86-575-6299 222   Website www.wfjt.com / www.rifa.com.cn

CHINA'S RICHEST PEOPLE WHO'S WHO IN CHINA

Huang Hongsheng (Stephen)
Skyworth Digital Holdings
"Aiming for the sky"

Corporate position	Founder and Chairman, Skyworth Digital Holdings
Net worth	RMB 1.3 billion (US$162 million)

"I came, I saw, I conquered."
Mr Huang Hongsheng's pledge during the National Business Manager Forum, September 2003

Born into a poor farming family in the Hainan Province, Mr Huang Hongsheng was sent to the countryside during the Cultural Revolution after high school in 1973. When China resumed its university entrance examination in 1977, Mr Huang was successfully admitted to the South China University of Technology and became one of the first group of university students in China after the Cultural Revolution.

In 1988, Mr Huang resigned from his job at a state-owned factory. With only RMB 50,000 (US$6,039), he founded a small factory specialising in the manufacturing of remote control devices[1]. After 15 years of sheer hard work and endurance, Mr Huang succeeded in building this small factory into one of China's leading producers and exporters of television sets - Skyworth Digital Holdings.

Today, Skyworth Digital Holdings has matured into a Group with several subsidiary companies, including a Hong Kong listed company (code: 0751, listed since April 2000). In 2002, the Group hit revenues of RMB 9.5 billion (US$1.1 billion) and net profits of RMB 227.1 million (US$27.4 million).

In line with the theme of globalisation, Skyworth Digital Holdings has set up two research centres for multi-media and digital video frequency technology. A laboratory in the Silicon Valley in the United States has also started operations. A new research centre in Shenzhen is constructed at an estimated cost of RMB 50 million (US$6 million).

Mr Huang envisions Skyworth Digital Holdings to be the leading brand in digital entertainment industry.

"We now announce that we are at war with Japanese and Korean manufacturers in the high-end TV set market. The final objective is to rid China of TV sets made in Japan. I will be the Sony in China," declared Mr Huang triumphantly in 2002 when he slashed the price of one of Skyworth's high end plasma TV models by a steep 30% to RMB 29,800 (US$3,600).

His motto is to never wait for opportunities. Mr Huang learned from experience that perseverance means victory. "It is like kicking balls. You have players of the competing team blocking you in the front, and chasing you from behind. You are on the brink of falling. If you fall, you will get nothing. But if you stretch out and kick the ball, you might score a goal," said Mr Huang.

Mr Huang is also known to be a filial son. There are many anecdotes about him, but the one of his mother and electronic "chicken pets" is perhaps the most well known. It is said that each time he returns to Hong Kong, he would take his mother for strolls on her wheelchair. His mother once

---
[1] Hu Jiali, *China Industrial and Business Times*, 6th December 2001

CHINA'S RICHEST PEOPLE WHO'S WHO IN CHINA

casually remarked that electronic chickens would make a good "pet" for many people. Being the respectful son, Mr Huang started making the electronic "pets". He ended up losing money on the venture.

Birth date	1957
Hometown	Lin'gao City, Hainan Province
Education	Bachelor of Engineering, majoring in Radio Engineering, South China University of Technology, 1981

Background
1973-1978	Sent down to the countryside in the Hainan Province during the Cultural Revolution
1978-1981	Studied at the South China University of Technology, Guangzhou City
1981-1988	Worked at a state-owned factory in Guangdong Province
1988-	Founded Skyworth Digital Holdings

Political affiliations
Member of the Chinese People's Political Consultative Conference

Member of the People's Political Consultative Conference of Guangdong Province and of Shenzhen city

Main industries of Skyworth Digital Holdings
Colour televisions and digital appliances

Corporate structure of Skyworth Digital Holdings

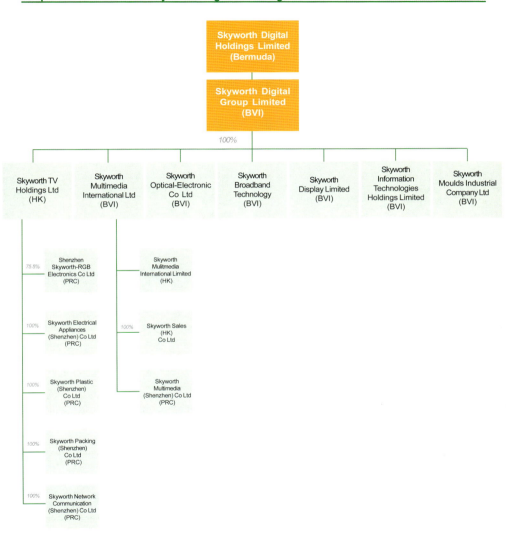

Contact information

Address Skyworth Digital Holdings, Gongmin Town, Shenzhen, China, 518106
Telephone 86-755-2773 1056 Facsimile 86-755-2773 2624 Website www.skyworth.com.cn

CHINA'S RICHEST PEOPLE WHO'S WHO IN CHINA

Gu Chujun Greencool Group
"Guardian of China's next generation"

Corporate position	Founder and Chairman, Greencool Group
Net worth	RMB 1.3 billion (US$152 million)

"We are doing more than just a business; we are doing it for our future."

Mr Gu Chujun and Greencool's axiom

Mr Gu Chujun founded the Greencool Group in 1998 and remain the driving force behind the company.

Prior to establishing the Greencool Group, Mr Gu, who holds a master's degree in engineering from Tianjin University, also lectured at Tianjin University where he was active in the research of thermodynamics and refrigeration engineering. After over 15 years of research and development of refrigeration engineering, Mr Gu made a breakthrough when he invented the revolutionary Greencool Refrigerants and founded the Greencool Group.

Beijing-based Greencool Group replaces harmful ozone refrigerants in air conditioners and refrigerators with a new formulation. Greencool was touted as a first mover in a lucrative business at a time when China is phasing out chlorofluorocarbons (CFCs) refrigerants used in millions of households, hotels, offices and factories across the country.

In the last five years, the Greencool Group has been actively encouraging environmental protection in China. It's refrigerants are categorised as a top-tier environmentally friendly product by the State Environmental Protection Administration of China and is recommended by a number of local governments in China.

Today, Greencool Group controls three listed companies: Greencool Technology Holdings (HK GEM, code: 8056, listed since July 2000), Guangdong Kelon Electronic Holdings (Shenzhen, code:

000921, listed since April 2002), and Hefei Meiling Co Ltd (Shenzhen, code: 000521, listed since May 2003).

Looking to vertically diversify his business, Mr Gu bought a 20.6% stake in appliance maker, Guangdong Kelon for RMB 558.9 million (US$67.5 million). Subsequently, Greencool Enterprise Development Company Limited also acquired a 29.8% equity interest in Hefei Meiling Co Ltd, a listed domestic refrigeration appliance manufacturer in the PRC since May 2003. These two new acquisitions is aimed at making Mr Gu one of the largest refrigerator manufacturers in China.

In 2002, Greencool Group's turnover reached RMB 331.1 million (US$40 million) and the Group paid taxes of around RMB 13.2 million (US$1.6 million).

Mr Gu's goal is to turn Greencool into Asia's largest and the world's second largest refrigerator manufacturer[1]. His Greencool Group has also expanded into the automobile industry through a merger with Ya Xin Bus in Yangzhou City, Jiangsu Province[2].

Birth date	1959
Hometown	Yangzhou City, Jiangsu Province
Education	Bachelor of Engineering, majoring in Thermal Engineering, Jiangsu Institute of Technology, 1981
	Master of Engineering, majoring in Power Engineering, Tianjin University, 1984

Background

1975-1977	Sent down to the countryside in Tai county, Jiangsu province during the Cultural Revolution
1977-1981	Bachelor's degree, Jiangsu Institute of Technology
1981-1984	Master's degree, Tianjin University
1985-1988	Researcher, Institute of Thermal Power, Tianjin University
1988	Invented Greencool refrigerants
1989-	Entered the business world
1995-1998	Founded Greencool China Co Ltd
1998-	Founded Greencool Technology Holdings

Main industries of Greencool Group

Refrigerants and refrigerators

---

[1] *Economic Observer*, 20th September 2003
[2] *Security Markets Weekly*, 6th July 2003

CHINA'S RICHEST PEOPLE WHO'S WHO IN CHINA

Corporate structure of Greencool Group

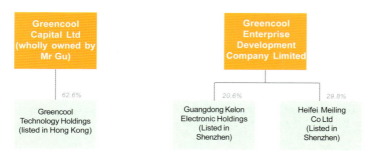

Corporate Structure of Greencool Technology Holdings

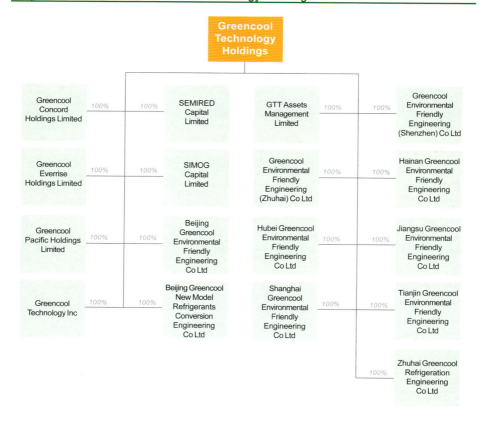

Corporate structure of Guangdong Kelon Electronic Holdings

Name	Directly	Indirectly
Guangdong Zhujiang Refrigerator Co Ltd	-	100%
Kelon Electronic Co Ltd	-	100%
Shunde Rongsheng Plastics Co Ltd	45%	25%
Kelon Development Co Ltd	100%	-
Guangdong Kelon Mould Co Ltd	40%	30%
Guangdong Kelon Refrigerator Co Ltd	70%	30%
Guangdong Kelon Air-conditioning Co Ltd	60%	-
Japan Kelon Corporation	-	100%
Chengdu Kelon Refrigerator Co Ltd	45%	25%
Yingkou Kelon Refrigerator Co Ltd	42%	6.79%
Guangke Tuozhan Co Ltd	-	100%
Kelon International Incorporation	-	100%
Guangdong Kelon Component Co Ltd	70%	30%
Sichuan Rongsheng Kelon Refrigerator Marketing Co Ltd	76%	-
Beijing Hengsheng Xinchuang Technology Co Ltd	80%	-
Beijing Kelon Tiandi Intelligent Network Technology Co Ltd	-	64%
Beijing Kelon Shikong Information System Technology Co Ltd	-	64%
Guangdong Kelon Refrigeratory Tank Co Ltd	44%	56%
Shunde Jiake Electronic Co Ltd	70%	30%
Shunde Kelon Home Appliance Co Ltd	25%	75%
Shunde Wangao Import & Export Co Ltd	20%	80%
Shunde Huaao Electronic Co Ltd	-	70%
Shunde Qihui Service Co Ltd	-	100%
Jiangxi Kelon Enterprise Development Co Ltd	60%	40%
Jiangxi Kelon Kangbaien Electronics Co Ltd	-	55%
Jilin Kelon Electronics Co Ltd	90%	10%
Kelon (USA) Inc	-	100%

Corporate structure of Hefei Meiling Co Ltd

Contact information
Address Unit 1406-7, 14/F, West Tower, Shun Tak Centre, 168-200 Connaught Road Central, Hong Kong
Telephone 852-2525 9193   Facsimile 852-2525 9191   Website www.greencool.com.hk

CHINA'S RICHEST PEOPLE WHO'S WHO IN CHINA

Duan Yongping BBK Electronics Corp
"Unleashing his trade prowess"

Corporate position	Founder, President and Chairman, BBK Electronics Corp
Net worth	RMB 1.1 billion (US$132 million)

"When you decide to accomplish a goal, always dedicate your heart and soul to the very end."

Mr Duan Yongping's motto as well as BBK Electronics Corp's advertisement message

Never one to let any trouble get the better of him, Mr Duan Yongping has built a brilliant career and an enviable reputation over the years. After graduating with a master's degree in 1989, Mr Duan Yongping left for the south of China in a quest for better opportunities. A decade later, he succeeded in building up two of the most famous brands in China – Subor (Xiao Ba Wang) and BBK (Bu Bu Gao) and became the stuff of legends in China.

In 1989, he was appointed the director of Yihua Electronics Factory, a small factory in Zhongshan city, Guangdong province. Mr Duan led the company to develop electronic game machines. The company was highly successful and was subsequently renamed Xiao Ba Wang in 1991.

By 1995, Xiao Ba Wang became the market leader in the hand-held electronic games market with annual production of more than RMB 1 billion (US$120.8 million). In the same year, Mr Duan proposed a management buyout (MBO) of the company but was rejected by the owners of Xiao Ba Wang. In July 1995, Mr Duan handed in his resignation.

In September 1995, Mr Duan founded BBK Electronics Corp Ltd China (BBK) and soon captured some of Xiao Ba Wang's customer base, carving out a 20% market share in China. BBK mainly focuses mainly on three business segments; digital video/audio products, telecommunication products and electronic education products. Today, BBK has evolved into a nationwide brand, with the help aggressive marketing and high profile advertising campaigns that included international celebrities such as Arnold Schwarzenegger and Jet Li.

Credited with his "clear foresight and innovative ability", Mr Duan was listed by *AsiaWeek* as one of the 20 Millennium Leaders in Asian commercial and financial circles in 1999. Mr Duan is "retired" from actual management and has instead tasked his senior management to run the company when they were still under 30 years of age, a very rare occurrence in China, especially in a large organisation like BBK. Mr Duan once said, "I should always try to figure out goals for my colleagues to keep them interested and active in their jobs and share my joy."

CHINA'S RICHEST PEOPLE WHO'S WHO IN CHINA

Birth date	1961
Hometown	Nanchang City, Jiangxi Province
Education	Bachelor of Engineering, majoring in Radio Engineering Department, Zhejiang University, 1982
	Masters of Economics, majoring in Econometrics, People's University of China, 1989
	MBA, CEIBS (China Europe International Business School), Shanghai, 2003

Background

1978-1982	Bachelor's degree, Zhejiang University
1982-1986	Worked at the Beijing Electronic Tube Factory
1986-1989	Master's degree, People's University of China
1989-1991	Worked as the Director in Yihua Electronics Factory in Zhongshan City, Guangdong Province
1991-1995	Managed Xiao Ba Wang Industrial Co and resigned just when the company was experiencing tremendous success in 1995
1995-	Founded BBK Electronics Corp, acting as president and chairman

Main industries of BBK Electronics Corp

Investments and electronic appliances

Subsidiaries of BBK Electronics Corp

BBK AV Products Subsidiary

BBK Telecommunication Equipments Subsidiary

BBK Education Electronics Subsidiary

Contact information
Address No. 23 BBK Street, Wu Sha, Chang An, Dongguan City, Guangdong Province, China, 523860
Telephone 86-769-5545 555   Facsimile 86-769-5540 007   Website www.gdbbk.com

CHINA'S RICHEST PEOPLE WHO'S WHO IN CHINA

Zhang Yang Interchina Holdings
"China's security market visionary"

Corporate position	Founder and Chairman, Interchina Holdings
Net worth	RMB 1.0 billion (US$120 million)

Mr Zhang Yang's journey to become an icon of entrepreneurship began when he emigrated from his hometown, Shanghai, to Hong Kong in 1989 where he started a trading business between these two cities.

At a time when his trading business is taking off, Mr Zhang made a strategic decision to take the plunge and diversify into the real estate industry in the 1990s. The decision proved to be a correct one and his venture has since grown significantly and now stretches across the bustling and vibrant hubs of Hong Kong, Beijing and Shanghai.

Apart from expanding his real estate business into China's fast-developing second-tier cities, Mr Zhang has also invested in the environmental and water treatment businesses.

In 2000, Mr Zhang made several acquisitions and now controls two Hong Kong listed companies, Interchina Holdings (code: 0202, listed since August 2000) and the Guoxin Group[1] (code: 1215, listed since December 2001). Mr Zhang is also planning on more takeovers in Mainland China.

Interchina Holdings' principal activities are property development, construction of private clubhouse and hotels, financial services and environmental management.

In 2002, Interchina Holdings reported revenues of RMB 74.5 billion (US$9 billion) in 2002. Securities and commodities broking accounted for 73% of the Group's 2002 revenues whilst property development accounted for the rest.

Birth date	1963
Hometown	Shanghai
Education	Bachelor of Engineering, majoring in Industrial Automation, Shanghai Second Staff University

[1] Guoxin Group was previously known as Wah Lee Resources Holdings Ltd.

CHINA'S RICHEST PEOPLE WHO'S WHO IN CHINA

Background

1989- Emigrated to Hong Kong and started the trading business; later changing the company name into Interchina Holdings and entered the real estate, environmental protection and water treatment industry, and securities market

Main industries of Interchina Holdings

Environmental protection and water treatment, real estate

Corporate structure of Interchina Holdings (Listed in Hong Kong)

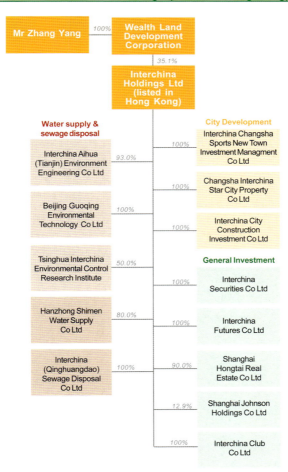

CHINA'S RICHEST PEOPLE WHO'S WHO IN CHINA

Corporate structure of Guoxin Group (Listed in Hong Kong)

Contact information

Address 45/F Far East Finance Centre, 16 Harcourt Road, Admiralty, Hong Kong
Telephone 852-2528 9910   Facsimile 852-2528 9737   Website www.interchina.com

CHINA'S RICHEST PEOPLE WHO'S WHO IN CHINA

Yin Mingshan Lifan Group
"Motorcycle magnate"

Corporate position   Founder and Chairman, Lifan Group

Net worth   RMB 940 million (US$113 million)

  "The Party is evolving in line with the changes in China. It is no longer interested in making the whole world believe in communism. Today, the main aim of the Party is to make the country and the people prosperous."

Mr Yin Mingshan on China's ideological transformation

Mr Yin Mingshan's career include stints as a factory worker, college teacher and book editor. At an age when Mr Yin Mingshan's retirement plans should be well underway, his ever-insatiable quest for challenges led him to embark a new motorcycle business at age 55.

Despite the roller coaster ride, Mr Yin has maintained a very optimistic philosophy: "Pick yourself up wherever you are, never cease to improve yourself and pursue excellence. Without the challenges and obstacles I had to face, I would not be able to establish what I have today. "

By capitalising on technology, Mr Yin established the Lifan Group with only RMB200,000 (US$24,155) and nine staff in 1992. In a mere 11 years, Lifan Group now has the highest production output of motorcycle engines anywhere in the world. During this time, the company has created over 40,000 jobs. Lifan Group today has become one of China's leading exporters.

The ambitious Mr Yin also has plans to enter the car market. Due to lower profits and fierce competition in the two-wheel industry, Lifan Group is gearing up to roll out cars by end of 2004.

"My role model is Honda," Mr Yin says. "It's a motorcycle maker turned carmaker, with car sales 10 times that of motorcycle sales."

Mr Yin is betting on the fast growing automobile market and plan to list in Hong Kong or in China by the end of 2004 to raise between RMB 300 million to RMB 400 million (US$36 million to US$48 million). The Lifan Group has invested RMB 828 million (US$100 million) in a car plant in Southwestern China and expects to produce its first sedan by the end of 2004.

"We want to call this first sedan 'Doodoo' because it sounds like the noise car horns make," said Mr Yin, who is 66 years old this year. "The name sounds round and fat, like Audi, and works for the Chinese market. Cars with names that sound 'thin' and 'hard' don't do as well."

Mr Yin hopes optimistically that 2004 sales will exceed RMB 5 billion (US$603 million), with net profit of around 5% of sales. Like Honda, the Lifan Group aims to expand into developed countries such as the United States.

Adaptability and diversity are but a way of Mr Yin's life. Harnessing this philosophy to the Lifan Group, Mr Yin has also invested in a local football club as well as in the financial and real estate sectors.

CHINA'S RICHEST PEOPLE WHO'S WHO IN CHINA

As the head of the Chongqing business chamber, Mr Yin is also proposing the establishment of a new private bank to help small and medium-sized entrepreneurs in Chongqing. In 2002, the company has 5,000 employees, reported revenues of RMB 4 billion (US$480 million) and paid taxes of RMB 115.9 million (US$14 million).

One of Mr Yin's beliefs is to impart his own experience on how he manages his business. A slogan in bold red letters on a Lifan building reads prominently, "One who earns money in China is a winner; one who earns money overseas is a hero." Such are the guiding principles that has formed the basis of Lifan's corporate culture, making Lifan a brand name synonymous with roots and sustenance.

Mr Yin describes himself as a conscientious student. No matter how busy he gets, he never neglects his homework – reading.

Birth date	1938
Hometown	Chongqing
Education	High school

Background

Before 1985	Editor, Chongqing Publication
1985-1992	Started his own business in educational publications
1992-	Founded Lifan Group

Other titles and positions

Head, Chongqing business chamber

Political affiliations

Member of the Chinese People's Political Consultative Conference

Vice president, Second Chongqing Municipal Committee of the CPPCC

Honours and awards

Outstanding entrepreneurs of Chongqing High-tech Industrial Zone, 1994-2003

National awards on quality management, 2002

Redbud Cup Entrepreneurs, Hong Kong Polytechnic University and China Business Chamber, 2000

Re-employment Star of Chongqing City, 1999

Main industries of Lifan Group

Motors and motorcycles, football

Contact information
Address Lifan Industrial Group, Shangqiao, Chongqing, China, 400037
Telephone 86-23-6520 7228 Facsimile 86-23-6521 3166 Website www.lifan.com.cn

CHINA'S RICHEST PEOPLE WHO'S WHO IN CHINA

Ren Zhengfei Huawei Technologies
"Technologist extraordinaire"

Corporate position   Founder, President and CEO
Huawei Technologies Co Ltd

 "Critical decisions should be made by the wise, not by the majority. The truth is usually in the hands of minority."
Mr Ren Zhengfei on the basic principles of Huawei Technologies

Mr Ren Zhengfei, the founder and CEO of Huawei Technologies Co Ltd is as much an enigma as he is an inspiration.

Much of what is said of the former People's Liberation Army (PLA) man behind one of China's leading companies in the telecommunications equipment market is shrouded in mystery. Suffice to say, Huawei Technologies' growth in the industry has been nothing short of phenomenal. From its humble beginning almost 16 years ago in Shenzhen, the first economic reform base in China at the time, Huawei has grown in leaps and bounds from a RMB 20,000 (US$2,415) company to a force to contend within the industry.

Today, Huawei Technologies is China's largest manufacturer of telecommunications equipment. The company makes a broad range of products, including core voice and data switching platforms for communications service providers. Huawei Technologies also makes optical networking systems, wireless products, corporate networking equipment, and network management and messaging software. The company primarily serves Asian carriers such as China Telecom, China Unicom, and SingTel. Other customers include Hutchison Telecom and Telecom Egypt. Huawei has joint ventures with 3Com as well as manufacturers in Russia and Japan. It also has a distribution agreement with IBM.

At last count, for the year 2002, Huawei weighs in with a hefty revenue of RMB 2.21 billion (US$266.9 million) and Mr Ren is key to this success.

However, the man behind the company remains as much an enigma as his company. Huawei is managed in a very traditional way, which harks back to Mr Ren's days in the PLA prior to 1978. The employees of the hi-tech company still congregates to sing patriotic Chinese revolutionary songs.

He is known more for what others say about him in industry circles than what he actually says about himself. He remains as tight-lipped as he was when he founded Huawei in 1988, sticking to his practice of never granting an interview to any media, broadcast or print. Even in the face of public criticism and rife speculation, Mr Ren remained steadfast in not responding to the barbs thrown in his direction.

That only fuels the public imagination of the man who delivers astounding results in a highly

CHINA'S RICHEST PEOPLE WHO'S WHO IN CHINA

competitive market in China. The extent of his personal wealth is also an object of speculation. In 2002, Forbes ranked him the third richest man in China, with a net worth of RMB 4.1 billion (US$500 million).

But officially, he only owns 1% of Huawei's shares. Huawei Labour Union Commission holds most of Huawei's shares. But as to the number of shares Mr Ren and other high-level managers hold in that commission, no one knows.

For a company to grow, Mr Ren believes that it must have three qualities; a sense of sensitivity, determined fighting spirit and team effort.

A quiet man, Mr Ren has written a book dedicated to the memories of his late parents. He was grateful to his parents for providing for him in a large family of nine. He felt remorseful about not having had the opportunity to spend quality time with his parents before they passed away.

Birth date	1944
Education	Bachelor's degree

Background

Before 1978	Served in the PLA as a military officer
1978-1988	Worked in Shenzhen
1988-	Founded Huawei Technologies Co Ltd, acting as President and CEO

Contact information
Address Banxuegang Industrial Park, Buji Longgang, Shenzhen, Guangdong, China, 518129
Telephone 86-755-2878 0808   Facsimile 86-755-2878 9251   Website www.huawei.com

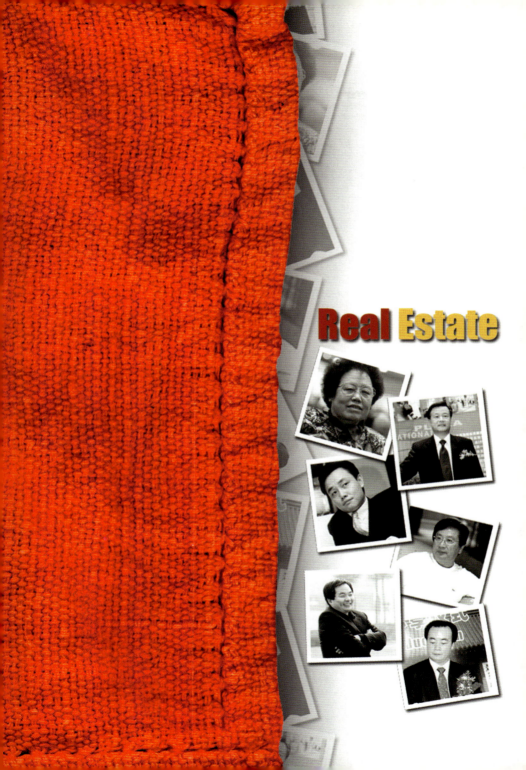
Real Estate

CHINA'S RICHEST PEOPLE WHO'S WHO IN CHINA

Xu Rongmao Shimao Group
"The rise and rise of China's biggest property player"

Corporate position   Chairman, Shimao Group

Net worth   RMB 6.7 billion (US$810 million)

 "Life is like a stage; once you are cast as a leading character, you must fully understand your role and play it well. Each time I spot an opportunity, I will try my utmost to seize it."

Mr Xu Rongmao

Mr Xu Rongmao, the founder of Shimao group, ranks third among China's richest people and is estimated to possess a net worth of RMB 6.7 billion (US$810 million).

Unlike other tycoons who were constantly making headlines with their business pursuits, it was not until Mr Xu acquired a 26.4% share in Shanghai Wanxiang Group that the world started taking notice of him.

In his view, opportunity presents itself in a depressed market. He says, "The key is whether you dare to take a chance, whether you know how to seize the opportunity when it presents itself."

Back in the 1970s, Mr Xu was captivated by the dynamics of the market in Hong Kong. As a broker, he exhibited his business adroitness in textile and garment business. After several triumphant business ventures in Australia's property market, he began to focus on China's high-end property market.

"The financing of large scale real estate projects usually comes from four sources," he shares. "Existing company funds, rollover cashflow from sales, bank financing and capital markets. We excel in the first and second type."

Over time, he has become one of the most prominent players in the Beijing, Shanghai and Fujian region. Currently Shimao is listed in Shanghai (code: 600823, listed since August 2000) and China Shimao in Hong Kong (code: 0649, listed since March 2002).

The Shimao Group owns major projects in Shanghai, Nanjing and Fuzhou. The corporation also employs 1,500 staff and recorded sales of over RMB 4.5 billion (US$540 million) in 2002, an increase of 8% over 2001, and paid taxes of more than RMB 99.4 million (US$12 million).

Mr Xu, who started his career as a Chinese physician, felt that it has benefited him in business. He stated, "Chinese medication relies on being at peace with oneself, hence we are not easily agitated over minute issues. There are people who are really smart, but due to their impulsive and irrational behaviour, their businesses have been negatively affected."

On his fortune, Mr Xu says, "There is actually no secret to my success. Compared to others, I try harder, I pay more attention to details and I am more committed - we take trivial details seriously."

Birth date	1949
Hometown	Shishi City, Fujian Province
Education	MBA

Background

Late 1970's	Came to Hong Kong and later on became a stock broker
1988	Invested in a textile and garment factory in Hong Kong and Mainland China
1989-1993	Invested RMB 16.6 million (US$2 million) into a holiday resort in his home province of Fujian
1995	Expanded into the Beijing property market
2000	Acquired 26.4% of Shanghai Wanxiang Group, becoming its major shareholder

Political affiliation

Member of the Chinese People's Political Consultative Conference

Contact information

Address No. 1 Weifang Road, West PuDong, Shanghai, China
Telephone 86-21-6888 8888   Facsimile 86-21-5888 8811   Website www.shimaogroup.com

SIMPLY GRAND

Spectacularly positioned on the upper floors of the landmark Jin Mao Tower. The city's most luxurious accommodation with views to take your breath away.

FEEL THE HYATT TOUCH®

上海金茂君悦大酒店
GRAND HYATT
SHANGHAI

www.hyatt.com

CHINA'S RICHEST PEOPLE WHO'S WHO IN CHINA

Ye Lipei (Eddie) Super Ocean Group
"On the super highway of fortune"

Corporate position	President, Super Ocean Group
Net worth	RMB 4.2 billion (US$501 million)

 "There is no niche in real estate, we depend mainly on three essential factors: calmness, steadfastness and boldness."

Mr Ye Lipei

Mr Ye Lipei, dubbed "Shanghai Property King", has kept a low profile but his success in developing Shanghai's high-end residential properties is well known. He is ranked No. 6 among China's richest people and is estimated to possess a net worth of RMB 4.2 billion (US$501 million).

Prior to entering business, Mr Ye was a mathematics teacher and was later involved in the food logistics business. He emigrated to Australia in 1980 where he ran a grocery delivery and garment businesses. There he accumulated nearly RMB 99.4 million (US$12 million) over the next 10 years. In 1989, he returned to China with an Australian passport and snapped up several prime properties at a bargain during the post-Tiananmen slump. In the 1990s, he rode the construction boom, which transformed Shanghai, Shenzhen and other China cities.

His philosophy regarding business can be summed up as follows. Focus on the business that one is familiar with and focus on what is easier for one to do. For instance, he chose the trading business given the low start-up capital required.

Betting on China's accession to WTO and the 2010 Shanghai Expo, Mr Ye's Super Ocean Group announced the launch of three major developments in Shanghai with a total investment of just over RMB 8.3 billion (US$1 billion).

Mr Ye commented, "Shanghai's RMB 1.8 billion (US$327 million) Super Ocean Commercial Centre will be the biggest shopping mall in Asia outside Japan, with 280,000 sq m of floor space."

Mr Ye revealed that gambling in casinos is his chief recreational activity. "Going to casinos is a part of my life. It's a form of relaxation. When I have extra money, my ieda of a vacation is simply a trip to the casino."

But when quizzed in June 2003 by an Australian reporter on the huge sums wagered at the Crown Casino in Australia, Mr Ye nonchalantly refused to comment and explained, "We are all born equal and there's no need to show off."

Other than being a highflyer, another activity also gratifies Mr Ye. "Going to the construction site gives me a deep sense of satisfaction too," he admits.

CHINA'S RICHEST PEOPLE WHO'S WHO IN CHINA

Birth date	1944
Hometown	Shanghai
Education	MBA

Background

Before 1979	Worked as a salesman
1979-1989	Emigrated to Australia and started a food processing and trade business
1989-	Founded Super Ocean and invested in Shenzhen property market
1990-	Moved business back to Shanghai

CHINA'S RICHEST PEOPLE WHO'S WHO IN CHINA

Chen Lihua Fu Wah International HK Group
"Chiselling wood into a multi-million empire"

Corporate position	President, Fu Wah International HK Group
Net worth	RMB 3.9 billion (US$471 million)

  "You need to learn the art of parting with what you have before you can expect to reap the riches."

Ms Chen Lihua

Ms Chen Lihua is ranked ninth among China's richest people and is estimated to possess a net worth of RMB 3.9 billion (US$471 million).

Ms Chen, of Manchurian descent, entered the furniture making trade when she became involved with the furniture repair business after she dropped out of school. Years of gruelling work and astute business instincts steeled her for the running of a furniture factory later.

In 1981, Ms Chen departed for Hong Kong where she made a fortune in the real estate market. Soon after, she returned to Beijing where her company, the Fu Wah Group, set up the Changan Club and launched several residential projects.

As the Fu Wah Group's business grew steadily, Ms Chen worked on her lifelong passion, red sandalwood. She constructed the first privately owned museum in Beijing, exclusively showcasing the lavish red sandalwood furniture and exquisite crafts.

On her speciality redwood carvings and furniture pieces, Ms Chen says, "Many people admire technology from western countries. I want to create unique Chinese artifacts that Westerners can marvel at." Ms Chen's own collection has been estimated to be around RMB 200 million (US$24.6 million).

Ms Chen currently serves as the president of the Fu Wah Group, giving strategic directions to the group, which is run by her son. With 2,000 employees, Fu Wah Group focuses mainly on the property market in Beijing. Ms Chen is currently developing a RMB 4 billion (US$ 483 million) on Beijing's main shopping street which is scheduled to be completed before the 2008 Olympics.

For a person surrounded by immense wealth and possessions, she believes that the greatest "invisible assets" a person can have are their friends.

Birth date	1941
Hometown	Beijing
Education	High school

Background

1976-	Started a furniture repair business in Beijing
1981-	Moved to Hong Kong and involved in trading and real estate
1982-	Returned to Beijing and entered the real estate market
1995-	Established the Changan Club in Beijing
1999-	Founded the China Red Sandalwood Museum in Beijing

Contact information

Address No. 10 Dong Chang An Avenue, Beijing, China, 100006
Telephone 86-10-6522 9988   Facsimile 86-10-6522 6980   Website www.fuwahgroup.com   Email gmoffice@fuwahgroup.com

CHINA'S RICHEST PEOPLE WHO'S WHO IN CHINA

Zhu Mengyi Hopson Development Holdings Ltd
"The real estate squire"

#11

Corporate position	Chairman, Hopson Development Holdings Ltd
Corporate revenue	RMB 3.3 billion (US$397 million)

"By law of nature, crisis is unavoidable, and death is inevitable. We are unable to refute this law. However, if we can discover the purpose of our lives, we can all lead more fulfilling lives."

Mr Zhu Mengyi

Mr Zhu Mengyi, Southern China's "Real Estate King", has been making a name for himself in the real estate market since the 1980s. He is ranked No. 11 among China's richest people and is estimated to possess a net worth of RMB 3.3 billion (US$397 million).

More than 20 years ago, Mr Zhu resided in a small town called Fengshun in Guangdong province where he worked as a construction contractor during the mid-1980s. Through his profound understanding of market developments, he slowly broadened his repertoire to become a property developer. By 1992, his extensive experience in the real estate market equipped him with the necessary knowledge, experience and capital to establish Hopson Development (a listed company) in Hong Kong.

A decade later, Mr Zhu steadily led his property group to reel across Beijing, Guangzhou and Shanghai. Hopson Development's total developed property area in Guangzhou alone covers six million square metres, rivalling the developed property area of China Vanke in the five largest cities of China.

"Hopson Development is the real aircraft carrier in China's real estate market," concedes Mr Wang Shi, the chairman of China Vanke.

Mr Zhu's main business associate is his brother Mr Zhu Muzhi, who is the major shareholder of Guangdong Southern Construction Engineering Co Ltd.[1] The pair also control a China investment vehicle, Guangdong Zhujiang Investment Co Ltd.

While Mr Zhu prefers to keep Hopson Development out of the spotlight, his company exerts a strong presence in the Hong Kong stock market. Mr Zhu has also diversified his business into infrastructure projects and investments.

Including their subsidiaries, Hopson Development employs more than 4,000 employees. It reported sales of RMB 2.1 billion (US$250 million) in 2002, paid taxes of RMB 99.4 million (US$12 million).

---

[1] Hopson Development and Guangdong Zhu Jiang Investment Co Ltd share many of their construction projects. Guangdong Southern Construction Engineering Co Ltd is one of the shareholders of Guangdong Zhu Jiang Investment Co Ltd. Another shareholder of Southern Construction Engineering Co Ltd is a company from Mr Zhu's hometown, called Han Jiang Construction Installation Engineering Co Ltd.

CHINA'S RICHEST PEOPLE WHO'S WHO IN CHINA

Birth date	1959
Hometown	Fengshun County, Guangdong Province
Education	High School

Background

Late 80s	Construction contractor
1992-	Founded Hopson Development with several partners in Hong Kong
1998-	Hopson listed on Hong Kong's stock market

CHINA'S RICHEST PEOPLE WHO'S WHO IN CHINA

Corporate structure of Hopson Development Holdings Ltd (listed in Hong Kong)

Hopson Development Holdings Ltd

Subsidiary	%	Subsidiary	%	Subsidiary	%	Subsidiary
Hopson Development International Limited	100%	Archibald Properties Limited	100%	Guangzhou Hopson Xingjing Business Services Limited	85.9%	60%	Guangzhou Hopson Yijing Real Estate Limited
Beijing Hopson Beifang Real Estate Development Limited	70%	Beijing Hopson Lu Zhou Real Estate Development Limited	70%	Guangzhou Hopson Yujing Real Estate Limited	70%	49.5%	Guangzhou Xinhua Information Development Limited
Beijing Hopson Yujing Real Estate Development Limited	70%	Ever New Properties Limited	100%	Guangzhou Yijing Arts and Culture Company Limited	49.5%	100%	Hopson Holdings Limited
Funland Properties Limited	100%	Galloping Properties Limited	100%	Hopson Development (Consultants) Limited	100%	100%	Hopson Development (Properties) Limited
Guangdong Esteem Property Services Limited	90%	Guangdong Hopson Lejing Real Estate Limited	53.5%	Hopson E-Commerce Limited	100%	100%	Hopson (Guangzhou) Industries Limited
Guangdong Hopson Minghui Real Estate Limited	90%	Guangdong Hopson Yuehua Real Estate Limited	90%	Hopson Industries (Shenzhen) Limited	100%	100%	Hopson Infrastructure (BVI) Limited
Guangdong Huajingxincheng Real Estate Limited	90%	Guangdong Huanan New City Real Estate Limited	60%	Hopson Properties (China) Limited	100%	100%	Nambour Properties Limited
Guangdong Huanan Real Estate Limited	70%	Guangdong Jinan Real Estate Limited	90%	Outward Expanse Investments Limited	100%	100%	Pomeroy Properties Limited
Guangdong New Tai An Real Estate Limited	52%	Guangzhou Hopson Cuijing Real Estate Limited	97%	Shanghai Hopson Property Development Company Limited	100%	100%	Solawide Properties Limited
Guangzhou Hopson Dongyu Real Estate Limited	100%	Guangzhou Hopson Junjing Real Estate Limited	95%	Sound Zone Properties Limited	100%	100%	Sun Yick Properties Limited
Guangzhou Hopson Keji Garden Real Estate Limited	95%	Guangzhou Hopson Qinghui Real Estate Limited	100%	Tianjin Hopson Zhujiang Real Estate Development Limited	70%	100%	Timbercrest Properties Limited
Guangzhou Hopson Qingyuan Water Supply Limited	93%	Guangzhou Hopson Yihui Real Estate Limited	100%	Tumen Properties Limited	100%	100%	World Sense Industries Limited

Contact information

Address 19th Floor, Wyndham Place, 40-44 Wyndham Street Central, Hong Kong
Telephone 86-20-8556 3373, 8556 3384   Facsimile 86-20-8556 0546, 8556 0435

Zhou Jianhe Junefield Group
"Manoeuvring the right moves on the field"

#10

Corporate position	Chairman, Junefield Group
Net worth	RMB 3.5 billion (US$420 million)

None other than Mr Zhou Jianhe owns the renowned Junefield Plaza, the largest residential and business centre in Beijing. He is ranked No. 10 among China's richest people and is estimated to possess a net worth of RMB 3.5 billion (US$420 million).

Born into a family of farmers, Mr Zhou joined the ranks of textile traders during the 1980s. In 1989, he acquired his Peruvian citizenship after residing there for a number of years. After which Mr Zhou set forth for Hong Kong in 1990 and soon founded the Junefield Group to develop properties in China.

Junefield was registered in Beijing in 1992 with a capital of RMB 397.4 million (US$48 million) and is now the second largest joint venture property development company in China.

In 1998, Junefield Group successfully clinched the exclusive rights to establish Beijing Sogo, with the 170-year-old Japanese company, Sogo. Beijing Sogo is currently the largest departmental store in Beijing, occupying a whopping 80,000 square meters. The Sogo project was cemented during a time when many were not optimistic of the economic future of Beijing. Mr Zhou was widely accredited with the triumph and his standing in the business circle was further elevated.

Currently Junefield Group's businesses include real estate, departmental stores and hotels. The group consists of 38 subsidiary companies from all over the world. The recent acquisition of a 51.0% stake in Hudson Holdings Limited by a wholly owned subsidiary of Junefield Group, enabled Junefield to tap into the profitable Yaohan departmental store, located next to a Sogo departmental store in Wuhan.

Mr Zhou remains low profile, rarely appearing in the public and refusing most interviews.

Birth date	1963
Hometown	Shuangfeng County, Hunan Province
Education	High school

Background

1980-1989	Textile trading business in China and Peru
1989	Granted Peruvian citizenship
1990	Moved to Hong Kong and founded Junefield Group
1992	Entered Beijing real estate market
1999	Started Beijing Sogo department store project in Beijing

Corporate structure of Junefield (Holdings) Ltd

[1] On 29th December 2003, Prime Century Investment Limited, a wholly owned subsidiary of Junefield (Holdings) Limited bought 51.0% shares of Hudson Holdings Limited. Hudson Holdings Limited was renamed Junefield Department Store Limited on 6th January 2004. Subsequently, it was again renamed to Junefield Group on 15th January 2004.

Contact information

Address 16 F, Office Tower 1, Junefield Plaza, Beijing, China, 100052
Telephone 86-10-6310 2288   Facsimile 86-10-6310 2860   Website www.junefield.com

Tong Jinquan Changfeng Group
"The savvy Shanghai property mogul"

Corporate position	Founder and President, Changfeng Group
Net worth	RMB 2.3 billion (US$275 million)

Mr Tong Jinquan is the founder and president of Changfeng Group, one of the largest real estate companies in Shanghai. His expedition into the competitive real estate business was one fraught with hardship and at times, dejection. But so determined was this man's strive to succeed, he scaled one hurdle after another to arrive at his current position as one of China's most affluent persons.

Born into a poor family, Mr Tong did not receive much formal education. After graduating from high school, he worked in his parents' small business when they moved to Suzhou. Two years later, Mr Tong was appointed general manager of a local ping-pong ball factory.

In 1994, he departed for Shanghai where he started the Changfeng Group. Since then, the Changfeng Group has developed over two million square meters of real estate, with a total investment of over RMB 8.3 billion (US$1 billion). Mr Tong and his Changfeng Group are currently developing two major projects in Shanghai.

Changfeng Group is rated Triple A in terms of its credit. The group is mainly involved in property development and logistics management, focusing on the Changning District of Shanghai. Most of its real estate projects are commercial buildings and residential hubs. The Changfeng Group also helped build the Number 2 Line of the Shanghai subway. It also donated funds for building a community centre for the aged in Changning District.

Like many of the rich and powerful in China, Mr Tong remains a low-key person. He seldom accepts media interviews.

Birth date	1955
Hometown	Shaoxing City, Zhejiang Province
Education	High school

Background

Before 1991	Worked in his family's business
1991-1992	General manager and vice chairman of a local ping-pong ball factory
1992-1994	Manager, development department, Minghang Trading House Development Co Ltd
1994-	Founded Changfeng Group, acting as president

Main industries of Changfeng Group

Shanghai real estate

Zhou Zerong Kingold Group
"Mr Zhou's midas touch"

Corporate position   President, Kingold Group

Net worth   RMB 2.0 billion (US$240 million)

#27

Mr Zhou Zerong, a low-profile tycoon, is known for his unorthodox business methods. He is ranked No. 27 among China's richest people and is estimated to possess a net worth of RMB 2 billion (US$240 million).

Like many other successful Chinese businessmen, Mr Zhou went overseas in search of business ventures. Moving first to Hong Kong in the 1970s and then emigrating to Australia in the 1980s, Mr Zhou made his fortune exporting a variety of products, including Australian minerals, seafood, frozen foods and fruits to China. He returned to the Guangdong province in 1988 and expanded into the real estate business.

It was during this momentous period that he made investments in real estate, investments which insiders dubbed "high risk miracles".

He is best remembered for his first gutsy investment, the Guangdong Foreign Business Club, one of China's luxurious projects, launched in 1989 during a time when many were careful about China's economic future. His second big venture was the RMB 1 billion (US$120.8 million) Guangzhou World Trade Centre project, also at a time when the outlook of high-end projects was seemingly bleak.

However, Mr Zhou persisted, focusing on high end property development in the Guangdong region, while others headed north of China for development.

Mr Zhou has also invested in the education business in 1999 where he contributed RMB 100 million

(US$12 million) in 1999 to build the Kingold Senior Management Training Centre. The centre's MBA programme is endorsed by Shanghai Jiaotong University and it charges RMB 238,000 (US$28,744) for its MBA programme, making it one of the most expensive courses in China.

The Kingold Group has invested more than RMB 10 billion (US$1.2 billion) in China across a wide range of businesses, including education, culture, intelligent systems integration, telecommunication, pharmaceuticals, hotels, restaurants, health and beauty, foods, interior decoration, trade and high-tech agriculture. Mr Zhou's upcoming project is to develop a six-star hotel that is slated to become a major landmark in Guangzhou.

The Kingold Group's investment motto is "Succeed in the first project before proceeding to the second." And the next objective is to invest RMB 2 billion (US$240 million) to build a five-star hotel in Zhujiang New Town.

Birth date	1954
Hometown	Chaoyang City, Guangdong Province
Education	College

Background

1970	Moved to Hong Kong, ventured into trading business
1980	Emigrated to Australia focusing on trading Australian products and technology to China
1988	
1999	Moved back to Guangdong and started investing in real estates
	Established joint collaboration with Sydney University and local universities to introduce the MBA course in Guangzhou
2003	Co-operated with Shanghai Jiaotong University to promote the MBA programme

CHINA'S RICHEST PEOPLE WHO'S WHO IN CHINA

Corporate structure of Kingold Group

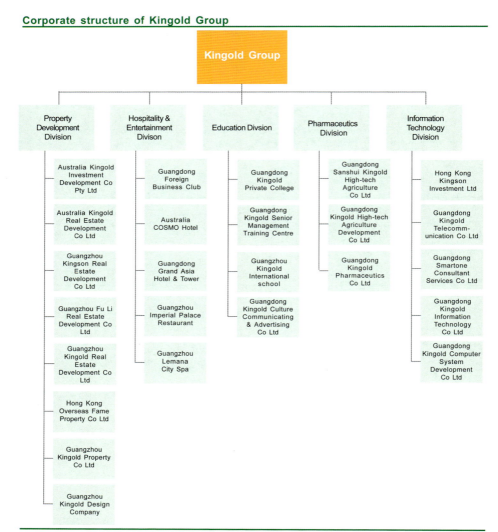

Contact information

Address Guangzhou International Trade Centre No. 1, Linhe Xi Road, Guangzhou, China
Telephone 86-20-8755 3818   Facsimile 86-20-3878 3798   Website www.kingold.com

Chen Jinfei — Tongchan Investment Group
"Of conquests and triumphs"

Corporate position	President, Tongchan Investment Group
Net worth	RMB 1.8 billion (US$ 215 million)

How did this man's meagre funds turn into a fortune? The tale of how Mr Chen Jinfei's first business deal of printing numbers on the jerseys of the Beijing basketball team made him a paltry profit of RMB 35 (US$4.2), never ceases to astonish. Today, he is ranked No. 36 among China's richest people and is estimated to possess a net worth of RMB 1.8 billion (US$ 215 million).

Mr Chen joined the former Ministry of Posts and Telecommunications after graduating from university. In 1987, he started his textile export business together with three other partners with a capital of only RMB 600 (US$73.5). Mr Chen also made his money trading high quality building bricks.

Through his unwavering spirit and endless toil, Mr Chen's business grew steadily and the company managed to make a profit of RMB 700,000 (US$84,541) by 1988.

Under his guidance, his company, the Tongchan Investment Group, became the first private company to form a Sino-foreign joint venture, as well as wield a controlling stake in a securities company[1]. Mr Chen also established a bank, "First Kerry Investment Bank" on Wall Street. While keen to invest, Mr Chen is also a pragmatic businessman and was one of the first few people to divest his interests in the Hainan property market when the tide turned.

Mr Chen is an admirer of Mao Zedong and has an avid interest in the latter's writings. His office reflects this with a display of nine large portraits of this revolutionary icon. A strong nationalistic person, he once tore up a contract involving millions of yuan due to a condescending display of attitude by an American businessman towards the Chinese. Chairman Mao's quotations are also known to plaster the walls of Tongchan's office reception area.

This businessman's favourite slogan is, "This army has an unbeatable spirit; it will fight any enemies and will not give in. No matter how harsh the environment, even if there is only one person left, he will keep on fighting."

Mr Chen is also lauded and praised by many Chinese for his contributions to the less privileged in society. In 1993, he donated his decoration-manufacturing factory to Huanro County's villagers.

Interestingly, he helped set up a German shepherd dog club given his passion for German shepherd dogs. Mr Chen is also a member of the Chinese People's Political Consultative Conference for a second term.

---

[1] Tongchan Investment Group is one of the major shareholders of Hong Kong Jin Tai Security Investment Co Ltd.

CHINA'S RICHEST PEOPLE WHO'S WHO IN CHINA

The Tongchan Investment Group, with over 1,000 staff, is set on transforming its core business from the more conventional real estate business, to a more dynamic holding group that will invest in high and new technology industries.

Birth date	1962
Hometown	Beijing
Education	People's University of China

Background

1987	Founded his textile factory
1988	Founded Tongchan Group
1988-1991	Invested in the Hainan property market

Subsidiaries of Tongchan Investment Group

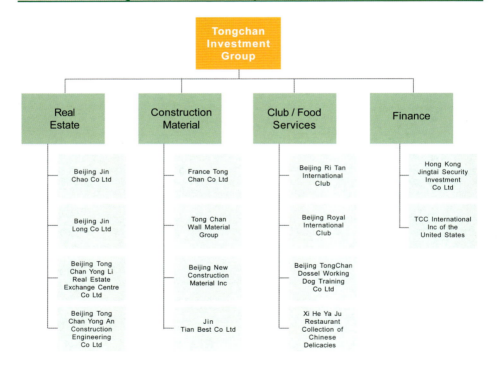

Contact information

Address Room 3509, Jing Guang Centre, Beijing, China, 100020
Telephone 86-10-6597 3388-3509   Facsimile 86-10-6597 8813   Website www.tongchan.com.cn

CHINA'S RICHEST PEOPLE WHO'S WHO IN CHINA

Chen Zhuoxian Agile (Holdings) Co Ltd
"Maintaining an agile stance"

Corporate position   President, Agile (Holdings) Co Ltd (Agile Holdings)

Net worth   RMB 1.8 billion (US$215 million)

Mr Chen Zhuoxian is reputed for his high-end residential projects in the Guangdong province. He is ranked No. 38 among China's richest people and is estimated to possess a net worth of RMB 1.8 billion (US$215 million).

Back in 1985, Mr Chen started a furniture workshop together with his brothers. Business prospered and the company soon became a major player in the Guangdong region.

Before long, Mr Chen recognised the huge potential of the property market especially with the influx of investors from Hong Kong and Macao who are interested in Guangdong. He founded Agile Holdings in 1992 and his first project was mainly targeted at Hong Kong and Macao buyers.

The marketing strategy that Mr Chen championed proved to be extremely successful. Since then, he continued to develop various high quality property projects. Agile Holdings' businesses also include golf courses, international trading, furniture, hotels and ornamental materials.

After 10 years in the real estate business, Mr Chen unveiled the "Green Architecture" concept. He pointed out, "A building should be harmonious and natural, developed with its occupants in mind. A healthy and environmental friendly living space is thus created for all."

With staff strength of more than 3,000 in 10 different subsidiaries, the company develops land area reaching 1.4 million square metres every year.

Birth date	1965
Hometown	Zhongshan City, Guangdong Province
Education	High school

Background

1985	Started a furniture manufacturing business
1992	Founded Agile Holdings
1997	Formed Agile Group

Contact information
Address Agile (Holdings) Co Ltd, Agile Hotel, Sangxiang Town, Zhongshan City, Guangdong Province, China, 528463
Telephone 86-760-6683913 / 6687188   Website www.agile.com.cn

Han Guolong Citichamp Holdings
"The property and soccer champion"

Corporate position	President of Citichamp Holdings
Net worth	RMB 1.5 billion (US$186 million)

Mr Han Guolong, who hails from the Fujian province, is one of the most successful property players in Beijing. His Citichamp Palace development generated a high degree of interest amongst the social elite in Beijing. He is ranked No. 48 among China's richest people and is estimated to possess a net worth of RMB 1.5 billion (US$186 million).

Mr Han's accomplishments culminated from his overseas experience. He worked in Indonesia for a few years before moving to Hong Kong in 1974. Mr Han got his big break when he invested in the booming real estate market in Hong Kong.

In 1988, he returned to his hometown in Fujian where he started his first project three years later. Subsequently, he moved to Hangzhou to take over an old government office site for redevelopment.

Shortly after, he acquired a listed company in Hong Kong. The year 1993 was a milestone for Mr Han when he successfully won the bid for the rights to develop Beijing's Haidian district. The project lasted nearly a decade. In 2003, he invested in a RMB 7 billion (US$850 million) project in Beijing.

Mr Han's success has been attributed to his aggressive forward-looking approach. Under his leadership, Citichamp Holdings has been constantly launching new prestigious projects.

His Citichamp Group now owns interests in a power cable firm, a Hong Kong securities firm, as well as Chengdu's soccer club which was acquired in 2003 for RMB 10 million (US$1.2 million).

Birth date	1955
Hometown	Fuqing City, Fujian Province
Education	High school

Background

1975	Emigrated to Hong Kong
1988	Moved back to China and invested in Fujian's property market
1991	Entered the Hangzhou property market
1993	Entered the Beijing property market with the contract awarded for developing Haidian district
2003	Concurrently appointed as chairman of Guancheng Datong Co Ltd

Corporate structure of Citichamp Holdings

[1] Fuzhou Yingrong Investment Co Ltd is a subsidiary of Citichamp Holdings through Fuzhou Zhongxin Investment Corporation.

[2] Guancheng Datong Co Ltd was renamed from Fuzhou Datong Co Ltd. Mr Han Guolong is the chairman of Guancheng Datong Co Ltd.

Contact information
Address First Floor, Guan Hai Building, Madian, Haidian District, Beijing, China
Telephone 86-10-8201 1333 / 8201 1777   Website www.citichamp.com

CHINA'S RICHEST PEOPLE WHO'S WHO IN CHINA

Huang Guangyu Pengrun Group
"The wizard of retailing"

Corporate position   President, Pengrun Group

Net worth   RMB 1.7 billion (US$204 million)

  "Always reach higher than you can reach. Only then, can one fly towards his dreams."

Mr Huang Guangyu

Mr Huang Guangyu is the president of Pengrun Group whose wizardry in Beijing's retail sector earned him a hefty RMB 1.5 billion (US$181.2 million) over 15 years. He is ranked No. 40 among China's richest people and is estimated to possess a net worth of RMB 1.7 billion (US$204 million).

Many in China know of the brand Gome which is associated with the largest home electrical appliance retailer in the country, but may not know of its relationship to the 35-year-old Mr Huang. In fact, Gome Home Appliance Co Ltd is only one company affiliated with the conglomerate, Pengrun Group, which is headquartered in Beijing.

Mr Huang was only 15 years of age when he left for Inner Mongolia together with his 18-year-old brother Huang Junqin with only RMB 4,000 (US$490) in their pockets to set up a trading business in the Inner Mongolia Autonomous Region in 1988. Soon after, they moved to Beijing to seek other opportunities.

When the Huang brothers noticed a perpetual shortage in the supply of home appliances, they decided to fill this gap and become home appliance retailers. They rented a small shop to sell their wares. "The reason why we shifted to home appliance retailing is that we predicted electrical appliances will have the greatest potential in changing people's daily life in the future," Mr Huang recalled.

Based on Mr Huang's business model of "low margin and high volume," sales mushroomed.

His drive to make a name for his company led him to expand his business to Beijing. In six years, Gome (pronounced as *guo mei*), became a household brand and Mr Huang is now the owner of the leading retailing chain in China with 150 stores across the country with an annual turnover of over RMB 20 billion (US$2.4 billion). In November 2003, the first Gome Hong Kong branch was established. Today, it enjoys a 35% market share in China.

By the end of 1993, the two brothers decided to divide their joint property. No exact reason has been offered for this move except Mr Huang's straightforward comment, "A company cannot have two bosses."

His brother decided to enter the Beijing real-estate market while Mr Huang decided to continue selling appliances. In addition to several hundred million yuan in assets, Mr Huang obtained the Gome brand name.

In 1996, with the establishment of Pengrun Real Estate Development Co Ltd, Mr Huang also diversified into the Beijing real-estate market. With a total investment of about RMB 1.3 billion (US$156 million), he built Pengrun Garden, a commercial and residential district. But Mr Huang's biggest real-estate property, the Pengrun Mansion, a modern office building spanning across 200,000 square meters, was not built by him but purchased from his brother.

In 1998, Mr Huang established Beijing Pengrun Investment Co Ltd, which concentrated on the funding aspects of his two core businesses, appliance retailing and real-estate development.

In February 2002, Pengrun Group stalked into the Hong Kong stock market after acquiring a 85.6% stake of a Hong Kong listed company, Capital Automation Holdings Ltd, for HK$1.5 billion. The company was later renamed the China Eagle Group. In November the same year, Pengrun Group acquired the Inner Mongolia Ningcheng Laojiao Co Ltd, which was listed on the Shanghai Stock Exchange.

Mr Huang has long admired Hong Kong tycoon Mr Li Ka-Shing, whose main businesses comprises ports, telecom, property and retail. "Li could break up the barriers between different industries to enable all the companies in his business empire to complement each other," he says.

"When it comes to making the right investment decisions, 'synergy' is the buzzword," Mr Huang stresses. "Only then can one plus one yield more than two". He does not subscribe to diversifying his investments too much.

Mr Huang's next goal is to have both his home appliance retailing and real estate development companies list on the Hong Kong Stock Exchange. "After China's accession into the WTO, we cannot regard home appliance retailers within the country as our real competitors anymore because giant retailers from abroad are preparing to march into China's markets," Mr Huang says.

Today, his Pengrun Group owns the biggest single office block building including a five-star hotel in Beijing. Mr Huang is now more involved in corporate strategic development and the capital markets.

When commenting on the problems he faces with his investments, Mr Huang has this to say, "Firstly, there are very few professionals with operational experience, especially technical experts. Secondly, there are even fewer talents with the requisite industry knowledge."

"Lastly, and most unfortunately, our people regrettably do not have high expectations of themselves," he lamented. "At the sight of the slightest improvements or results, they become complacent and think the world of themselves."

Birth date	1969
Hometown	Shantou City, Guangdong Province
Education	College

CHINA'S RICHEST PEOPLE WHO'S WHO IN CHINA

Background

1988	Trading in Inner Mongolia
1988	Moved to Beijing and started a home appliance retail business
1993	Expanded in Beijing with more branches; expanded to whole of China
1996	Established Pengrun Real Estate Development Co Ltd
1998	Established Beijing Pengrun Investment Co Ltd
2002	Purchased 85.6% shares of Hong Kong listed company, Capital Automation Holdings Ltd, and subsequently changed name to China Eagle Group
2003	Established its first Gome Hong Kong branch

Contact information
Address 18 F, Zone B, Pengrun Building, 26 Xiaoyun Road, Cao Yang District, Beijing, China

Corporate structure of Pengrun Group

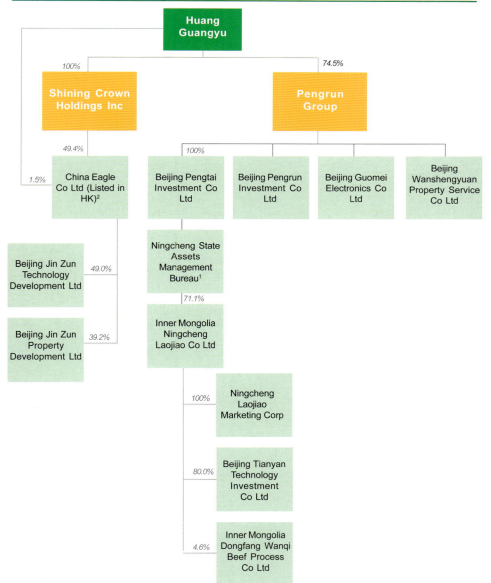

[1] Beijing Pengtai Investment Co Ltd is contracted by Ningcheng State Assets Management Bureau to manage the 71.1% shares of Inner Mongolia Ningcheng Laojiao Co Ltd from November 2002.
[2] Shareholding amount as of 2003

Miao Shouliang Shenzhen Fuyuan Group
"The forerunner who laid his own track"

Corporate position	Founder, Chairman and CEO, Shenzhen Fuyuan Group
Net worth	RMB 2.0 billion (US$240 million)

" With baby steps, fame and fortune will eventually be within grasp."

Mr Miao Shouliang

Mr Miao Shouliang's winding road to riches was one pelted with gruelling tasks and uphill mazes. But of the toils and troubles, emerged a man who wears many feathers in his cap.

The 49-year-old is the president of the Shenzhen Fuyuan Industrial Group, which controls over 300,000-square-metres of real estate, 15 wholly owned subsidiaries and 33 joint ventures. He is also vice chairman of China Young Township Entrepreneurs' Society.

Born into a poor Hakka family, Mr Miao did not receive much formal education. He spent his formative years trading local products, including wood and tobacco. By 1987, he moved to Shenzhen and took over a bankrupt stone quarry with a loan of RMB 30,000. During the first year, Mr Miao made his pile and by 1989, he had earned RMB 10 million (US$1.2 million).

From 1989 to 1990, the boom of Shenzhen's real estate industry resulted in a crippling shortage of electricity. Like a sharp-eyed falcon, Mr Miao swooped in on this crisis and installed his own power generator. Productiveness soared while his counterparts in the business struggled with power failures in their building projects. This strategy won Shenzhen Fuyuan Group several key projects, including supplying a third of the stones needed for the Shenzhen airport runway in 1988. His company is currently in a league of its own.

When land prices in Shenzhen began to plummet in 1993, resulting in financial woes for many construction companies, Mr Miao was prompt to curtail his RMB 100 million (US$12.1 million) investment in various skyscraper construction projects. He channelled his resources to developing factories instead. When property prices recovered several years later, he resumed his previous projects.

Mr Miao's foresight salvaged his company from suffering the brunt of the property crash and has instilled much confidence in his company.

Not content to rest on his laurels, Mr Miao says, "I'm a man on a quest for success and I'm always on the lookout for new challenges."

His conviction to foster a learning culture amongst his fellow countrymen has even spurred him to establish a university and schools, which offer martial arts and English courses. Opened in June 1999, Fuyuan Culture & Martial Art School consists of a middle school, primary school and kindergarten. The culture and martial arts school enrolls more than 2,000 students. Although it is still an unprofitable business, Mr Miao has insisted on subsidising top students from financially distressed families. In recent years Mr Miao have donated RMB 30 million (US$3.7 million) to educational causes.

" A person's material desires are limited. And I do not believe that fortune can bring you happiness. It's in the process of work that you find happiness," attests Mr Miao.

Mr Miao is known to be an avid reader and also likes to write poetry. "Just because I'm busy doesn't mean I have to stop reading. Learning enriches the mind and helps put my work in perspective."

On wealth, Mr Miao has this to say, "I want to use money to create wealth for society. When I am old and retired, I will leave only five million yuan for myself and donate the rest."

Today, Shenzhen Fuyuan Group is in the height of success in the real estate sphere in South China. Its interest includes the Shenzhen residential and commercial real estate, as well as manufacturing sectors.

Birth date	1955
Hometown	Meizhou City, Guangdong Province
Education	College level

Background

Before 1987	Trading in local products, including wood and tobacco in his hometown of Meizhou city
1987-1988	Moved to Shenzhen, taking over a bankrupt stone quarry
1988-1994	Founded Shenzhen Fuyuan Industrial Company, acting as General Manager
1994-	Founded Shenzhen Fuyuan Group, acting as Chairman and CEO

Honours and awards

Outstanding Private Entrepreneurs of China

Ten Outstanding Entrepreneurs of Guangdong Province

Ten Outstanding Youth of Shenzhen City

Ten Outstanding Young Entrepreneurs of Shenzhen City

Political affiliation

Member of the Chinese People's Political Consultative Conference

Main industries of Shenzhen Fuyuan Group

Shenzhen real estate, household electronic products and shopping malls

CHINA'S RICHEST PEOPLE WHO'S WHO IN CHINA

Subsidiaries of Shenzhen Fuyuan Group
Fuyuan Real Estate Development Co Ltd
Fuyuan Property Service Co Ltd
Fuyuan Industry City
Haibin Market
Fuyuan Park
Fuyuan Industry Zone
Fuyuan Garden
Fuyuan Commerce Centre
Fuyuan School

Contact information
Address 9th Floor, Fuyuan Building, 45 Fanshen Road, New Town No. 45 District, Baoan District, Shenzhen, China, 518133
Telephone 86-755-2781 6238 Facsimile 86-755-2781 7898 Website www.szfuyuan.com

"I am a very stubborn person: from a positive angle you can say that I am persistent; from a negative perspective I can be considered wilful."

Mr Song Weiping

CHINA'S RICHEST PEOPLE WHO'S WHO IN CHINA

Song Weiping Greentown Group
"Sportsmanship not just for football"

Corporate position	Founder and Chairman, Greentown Group
Net worth	RMB 1.3 billion (US$154 million)

Mr Song Weiping is the founder and chairman of the Greentown Group, which has evolved into a leading player in both the real estate and the education business.

Mr Song was previously quoted as saying that he is currently involved in "two and a half industries", namely real estate, education and a soccer team respectively.

An arts graduate from Hangzhou University (now Zhejiang University), he spent five years as a teacher in the CPC Party School of the Zhejiang province. In 1987, he resigned from his teaching position and left for Guangdong. He was hired by an IT firm in Zhuhai City.

His propensity for business surfaced quickly. From a junior staff, he rose through the ranks to become the general manager of the company.

Mr Song returned to Hangzhou City in 1994 with RMB 150,000 (US$18,115) and founded the Greentown Group to develop real estate in the city. Within eight years, the assets of Greentown Group peaked to around RMB 2 billion (US$242.5 million). Today, Mr Song has 12 developments currently underway outside his home province.

In 2002, the Group reported revenues of RMB 1.8 billion (US$220 million). The Greentown Group's investments include a kindergarten and a foreign language school. As an avid soccer enthusiast, Mr Song has also invested in a football school apart from the football club.

Birth date	1957
Hometown	Shaoxing City, Zhejiang Province
Education	Bachelor of Arts, majoring in History, Hangzhou University (now Zhejiang University), 1982

Background

1978-1982	Student at Hangzhou University
1982-1987	Teacher, CPC Party School of Zhejiang Province
1987-1994	Moved to Zhuhai City and worked in an IT company
1994-	Returned to Hangzhou City and founded the Greentown Group

Main industries of Greentown Group

Hangzhou, Shanghai and Beijing real estate and education

Contact information
Address Huanglong Century Square, 1 Hang Da Road, Hangzhou, China
Telephone 86-571-8898 8888 Website www.chinagreentown.com Email songweiping@chinagreentown.com

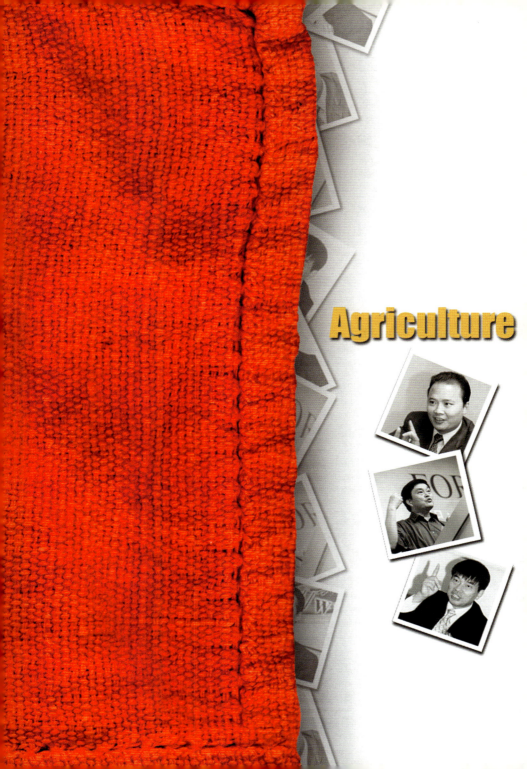
Agriculture

CHINA'S RICHEST PEOPLE WHO'S WHO IN CHINA

Liu Yonghao New Hope Group
"The beginning of hardship can only breed hope"

Corporate positions	Managing Director, New Hope Group President, Hope Group
Net worth	RMB 4.7 billion (US$565 million)

"You must have an entrepreneurial spirit to succeed."

Mr Liu Yonghao on what it takes to be successful

His childhood was so impoverished that he could not even afford any shoes. Today, Mr Liu Yonghao is one of the most active and respected private businessmen in China.

He owns the biggest animal feed business in the country, ranking him the fifth amongst China's richest people. Mr Liu is estimated to possess a net worth of RMB 4.7 billion (US$565 million).

Mr Liu is the youngest of four brothers. Before he went into business, he was a teacher earning a monthly salary of RMB 38 (US$4.6). Together with three other brothers in the family, they each left steady jobs in government departments, educational institutions and state-owned enterprises to start a quail farming business in 1982. To raise RMB 1,000 capital, they had to pawn their watches and bicycles. Six years later, they managed to amass RMB 10 million (US$1.2 million) and changed their business focus to providing bird feed to quail farmers. By 1990s, their operations had spanned the whole of China.

Eight years later, they made the timely switch to become animal feed manufacturers. Hope Group was thus founded in 1992. Through their relentless efforts, Hope Group emerged as China's foremost animal feed manufacturer, and in 1995 was ranked No. 1 by China's Bureau of Industry and Commerce among the top 500 largest privately owned enterprises.

The brothers soon realised that in order for the family business to flourish, it was imperative to bring in new talents. As a result, the company underwent two major restructuring exercises and the New Hope Group was established. The animal-feed business was split into two in 1995. Mr Liu Yongxing in Shanghai is running East Hope, and Mr Liu Yonghao in Sichuan is managing New Hope. The Liu brothers have since then also diversified into real estate, electronics, banking and insurance.

Under Mr Liu's sagacious management, New Hope Group grew to become another important market leader in the agricultural sector. Its non-agricultural business scope, which included dairy products, retail, finance, real estate and other strategic investments also proved to be highly viable.

Presently, animal feed manufacturing remains New Hope Group's core business. In the last couple of years, it hit sales of around RMB 4.1 billion (US$500 million), paid taxes of RMB 91.1 million (US$11 million) and employs 10,000 workers.

In 1996 Mr Liu set up Minsheng Bank, the first predominantly private enterprise funded bank, limited by shares, in China. Minsheng Bank was listed in early 2000 on the Shanghai Stock Exchange, with

New Hope Group as the largest shareholder. Mr Liu was the vice-chairman for two terms.

"An entrepreneur should have a vision to fulfil. I often analyse what international CEOs think about and it is uncanny how alike our thinking are. Their lives are often simple and it can be a humbling experience to know how frugal they can be."

On amassing great riches, he says, "A man hungers the most for riches when he has RMB 100,000 (US$12,000) – this is when money matters most to him. Once he acquires 10 times that amount, he becomes smug and believes he can get whatever he desires – this is also the point when a man loses most of his drive."

"An extra 100 million or a few hundred dollars makes no difference to me as long as the basics of my life can be fulfilled. I have been a teacher and a farmer," he mulls. "Even if I were to lose all my riches one day, I can still be a farmer. The bottomline is money is no longer the end goal."

"Wealth to me has lost its meaning. It is only a symbol. The accumulation of wealth to me is to contribute to society," he adds philosophically. "Many people fail to self-reflect after attaining their fortunes, forgetting their duty to the society. I am not such a person."

Mr Liu is also a founding member of Guangcai, a charity organisation set up by Chinese entrepreneurs to fight poverty. He is also a former vice-chairman of the All China Federation of Industry and Commerce (ACFIC) and a member of the Chinese People's Political Consultative Conference for a third term.

Birth date	1951
Hometown	Xinjing County, Sichuan Province
Education	Graduate, Sichuan University

Background

1982	Co-founded the Yuxin Quail Farm
1989	Developed the 'Hope' animal feed formula
1993	Co-founded the Hope Group focusing on the animal feed business
1995	Founded the New Hope Group
2000	Became one of the largest shareholders of listed private enterprise funded bank Minsheng Bank

CHINA'S RICHEST PEOPLE WHO'S WHO IN CHINA

Honours and awards

Best 10 Private Entrepreneurs in China
Man of the Time in China Reform
Top 10 Poverty Fighters of China
Outstanding Awards for Corporation Management in China
Top 10 Men of the Times in China Real Estate Industry
Year 2000 Asia Stars, by *BusinessWeek*

Corporate structure of New Hope Group

Contact information

Address No.1 Jinzhu Building, Xinkai Road, Chengdu, China, 610016
Website www.newhopegroup.com

CHINA'S RICHEST PEOPLE WHO'S WHO IN CHINA

Liu Yongxing East Hope Group
"Looking to the east for hope"

Corporate position President, East Hope Group

Net worth RMB 4.1 billion (US$490 million)

"Fame and fortune represent not only glories and achievements of yesteryear. My elevation in this society represents the possibilities that tomorrow can hold."
Mr Liu Yongxing

Mr Liu Yongxing, the second of the four brothers who co-founded the famous Hope Group, has proven himself a man of mark. He has also been heaped with commendations for his new primary metals business. He is ranked No. 7 amongst China's richest people and is estimated to possess a net worth of RMB 4.1 billion (US$490 million).

Like the rest of the Liu brothers who left their steady jobs, he resigned as an electronics spare-part designer to run the family quail farming business. Subsequently, he became the President of the Hope Group which was founded in 1991.

An internal corporate restructuring in 1995 led to Mr Liu to establish the East Hope Group, pulling together more than 10 factories during the reorganisation.

At the Shanghai government's invitation, East Hope Group moved their headquarters to the Pudong area in Shanghai in 1999 for future strategic development. The East Hope Group's decision to diversify into primary metals in 2000 was met with roaring success. The company currently consists of about 70 companies across 16 provinces. With 60 feed factories around the country and two in Vietnam, East Hope's feed sales amounted to RMB 3 billion (US$360 million) last year with 6,000 employees. Other investments include a lysine[1] plant, a finance company, a dairy products company and a small ski resort in the north of China

Mr Liu plans a second phase investment of RMB 4.6 billion (US$550 million) into the primary metal business and an investment into a South Korean fast food chain.

Mr Liu says, "Wealth is merely a symbol, the real wealth is the growth of a company built on good products nurtured by a capable organisation and managed by talented managers". He views his riches and fortunes as a "balanced" one, as "wealth signifies past successes and stands as a platform for future business enterprises". Mr Liu remains frugal in spite of his tremendous wealth and does not believe in purchasing branded clothing.

While there is no secret to his success, he claims there are factors that have been beneficial - "Firstly, revolutionary economic reforms led by the late Chairman Deng Xiaoping; secondly, positive attitudes: and thirdly, venturing into business at a time when there is less competition."

Mr Liu is also actively involved in the Guangcai charity organisation and like his brother, he believes

[1] Lysine is an animal feed ingredient.

CHINA'S RICHEST PEOPLE WHO'S WHO IN CHINA

that the wealth that they create should enable more farmers to attain financial well being, nurture workers' potential to become outstanding managers, thus creating value for society. "Through our collective efforts, we want to repay society in whatever means we can."

Mr Liu is well known for his instinct in spotting business opportunities. One striking instance was East Hope Group's move to register the trademark of *Harry Potter*, the critically acclaimed fictitious character depicted in a series of books and movie blockbusters created by British author J.K. Rowling.

Birth date	June 1968
Hometown	Xinjing County, Sichuan Province
Education	University

Background

1982	Left his electronic components designing work to start a quail farming business together with his three brothers
1986	Co-founded the Hope Science Centre focusing on the research and development of animal feed
1991	Co-founded the Hope Group and acted as Group Chairman
1995	Founded the East Hope Group and acted as Group Chairman
1999	Moved the Group headquarters to Pudong, Shanghai
2000	Diversified into the primary metals business

Contact information

Address Block 3, 1255 Shang Cheng Road, Pudong, Shanghai, China, 200120
Telephone 86-21-6876 9456   Facsimile 86-21-5830 3333

CHINA'S RICHEST PEOPLE WHO'S WHO IN CHINA

Liu Hanyuan Tongwei Group
"Setting the pace to revolutionize the aquatic industry"

Corporate position Founder and President, Tongwei Group

Net worth RMB 2.7 billion (US$330 million)

"Honesty, credibility, fairness and excellence."

The motto of Mr Liu Hanyuan and his company

Mr Liu Hanyuan was born into a poor family and graduated from Sichuan University with a master's degree. In 1984, he came up with a new technique for fish farming in his hometown. To finance his experiment, his parents sold their pigs for US$60. Soon after, he changed his business focus to selling fish feed.

Within 10 years, Mr Liu's Tongwei Group has grown into China's leading brand for fish feed with sales of over RMB 5 billion (US$600 million) in 2003. Tongwei Group is also China's largest aquatic feed production enterprise as well as a major player in poultry and livestock production, with sales in year 2000 reaching RMB 6.1 billion (US$735 million).

From being a major aquatic feed production enterprise to making sound investments in construction and real estates in Sichuan province, Tongwei Group is making its unfaltering presence felt on the China map.

Perhaps, what stands to awe most of all, is that for a man so deeply rooted in a traditional agricultural business, Mr Liu has dived into high-tech fields, sinking money into IT, biotechnology and mega-agriculture developments. Foreseeing a possible crisis that China's WTO entry might bring to his company, his answer was the diversification of his business. In 2003, Tongwei Group also ventured into pet food and other animal feeds, as well as invested RMB 2.1 billion (US$250 million) into the semi-conductor chip-making business and a further RMB 414 million (US$50 million) into real estates in Liuzhou, Guangxi. He also set up an IT joint venture with a German partner with an investment of RMB 2 billion (US$242 million). Among other strategies, Tongwei Group will also increase the feed production to 10 million tonnes in year 2010 from the present two million tonnes. The annual revenue by 2010 is projected to be RMB 30 billion (US$3.6 billion).

Such moves have proven to be truly beneficial for Tongwei Group. Mr Liu was awarded the title 'National Pacemaker of the Spark Plan for Science and Technology', a national movement aimed at the development of new technologies across industries.

Tongwei's corporate culture has been described as "working hard to help the impoverished shake off poverty, therefore good creditability is Tongwei's number one priority". While he concedes that one of the current problems Tongwei faces is perfecting its management system, he declared his ultimate goal for Tongwei Group is to "become the greatest aquatic product company, and to be king of this industry. "

CHINA'S RICHEST PEOPLE WHO'S WHO IN CHINA

Mr Liu is a member of the Chinese People's Political Consultative Conference for a second term and is currently undertaking an MBA at Peking University's Guanghua School of Management.

Mr Liu has plans to take Tongwei Group for a public listing soon.

Birth date	1964
Hometown	Meishan City, Sichuan Province
Education	Masters, Sichuan University

Honours and awards
National Excellent Young Entrepreneur
National Top Ten Private Entrepreneur
National Pacemaker of the Spark Plan for Science and Technology
Technical Expert in the National Feed Industry
Outstanding Entrepreneur of National Private Businesses

Political affiliations
Commissioner of Chinese People's Political Consultative Conference
Standing Commissioner of the Central Committee of the China Democratic National Construction Association
Vice-president of China Feed Industry Association
Vice-president of Academy of Forestry, Livestock and Fishery Sciences in China
Vice-president of China Fishery Association
Vice-president of the Private Investment Committee of IAC
Senior staff member of National Agricultural Science & Technology Association

Main industries of Tongwei Group
Fish feed and farming

Corporate structure of Tongwei Group

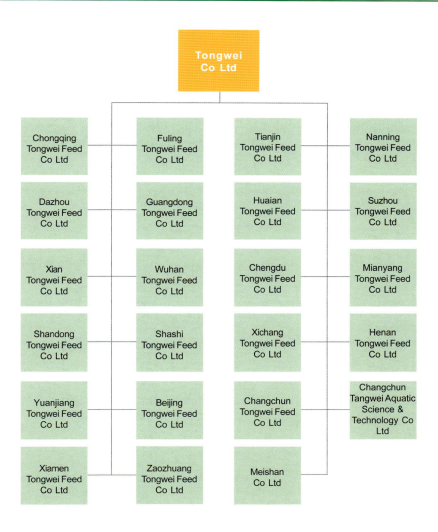

Contact information

Address No. 618, Chengdu Hi-tech Development Zone, Sichuan, China, 610041
Telephone 86-28-8518 8888   Facsimile 86-28-8519 9999   Webiste www.tongwei.com

CHINA'S RICHEST PEOPLE WHO'S WHO IN CHINA

Guo Hao   Chaoda Modern Agriculture Holdings
"Success has a bitter root, but yields sweet fruit"

Corporate position   President, Chaoda Modern Agriculture Holdings

Net worth   RMB 1.9 billion (US$225 million)

He is a self-made businessman whose wealth stems from harvesting nature's produce. Dubbed the "Fruits and Vegetables King" of China, Mr Guo Hao ranks No. 32 on the list of China's richest people and is estimated to possess a net worth of RMB 1.9 billion (US$225 million).

When the Cultural Revolution broke out in the 1960s, the young Mr Guo had to quit his studies and join the army. Perhaps it was this gruelling military training that fostered in him the stamina and mental agility to tackle Herculean tasks in the later part of his life.

In 1979, he became a sales agent for Intel Corporation after spending a few years working in the military factory.

Mr Guo then opened his own electronics trading company that gave him his first big break five years later.

Noting how much more inexpensive China's agricultural products were compared to most other countries, Mr Guo began investing in agriculture in 1994. Spotting the trend towards healthy living in China and abroad, he began supplying organic foods (grown without chemical pesticides). His organic products are mainly for export, especially to Japan.

Over the years, Mr Guo's stronghold as the "Fruits and Vegetable King" has been fortified. Chaoda Modern Agriculture Holdings was listed on the Hong Kong Stock Exchange in December 2000.

The infamous Yang Bin saga momentarily weakened Mr Guo's business but the latter's business has stood unwavering ever since.

Mr Guo also extended his business to the retail sector. There are currently five supermarkets under his company selling organic green vegetables and fruits, together with a variety of fresh foods.

Chaoda Modern Agriculture Holdings' businesses range from the supply of agricultural produce, the construction of green farm produce bases, deep processing, storage and transportation, exports of produce to the development of community chain sales network. The company's mission is, "Going the green path, creating the culture of going natural".

With Mr Guo at helm, his company has also established strategic partnerships with many chain store supermarkets including Wal-Mart (China).

CHINA'S RICHEST PEOPLE WHO'S WHO IN CHINA

Birth date	1955
Hometown	Fuzhou City, Fujian Province
Education	Junior High School

Background

1967-	Joined the People's Liberalization Army
1970's	Worked in a military factory
1989-	Became a sales agent for Intel Corporation
1993-	Set up his own electronics trading company
1994-	Commenced his investment on organic agriculture

Corporate structure of Chaoda Modern Agriculture Holdings (listed in Hong Kong)

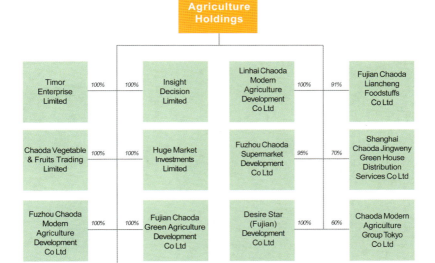

Contact information

Address No. 29 Tong Pan Road, Fuzhou, Fujian, China, 350003
Telephone 86-591-7835 933   Facsimile 86-591-7833 208

Information Technology

CHINA'S RICHEST PEOPLE WHO'S WHO IN CHINA

Ding Lei (William) Netease.com
"The wired kingdom"

Corporate position   Founder and Chief Technology Officer, Netease.com Inc

Net worth   RMB 7.6 billion (US$918 million)

"Life is like sailing in the vast ocean sea. If you lose your compass, any direction can plunge you in jeopardy."

Mr Ding Lei on the importance of setting goals in life

Mr Ding Lei, the 32-year-old founder of the NASDAQ listed Internet company, Netease.com Inc (www.163.com), is ranked the second amongst China's richest people. Holding 58.5% of Netease.com Inc's stocks, he is estimated to possess a net worth of RMB 7.6 billion (US$918 million). Netease.com Inc is a China-based provider of Chinese language online content services.

Unlike most other Internet tycoons who went overseas, Mr Ding studied and worked in China, initially in a local China Telecom bureau.

Paying no heed to his family members' objections, he quit an enviable job at Sybase, a United States software company to join a start-up IT company as their technical expert in 1996. Upon reflection, he says, "One will encounter many opportunities in one's life, but every opportunity comes with a price. The watershed of one's life is whether one has the courage to take the first step." However, this company proved to be short-lived.

Eventually, with money scrimped and saved from his four years of computer programming, the talented Mr Ding decided to set up his own business in May 1997.

As a leading Internet technology company in China, Netease.com Inc. have contributed immensely to China's IT progress. It has developed a number of popular web-based products, including China's first web-based message distribution system, the first free e-mail service, the first online community, the first personalised information service and the first online auction. It also launched business-to-consumer and consumer-to-consumer platforms. Other than relying on traditional Internet revenue sources like banner advertisement sales and e-mail subscriptions, Netease.com Inc has two other revenue streams which includes wireless downloads of SMS content such as ring tones, screen graphics, news, weather and horoscopes and online games.

"Online games let me earn more money easily, even if I did nothing but lie in bed all day long," joked Mr Ding.

According to some sources, Netease's mailbox www.163.com is the second most visited portal in China, with over four million page views per day. There is a popular saying in China, "The North has Sohu and the South has Netease." The company employs approximately 200 people in Beijing, Shanghai and Guangzhou.

Not surprisingly, many considered Mr Ding to have played a pivotal role in revolutionising the

CHINA'S RICHEST PEOPLE WHO'S WHO IN CHINA

Chinese's perception of IT. The earnest millionaire concedes that in an industry that could go from boom to bust overnight, he would rather be known for his passion and skills, not his riches. In March 2000, he relinquished the CEO title to concentrate on technology development, just as Bill Gates did with Microsoft. Sources in the company reveal that Mr Ding remains very much involved in the technology aspect of the company, and is regarded by many engineers who work for him as their mentor.

Netease.com Inc. was listed on NASDAQ on 30 June 2000 (Ticker Symbol: NTES). In 2002, the company reported a net profit of RMB 16.3 million (US$2.0 million) and generated positive operating cash flows of RMB 26.8 million (US$3.2 million).

Birth date	October 1971
Hometown	Ningbo City, Zhejiang Province
Education	Bachelor of Engineering in Communications Technology, University of Electronic Science and Technology of China (Chengdu)

Background

1993/07-1995/05	Technical engineer, China Telecom's Ningbo Branch
1995/05-1996/05	Regional project manager, Sybase Guangzhou Co
1996/05-1997/05	Worked at Guangzhou Feijie Co
1997/05-2000/03	Founder and CEO, Netease.com Inc
2000/03-	Chief Technology Officer, Netease.com Inc

Honours / awards

One of the 10 most influential Internet celebrities in China, 1999

China's Top Ten IT Figures, 2001 and 2002

Corporate structure of Netease.com Inc

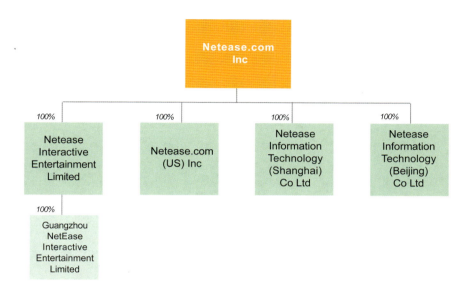

Contact information

Address NetEase.com Inc, Room 1901, Tower E3, The Towers, Oriental Plaza No. 1, East Chang An Ave, Dong Cheng District Beijing 100738, P.R. China
Telephone 86-10-85180163 Facsimile 86-10-85183618

CHINA'S RICHEST PEOPLE WHO'S WHO IN CHINA

Chen Tianqiao (Timothy)
Shanda Networking Development
"A multimillion multimedia legacy"

Corporate position	Managing Director & President, Shanda Networking Development
Net worth	RMB 4.0 billion (US$485 million)

In the clique of private businessmen, Mr Chen Tianqiao is a legend to behold. His Shanda Networking Development's growth is unprecedented. In just four years, Mr Chen increased his wealth by a staggering 8,000 fold.

He was only 30 when he created an online gaming business. This computerised empire is now worth millions and Mr Chen is placed No. 8 amongst China's richest people. He is estimated to possess a net worth of RMB 4.0 billion (US$485 million).

Mr Chen's budding business acumen was already evident during his university days. Due to his exceptional grades, he graduated one year earlier than his fellow classmates.

His first job after graduation was as a vice general manager for a real estate company under the Lu Jia Zui Group. He was soon promoted from assistant to the group chairman three years later. Despite the prospects that beckoned, he rejected his boss's invitation to join the government management.

He spent the next three years with a security brokerage company and it was during this time he discovered the huge potential of online gaming.

In 1999, he founded Shanda Networking Development. Within months of inauguration, the then animated cartoon website achieved close to a million registered users. Due to this initial success, Mr Chen successfully secured RMB 24.8 million (US$3 million) in venture capital for greater expansion.

In 2001, he shifted his core business to Massively Multiplayer Online Role-Playing Games (MMORPGs) together with the promotion of the popular online game "Legend of the Mir II" which was licensed from Korean company Actozsoft. Many deem that this decisive undertaking led to Mr Chen's underlying success.

Shanda Networking Development subsequently took a big leap forward by ploughing in millions to develop an in-house game called "New Legend", released in June 2003.

Eventually, after signing up 150 million users and an additional second phase injection of RMB 331.2 million (US$40 million) of venture capital, Mr Chen is now considered a pioneer in one of the rapidly growing businesses in China.

China's online game market is growing fast, and Shanda Networking Development holds a reported 68% market share with its MMORPGs logging over one million concurrent users playing on over 5,000 servers in 22 provinces.

Shanda Networking Development has grown from a staff-base of 50 in year 2000 to 650 three years later. Mr Chen owns more than half of the company's equity.

Birth date	1973
Hometown	Xinchang City, Zhejiang Province
Education	Bachelor of Economics, Fudan University, 1993

Background

1993-	Graduated from Fudan University
1993-1996	Vice general manager, Real Estate Company of Lu Jia Zhui Group & Assistant to Group Chairman
1996-1999	Manager in a security firm
1999-	Founded Shanda Networking Development in Shanghai
2001-	Transferred core business to on-line gaming
2003-	Released self-developed MMORPG game "New Legend"

Contact information

Address 21/22 F Hua Rong Building, Pudong, Shanghai, China, 200122
Telephone 86-21-5050 4720 Facsimile 86-21-5050 4720 - 8088   Website www.shanda.com.cn

Zhang Chaoyang (Charles) Sohu.com
"The guru of cyber space"

Corporate position	Founder, CEO, President and Chairman, Sohu.com
Net worth	RMB 2.2 billion (US$268 million)

Dr Charles Zhang is the founder of Sohu.com and has been its chairman of the board, president and chief executive officer since August 1996.

Sohu.com is visited by an average of 20 million users a day, surpassing rivals Netease and Sina. In year 2003, third-quarter revenues at Sohu rose 194% year-on-year to reach RMB 183 million (US$22.1 million), marking the 13th consecutive quarter of double-digit quarterly growth.

Says Dr Zhang on Sohu.com's success: "Among the key drivers of our success in the second quarter of 2003 were the growth in brand advertising and search/paid listings as well as our ongoing ability to have our users adopt a broadening variety of free products and services into their daily lifestyle."

Sohu.com recently launched a slew of Disney cartoon characters that are made available for download via the Sohu.com web portal and over mobile phones. In another initiative earlier this year, Dr Zhang started offering online games, which proved to be very profitable.

As a child, Dr Zhang says that he has always been "living in anticipation of bigger things to come." He even recalls his somewhat forlorn days of his teenage years when he spent night after night cramming for examinations under a dim kerosene lamp. The hardships he endured have certainly prepared him for the challenges ahead. Today, his list of accolades is testimony to his astronomical contributions to the IT landscape in China.

As a student, he excelled academically and received a scholarship after his tertiary studies at Tsinghua University in Beijing to pursue a Ph.D. degree in experimental physics from the Massachusetts Institute of Technology (MIT) in the United States. He was the country's liaison officer for MIT.

On life, Dr Zhang has this to say, "A person in my age group should have found a reason for living, whether it's a house, car, kids - but I cannot find that reason, and sometimes I know not for what I am striving. One who is nearing middle age is usually anchored by bosses, family and such trivial social structures, but I have none of these."

On fame, he says, "I have been numb to fame in China, perhaps my values and perspectives are changing. What is the definition of success? Does success in a particular group equate to success?"

Prior to founding Sohu.com, Dr Zhang worked for Internet Securities Inc (ISI) and helped establish its China operations.

In view of his outstanding performance, *Time Digital* as one of the world's top 50 digital elite in named Dr Charles Zhang in October 1998.

CHINA'S RICHEST PEOPLE WHO'S WHO IN CHINA

The World Economic Forum as a Global Leader of the Future has also recognised him. Dr. Zhang is also a regular participant in leading international conferences, including the *Fortune Global 500* Forum, *Fortune* Magazine roundtables and World Economic Forum meetings.

Dr Zhang wields so much influence that in July 2001, he was appointed to co-lead a delegation to support Beijing's successful 2008 Olympic bid at the 112th International Olympic Committee in Moscow.

Dr Zhang is also no stranger to powerful international political figures. In December 2001, he joined the International Advisory Board of the Global Attitudes Survey as an inaugural member upon the invitation by former U.S. Secretary of State Madeleine K. Albright, chairman of the project.

In March 2003 Charles Zhang became a member of the All-China Federation Of Industry & Commerce.

In May 2003 Charles Zhang joined the sohu-sponsored China Mount Everest team to climb to a height of 6,666 meters in an expedition celebrating the 50th anniversary of the human conquest of the world's highest mountain.

In July 2003 *Time Magazine* featured Charles Zhang as one of 15 Global Tech Gurus. And in September 2003, *Business Week* listed Dr Zhang as one of 25 global E-biz CEOs.

Birth date	1964
Hometown	Xi'an City, Shaanxi Province
Education	Bachelor of Science, majoring in Physics, Tsinghua University, 1986
	Ph.D., majoring in Experimental Physics, Massachusetts Institute of Technology, United States, 1993

Background

1982-1986	Bachelor degree, Tsinghua University
1986-1993	Ph.D., Massachusetts Institute of Technology
1993-1995	Post Doctoral at Massachusetts Institute of Technology
1995-1996	Worked for Internet Securities Inc
1996-	Founded Sohu.com

Awards and Honours

One of the world's Top 50 digital elite, named by *Time* magazine, 1998

Awarded by the World Economic Forum as a "Global Leader of the Future"

Joined the international advisory board of the Global Attitudes Survey as an inaugural member upon the invitation of former US Secretary of State Madeleine Albright, 2001

Initiated into the All-China Federation of Industry and Commerce, 2002

Main industries of Sohu.com Inc

SMS-messaging, online games and Internet portal

Corporate structure of Sohu.com Inc (NASDAQ listed)

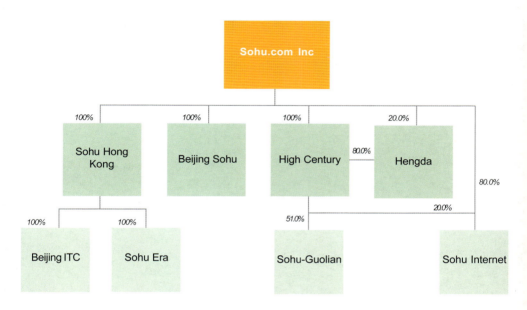

Contact information
Address 15th Floor, Tower 2, Bright China Chang An Building, 7 Jianguomen Nei Avenue, Beijing, China, 100005
Telephone 86-10-6510 2160   Facsimile 86-10-6510 1377   Website www.sohu.com

CHINA'S RICHEST PEOPLE WHO'S WHO IN CHINA

Tang Wanli

Tang Wanxin

D'Long International Strategic Investment
"Band of brothers"

Corporate position   Chairman (Tang Wanli) and President (Tang Wanxin), D'Long International Strategic Investment

Net worth   RMB 1.8 billion (US$212 million)

The Tang brothers are deeply respected for their accomplishments in various investments. They are ranked No. 39 among China's richest people and are estimated to possess a net worth of RMB 1.8 billion (US$212 million) as of October 2003.

Born into a family of intellectuals and armed with a teaching background, Mr Tang Wanli set up a film developing business together with four university friends and his brother Mr Tang Wanxin, a fresh graduate then.

This business soon developed into a computer trading and entertainment business. The turning point for the Tang brothers was the decision to enter the securities business.

In 1996, the company became one of the first private companies in China to take over a publicly listed company. The company's subsequent moves included diversifying into tomato sauce production and a cement business in North West China.

Modelled after the United States' General Electric Capital's business structure, they started fund raising and investing in various companies.

The D'Long Group is a leader in the heavy trucks industry and is also developing a retail superstore for the countryside. The Group recorded sales of over RMB 10 billion (US$1.2 billion), employing more than 100,000 employees under the management of 37 shareholders.

The company has also invested in other sectors including agriculture, animal husbandry, electromechanical manufacturing, automobile parts, building materials, mining, tourism, retailing, and financial services. Currently, D'Long Group controls five listed companies, whose total market capitalisation exceeds RMB 20 billion (US$2.4 billion). The D'Long group has also taken over the Fairchild-Dornier's project to build the 728-passenger jet, saving thousands of jobs threatened when the aircraft maker filed for bankruptcy in 2002. The new company is renamed Fairchild Dornier Aeroindustries.

Mr Tang Wanli is a member of the Chinese People's Political Consultative Conference for a second term and vice-chairman of the All China Federation of Industry and Commerce.

CHINA'S RICHEST PEOPLE WHO'S WHO IN CHINA

Birth date	1956 (Tang Wanli), 1964 (Tang Wanxin)
Hometown	Urumqi City, Xinjiang
Education	University

Background

1986	Urumqi New Product & Technology Development Company and Tianshan Business & Trade Company, predecessors of D'Long, were set up
Late 1980s	Entered the China stocks and securities market
1992	Xinjiang D'Long Industry Company was set up
1996	Successfully took over a public listed company

Corporate structure of D'Long International Strategic Investment

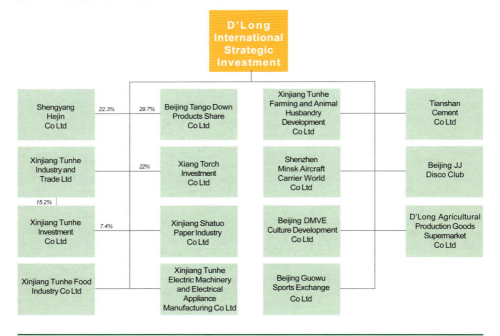

Contact information
Address No.1166 Yuan Shen Road, Pudong, Shanghai, China, 200135
Telephone 86-21-6862 4600   Facsimile 86-21-2664 8046   Website www.d-long.com

Lv Xiangyang — Youngy Investment & Management Group
"Banking on China's real estate"

Corporate position	Founder and Chairman, Youngy Investment & Management Group
Net worth	RMB 1.5 billion (US$181 million)

Mr Lv Xiangyang was only 16 when he stepped into the banking industry. He worked for 15 years at the Guangzhou branch of the People's Bank of China.

Albeit having little formal education, he was able to garner a wealth of financial experience before founding Youngy Investment & Management Group ("Youngy") at the age of 31. Youngy specialises in providing investment advisory services for its clients.

Chancing upon China's fledgling stock market and the local real estate boom, Mr Lv's break came in 1995 when he invested in his cousin's, Mr Wang Chuanfu, battery manufacturing business, BYD Co Ltd[1].

BYD Co Ltd subsequently floated on the Hong Kong stock exchange (code: 1211, BYD, listed since June 2002). Currently Mr Lv holds 21% of the stock of the listed company.

Youngy's main business today is divided into finance and manufacturing. With a private fund of several hundred million dollars, Youngy invests and manages on behalf of clients, and has interests in various industries in Guangzhou and Shanghai, including real estate, raw materials for batteries and paint emulsions.

Under Mr Lv's management, Youngy also partnered with the Shenzhen International Airport to set up a building materials trading market.

In the field of fund management, Youngy builds on a variety of investment partnerships with many financial institutions. Currently, Youngy is in talks with both China and foreign investment institutions to raise funds and to set up an investment management company specialising in investing in the automobile industry.

Birth date	1962
Hometown	Wuwei County, Anhui Province
Education	College level

Background

1978-1993	Worked at the Anhui branch of the People's Bank of China
1993-	Founded Youngy Investment & Management Group, acting as chairman

---

[1] His cousin, Mr Wang Chuanfu, was the founder, chairman and president of BYD Company Limited. Mr Wang was ranked 24 among China's richest people and was estimated to possess a net worth of RMB 2.8 billion (US$338 million) as of October 2003.

Main industries of Youngy Investment & Management Group

Finance, real estate

Contact information
Address No. B-7, Yanying Building, Shui Yin Si Heng Road, Guangzhou, China, 510075
Telephone 86-20-8704 7020, 8704 96500   Facsimile 86-20-8704 7910   Website www.youngy.com.cn

Dai Zhikang — Zendai Investment Group
"Fiscal matters"

#55

Corporate positions Founder and Chairman, Zendai Investment Group

Net worth RMB 1.5 billion (US$180 million)

"Life is like plotting your own novel. You will not know what the last chapter holds until you work your way through the twists and turns of the script."

Mr Dai Zhikang

Mr Dai Zhikang, the fourth of six children, was born into a farming family in the Jiangsu province. He went to Beijing in 1981, first studying international finance at the prestigious People's University of China, and later enrolling in economics at the graduate school of the People's Bank of China.

After graduation, he worked at the People's Bank of China, China International Trust & Investment Corporation (CITIC) and Dresdner Bank, a German and Dutch investment bank.

In the early days of 1990, Mr Dai headed down to the Hainan Province. It was there that he set up one of China's first fund management firms and embarked on his career in the financial industry. At the same time, Mr Dai started to venture into the real estate industry in Hangzhou.

However, the 1993 stock market downturn sent his business plummeting. Following a resurgence of the stock market, Mr Dai bounced back in 1998. In the same year, Mr Dai invested in the Shanghai property market when he realised that the property value in Shangai was undervalued given the economic growth of the city. At the same time he was looking to invest in a listed property company but he did not find any that met his requirements then.

In 2000, he started a private equity fund, taking over a Hong Kong listed vehicle (Shanghai Century Holdings Limited, code: 0755, listed since March 2003).

While financial management remains Zendai Investment Group's core business activity, the Group also has vested interests in the real estate industry. Mr Dai's plans to build a five-star hotel are also underway.

CHINA'S RICHEST PEOPLE WHO'S WHO IN CHINA

On success, Mr Dai once said during an interview, "Successful people must have the following qualities, passion, ambition and agility. At the same time, these qualities alone will never be enough, you must also have the poise and cool-headedness of a realist, finishing a task in a down-to-earth fashion."

To him, Chinese culture "does not teach you how to make money, compete and fight. Being a good person matters above all. Chinese are also inculcated with the notion that money is not everything and life can be rendered meaningless and fearful with too much fortune to handle," Mr Dai thus feels that, "Although modern society cannot be separated from money, we need to be able reconcile the importance of material assets with the value of life."

A subsidiary of Zendai Investment Group, Shanghai Zendai Century (Group) Co Ltd, recently purchased French sculptor Cesar Baldaccini's "Thumb" sculpture for RMB 2.6 million (US$314,300) in 2002 at the Shanghai Art Fair. "Shanghai is a cosmopolitan city, but the current sculptures in the city are far from impressive. We lack a defining sculpture, such as the Statue of Liberty in the United States," says Mr Dai, who is also president of Shanghai Zendai Century (Group) Co Ltd. "I hope the 'Thumb' will be a good start."

Birth date	1964
Hometown	Haimen City, Jiangsu Province
Education	Bachelor's degree, majoring in International Finance, People's University of China, 1985
	Master's degree, majoring in Economics, Graduate School of People's Bank of China, 1988

Background

1981-1985	Bachelor's degree, People's University of China
1985-1988	Master's degree, Graduate School of People's Bank of China
1988-1990	Worked at the People's Bank of China, CITIC and Dresdner Bank
1993-	Relocated to Hainan Province and set up the Hainan Zendai Investment Management Co Ltd, Shanghai Zendai Investment Management Co Ltd, and Zendai Investment Group, acting as chairman

Main industries of Zendai Investment Group
Real estate in Shanghai and Hangzhou, and financial management

Corporate structure of Zendai Investment Group

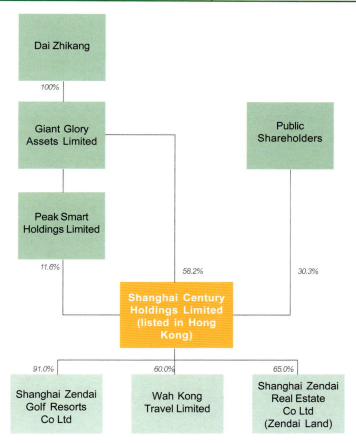

Contact information
Address 24-A-F, Huadou Building, 838 Zhangyang Road, Pudong District, Shanghai, China, 200122
Telephone 86-21-6876 2401 / 6876 2402 / 6876 3946   Facsimile 86-21-6876 4884   Website www.zendai.com

Food & Beverage

Ming Jinxing People's Food Holdings
"Savouring the corporation's exponential growth"

#16

Corporate positions	Co-founder and Chairman, People's Food Holdings
Net worth	RMB 2.5 billion (US$307 million)

Mr Ming Jinxing is the founder and executive chairman of People's Food Holdings, which is dually listed on the Singapore Stock Exchange (code: PFOOD, listed since March 2001) and Hong Kong's main board (code: 0708, listed since October 2002).

Holding 5.9% of People's Food Holdings' shares, Mr Ming is the largest individual shareholder of the company. His net worth was estimated to be around RMB 2.5 billion (US$307 million) at the end of 2003.

A graduate of Shandong Medical University, Mr Ming was a practising medical doctor for 12 years before he decided to venture into the business world of medical equipment trading in 1993.

A year later, he co-founded People's Food Holdings with two brothers, Mr Zhou Liankui and Mr Zhou Lianliang.

People's Food Holdings became China's most successful company in the meat products market with the "Jinluo" brand as its flagship brand. The Jinluo brand was recognised as one of the top 10 brands in China in terms of brand recognition, goodwill and market share in the year 2000.

In 2002, the company recorded revenues of RMB 5.1 billion (US$615.9 million) and a net profit of RMB 822.8 million (US$99.4 million).

Regarded as a low-profile figure, as chairman of the board of directors since 1994, Mr Ming is in charge of conceptualising overall strategy and direction of the group.

Birth date	1958
Hometown	Zibo City, Shandong Province
Education	Bachelor's degree, majoring in Medicine, Shandong Medical University, 1981

Background

1977-1981	Studied at Shandong Medical University, majored in Medicine
1981-1993	Served as a doctor at Beijing Medical University Hospital and subsequently at Xiehe Hospital
1993-1994	Started his own business in medical equipment trading
1994-	Founded People's Food Holdings

CHINA'S RICHEST PEOPLE WHO'S WHO IN CHINA

Main industries of People's Food Holdings
Meat products

Corporate structure of People's Food Holdings (Listed in Singapore and Hong Kong)

Contact information
Address Bancheng Town, Linyi, Shangdong, China, 276036
Telephone 86-539-869 2888 Facsimile 86-539-869 2875 Website www.peoplesfood.com.sg

Zhu Yicai — Jiangsu Yurun Food Group
"China's food manufacturing baron"

Corporate positions	Founder and CEO, Jiangsu Yurun Food Group
Net worth	RMB 1.8 billion (US$222 million)

Like many self-made men in China, Mr Zhu Yicai came from humble beginnings. Impoverishment in his childhood imbued in him an aptitude to tackle the hardships of life.

In 1989, after graduating from the Hefei University of Technology, he was assigned to work in an ocean shipping company at the Anhui Transportation Bureau.

His lofty ambitions led him to start his own seafood business. In the same year, with a meagre capital of RMB 200 (US$24), he began exporting shrimps and crabs to Japan. So lucrative was this business, he managed to amass a fortune of RMB 3 million (US$362,000).

Following his first successful venture, Mr Zhu left his hometown in search of even more opportunities. Hence, Jiangsu Yurun Group was established. The company began focusing on the meat business.

Within several years, he has developed the Jiangsu Yurun Group into China's leading company in the low temperature meat processing industry. Today, the Yurun brand of meat products can be found virtually in every supermarket all over China.

With 12,000 employees, the Jiangsu Yurun Group reported revenues of RMB 4 billion (US$490 million) and paid taxes of RMB 289.8 million (US$35 million) in 2002. To cater to the towering demand, Mr Zhu has been significantly expanding the group.

The Jiang Yurun Group has one listed company in Hong Kong (Oriental Investment Corporation Limited, Code: 0735, listed since April 2002). Mr Zhu has also acquired 20 state-owned enterprises in the process.

While his meat business continues to enjoy stable growth, Mr Zhu has also injected his resources into the real estate field. His first projects have already taken root in Nanjing, Beijing and Hefei.

The central principle that the "food industry is a moral industry" is inducted into each Yurun staff.

Jiangsu Yurun Food (Group) Co Ltd earned widespread accolades such as 'The Most Influential Food Enterprise in 21st Century', 'One of the top 20 outstanding food enterprises in China food industry', and 'The enterprise with outstanding contribution to Chinese food industry 1998-2001' awarded by the China Food Industry Association in December 2001. Mr Zhu was also awarded the 'One of the top 20 outstanding entrepreneurs' amongst other accomplishments.

Mr Zhu is the president of Nanjing Association of Industry and Commerce.

CHINA'S RICHEST PEOPLE WHO'S WHO IN CHINA

Birth date	1964
Hometown	Tongcheng City, Anhui Province
Education	Bachelor of Engineering, Hefei University of Technology, 1989

Background

1985-1989	Bachelor of Engineering, Hefei University of Technology
1989-1989	Started work in an ocean shipping company at the Anhui Transportation Bureau
1989-1992	Started his seafood trading business

Political affiliation

Delegate to the National People's Congress

Main industries of Yurun Group

Meat products and real estate

Corporate structure of Yurun Group[1]

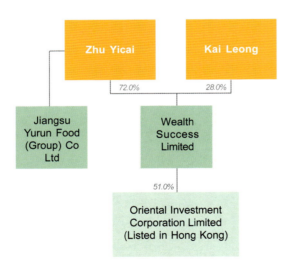

Contact information

Address Bancheng Town, Linyi, Shangdong, China, 276036
Telephone 86-025-6800 888   Facsimile 86-025-6802 612   Website www.yurun.com

---

[1] Mr Zhu is also the executive director of Oriental Investment Corporation Limited. Mr Kai Leong, the chairman of Oriental Investment Corporation Limited, is a business associate of Mr Zhu.

CHINA'S RICHEST PEOPLE WHO'S WHO IN CHINA

Zong Qinghou Wahaha Group
"Brewing the potion of success"

Corporate position   Founder and Chairman, Wahaha Group

Net worth   RMB 1.3 billion (US$151 million)

  "The key to entrepreneurship is sharpening your intuition."
                                                            Mr Zong Qinghou

It was the sweltering summer of 1987 when Mr Zong Qinghou was pushing a wooden mobile stall peddling ice cream on the streets of Hangzhou City. It is hard to imagine that this man would one day assume the position of chairman of China's largest soft drink company.

While Coca Cola may be the best-known soft drink brand in the world, the Wahaha brand is more familiar to the billions in China. Such is the crowning point in Mr Zong's career.

Back then, his family was affiliated with high ranking officials. During the Cultural Revolution's purge of the bourgeois influence, the young Mr Zong was sent down to the remote countryside to do hard labour.

Deprived of a formal education, he resolved to work doubly hard. When he returned to Hangzhou 15 years later, he ran a small business in the school where his mother taught.

From 1987, he started selling school stationery. Later, he switched to drinks and ice cream targeted at students.

Business boomed and since then, the Wahaha Group has developed seven more product ranges. Their key products include bottled milk, water, and soft drinks.

Wahaha Group's track record has been so impressive that in 1996, a French-based beverage company invested in a joint venture with the company.

More recently in 1998, his company launched 'Future Cola', a carbonated soft drink to compete against the big multinational carbonated drinks brands like Coca Cola and Pepsi. Since the launch, Future Cola's sales volume has exceeded 100,000 tonnes and demand is greater than supply, with shortages estimated at 3 million boxes per month.

The Wahaha Group reported revenues of RMB 8.8 billion (US$1.06 billion) and net profits of RMB 1.2 billion (US$144.9 million) in 2002.

On China-created brands, Mr Zong says, "China brands are worthless." As ruthless as this may sound, he believes that "China has not reached the age of brand recognition. Although one can create brand recognition with advertisements, the man on the street does not exhibit strong brand loyalty – they are realistic and habitually purchase things which are cheap and good." He also reckons it will take another few decades before China enters the era of brand recognition.

CHINA'S RICHEST PEOPLE WHO'S WHO IN CHINA

The success of Future Cola was undoubtedly due to its attractive price. Mr Zong says, "We are in the business of fast moving consumer goods, pricing is important, prices cannot be too high. To be profitable we need to achieve sales volume and lower production costs with automation and distribution channels."

"What we lack now is not credibility, but courage to compete with foreign brands." Having said that, Mr Zong also says that the problem with foreign multinational companies is that they are not well adapted to do business in China. For instance, Coca Cola is said to report RMB 500 million (US$60 million) annually, which is less than what a single company under the Wahaha Group can earn. The reason for this, says Mr Zong is that Wahaha Group has established an extensive distribution network which he referred as the "spider network" across China. This is precisely what enables Wahaha Group to control the end retail points.

Birth date	October 1945
Hometown	Hangzhou City, Zhejiang Province
Education	Vocational School

Background

1961-1964	Manual work in Makou Farm, the countryside of Zhoushan County, Zhejiang Province, during the Cultural Revolution
1964-1978	Yardman, Lvxing Farm, Zhejiang Province
1978-1979	Business executive, Paper Box Factory of Hongzhou Industrial & Agricultural School
1979-1980	Worked at Hangzhou Guangming Electric Instrument Factory
1981-1982	Worked at Hangzhou Shengli Electric Instrument Factory
1982-1986	Business executive, Hongzhou Industrial & Agricultural School Factory
1986-1987	Manager, Hangzhou Shangcheng District School Factory
1987-1991	Founded the Wahaha Nutrition Food Factory, acting as the director
1991-	Restructured Wahaha Nutrition Food Factory into the Wahaha Group

Political affiliation

Delegate to the National People's Congress

Main industries of Wahaha Group

Soft drinks and children clothing

Contact information
Address No. 128-1, North Qiu Tao Road, Hangzhou, China
Telephone 86-571-8603 2866   Facsimile 86-571-8695 1532   Website www.wahaha.com.cn

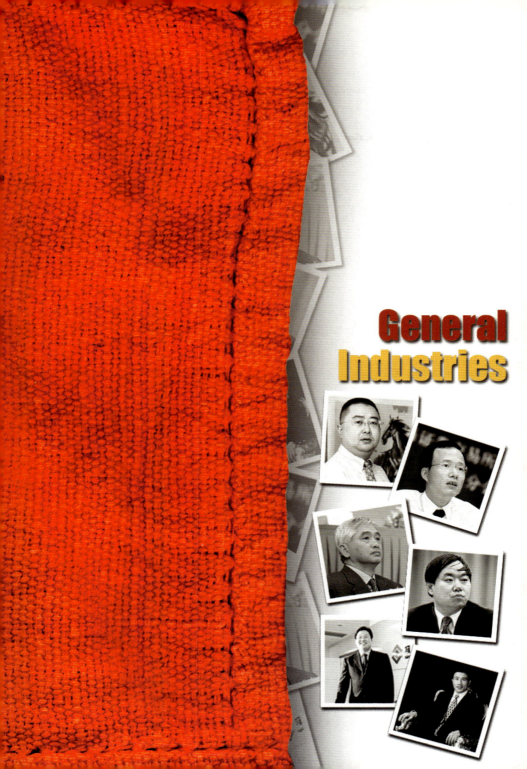

General Industries

CHINA'S RICHEST PEOPLE WHO'S WHO IN CHINA

Rong Zhijian (Larry) CITIC Pacific
"A capitalist like no other"

#1

Corporate position	Executive Director, China International, Trust & Investment Corporation (CITIC) Chairman, CITIC Pacific & CITIC Hong Kong (Holdings) Ltd (CITIC HK)
Net worth	RMB 8.1 billion (US$975 million)

 "I've learnt not to bear resentment towards the Cultural Revolution. In many ways, I've become a stronger person."

Mr Rong Zhijian on how the Cultural Revolution left a profound impact on him

Shanghainese Rong Zhijian is the son of former vice president of CITIC Pacific, Mr Rong Yiren. He is ranked first among China's richest people and is estimated to possess a net worth of RMB 8.1 billion (US$975 million).

He is from a well-heeled family but many have attributed his ascent to his current position of power entirely to his own calibre.

During the Cultural Revolution, he worked in the countryside for eight years from 1966 to 1973 where he endured hard labour. "I feel that the biggest impact to my life had been the Cultural Revolution. Before this, I can say that I have never suffered." When recalling those years, he says with emotions, "I suffered a lot during those 8 years, and learnt many things. One becomes stronger, and is no longer as naïve about society. This taught me many deep truths of life, and I gained knowledge that I could never get in school."

His previous stint also included 14 years of experience with the Ministry of Electric Power.

Admittedly, riding on his family's name may have opened windows of opportunities. However, Mr Rong asserts that this is not permanent. To prove himself, he left his wife and family behind when he was 36 years old to relocate to Hong Kong in 1978, where his father still had some assets mostly in the textile industry. With these assets, he set up Elcap Electric Pte Ltd with two cousins, which eventually made him a return of 56 times his initial investment when he sold it years later to an American electronics firm.

His subsequent US$2 million investment in a software company in the United States marked his next triumph, bringing him a 40 times return in investment on his original 60% stake when the company was listed in 1984. His partners in this venture included Mr Michael Feuer and other famous American software designers.

After joining CITIC Pacific where his father worked as the vice president and general manager, Mr Rong made calculated investments, including the acquisition of 12.5% of Cathay Pacific Airways and 20% of Hong Kong Telecom.

Under Mr Rong's discerning management, CITIC grew into a HK$20 billion (US$2.6 billion) business empire with businesses in infrastructure, real estate, marketing and distribution.

An avid lover of horse racing, Mr Rong is also a steward of the Hong Kong Jockey Club.

CHINA'S RICHEST PEOPLE WHO'S WHO IN CHINA

Birth date	1942
Hometown	Wuxi City, Jiangsu Province
Education	Bachelor of Electrical Engineering, Tianjin University

Background

1965-1966	Worked in a small water electric power station (Jiling province, countryside)
1966-1972	Worked in the countryside during the Cultural Revolution (Sichuan province)
1972	Returned to Beijing
1978	Moved to Hong Kong
1987	Ran a venture capital firm and founded CITIC Pacific

Other information

Mr Rong is the only son in his family, with two elder sisters and two younger sisters.

List of subsidiaries of CITIC Pacific

Power Generation	Inner Mongolia Electric Power Generation Company Limited - 35% (Indirect) Jilin Xinli Power Cogeneration Co., Ltd. - 60% (Indirect) Wuxi Taihu Lake Pumped Storage Power Co., Ltd. - 70% (Indirect) Inner Mongolia Mong Hua Tai Re Dian Private Limited - 50% (Indirect) Jiangsu Ligang Electric Power Company Limited - 56.31% (Indirect) Kaifeng Xinli Power Generation Co., Ltd. - 50% (Indirect) Zhengzhou Xinli Electric Power Co., Ltd. - 50% (Indirect)
Tunnels	New Hong Kong Tunnel Company Limited - 70.8% (Indirect) Eastern Harbour Crossing Company Limited - 50% (Indirect) Hong Kong Tunnels and Highways Management Company Limited - 35% (Indirect) Western Harbour Tunnel Company Limited - 35% (Indirect) Ecoserve Limited - 50% (Indirect)
Environmental	Enviropace Limited - 20% (Indirect) Green Valley Landfill, Limited - 30% (Indirect) South China Transfer Limited - 30% (Indirect)
Communications	AAA Internet Limited - 100% (Indirect) CITIC Concept 1616 Limited- 100% (Indirect) CITIC Consultancy 1616 Limited - 100% (Indirect) CITIC Data 1616 Limited - 100% (Indirect) China Interactive Sports Technology Company Limited - 100% (Indirect) CITIC Networks 1616 Limited - 100% (Indirect) CITIC Pacific Communications Limited - 100% (Indirect) CITIC Telecom 1616 Limited - 100% (Indirect) CITIC TeleSoft 1616 Limited - 100% (Indirect) CPCNet Hong Kong Limited - 100% (Indirect) CPCNet Japan Limited - 100% (Indirect) CPCNet Macau Limited - 100% (Indirect) CPCNet Singapore Private Limited - 100% (Indirect) Data Communication Services Limited - 100% (Indirect) Global Link Information Services Limited - 100% (Indirect) Vision Network Limited - 100% (Indirect) World Navigation Limited - 100% (Indirect) Guangzhou Taifu Science and Technology Private Limited - 100% (Indirect) Guangzhou Taifu Technology Private Limited - 100% (Indirect) CITIC Guoan Co., Ltd. - 50% (Indirect) Companhia de Telecomunicacoes de Macau S.A.R.L. - 20% (Direct)

CHINA'S RICHEST PEOPLE WHO'S WHO IN CHINA

Aviation	Air China Cargo - 25% (Direct)
	Cathay Pacific Airways Limited - 2.14% (Direct) - 23.56% (Indirect)
	Hong Kong Dragon Airlines Limited - 28.5% (Indirect)
	Swire Aviation Limited - 33.3% (Indirect)
Marketing & Distribution	Adachi Trading Company Limited - 100% (Indirect)
	Confidence Motors Limited - 100% (Indirect)
	Consolidated Parts & Accessories Sales Centre Limited - 100% (Indirect)
	Dah Chong Hong (Canada) Ltd. Dah Chong Hong (China) Limited - 100% (Indirect)
	Dah Chong Hong – Dragonair Airport GSE Service Limited - 70% (Indirect)
	Dah Chong Hong (Engineering) Limited - 100% (Indirect)
	Dah Chong Hong Holdings Limited - 100% (Indirect)
	Dah Chong Hong, Limited - 100% (Indirect)
	Dah Chong Hong (Japan) Limited - 100% (Indirect)
	Dah Chong Hong Motors (China) Limited - 100% (Indirect)
	Dah Chong Hong (Motor Leasing) Limited - 100% (Indirect)
	Dah Chong Hong (Motor Service Centre) Limited - 100% (Indirect)
	Dah Chong Hong Motors (Nissan – China) Limited - 100% (Indirect)
	Dah Chong Hong Trading (Singapore) Pte. Ltd. - 100% (Indirect)
	DAS Aviation Support Limited - 70% (Indirect)
	DAS Nordisk Limited - 49% (Indirect)
	DCH Beverage Solutions Limited - 100% (Indirect)
	DCH Food Industries Limited - 100% (Indirect)
	DCH Healthcare Products Limited - 100% (Indirect)
	DCH Motors (Bentley) Limited - 100% (Indirect)
	DCH Motors Ltd. - 100% (Indirect)
	Gentech Vehicle Engineering Limited - 100% (Indirect)
	Guangdong Jing Yun Distribution Co., Ltd. - 90% (Indirect)
	Harmony Motors Limited - 100% (Indirect)
	Honest Motors, Limited - 100% (Indirect)
	Japan Auto Parts Company Limited - 100% (Indirect)
	Premium Motors Limited - 100% (Indirect)
	Regal Motors, Limited - 100% (Indirect)
	Reliance Motors, Limited - 100% (Indirect)
	Sims (China) Limited - 100% (Indirect)
	Sims (Guangdong) Limited - 100% (Indirect)
	Sims Trading Company Limited - 70% (Indirect)
	Shanghai DCH Food Industries Ltd. - 100% (Indirect)
	Triangle Auto Pte Ltd - 100% (Indirect)
	Triangle Motors Limited - 100% (Indirect)
	Triangle Motors (China) Limited - 100% (Indirect)
	Twin Tiger International Limited - 100% (Indirect)
	Jiangmen Dachang Shenchang Food Processing Private Limited - 90% (Indirect)
	Jiangmen Shenchang Trading Private Limited - 100% (Indirect)
	Qingdao Adachi Paints and Chemical Materials Co., Ltd. - 75% (Indirect)
	Shiseido Dah Chong Hong Cosmetics Limited - 50% (Indirect)
	Alto China Limited - 50% (Indirect)
	Shanghai Shineway DCH Tyson Co., Ltd. - 22% (Indirect)

Property	Admarch Limited - 100% (Indirect)
Admarch Property Management Company, Limited - 100% (Indirect)
Borgia Limited - 100% (Indirect)
Broadway Centre Property Management Company Limited - 100% (Indirect)
Campbellton Development Limited - 100% (Indirect)
Famous Land Limited - 100% (Indirect)
Glenridge Company Limited - 100% (Indirect)
Goldenburg Properties Limited - 70% (Indirect)
Hang Luen Chong Investment Company, Limited - 100% (Indirect)
Hang Luen Chong Property Management Company, Limited - 100% (Indirect)
Hang Wah Chong Investment Company Limited - 100% (Indirect)
Lindenford Limited - 100% (Indirect)
Neostar Investment Limited - 100% (Indirect)
Pacific Grace Limited - 100% (Indirect)
Shanghai Super Property Co., Ltd. - 100% (Indirect)
Tendo Limited - 100% (Indirect)
Yee Lim Godown & Cold Storage Limited - 100% (Indirect)
Shanghai Citic Taifu Square Private Limited - 80% (Indirect)
Shanghai Lauximen Xinyuan Properties Private Limited - 100% (Indirect)
Wuxi Taihujin Development Private Limited - 70% (Indirect)
Wuxi Taihuyuan Properties Private Limited - 70% (Indirect)
Wuxi Taihumei Environment Protection Private Limited - 70% (Indirect)
CITIC Tower Property Management Company Limited - 40% (Indirect)
Festival Walk Holdings Limited - 50% (Indirect)
Goldon Investment Limited - 40% (Indirect)
Hong Kong Resort Company Limited - 50% (Indirect)
Kido Profits Limited - 15% (Indirect)
Shinta Limited - 20% (Indirect)
Sun Kong Investment Company, Limited - 40% (Indirect)
Industrial Manufacturing	Jiangyin Xingcheng Special Steel Works Co., Ltd. – 54.94% (Indirect)
Jiangyin Xingcheng Steel Products Co., Ltd. - 55% (Indirect)
Jiangyin Xingcheng Storage and Transportation Co., Ltd. - 55% (Indirect)
Jiangsu CP Xingcheng Special Steel Co., Ltd. – 54.72% (Indirect)
Wuxi Huada Motors Co., Ltd. - 50% (Indirect)
Jiangyin Tai Fu Xing Cheng Special Materials Private Limited - 54.87% (Indirect)
Finance	CITIC Pacific Finance (2001) Limited 100% (Direct)
Idealand Investment Inc. 100% (Indirect)
Top Trend Investments Holdings Corp. 100% (Direct)
Cheer First Limited - 40% (Indirect)
Treasure Trove Limited - 50% (Indirect)
Way Chong Finance Limited - 50% (Indirect)
Others	Botanitown Pharmaceuticals Limited - 62% (Indirect)
Beijing Botanitown Biotechnologies Limited - 62% (Indirect)
CITIC Pacific China Holdings Limited - 100% (Indirect)
Winway Investments Holdings Corp. - 62% (Indirect)
CITIC Capital Markets Holdings Limited - 50% (Indirect)
CP Adaltis Hong Kong Company Limited - 50% (Indirect)
Shanghai Citic Yataisi Testing Private Limited - 50% (Indirect)
Sichuan Luzhou Ketai Biotechnology Development Private Limited - 31% (Indirect)

Contact information

Address 32nd Floor, CITIC Tower, 1 Tim Mei Avenue, Central, Hong Kong
Telephone 852-2820 2111　Facsimile 852-2877 2771　Website www.citicpacific.com

CHINA'S RICHEST PEOPLE WHO'S WHO IN CHINA

Sun Guangxin Guanghui Enterprise Group
"A man of enterprising undertakings"

Corporate position	Founder and CEO, Guanghui Enterprise Group
Net worth	RMB 3.1 billion (US$379 million)

" To make it big in your career, you need to initiate, not to be instructed."

Mr Sun Guangxin's motto

Mr Sun Guangxin is the founder and CEO of the Guanghui Enterprise Group, headquartered in Urumqi City, Xinjiang Municipality. With more than 23,000 employees, the Group reported sales of RMB 7 billion (US$840 million) in 2002.

Even after relinquishing 25% of his shares to his management team, he remains the major shareholder of the company and is estimated to possess a net worth of RMB 3.1 billion (US$379 million).

Mr Sun enlisted at the tender age of 18 to become an army officer in the People's Liberation Army (PLA). Later on, he fought in the 1979 border war with Vietnam.

When the war ended, he quickly established himself in business with the founding of Guanghui Enterprise Group in 1989. He said to himself then, "I want to build a top quality company within 15 years."

With only RMB 3,000 (US$362) for capital, the company first channelled its investments into restaurants and leisure ventures. His first venture was a seafood restaurant in Urumqi city. The seafood restaurant was a hit with large companies throwing business banquets and dinner functions. The shrewd Mr Sun noticed that most of the guests who wined and dined at his restaurant were from the oil industry. He took the opportunity to build relationships with these guests and was subsequently given an opportunity to distribute oil drilling spare parts. Within three months, he turned a profit of RMB 230,000 (US$27,700). Gradually, the company changed its focus to the trading of oil equipment, including deals with companies from the former Soviet Union.

He also ventured into marble stone trading and refining, tapping on the large reserves of marble in Xinjiang and the rising demand for marble in China. Mr Sun ploughed profits from his various businesses into the real estate industry in Xinjiang. Soon, his company dominated the local market in Xinjiang, providing homes to one quarter of the citizens in Urumqi. Inevitably, this success led the organisation to become one of the leading real estate company in China.

The company was listed at the Shanghai Stock Exchange in May 2000 (code: 600256). In 2002, Guanghui was ranked sixth amongst China's private enterprises.

In 2001, Mr Sun invested in a US$1 billion five-year natural gas refinery project and a US$310 million exhibition and logistics centre project to accentuate the growth of the company.

Mr Sun smiled when asked how a private company like his managed to get permission to develop the natural gas market in China.

"The government wouldn't give this project to a Fortune 500 company," he said. "They're not paying 10% of the taxes here, they are not employing 10% of the workforce. We're providing a huge service to society. We've got roots."

Guanghui Enterprise Group has been very successful as a result of these projects and has expanded rapidly since 2003.

To Mr Sun, talent is the biggest capital of any organisation. He says, "An entrepreneur's responsibility is to choose good people, use them well and manage them well. One must place the right specialists in positions where they can fully realise their potential."

Birth date	December 1962
Hometown	Pingdu City, Shandong Province
Education	Postgraduate degree, Anhui Military College
Professional qualification	Senior economist

Background

Before 1989	Served in the PLA as a military officer
1989-	Founded Guanghui Enterprise and Trading Co. Ltd. (formerly known as Guanghui Enterprise Group) and acted as CEO

Main industries of Guanghui Enterprise Group

Real estate, building materials and natural gas

Corporate structure of Guanghui Enterprise Group

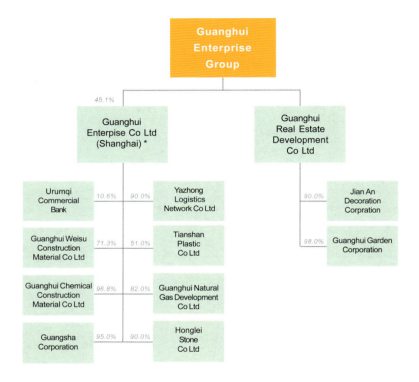

* "Guanghui Enterprise Co Ltd" was known as "Guanghui Granite Mine Development Co Ltd" before March 2002.

Contact information
Address No. 6, Urumqi Economic and Technological Development Area, Xinjiang Municipality, China, 830026
Telephone 86-991-373 5597 Facsimile 86-991-371 8150 Website www.guanghui.com

CHINA'S RICHEST PEOPLE WHO'S WHO IN CHINA

Guo Guangchang
Shanghai Fosun High-Tech Group
"The power of technology to enrich"

#12

Corporate position	Co-founder and Chairman, Shanghai Fosun High-Tech Group
Net worth	RMB 3.2 billion (US$380 million)

 "What the youth needs is not individual heroism, but collective heroism."
Mr Guo Guangchang

Mr Guo Guangchang graduated from China's prestigious Fudan University in 1989 where he studied philosophy and thereafter worked at the university for the next three years.

In 1992, Mr Guo entered business at the age of 25 and founded a consulting company with four partners who were all younger than him. In June of 1993, he decided to shift focus from market research to real estate and biotechnology.

With only RMB 100,000 (US$12,000), he and his partners decided to focus primarily on the biotech industry. Shanghai Fosun High-Tech Co Ltd was thus born.

The company progressed successfully and soon became the first privately owned high technology company in Shanghai in 1994.

With support garnered from different cliques of communities in China, the Shanghai Fosun High-Tech Group ventured successively into the industries of biotech, property, IT, commerce and trade, finance, and steel manufacturing. In the past decade, Mr Guo has made indelible marks in these various sectors.

Mr Guo says, "A businessman should be logical. Similar to an artist, he should possess both talent and passion - qualities that cannot be cultivated from a man-made mathematical process." He adds that a businessman's talent lies in whether he can spot the opportunity in the market, although passion is equally important as it enables one to surmount many difficulties. He quips, "Like fighting a battle, a big victory is built on many small victories. Passion will arm one with patience in surmounting difficulties."

In 2002, the sales volume of Fosun Group reached RMB 10.1 billion (US$1.2 billion) and total assets measured RMB 11.5 billion (US$1.4 billion).

Meanwhile, the Shanghai Fosun High-Tech Group ranked 144th amongst the top 500 enterprises in China and ranked sixth amongst the top 10 private enterprises in China in 2003.

In 2002, the sales volume of the company and its associated parties reached RMB 34 billion (US$4.1 billion) and total assets amounted to RMB 20.2 billion (US$2.4 billion).

The company also controls three companies listed on Shanghai's Stock Exchange Shanghai

CHINA'S RICHEST PEOPLE WHO'S WHO IN CHINA

Fosun Industrial (code: 600196; listed since August 1998), Yuyuan Tourist Mart (code: 600655; listed since November 2001), and Nanjing Iron and Steel (code: 600282; listed since April 2003).

As one of China's most outstanding private technological entrepreneurs, Mr Guo has often been hailed as "Shanghai's Bill Gates".

He was a member of the previous session of Chinese People's Political Consultative Conference. Currently, he serves as a delegate to the National People's Congress.

Birth date	1967
Hometown	Dongyang City, Zhejiang Province
Education	Bachelor's degree, Department of Philosophy, Fudan University, 1989
	MBA, Management School, Fudan University
Professional qualification	Senior engineer

Background

1989-1992	Worked at Fudan University
1992-	Founded Shanghai Fosun High-Tech (Group) Co Ltd

Honours and awards

China's outstanding private entrepreneur
1997 Model works of Shanghai
One of the ten 'Outstanding young persons' in Shanghai
Winner of the May Fourth Movement Medal for Chinese Youth
Winner of the 2000 'Chinese Redbud Cup' achievement award for outstanding entrepreneurs
2001 'Opens up awards' for China's outstanding private technological entrepreneurs
2002 China's outstanding private technological entrepreneur

Political affiliations

Delegate to the Tenth Session of the National People's Congress
Standing commissary, Ninth Executive Council of All-China Federation of Industry and Commerce
Committee member, Eighth committee of Chinese Youth Union Conference
Vice chairman, Chinese Youth Entrepreneur Association
Deputy chairman, Shanghai Federation of Industry and Commerce
Deputy chairman, Shanghai Enterprise Director Association
Deputy chairman, Shanghai Youth Union Conference

Main industries of Shanghai Fosun High-Tech Group

Shanghai real estate, steel, and pharmaceuticals

Corporate structure of Shanghai Fosun High-Tech Group

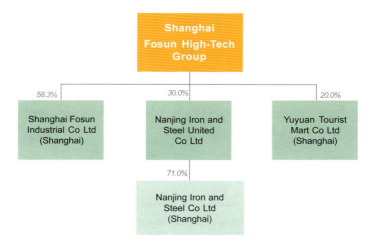

Contact information

Address No 2, East Fu Xing Road, Shanghai, China, 200010
Telephone 86-21-6332 5858   Facsimile 86-21-6332 5028   Website www.fosun.com

Xu Ming Shide Group
"Opening the windows to wealth"

Corporate position	Founder and President, Shide Group
Net worth	RMB 2.8 billion (US$338 million)

Mr Xu Ming is the founder and president of Shide Group, which is a leading company in the construction materials market in China. At 33, Mr Xu is one of the youngest on the list of the China's richest.

Although polyvinyl chloride (PVC) manufacturing remains the core of Shide's business, Mr Xu and his Shide Group have undoubtedly made a name for themselves with their soccer club, which has won seven championships in the nine-year history of China's top soccer league.

"Soccer is a faster and more efficient form of advertising for us. As a matter of fact, most people are acquainted with Shide through the popularity of our soccer club," he states, "I believe that after China has joined WTO, many foreign companies will be inclined to invest in soccer clubs to publicise their brands."

In 2000, Shide Group shelled out RMB 120 million (US$14.5 million) for full ownership of Wanda soccer club in Dalian. This saved Shide Group RMB 40 million (US$4.8 million) of advertising budget and brought in RMB 70 million (US$8.4 million) worth of publicity.

Throughout his primary, secondary and tertiary studies, the talented Mr Xu excelled academically and graduated a full year ahead of his classmates. This head start in life no doubt propelled him to eventually become one of the pillars of the Chinese economy.

Mr Xu graduated from Shenyang Aviation College with a master's degree in international trade. After working for a year, Mr Xu, then only 22 years old, won the bid in 1992 to provide soil for a reclamation project, which earned him RMB 30 million (US$3.5 million).

In 1995, Mr Xu founded the Shide Group in 1994 and began manufacturing PVC materials used for panelling in windows and doors. The government's support for the real estate development during those years proved to be a boon to Mr Xu's business. The company was able to expand swiftly and eventually, Shide Group also acquired a bus factory and a water heater business.

"I think everything can serve as an opportunity. The real challenge is how to seize them in a timely manner." Mr Xu, explaining his business philosophy.

Today, Shide Group is the world's largest manufacturer of PVC. The company has also expanded its soccer game ventures and has made further inroads into the financial industry.

The group presently controls a local commercial bank, and made investments in two insurance companies, a private equity fund and several small listed companies.

Under Mr Xu's direction, Shide Group now controls two Shanghai listed companies: Ningxia

CHINA'S RICHEST PEOPLE WHO'S WHO IN CHINA

Dayuan Chemicals (code: 600146, listed since December 2000) and Lingyun (code: 600480, listed since July 2003). In 2002, the group reported revenues of RMB 4.8 billion (US$580 million) and paid taxes of RMB 207 million (US$25 million).

Birth date	1971
Hometown	Zhuanghe City, Liaoning Province
Education	Master's degree, majoring in International Trade, Shenyang Aviation College, 1990

Background

1990-	Graduated from Shenyang Aviation College
1990-1991	Worked at Zhuanghe Foreign Trading Commission
1991-1992	Started his own business in the construction industry
1992-	Founded the Shide Group, acting as president

Main industries of Shide Group

PVC manufacturing, soccer and finance

Corporate structure of Shide Group

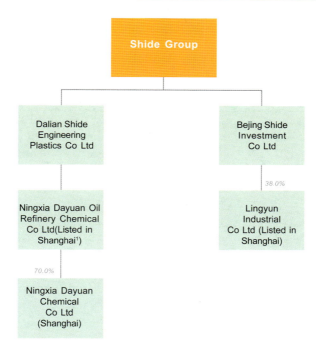

[1] In September 2002, Dalian Shide Engineering Plastics Co Ltd injected RMB 256.8 million (US$31 million) worth of goods (in terms of PVC profiles and other products) into Ningxia Dayuan Oil Refining Chemical Co Ltd.

Contact information

Address 38 Gao Er Ji Road, Xigang District, Dalian, Liaoning, China, 116011
Telephone 86-411-362 2218   Website www.shide.com

CHINA'S RICHEST PEOPLE WHO'S WHO IN CHINA

Zhang Yong Linfeng Group
"Fuelling the assets"

Corporate position   President, Linfeng Group

Net worth   RMB 2.5 billion (US$301 million)

  "The journey that Linfeng Group is about to undertake spans as long as the Great Wall of China. This acquisition marks only the first baby step."

Mr Zhang Yong, on his energy industry investment

Mr Zhang Yong is the first person in China to take over a *Fortune 500* enterprise's China asset - Enron's share in a Chengdu power station through his private enterprise, Linfeng Group.

He is ranked No. 17 amongst China's richest people and is estimated to possess a net worth of RMB 2.5 billion (US$301 million).

Being one of the richest men at only 38, Mr Zhang is regarded as the epitome of success.

He was born into a military family in the Xinjiang province. As a small boy, he moved to Chengdu. In 1986, he left for Hong Kong and found work in a hotel.

His first business venture was in textiles trading, followed by real estate investments in Guangdong in 1988. He was later involved in alcohol trading in northern part of China, a business that was rigidly controlled by the state government.

He established Linfeng Group in Beijing in 1993. In three years' time, Mr Zhang's restaurant cum entertainment centre gained immense popularity in Chengdu. Linfeng Group has never looked back since.

Following the acquisition of a state-owned real estate company in 1995, Linfeng Group swelled to a corporation with 5,000 employees and US$1 billion sales.

At a signing ceremony, Mr Zhang once said in mirth, "Foreign companies sink money into China so that we can lay hands on their assets."

The Linfeng Group consists of three regional centres, namely in Beijing, Chengdu and United States (Hawaii). It is actively involved in the energy industry, real estates in Chengdu, Beijing and Dalian, trading, a hotel in Hawaii, petrochemicals and a dinosaur theme park.

Birth date	1966
Hometown	Yilin City, Xinjiang Municipality
Education	Bachelor degree, majoring in Economics and Management, Peking University

Background

1986-1988	Worked in a hotel in Hong Kong after graduation from university
1988-	Moved back to China and began alcohol trading and textile import/export business
1993-	Founded Linfeng Group
1994-	Set up restaurant and entertainment centre in Chengdu
1995-	Took over a state-owned real estate company

Contact information

Address No. 5 Gao Qiao Dong Road, Chengdu City, Sichuan Province, China
Telephone 86-28-8515 7780 / 8517 1180

CHINA'S RICHEST PEOPLE WHO'S WHO IN CHINA

Wang Yusuo XinAo Group
"Powered by gases"

Corporate position   President, XinAo Group

Net worth   RMB 1.9 billion (US$230 million)

Mr Wang Yusuo, who thrice flunked his university entrance examinations, found his calling in the natural gases industry.

He is ranked No. 29 among China's richest people and is estimated to possess a net worth of RMB 1.9 billion (US$230 million).

Mr Wang, who always had a strong desire to make it on his own, never had a taste of slogging for others in his younger days. His first small business was selling sunflower seeds and beer.

A few years later, he set up a taxi company and soon caught onto the accelerating demand for oil products. He subsequently closed down his taxi company in 1984 to start a canned gas trading business. His company, thus, became one of the first pioneers in the natural gas industry.

In 1992, he founded XinAo Gas Company and began investing in city-gas projects. His was the first private enterprise to be involved in a public utilities project. XinAo Gas was one of the first non state-owned piped gas distributors in Mainland China. The principal business of XinAo includes the operation and management of gas pipeline infrastructure, as well as sales and distribution of piped gas and gas appliances. A couple of years later, his XinAo Group made Langfang the first city in the Hebei province to use a natural gas pipeline.

"In line with the support of use of natural gas by the Chinese government, with the aim of alleviating pollution problems from coal combustion, we believe that the natural gas market presents tremendous potential for growth" says Mr Wang. Through the Chinese government's economic policies and inauguration of the "West to East China plan for natural gases" policy, Mr Wang's XinAo Group has become the biggest non state-owned city gas operator in China.

According to Mr Wang, the Group possesses clear business focus and strategies, "As a leading non state-owned piped gas distributor in the China, we enjoy competitive advantages and promising business prospects." He adds that their experienced management team coupled with a diversified clientele including residential, commercial and industrial users enable XinAo "to have a balanced mix of revenues."

XinAo Group is focusing on China's major cities for its further expansion backed by its extensive network across more than 30 cities. With staff strength of 4,000, the company has been chalking up sales of up to RMB 571.3 million (US$69 million).

Mr Wang is also owner of two golf courses in China.

Birth date	1964
Hometown	Bazhou City, Hebei Province
Education	Master's degree, Tianjin University of Finance and Economics
	Bachelor's degree, Renmin University of China

Background

Before 1984	Small retail business and operated a taxi company
1984-	Canned gas trading business
1992-	Founded the XinAo Group
1994-	Made Langfang the first city in the Hebei province to use a natural gas pipeline
2002-	Successfully entered the capital market in the Hong Kong stock exchange and secured loans from international banks

Contact information
Address Huaxiang Road, Langfang Economic & Technological Development Zone, Hebei Province , China, 065001
Telephone 86-316-6079 999   Facsimile 86-316-6080 999   Website www.xinaogroup.com

CHINA'S RICHEST PEOPLE WHO'S WHO IN CHINA

Jian Yinghai Jian Enterprise Group

Corporate positions	Founder, Chairman and President, Jian Enterprise Group
Net worth	RMB 1.5 billion (US$179 million)

Born in Hunan Province, Mr Jian Yinghai is of Uyghur ethnicity. Similar to many others in businesses in the late eighties, Mr Jian started his business by buying electronics in Shenzhen and trading them in Beijing.

He headed out briefly to the United States to 'broaden his mind' in 1991. Since then, he has ventured into a variety of industries including investments in the stock market and in the entertainment industry.

With more than 3,000 employees, the Jian Enterprise Group has developed rapidly since its founding. In 2001, the Group reported revenues of RMB 1.2 billion (US$145 million). Jian Enterprise Group currently has two listed companies: Jian ePayment Systems, listed in Hong Kong GEM (code: 8165, listed since December 2001) and Wuchangyu, listed in Shanghai (code: 600275, listed since July 2002).

Whilst the Group is still expanding its Beijing supermarket chain, Mr Jian proceeded to roll-out to his Hong Kong-listed e-payment systems to ten cities around China. Jian ePayment Systems Limited is one of the first developers and operators of the electronic payment system utilising contactless smart card technology in the PRC. He also injected some of his real estate into the Shanghai-listed company in 2002.

Mr Jian was one of the first entrepreneurs of the private sectors to start charitable activities. He led poverty-relief projects throughout China. In 1993 and 1995, he financed the drilling of two oil wells in an old revolutionary base area in northwest China's Shaanxi Province. In 1994, he provided economic assistance to more than 60 dropouts in Sichuan and Anhui provinces through "Project Hope", and set up a RMB 1 million "Huapu Charity Fund" to help poverty-stricken city students complete their education.

Birth date	1962
Hometown	Hunan Province
Education	Bachelor degree, Beijing Broadcast College

CHINA'S RICHEST PEOPLE WHO'S WHO IN CHINA

Background

Late 1980s	Trading electronics between Shenzhen and Beijing
1991	Stayed in the United States
1991-1994	Invested in the stock market and entertainment industry
1994-	Founded Jian Enterprise Group, acting as chairman and president of the Group

Political affiliation

Member of the Chinese People's Political Consultative Conference for a second term

Main industries of Jian Enterprise Group

Beijing real estate, electronic payment systems and retail

Corporate structure of Jian Enterprise Group

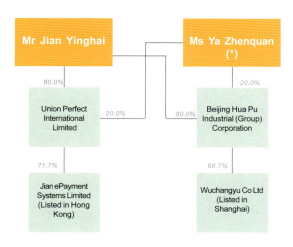

* Ms Ya Zhenquan is Mr Jian Yinghai's mother.

Contact information

Address Jian Enterprise International Building, 19 Chao Yang Men Wai Street, Beijing, 100020
Telephone 86-10-6599 3388 / 6599 6688   Facsimile 86-10-6599 1693   Website www.jiangroupco.com

Offshore Incorporation Services

- Offshore company incorporation
- Corporate secretarial services
- Shelf companies for purchase
- Nominee shareholders and directors
- Company administration and services
- Operation of bank accounts
- Bank signatory
- Invoicing
- Custodial services

Incorporate in:
Mauritius
British Virgin Islands
Bahamas
Jersey
Cayman Islands
Isle of Man
Netherlands Antilles
Singapore
Labuan
Hong Kong

CHINA BUSINESS INTELLIGENCE & CORPORATE SERVICES
5 Shenton Way
#37-02 UIC Building
Singapore 068808
Tel: (65) 6358 2289
www.1st-link.com

Leaders of China's Largest Companies

These are accounts of miracle workers, of men and women overcoming insurmountable obstacles: transforming small companies on the brink of disaster into global successes and reaping unimaginable riches.

But divine intervention, or even luck, has very little to do with the miracles they do;

Like the coal-miner who became a top banker,

Or the man, who dreamt of taking what is a local household name and turning it into a global brand,

Or the woman whose steely facade belies her flexible approach in running her organisation.

At the heart of each and every account is a simple tale of hope, perseverance and the triumph of those who never give up.

Smooth flowing distribution

Growth opportunities in China can be tapped more effectively with an efficient distribution network. For over 20 years, TNT enables the smooth flow of trade between China and more than 200 countries. Covering over 500 cities in China, TNT provides customers who want to do business with China with fast, reliable and innovative Express delivery and Logistics solutions. TNT, the leading Express and Logistics company in Europe, has the expertise to deliver distribution solutions to customers in China.

For more information, please call:

China 800 810 9868   Hong Kong 852 2331 2663   Indonesia 62 21 520 1157   Japan 81 3 5445 1301   Korea 82 2 6669 0401
Malaysia 603 5568 8888 Philippines 63 2 551 5632 Singapore 65 6214 1111   Taiwan 886 2 2791 8277
Thailand 66 2 249 8000   Vietnam 844 514 2574 (Hanoi) / 848 848 6820 (Ho Chi Minh)

or visit: www.tnt.com

Business Logistics Solutions that deliver

Top 100 Companies in China

Rank (Sales)	Company Name	Chairman	President	2002 Sales (billion) RMB	US$
1	China National Petroleum Corporation	Chen Geng*	Chen Geng*	379.20	45.80
2	Sinopec Group	Chen Tonghai*	Wang Jiming	378.00	45.65
3	China Mobile Communications Corporation	-	Zhang Ligui*	163.73	19.77
4	Industrial and Commercial Bank of China	Jiang Jianqing*	Jiang Jianqing*	161.62	19.52
5	SinoChem Corporation	-	Liu Deshu*	155.29	18.75
6	China Telecommunications Corporation	Zhou Deqiang*	Zhou Deqiang*	149.08	18.00
7	China First Automobile Works Group Corporation	-	Zhu Yanfeng*	127.24	15.37
8	China Life Insurance Company	Wang Xianzhang*	Wang Xianzhang*	126.91	15.33
9	Bank of China	Xiao Gang*	Xiao Gang*	126.18	15.24
10	China Construction Bank	-	Zhang Enzhao*	112.06	13.53
11	China National Cereals, Oils and Foodstuffs Imp & Exp Corporation	Zhou Mingchen*	Li Fuchun	109.71	13.25
12	Agricultural Bank of China	-	Yang Mingsheng*	96.46	11.65
13	Shanghai Baosteel Group Corporation	Xie Qihua*	Xie Qihua*	77.73	9.39
14	Guangdong Guang-dian Power Grid Group Co Ltd	Wang Yeping	Wu Zhouchun	76.95	9.29
15	Shanghai Automotive Industry Corporation	Chen Xianglin	Hu Maoyuan*	71.20	8.60
16	Haier Group	Zhang Ruimin*	Zhang Ruimin*	71.06	8.58
17	China Network Communications Group Corporation	-	Zhang Chunjiang*	66.03	7.97
18	China State Construction Engineering Corporation	-	Sun Wenjie	63.83	7.71
19	China Ping An Insurance Co Ltd	Ma Mingzhe*	Ma Mingzhe*	62.03	7.49
20	China Putian Corporation	-	Ouyang Zhongmou*	60.23	7.27
21	China Ocean Shipping (Group) Company	-	Wei Jiafu*	59.49	7.18
22	Philips (China) Investment Co Ltd	Rob Westerhof	Zhang Bian	58.42	7.06
23	Dong Feng Automobile Co (Second Automotive Works Corporation)	Miao Wei*	Miao Wei*	53.36	6.44
24	State Post Bureau	-	Liu Andong*	51.05	6.17
25	China United Communications Corporation	Wang Jianzhou	Yang Xianzu*	50.33	6.08
26	Motorola (China) Inc	Gene Delany	Shi Dakun	47.10	5.69
27	China Railway Engineering Corporation	-	Qin Jiaming	46.96	5.67
28	Shanghai Electronic (Group) Corporation	Wang Chengmin	Ma Xinsheng	46.94	5.67
29	China National Metals & Minerals Import & Corporation	-	Zhou Keren	46.30	5.59
30	China Railway Construction Corporation	-	Wang Zhenhou	45.20	5.46
31	Beijing Railway Bureau	-	Li Shutian	44.49	5.37
32	China Weapon Industrial Group Corporation	-	Wang Dechen	42.61	5.15
33	China South Industries Group Corporation	-	Ma Zhigeng	39.69	4.79
34	China Huaneng Group	-	Li Xiaopeng*	37.04	4.47
35	Shanghai Volkswagen Automotive Company Ltd	Chen Xianglin	Chen Zhixin	36.27	4.38
36	China Aviation Industry Corporation I	-	Liu Gaozhuo	36.00	4.35
37	Legend Group	Liu Chuanzhi*	Yang Yuanqing*	35.54	4.29
38	China National Offshore Oil Corporation	-	Fu Chengyu	34.34	4.15
39	Yuxi Hongta Tobacco (Group) Co Ltd	Liu Wandong	Yao Qingyan	33.60	4.06
40	SVA Group	Xu Weihu	Xu Weihu	33.15	4.00
41	China Worldbest Group Co Ltd	Zhou Yucheng	Zhou Zhengsheng	32.00	3.86
42	Shanghai Railway Bureau	-	Liu Lianqing	28.62	3.46
43	Zhonghuan Information Industrial Group	-	Chen Wu	28.41	3.43
44	Zhengzhou Railway Bureau	-	Xu Yifa	27.68	3.34
45	China Southern Airlines Co Ltd	Yan Zhiqing*	Wang Changchun	26.90	3.25
46	China Aviation Industry Corporation II	-	Zhang Yanzhong	26.30	3.18
47	Shenhua Group Corporation Ltd	Chen Biting	Chen Biting	25.79	3.11
48	Liaoning Electronic Power Corporation	Zhong Jun	Tang Shisheng	25.65	3.10
49	Shougang Group	Zhu Jimin	Wang Qinghai	25.38	3.07

* Featured in Who's Who in China

LEADERS OF CHINA'S LARGEST COMPANIES WHO'S WHO IN CHINA

Rank (Sales)	Company Name	Chairman	President	2002 Sales (billion) RMB	US$
50	Hualian Group	Huang Yue	Huang Yue	25.17	3.04
51	China Metallurgy Construction (Group) Corp	Yang Changheng	Ma Yanli	24.77	2.99
52	Anshan Iron & Steel Group Corporation	-	Liu Jie	24.56	2.97
53	Bank of Communications	Yin Jieyan	Fang Chengguo*	24.56	2.97
54	Benxi Steel (Group) Co Ltd	-	Liu Guoqiang	23.42	2.83
55	Air China (Group) Corporation	-	Li Jiaxiang*	23.19	2.80
56	Shanghai Construction Group	Jiang Zhiquan	Xu Zheng	23.00	2.78
57	China-Aerospace Science and Industry Corporation	-	Xia Guohong	22.67	2.74
58	Zhejiang Wuzi Group	Hu Jiangcao	Wang Yudi	22.65	2.74
59	TCL Group	Li Dongsheng*	Li Dongsheng*	22.12	2.67
60	Huawei Technologies Co Ltd	Sun Yafang	Ren Zhengfei*	22.00	2.66
61	China Shipping (Group) Company	-	Li Kelin	21.60	2.61
62	China Development Bank	-	Chen Yuan	21.40	2.58
63	Aluminium Corporation of China	Guo Shengkun	Guo Shengkun	20.79	2.51
64	China National Coal Group Corp	-	Jing Tianliang	20.53	2.48
65	China Eastern Airlines Co Ltd	Ye Yigan*	Li Fenghua	20.48	2.47
66	China Railway Material Corporation	-	Dong Guifeng	20.39	2.46
67	Guangzhou Automobile Industry Group	Zhang Fangyou	Lu Zhifeng	20.19	2.44
68	Chengdou Railway Bureau	-	Qi Wenchao	20.18	2.44
69	China Harbour Engineering (Group) Corp	-	Liu Huaiyuan	20.15	2.43
70	China Shipping Industry Corp	-	Li Changyin	20.05	2.42
71	Shengyang Railway Bureau	-	Zhang Wei	19.99	2.41
72	Wuhan Iron & Steel (Group) Co Ltd	-	Liu Benren	19.76	2.39
73	China State Shipbuilding Corp	-	Chen Xiaojin	19.72	2.38
74	Hisense Group	Zhou Houjian*	Zhou Houjian*	19.31	2.33
75	Guangzhou Railway (Group) Corp	Jiang Linxiang	Zhang Zhengqing	18.72	2.26
76	China Aviation Oil Holding Company	-	Jia Changbin	18.61	2.25
77	Chunlan Group	Tao Jianxin*	Tao Jianxin*	18.58	2.24
78	Shanghai GM Co Ltd	Phil Murtaugh	Chen Hong	18.56	2.24
79	Lianhua Supermarket Holdings Co Ltd	Wang Zongnan	Wang Zongnan	18.33	2.21
80	China National Foreign Trade Transportation (Group) Corp	-	Zhang Jianwei	18.25	2.20
81	Guangdong Wuzi Group Corp	Zhuang Yao	Zhuang Yao	18.00	2.17
82	Jinan Railway Bureau	-	Zuo Shenxiang	17.59	2.12
83	Beijing Urban Construction Group Co Ltd	Dong Yonggui	Yu Zhitong	17.58	2.12
84	Haerbin Railway Bureau	-	He Hongda	17.53	2.12
85	China National Machinery & Equipment (Group) Corp	-	Ren Hongbin	17.32	2.09
86	Shanghai Huayi (Group) Corp	Zhang Peizhang	Xing Xuepu	16.54	2.00
87	Panda Electronics Group Co Ltd	Xi Yongmin	Li Anjian	16.39	1.98
88	Shanghai Tobacco (Group) Corp	-	Dong Haolin	16.31	1.97
89	Guangdong Guangxin Foreign Trade (Group) Corp	Li Dehe	Chen Jinshhui	16.19	1.96
90	China Beidahuang (Group) Corp	Sun Yongcai	Yu Hongzhou	15.89	1.92
91	Great Wall International IT Product (Shenzhen) Co Ltd	Wang Zhi	Jeffrey Gallinat	15.58	1.88
92	Shanghai Pharm (Group) Corp	Zhou Yucheng	Qian Jin	15.07	1.82
93	Media Group	He Xiangjian	Zhang Hechuan	15.05	1.82
94	Shanxi Coal Distribution (Group) Corp	-	Zhang Gengu	14.68	1.77
95	China National Postal and Telecommunications Appliances Corp	-	Yang Zhongliang	14.67	1.77
96	Yan Kuang (Group) Co Ltd	Geng Jiahuai	Geng Jiahuai	14.57	1.76
97	Jiangsu Shagang Group	Sheng Wenrong	Sheng Wenrong	14.51	1.75
98	Founder Group	Wei Xin	Zhang Zhaodong	14.50	1.75
99	Nanjing Iron & Steel Group	Xiao Tongyou	Yang Simin	14.49	1.75
100	Shenzhen Construction Investment Holding Corp	Zhang Yijun	Jiang Hongku	14.38	1.74

Note: President of Tsingtao Brewery Co Ltd, Mr Jin Zhiguo and Chairman of China Vanke, Mr Wang Shi are also featured although the company is not ranked top 100 in China

LEADERS OF CHINA'S LARGEST COMPANIES WHO'S WHO IN CHINA

Geographic Breakdown of China's Largest Companies[1]

Province	Number of Companies	Province	Number of Companies
Beijing	46	Shanghai	17
Guangdong	12	Shandong	4
Liaoning	4	Jiangsu	4
Hubei	2	Tianjin	2
Heilongjiang	2	Jilin	1
Yunnan	1	Henan	1
Shaanxi	1	Zhejiang	1
Sichuan	1	Shanxi	1

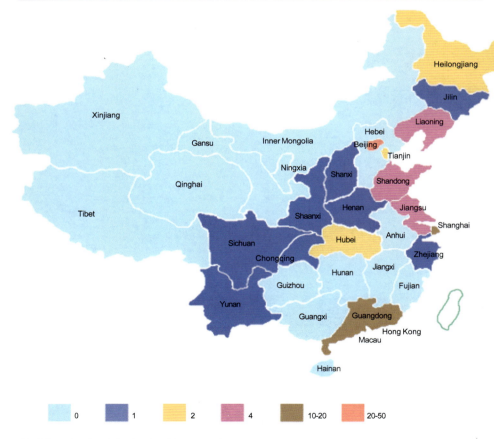

[1] Statistics are based on the headquarters of these companies

Where China's Largest Companies are Listed[1]

No.	Sales 2002 RMB Billion	Company name	Shanghai	Shenzhen	Hong Kong	New York	Others
1	379.20	China National Petroleum Corporation CHEN Geng			✓	✓	
2	378.00	Sinopec Group CHEN Tonghai			✓	✓	London ✓
3	163.73	China Mobile Communication Corporation ZHANG Ligui			✓		
4	161.62	Industrial and Commercial Bank of China JIANG Jianqing			✓		
5	155.29	SinoChem Corporation LIU Deshu					
6	149.08	China Telecommunications Corporation ZHOU Deqiang			✓		
7	127.24	China First Automobile Works Group Corporation ZHU Yanfeng	✓	✓✓			
8	126.91	China Life Insurance Company WANG Xianzhang			✓		
9	126.18	Bank of China XIAO Gang			✓		
10	112.06	China Construction Bank ZHANG Enzhao					
11	109.71	COFCO ZHOU Mingchen			✓✓✓		
12	96.46	Agricultural Bank of China YANG Mingsheng					
13	77.73	Shanghai Baosteel Group XIE Qihua	✓				
14	71.20	Shanghai Automotive Industry Corporation HU Maoyuan / JIANG Mianheng	✓				
15	71.06	Haier Group ZHANG Ruimin	✓			✓	
16	66.03	China Network Communications ZHANG Chunjiang					
17	62.03	China Ping An Insurance Co Ltd MA Mingzhe					
18	60.23	China Putian Corporation OUYANG Zhongmou	✓✓✓	✓	✓		
19	59.49	China Ocean Shipping (Group) Company WEI Jiafu	✓✓	✓✓	✓✓		Singapore ✓
20	53.36	Dong Feng Automobile MIAO Wei	✓				
21	51.05	State Post Bureau LIU Andong					
22	50.33	China United Communications Corporation YANG Xianzu	✓				
23	37.04	China Huaneng Group LI Xiaopeng	✓		✓	✓	
24	35.54	Legend Group LIU Chuanzhi & YANG Yuanqing			✓		
25	33.60	Hongta Group LIU Wandong	✓	✓			
26	26.90	China Southern Airlines Ltd YAN Zhiqing			✓		
27	24.56	Bank of Communications FANG Chengguo					
28	23.19	Air China (Group) Corporation LI Jiaxiang					
29	22.12	TCL Group LI Dongsheng		✓	✓		
30	20.48	China Eastern Airlines YE Yigan	✓		✓	✓	
31	19.31	Hisense Group ZHOU Houjian	✓				
32	18.58	Chunlan Group TAO Jianxin	✓				
33	4.60	China Vanke Co Ltd WANG Shi			✓		
34	1.50	Tsingtao Brewery Co Ltd JIN Zhiguo			✓		

[1] ✓ denotes number of listings including subsidiaries.

Electronics

LEADERS OF CHINA'S LARGEST COMPANIES WHO'S WHO IN CHINA

Zhang Ruimin Haier Group
"China's king of electronics"

Corporate position   Chairman and CEO, Haier Group

Corporate revenue   RMB 71.1 billion (US$8.6 billion)

  "Always cautious, always meticulous."

Mr Zhang Ruimin's philosophy towards achievements

Widely regarded as the man who single-handedly raised the profile of China's most successful home appliance brand, Mr Zhang Ruimin has been lauded both at home and overseas for his ideas and practices in management.

The chairman and CEO of Haier Group was the first Chinese business leader to be invited to give a lecture at the prestigious Harvard Business School. His international standing was further enhanced when the Haier Group was subsequently picked as the subject of a case study "Haier's Culture Activated a Shocked Fish" for Harvard Business School - a first among Chinese companies. A "shocked fish" refers to a company with the infrastructure or "hardware" but lacks the proper management or "software".

Mr Zhang's ascent to the dizzy heights in the business community started more than 20 years ago in 1984 when the vice manager of Qingdao Home Appliance Company was promoted to be the director-in-charge of Qingdao Refrigerator General Factory. There, he put forward his "famous brand strategy" and led his employees on a mission to develop Haier into a global brand. Part of his strategy included placing three core personnel in each subsidiary, one to manage the overall operations, a second to take charge of quality control and the third to be in charge of corporate management.

Under his guidance, Haier's transformation was nothing short of spectacular. From a small factory bleeding from debts of RMB 1.5 million (US$177,000), it grew to become the No. 1 Chinese household appliance manufacturer and the fifth largest white goods company worldwide. In 2002, its sales reached RMB 71.1 billion (US$8.6 billion).

Mr Zhang recalls, "The real problem was that workers had no faith in the company and did not care. Quality did not even enter into anybody's mind."

To motivate his employees, Mr Zhang once lined up 76 defective products in the factory, picked up a sledgehammer and told those responsible to smash them to bits. And he included himself in the task. The message got through.

"There is no A, B, C, or D quality. There is only acceptable and unacceptable," he said.

Haier's success was attributed to Mr Zhang's willingness to bring together management ideas from different schools of thoughts, amalgamating traditional Chinese culture with advanced

Western management concepts. Often referred to as the "scholar entrepreneur" for his extensive knowledge and innovative ideas, the culture of success developed by Mr Zhang runs deep in the company's 30,000 employees. He is also praised for his diversification plans into computers, TVs and DVD players. He was also behind the launch of a refrigerator plant in the United States and for the company's expansion plans into Europe.

The road to success for Haier has not always been an easy one. Mr Zhang had to bring floundering state-owned enterprises into Haier's fold and turn them around. "The real problem is that people do not have the right attitude. In Haier's business culture, time is money," he once said.

Another management practice adopted by Mr Zhang is the "Three Eyes" change management concept: "One eye on the company's internal management, to continuously motivate company employees; one eye on the changing market condition, to continuously innovate; one eye on the country's macro economic environment, to seize opportunities to move ahead."

For his achievements, he was given the highest accolades from marketing guru Phillip Kotler. "He is an outstanding Chinese entrepreneur and Haier is a really innovative brand," Mr Kotler once said of Mr Zhang while visiting the Haier Group in 2001.

Birth date	5 January 1951
Hometown	Laizhou City, Shandong Province
Education	MBA, University of Science and Technology, China, 1995
Professional qualifications	Senior economist

Background

1984-2000	Appointed chief plant manager (president), Qingdao Refrigerator Factory from Qingdao Municipal-owned Home Appliance Industry Company
2000-	Appointed the CEO of Haier Group

Other titles and positions

Member of National Industry and Commerce Association

Deputy chairman of China Enterprise Management Association

Deputy director of China Air Conditioner and Refrigerator Association

Honours and awards

The Master of Management in China, 1995

Annual Achievement Award for Entrepreneurs, by *Asiaweek*, 1997

The first Chinese business leader invited by Harvard University Business School to give a lecture at the university in March 1998

Ranked 26th in 'World's 30 Most Prestigious Entrepreneurs', by *Financial Times*, December 1999

Ranked ninth in 'The Top Global Appliance Manufacturers (in volume)' by *American Appliance Manufacturer* magazine in February 2001. Other top 10 appliance giants included Whirlpool, Electrolux, GE, Panasonic, Siemens, Sharp, Toshiba and Hitachi

Businessman of the Year (2001) in China, China Central Television (CCTV), 2002

Contact information

Address No. 1 Haier Road, High-tech Industrial Zone, Qingdao City, China, 266101
Telephone 86-532-8939 999   Facsimile 86-532-8938 666   Website www.haier.com

Corporate structure of Haier Group (October 2003)

Haier Group

- Qingdao Haier Co Ltd (listed in Shanghai) — 12.0%
- Haier-CCT Co Ltd (listed in Hong Kong) — 43.0%
- Haier International Electronic Product Co Ltd — 93.4%
- Qingdao Haier Air-conditioning Co Ltd — 99.9%
- Qingdao Haier Refrigerator Co Ltd — 75.0%
- Qingdao Haier Refrigerator (International) Co Ltd — 75.0%
- Qingdao Haier Special Type Refrigerator Co Ltd — 75.0%
- Qingdao Haier Freezer Co Ltd — 61.0%
- Qingdao Home Appliance Technical Equipment Research Institute — 100%
- Qingdao Haier Health Home Appliance Co Ltd — 98.3%
- Qingdao Haier Dishwasher Co Ltd — 83.3%
- Qingdao Haier Intelligent Digital Co Ltd — 95.0%
- Zhangqiu Haier Electronic Machine Co Ltd — 98.2%
- Haier Group E-commerce Co Ltd — 30.0%
- Haier Merloni (Qingdao) Washing Machine Co Ltd — 20.0%
- Qingdao Commercial Bank — 0.4%
- Qingdao Haier Electronic Plastic Co Ltd — 80.0%
- Dalian Haier Air-conditioning Co Ltd — 90.0%
- Dalian Haier Refrigerator Co Ltd — 90.0%
- Qingdao Haier Special Type Freezer Co Ltd — 51.0%
- Bank of Communications — 0.056%
- Shanghai Hualian Mall — 0.0085%

Liu Chuanzhi Legend Group
"Godfather of entrepreneurs"

Corporate position   Chairman and Co-founder, Legend Group
President, Legend Holdings Ltd
Chairman, Legend Capital
Corporate revenue   RMB 35.5 billion (US$ 4.3 billion)

Mr Liu Chuanzhi is the chairman of Legend Group, China's largest PC manufacturer and his foray into the Chinese information technology industry is nothing short of legendary.

After graduating from the Xi'an Military Academy of Telecommunications Engineering in 1966, Mr Liu first started his working life as a researcher in the State Commission for National Defence, Science and Industry. Shortly after, he was sent during the Cultural Revolution to work in Zhuhai.

In 1970 he joined the Institute of Computer Technology, Chinese Academy of Sciences where he worked until 1984. When he left the academy (which is currently a major shareholder of Legend Group) with 11 of his colleagues, he had a modest capital of only RMB 200,000 (US$24,000) to start the Beijing Computer Technology Development Corporation[1] (later renamed the Legend Group). The company grew rapidly where between 1994 and 2000 alone, the total number of PC units shipped rose 57-fold from 42,000 units to 2.4 million units, turning Legend Group into a PC manufacturing giant by the end of the millennium. By 2002, sales have reached RMB 35.5 billion (US$4.3 billion).

Today, the company not only dominates China's PC market with close to a third of the country's market share but it has also gone on to become the leading PC player in Asia Pacific (excluding Japan) with a 12% market share. To achieve its global ambition, the Legend Group has undergone a re-branding exercise to sell its PCs under the Lenovo brand and is now the third largest PC manufacturer in the world. Along the way, he inked a high-profile joint venture with AOL and pioneered the use of stock options in China. For his achievements, Mr Liu is widely referred to as "China's PC King" and the "Godfather" of Chinese entrepreneurs.

Mr Liu is a visionary business leader who couched in cinematic terms his corporate role of chairman – he likens the chairman's role to being a producer, an actor and a consultant in the production of a movie. Like the producer, he helps determine the strategic direction of his "work", like the actor he takes directions during the "shoot", performing the chairman's function as and when "directed" by the CEO, and like the consultant, he shares his knowledge and experiences with his colleagues.

In the China Business Summit in 2000, Mr Liu revealed that Legend's key to success include a good understanding of the market, sound knowledge of business conditions and development of product technologies. In the same conference in 2001, Mr Liu said that China faces two obstacles when developing its high-tech sector namely, insufficient investments and a lack of skilled managers and technicians. He believes that companies should give shares to their employees as a way to attract and retain workers and grow their businesses. The government must set up the

---

[1] Translated from original company name in Chinese.

right environment to help venture companies prosper. Mr Liu also believes that Chinese companies must adopt modern governance and organisation and learn from foreign competitors.

Mr Liu learnt many lessons on strategies from famous Western brands like Microsoft and Intel. Said Mr Liu during an interview in 2001 with *McKinsey Quarterly*, "Our earliest and best teacher was Hewlett-Packard. It was as Hewlett-Packard's distributor that we learnt, how to organise sales channels and how to market."

When commenting on Legend's success in China, Mr Liu says, "We want to focus on two areas, and in both cases we looked to companies in the United States as a model. The first was how to reorganise our business for raising funds on the stock market and the second was how to build a solid management foundation.

Mr Liu has also been singled out for numerous awards by various prestigious magazines, including *Fortune's* Asia's Businessman of the Year in 1999 and he was voted *Times* magazine's 25 Most Influential Global Executives.

Birth date	29 April 1944
Hometown	Zhenjiang City, Jiangsu Province
Education	Bachelor of Engineering, majoring in Radar Design, Xi'an Military Academy of Telecommunications Engineering, 1966
Professional qualifications	Senior engineer

Background

1961-1967	Xi'an Military Academy of Telecommunications Engineering
1967-1968	Researcher, State Commission for National Defence, Science and Industry
1968-1970	Sent during the Cultural Revolution to work in Zhuhai City, Guangdong Province
1970-1984	Researcher, Computer Peripherals, Institute of Computing Technology
1984-	Co-Founder, Beijing Computer Technology Development Corporation (later renamed to "Legend Group")
1988-	Founder, Hong Kong Legend Holdings

Other titles and positions

Vice chairman, All-China Federation of Industry and Commerce
Director of Institute of Computing Technology, Chinese Academy of Sciences

Political affiliations

Representative of the Ninth National People's Congress of the PRC in 1998
Reappointed a Representative of the 10th National People's Congress of the PRC in 2003

LEADERS OF CHINA'S LARGEST COMPANIES WHO'S WHO IN CHINA

Honours and awards

25 Most Influential Global Executives, by *Time* magazine, 2001
Stars of Asia, by *BusinessWeek* magazine, 2000
Asia's Businessman of the Year, by *Fortune* magazine, 1999
10 Most Influential Men of the Commercial Sector in China, 1996
Model of National Work Force, 1995
Man of Reform in China, 1995
The first prize of the Second National Technology Entrepreneurs Gold Award, 1990

Corporate structure of Legend Group Limited (listed in Hong Kong)

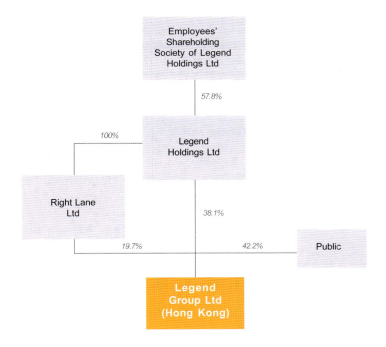

Contact information
Address Legend Tower, No. 6 Chuang Ye Road, Shangdi Information Industry Base, Haidian District, Beijing, China, 100085
Telephone 86-10-8287 8888   Facsimile 86-10-8287 6709   Website www.lenovo.com

LEADERS OF CHINA'S LARGEST COMPANIES WHO'S WHO IN CHINA

Yang Yuanqing Legend Group
"Scholar, dreamer, entrepreneur"

Corporate position Vice Chairman, President and CEO, Legend Group

Corporate revenue RMB 35.5 billion (US$4.3 billion)

 "Our goal is to educate the Chinese people on how best to use the PC."
Mr Yang Yuanqing

As Legend Group's president and CEO, Mr Yang Yuanqing's influence on China's IT industry is no less important than his chairman, Mr Liu Chuanzhi.

Therefore, it was quite inconceivable that the CEO of China's leading PC manufacturer had once thought of leaving the Legend Group to pursue a doctorate in the United States back in 1991. Like many in his generation in China then, he had wanted to go to the United States to further his postgraduate studies. His resignation was however, turned down and the rest was history.

He rose quickly from a sales position within the company to become Legend Group's top executive. Mr Yang is widely credited with helping the Legend Group become a multi-billion dollar company. Mr Yang's ability to compete in the highly competitive IT market is often reflected by the various corporate strategic initiatives driven by him such as bundling PCs sold with software and services.

Although Legend is the most popular desktop PC brand in China (recently rebranded as Lenovo), the company is set on ensuring more than 20% of its annual revenue comes from outside China by 2008. Overseas revenue currently accounts for less than 5%.

"It is Legend's long-term aspiration to become an international company. At the moment our main business focus will still be on China, where the robust growth of the China IT market still offers us growth opportunities," says Mr Yang. In 2003, 95% of Legend Group's turnover came from the China market.

"However, expansion into the international market is inevitable. That's why we took the proactive action of changing our English brand name to 'Lenovo' in April 2003, which will enable it to be without any restrictions in markets worldwide."

Mr Yang, however, believes that competition will not be China's largest PC maker as much as complacency. "Competition always exists," he says. "More importantly, we are our biggest competitor."

Mr Yang who graduated from the University of Science and Technology of China with a masters degree in 1989, has become the standard bearer of China's IT industry. Some of his influential speeches made between 1999 and 2001, in particular "The Third Revolution of IT Industry" and "Legend and the growth of China's e-commerce" provided guiding principles for the development of the Chinese IT industry.

Birth date	November 1964
Hometown	Ningbo City, Zhejiang Province
Education	Bachelor of Engineering, majoring in Computer Science, Shanghai Jiaotong University, 1986
	Master of Science, majoring in Computing Science, University of Science and Technology of China, 1989

Background

1982-1986	Shanghai Jiaotong University
1986-1989	University of Science and Technology of China
1989-	Joined the Legend Group
1989-1993	Sales executive, CAD department of Legend Group, promoted to general manager of the Group in 1991
1994-1995	Head of Personal Computer Division, Legend Group, in charge of sales and marketing
1995-2000	Vice president, Legend Group
2000-	Vice chairman, president and CEO, Legend Group

Other titles and positions

Member of the National Youth Committee

Professor at the University of Science and Technology of China

Non-executive director of Beijing Ufsoft Co Ltd, which is engaged in software development and manufacturing.

Honours and awards

Stars of Asia, by the *BusinessWeek* magazine, 1999 and 2001

Medal of May Fourth Youth in China (the highest honour given to youths by the Chinese government), 1999

One of the Top 10 Most Outstanding Youths of Beijing, 1998

Contact information
Address Legend Tower, No. 6 Chuang Ye Road, Shangdi Information Industry Base, Haidian District, Beijing, China, 100085
Telephone 86-10-8287 8888   Facsimile 86-10-8287 6709   Website www.lenovo.com

LEADERS OF CHINA'S LARGEST COMPANIES WHO'S WHO IN CHINA

Li Dongsheng TCL Group
"Bright spark of talent"

Corporate position Chairman and President, TCL Group

Corporate revenue RMB 22.1 billion (US$2.7 billion)

"My dream is to establish a world-class Chinese company."
Mr Li Dongsheng

Turning one of China's top electronics companies into the world's largest TV manufacturer through a merger of TCL's and Thomson's TV business in November 2003 is evidence of Mr Li Dongsheng's ambition and talent.

Mr Li was voted Asia's Businessman of the Year for his daring and vision by *Fortune* magazine in 2004. The US$560 million joint venture company, TCL-Thomson Electronics Co Ltd is 67% owned by TCL Group and is expected to produce more than 18 million TV sets representing US$3.5 billion of sales during its maiden year.

Mr Li entered technical college after spending time in an agricultural cooperative during the Cultural Revolution. In 1982 he graduated from the South China University of Technology in Guangzhou as an electrical engineer. Mr Li joined the Huizhou TTY Electronic Co Ltd as a technician in the same year and he was quickly promoted to be the general manager of the company in 1985. In 1986, he left the company and joined Huizhou Electronic Industrial Corporation in Hong Kong.

Three years later, he re-joined his former company, which subsequently reorganised and listed its main businesses on the Shenzhen Stock Exchange as TCL Communication Equipment Co Ltd in 1993. In that same year, Mr Li was promoted to be the general manager of the holding company of TCL Communication Equipment Co Ltd and by 1997, the former technician has risen to become the chairman and president of the entire TCL Group. By then, the TCL brand was valued at more than RMB 18.8 billion (US$2.3 billion) and its products such as TCL mobile handsets have become dominant market leaders in China.

Mr Li is known for aggressive marketing and his relentless focus on cost control. At the Fortune Global Forum in Shanghai in 1999, Mr Li confidently declared that over the following decade TCL would increase sales tenfold and vault into the Global 500 list of companies as a "world class enterprise." Mr Li currently focuses his attention as chairman and president on growing the TCL Group and building the TCL brand.

Birth date	July 1957
Hometown	Huizhou City, Guangdong Province
Education	Bachelor of Engineering, majoring in Radio Technology, South China University of Technology, 1982

Background

1978-1982	Shanghai South China University of Technology
1982-1997	Technician, salesman, sales manager of Huizhou TTY Electronic Co Ltd
	Operations manager of the Hong Kong Branch, Huizhou Electronic Industrial Corp, general manager of TCL group
1997-	President and chairman of TCL group

Honours and awards

Asia's Businessman of the Year (2003), February 2004
Top 10 Stars in Merger & Acquisition, by the *Talent* magazine, 2002
Top 10 Stars in IT Industry, 2001
Businessman of the Year, China Central TV Station, 2002
National Model of Labour (the highest honour from Chinese government), 2000
Outstanding Young Entrepreneur, 1995

Political affiliations

Mr Li is a member of the National People's Congress of China.

Corporate structure of TCL Group

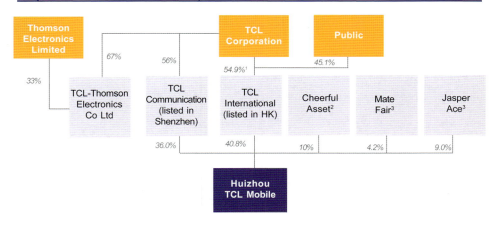

[1] Through a wholly-owned subsidiary
[2] A BVI company controlled by the management of Huizhou TCL Mobile
[3] Mr Wong Toe Yeung, non-executive director of TCL International, controls Mate Fair and Jasper Ace

Contact information

Address TCL Industrial Building, 6 South E Ling Road, Huizhou City, China, 516001
Telephone 86-752-2288 333   Facsimile 86-752-2278 018   Website www.tcl.com

LEADERS OF CHINA'S LARGEST COMPANIES WHO'S WHO IN CHINA

Zhou Houjian Hisense Group
"Key TV maker"

Corporate position   Chairman, Hisense Group

Corporate revenue   RMB 19.3 billion (US$2.3 billion)

Although Mr Zhou Houjian is the only son of a family with strong business traditions, his inclinations were towards the academia. A graduate of the Shandong University in 1982, he aspired to be a university lecturer.

However, academia's loss became the electronics sector's gain when Mr Zhou was assigned to technical work in Qingdao TV Factory, a local state-owned enterprise.

Over a 12-year period, he rose quickly from the rank of a deputy manager of its design department to eventually head the company in 1992. When he took over as the top executive, there were no major Chinese companies that could effectively compete against foreign companies producing colour TVs. This was an especially challenging period for Mr Zhou.

However, adhering to a vigilant philosophy of high-quality, superior service and a focus on high technology, he built Hisense into an international brand name with a diversified portfolio of household appliances, telecommunications and IT. Mr Zhou is a meticulous and detailed person. A hint of his persona is best given when he once revealed how much he was influenced by the fiction *The Dvovak*[1].

Under his leadership, the company, later renamed Hisense, was listed on 22 April 1997 on the Shanghai Stock Exchange (code: 600060). It grew to become the largest electronics enterprise in the Shandong province with its revenue growing 47-fold over a 10-year period to reach RMB 19.3 billion (US$2.3 billion) by 2002.

It is clear that Hisense is aiming to master its own core technology. "Which world-class company has ever produced low quality products?" challenged Mr Zhou.

On 13 September 2003, Hisense Group held the "Global Agents Conference" under the theme of "Our Hisense, Our Future" in Qingdao City. Mr Zhou stressed that exports of Chinese colour TV sets and air-conditioners are rapidly growing, and will probably exceed the expected export targets this year. While referring to the past when the Chinese home appliances used to be branded as "low quality", he emphasised that the situation has changed greatly for the better, thanks to the adoption of world class technologies, excellent staff, core technologies, technological innovations and other endeavours.

[1] By Ethel Lilian Voyuich

LEADERS OF CHINA'S LARGEST COMPANIES WHO'S WHO IN CHINA

Birth date	August 1957
Hometown	Muping County, Shandong Province
Education	Bachelor of Engineering, majoring in Electronics, Shandong University, 1982
Professional qualifications	Research fellow

Background

1978-1982	Shandong University
1982-1992	Deputy manager of Design Department, assistant director and associate director of Qingdao Television Factory
1992-1994	Director of Qingdao Television Factory
1994-1995	General manager of Qingdao Hisense Electric Corp
1995-2000	Chairman of Board of Directors, Party secretary and general manager of Qingdao Electronic & Meter Industrial Corp (concurrent posts)
	Party secretary and president of Qingdao Hisense Group Corp
	Director of Qingdao Electronic Industrial Administrative Office
2000-	Chairman of Board of Directors, Hisense Group

Honours and awards

Top-notch Technical Expert of Qingdao City and Shandong Province

Outstanding Entrepreneur of Shandong Province

Outstanding Young Entrepreneur of China

Outstanding Entrepreneur of the Ministry of Electronic Industry

Golden Ox Award winner

May 1st Labour Medallist

National Model Worker

Outstanding Businessman and Young Expert for 1998

Special prize for Management Talent

Winner of 'Global Cup' World Young Entrepreneur competition (the only winner from China)

National winner of 'Outstanding Award for Scientific and Technological Innovation for Youths'

Political affiliation

Member of the National People's Congress

Shareholdings of Hisense Electrics Co Ltd (listed in Shanghai)

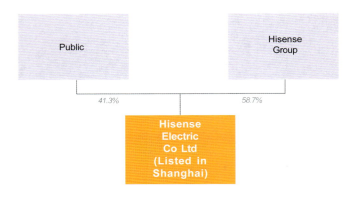

Contact information

Address No. 17 Donghaixi Road, Qingdao City, China, 266071
Telephone 86-532-3878 888 / 3895 188 / 3896 188 / 3897 188   Facsimile 886-532-3866 770   Website www.hisense.com

Tao Jianxin Chunlan Group
"Miracle worker"

Corporate position Chairman and CEO, Chunlan Group

Corporate revenue RMB 18.6 billion (US$2.2 billion)

From a small air-conditioner manufacturing company teetering on the brink of collapse, Mr Tao Jianxin transformed Taizhou Air Conditioning Factory into the Chunlan Group, one of China's top companies.

Mr Tao, a graduate of the prestigious Nanjing University, joined the company 19 years ago in 1985, helping it grow into the acknowledged leader for air-conditioning units and washing machines in China. Today, the company has 42 other subsidiaries and has diversified into various white goods, electronic products and automotive products (including specialised batteries, automotive engines, trucks and motorcycles).

Chunlan's rapid growth under his leadership led the media in China to refer to the Chunlan Group as the "Chunlan Phenomenon" or the "Chunlan Miracle".

As China's own answer to the United States' General Electric, the Chunlan Group has been steadily growing into a diversified corporate giant while remaining one of China's most profitable white goods manufacturers.

Under Mr Tao's guidance, Chunlan Group has developed a strong research and development capability by setting up various research organisations including the Chunlan Research Institute of Electronics, Chunlan Research Institute of Motor Vehicles, Chunlan Research Institute of Electrical Appliances and Chunlan College.

To sustain Chunlan Group's competitiveness, Mr Zhou also implemented his "innovative matrix management" which involves creating six platforms for innovation involving information, scientific research, business, funding, purchasing and logistics. These efforts have greatly improved Chunlan Group's scientific and technological capabilities and helped strengthen the group's global market competitiveness.

Birth date	December 1953
Hometown	Dantu County, Jiangsu Province
Education	Bachelor of Science, majoring in Mathematics, Nanjing University

LEADERS OF CHINA'S LARGEST COMPANIES WHO'S WHO IN CHINA

Background

1985-   Director of Taizhou Air Conditioning Factory, later renamed Chunlan Group, where he became CEO and Chairman

Honours and awards

One of the '10 Outstanding Employees'
Hu Yingdong Award
Businessman of the Year (2001), by CCTV, 2002

Political affiliations

Alternate member of the CPC Central Committee

Shareholdings of Jiangsu Chunlan Refrigerating Equipment Stock Co Ltd (listed in Shanghai)

Contact information

Address No. 7 Kou Tai Road, Taizhou City, China, 225300
Telephone 86-523-6220 588   Facsimile 86-523-6222 092   Website www.chunlan.com

Ouyang Zhongmou — China Putian Corporation
"Distinctive individual, distinguished company"

Corporate position   President, China Putian Corporation

Corporate revenue   RMB 60.2 billion (US$7.3 billion)

The company Mr Ouyang Zhongmou runs continues to draw recognition. Formerly the China Posts and Telecommunications Industry Corporation, the company was a subsidiary of the Ministry of Information Industry[1]. In 1998, it became a state-owned enterprise. China Putian Corporation has since gone on to distinguish itself. It was voted China's best international trading company for two years running in 2001 and 2002. It also topped the Top 100 Chinese Electronics & Information Enterprises awards.

For Mr Ouyang's achievements, the praises lavished on him are no less distinguished. The China Economic and Trade Guide voted the president of this multi-billion-turnover company one of China's top 500 entrepreneurs and top 100 industry leaders in 1994.

He has also received wide spread recognition abroad and was voted 'The Most Distinctive Individual in the World' by Cambridge International Biography Centre. In the United States, he was included in the *Who's Who in the World*[2].

China Putian Corporation employs over 54,000 employees and has five listed companies, namely, Shanghai P&T, Chengdu Cable, Nanjing Putian, Putian Eastcom and Ningbo Bird and over 50 subsidiaries, including Putian Capital Group, Putian Eastcom and Ningbo Electronics. Its diversified products and services include mobile communications systems, cell phone systems and test instruments. China Putian Corporation is a market leader in many products domestically, including the rapidly growing mobile handset market.

In March 2003, Nokia merged its four existing China joint ventures into a single joint venture. Nokia's largest China joint venture partner is China Putian Corporation.

During the signing ceremony, Mr Ouyang said on behalf of all joint venture partners, "We are extremely excited about the merger. It is a logical next step for what has so far been a very fruitful partnership. We have full confidence in the future development of the new company. As partners, we will continue to provide our most valuable resources to enhance the new company's overall strength. For us, the merger will not only bring increased opportunities for us in China, but also allow us to improve our competitiveness outside of China."

Education   Bachelor of Science, majoring in Physics, Tsinghua University

---

[1] Formerly the Ministry of Posts and Telecommunications
[2] Published by Marquis

Background

1974-1978	Worked at the 4433 Factory under the PLA
1978-1980	Worked at the Electronics Import and Export Department[1], Ministry of Electronics Industry
1980-1987	Officer, section chief, regional manager, deputy manager of the headquarters at China Electronics Importing Company
1987-1995	Managing director of China Electronics Importing Company
1995-2000	Managing director and vice president of China Posts and Telecommunications Industry Corporation
2000-	President of China Putian Corporation

Honours and awards

'The Most Distinctive Individual in the World' certificate by Cambridge International Biography Centre

Who's Who in the World published by Marquis in the United States

Other titles and memberships

Vice chairman of China Communication Industry Association

Board director of China Electronics Academic Association

Chairman of Information Product Chamber of China Machine and Electronics Importing Chamber of Commerce

Vice chairman of China Mobile Communication Association

Vice chairman of Electrical Information Science and International Relationship Academic Association

Board director of China Market Academic Association

Board director of China Policy Study Academic Association

---

[1] Later the China Electronics Import and Export Corporation

LEADERS OF CHINA'S LARGEST COMPANIES WHO'S WHO IN CHINA

Corporate structure of China Putian Group

China Putian Corporation

Subsidiary	Ownership		Subsidiary	Ownership
Shanghai Posts & Telecommunications Equipment Co Ltd (listed in Shanghai)	54.0%	Putian Eastcom Co Ltd (listed in Shanghai) — 51.6%	Beijing Putian Taili Telecommunications Technology Development Co Ltd	100%
				Wuhan Putian Telecommunications Equipment Co Ltd
Nanjing Putian Telecommunications Cable Co Ltd (listed in Shenzhen)	53.5%	Chengdu Putian Telecommunications Cable Co Ltd (listed in Hong Kong) — 60.0%	China Putian IT Industry (Guangzhou) Co	100%
				Houma Putian Telecommunications Cable Co Ltd
Ningbo Electronics Information Holdings Co Ltd	56.1%	Putian Shouxin Telecommunications Equipment Co Ltd — 100%	China Putian IT Industry (Zhenzhou) Co	100%
				Guiyang Putian Wanxiang Logistics Co Ltd
Xian Putian Telecommunications Equipment Co Ltd	100%	Beijing Posts, Telecommunications & Telephone Equipment Co Ltd — 100%	Beijing Ericsson Putian Mobile Communication Co Ltd	
				Beijing Putian Runhui Technology Co Ltd
Shanghai Telephone Equipment Co Ltd	100%	Guiyang Putian Telecommunications Equipment Co Ltd — 100%	Shenzhen Putian Lingyun Electronic Co Ltd	
				Putian Real Estate Development Co Ltd
Jinan Putian Telecommunications Equipment Co Ltd	100%	Luoyang Putian Huanghe Motorcycle Factory — 100%	Shanghai Xindianyuan Telecommunications Equipment Co Ltd	
				Beijing Lucent Technological Cable Co Ltd
Putian IT Research Institute	100%	Zhongxun Telecommunications Industrial Technology Service Centre — 100%	Beijing Hongna Post Product Co Ltd	
				Hangzhou Hongyan Electronic Product Co Ltd
Telecommunication Industry (Newspaper)	100%	China Putian IT Industry (Changchun) Co — 100%	Chongqing Putian Telecommunications Equipment Co Ltd	
				Beijing Panasonic Telecommunications Equipment Co Ltd
China Putian IT Industry (Xiamen) Co	100%	Tianjin Telephone Equipment Co Ltd — 100%	Julong Information Technology Co Ltd	
				Beijing Putian Huixun Information Technology Co Ltd
Chengdu Posts & Telecommunications Equipment Co Ltd	100%	Tianjin Putian Telecommunications Equipment Co Ltd — 100%	Putian Telecommunication Co Ltd	
				Shanghai Lucent Technological Cable Co Ltd
Jingdezhen Putian Telecommunications Equipment Co Ltd	100%	Zhuzhou Putian Telecommunications Equipment Co Ltd — 100%	Shandong Huari Battery Co Ltd	
				Beijing Haihong Communication System Co Ltd
Guilin Putian Telecommunications Equipment Co Ltd	100%	China Putian IT Industry Beijing Telecommunications Planning Institute — 100%	Beijing Haihong Communication System Co Ltd	
				Beijing Changxinjia Information Technology Co Ltd

Contact information

Address No. 28 West Street, XuanWu Men, Beijing, China, 100053
Telephone 86-10-6360 3001   Facsimile 86-10-6360 3002   Website www.china-putian.com.cn

Financial Services

LEADERS OF CHINA'S LARGEST COMPANIES WHO'S WHO IN CHINA

Jiang Jianqing — Industrial and Commercial Bank of China
"From coal to pennies"

Corporate position Chairman and President, Industrial and Commercial Bank of China

Corporate revenue RMB 161.6 billion (US$19.5 billion)

Shanghai-born Mr Jiang Jianqing could well be the only top banker in China who can boast of a three-year stint as a coal miner in his resume.

The president of China's largest commercial bank, the Industrial and Commercial Bank of China (ICBC), spent three years in the coalmines of Henan province at the tender age of 17 as a result of the Cultural Revolution. He was sent there to get a taste of "real life" as experienced by the people.

When he first started out as a young banker (aged 26) in the Jing'an office of the People's Bank of China in 1979, he quickly realised that he lacked the requisite banking experience. He decided to upgrade himself and to learn at every opportunity. Not only did this diligence culminated in him earning a doctorate from one of China's top universities, Shanghai Jiaotong University, he also became the youngest president of the biggest of the "Big Four" banks in China (Industrial and Commercial Bank China, Bank of China, Agricultural Bank of China, China Construction Bank) when he was appointed to head ICBC in year 2000 at age 47.

Mr Jiang, also the chairman of China Banking Association, happens to be a prolific writer. He has written several influential articles on financial markets including the *Analysis of overseas financial crisis*, *A look at financial crisis*, *The technology revolution and the US banking industry* and *A study of the development of financial technology and its influence*. These seminal articles on banking administration and management policies have been adopted by key Chinese policy makers.

In the 2002 China Business Summit, Mr Jiang commented, "The banks have assumed the cost of economic transition." Mr Jiang said this while explaining the massive burden of non-performing loans faced by China's four key commercial banks. He also said RMB 1.3 trillion (US$157 billion) in non-performing loans have already been taken off the books, but agreed aggressive reforms must continue. Mr Jiang cited poor management, lack of innovation and outmoded technology as some of the key challenges that continue to hinder China's commercial banks.

Under Mr Jiang's leadership, ICBC has been voted 'Best bank in China' by *The Banker* for three years running since 2000. The ICBC controls a quarter of the market share of the Chinese banking sector with total assets exceeding RMB 4 trillion (US$482 billion) and exerts business presence in all major international financial centres. Since 1999, it has also been included in *Fortune's Global 500* three years running and it is also become the 10th largest bank in the world in terms of tier-one capital.

LEADERS OF CHINA'S LARGEST COMPANIES WHO'S WHO IN CHINA

Birth date	February 1953
Education	Bachelor of Arts, majoring in Finance and Economics, Shanghai University
	Masters degree, majoring in Finance, Shanghai Jiaotong University
	Doctorate, Shanghai Jiaotong University

Background

1979-1995	Banker, Jing'an Banking Office, People's Bank of China and ICBC Shanghai Branch; deputy general manager of ICBC Shanghai Municipal Branch General manager of ICBC Pudong Branch, Shanghai
1995-1997	General manager of Shanghai City Cooperative Bank
1997-1999	General manager of ICBC Shanghai Municipal Branch
1999-2000	Vice chairman and executive vice president of ICBC
2000-	Chairman and president of ICBC

Other titles and memberships

Member of the Board of Monetary Policy
Member of the Board of The People's Bank of China
Vice president of The China Society for Finance and Banking
President of The China Urban Society for Finance and Banking
Guest professor and doctorate supervisor of Shanghai Jiaotong University
Guest professor of Shanghai International Studies University
Guest professor of Shanghai University of Finance and Economics
Chairman of China's Banking Association
Vice president of China Financial Institute
Director of the board of Fudan University

Shareholdings of ICBC (Asia) (listed in Hong Kong)

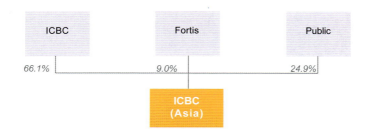

Corporate structure of ICBC

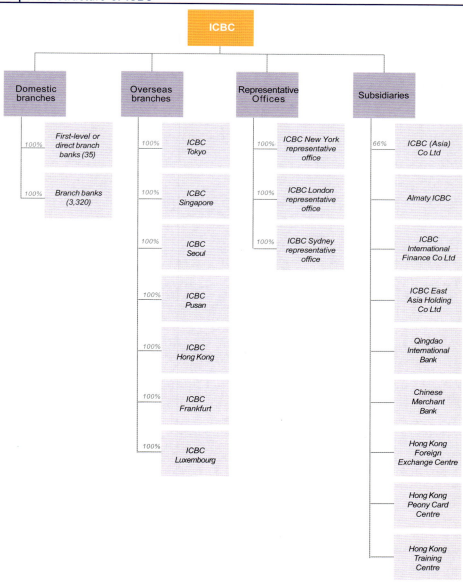

Contact information
Address ICBC Building, 55 Fuxingmen Street, Xicheng District, Beijing, China, 100032
Website www.icbc.com.cn

LEADERS OF CHINA'S LARGEST COMPANIES WHO'S WHO IN CHINA

Wang Xianzhang China Life
"Insurance industry veteran"

Corporate position Chairman and President, China Life Insurance Company Ltd

Corporate revenue RMB 126.9 billion (US$15.3 billion)

Mr Wang Xianzhang is the first businessman in China to grace the cover of the inaugural issue of the chinese edition of *Fortune* magazine[1]. The modest, collected and low profile executive, who was named Businessman of the Year in 2002, is the chairman and president of China Life, China's largest insurance company.

China Life, formerly the life insurance business of the People's Insurance Company of China (PICC), is dually listed on the New York Stock Exchange and Hong Kong Stock Exchange in late 2003 after a complex restructuring. Under the stewardship of Mr Wang, China Life is today the leading life insurance company in China with over 51% of the market share. China Life is the market leader in the life, annuity, accident and health insurance products, making it China's single most dominant insurance company.

Mr Wang was reported to have wept tears of joy in front of more than 60 people after the share offer was fixed at HK$3.63 for each share. It was close to the maximum of HK$3.65 that China Life targeted for. China Life priced its share offering during a meeting held at the basement of Credit Suisse First Boston's New York office.

At that time, Mr Wang was overjoyed and enthused that China Life may want to invest the US$3.5 billion it raised, in one of the largest share offering in 2003 in the overseas markets. "We are seeking permission to park the listing proceeds abroad," says Mr Wang. But he said it might be difficult to keep all of the funds overseas. "I can assure you that at least some of the listing proceeds should be allowed to sit overseas," he said.

This insurance veteran has been working in China insurance industry ever since he graduated from Liaoning Finance & Economic Institute in 1965. Having spent nearly 40 years in the insurance industry as an executive in PICC (and its various restructured entities) and China Life, he is widely respected for his industry knowledge and contribution to the development of Chinese insurance industry.

Mr Wang has held various positions in the past before assuming his current position including chairman and president of China Insurance Co Ltd, vice chairman and president of China Insurance HK (Holdings) Co Ltd, vice president of People's Insurance Company of China, vice president of PICC (Group) and general manager of the Liaoning branch of PICC. He remains as president of the holding company of China Life, China Life Insurance (Group) Company.

Birth date	May 1942
Hometown	Liaoning Province
Education	Bachelor degree, majoring in Foreign Economics and Trade, Northeast University of Finance and Economics (Formerly Liaoning University of Finance and Economics)

[1] January issue, 2003

LEADERS OF CHINA'S LARGEST COMPANIES WHO'S WHO IN CHINA

Background

1969-2000	General manager of People's Insurance Company of China, Liaoning Branch
	Vice chairman, vice president, PICC
	Vice chairman, president of China Insurance HK (Holdings) Co Ltd
2000-	Party secretary, president of China Life Insurance Company

Honours and awards

Businessman of the Year 2002, by *Fortune* Magazine

2003's Top 10 Chinese in Capital Markets, by First Chinese Capital Markets Forum in Beijing

Other titles and memberships

Vice president of China Insurance Academy

Chairman of Insurance Industry Association of China

Vice chairman of Insurance Institute of China

Political affiliations

Selected as a delegate of 16th CPC National Congress

Member of People's Political Consultative Congress in November 2003

Corporate structure of China Life (Listed in Hong Kong)

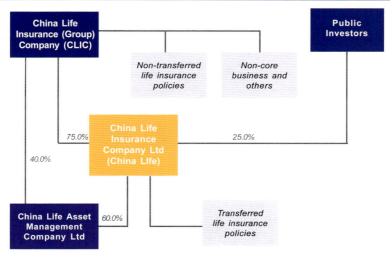

Contact information

Address China Life Insurance Company, No. 5 Guanying Park West, West District, Beijing, China, 100035
Telephone 86-10-6611 1567   Facsimile 86-10-6611 4423   Website www.chinalife.com.cn

LEADERS OF CHINA'S LARGEST COMPANIES WHO'S WHO IN CHINA

Xiao Gang Bank of China
"Reformer and pioneer"

Corporate position Chairman and President, Bank of China

Corporate revenue RMB 126.2 billion (US$15.2 billion)

#9

Mr Xiao Gang graduated from the Hunan Institute of Finance and Economics in 1981 and in the same year he started his banking career with the China's central bank, the People's Bank of China. Over the next eight years, the meticulous and dedicated banker worked his way up to become the director general of the Policy Research Department.

In 1996, Mr Xiao was made assistant governor of the People's Bank of China (PBC) and two years later, he became PBC's deputy governor. In 2003, Mr Xiao was appointed chairman and president of China's most international and profitable bank, the Bank of China (BOC). Given his experience and reputation, Mr Xiao was carefully selected to lead China's oldest[1] and only foreign-exchange bank.

On his planned listing by 2005, Mr Xiao Gang mentioned to the *Shanghai Securities Post* that the Bank of China is exploring listing its business in its entirety as this would help guarantee transparency and decrease the relative amount of regulatory approvals that would be involved in listing of the bank.

Throughout his long and illustrious career with PBC, Mr. Xiao was actively involved in the formulation and implementation of key economic and fiscal policies in China and was often called upon by the government to help manage troubled financial situations in the country. He led the restructuring of the trust and investment companies in China and was involved in the closure of various troubled financial institutions including the China Rural Development Trust and Investment Company, Guangdong International Trust and Investment Company and the Hainan Development Bank.

Mr Xiao is viewed as a progressive central banker who was instrumental in the setting up of various financial institutions and systems. He helped established the China Foreign Exchange Trading Centre in 1994, China's advanced payment system in 2000 and China UnionPay Corporation Co Ltd[2] in 2002.

Birth date	1958
Hometown	Changsha, Hunan Province
Education	Bachelor of Finance, Hunan Finance and Economic Institute
	Masters of Law, Renmin University of China
	Visiting Scholar, Harvard University

[1] Established in 1912
[2] The first bankcard coalition organisation in China

Background

1981-1989	Director of Research Bureau, PBC
	Head of China Foreign Exchange Trading Centre
1989-1996	General manager of China Foreign Exchange Trading Centre
	Director-general of Policy Research Department, PBC
1996-1998	Assistant governor of PBC
	Director-general of Fund Planning Department
	Director-general of Monetary Policy Department
	President of the PBC's Guangdong Branch
	Director-general of Guangdong Branch of the State Administration of Foreign Exchange (SAFE)
1998-2003	Deputy governor of PBC
2003-	Chairman and president of Bank of China

Other titles and memberships

Member of Monetary Policy Committee of People's Bank of China

Political affiliations

Deputy to the Ninth National People's Congress
Alternate Member of Eighth Guangdong Provincial Committee of the CPC

Contact information
Address No. 1 Fuxingmen Nei Street, Beijing, China, 100818
Telephone 86-10-6659 6688   Facsimile 86-10-6601 4024   Website www.bank-of-china.com

LEADERS OF CHINA'S LARGEST COMPANIES WHO'S WHO IN CHINA

Corporate structure of Bank of China

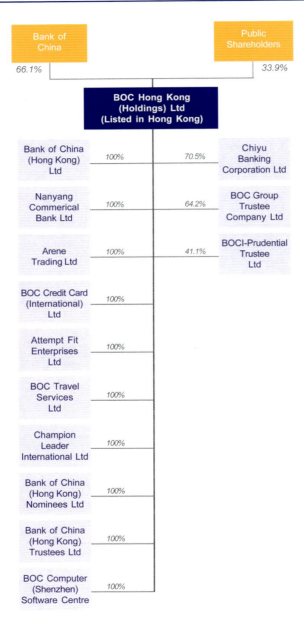

LEADERS OF CHINA'S LARGEST COMPANIES WHO'S WHO IN CHINA

Zhang Enzhao China Construction Bank
"Quiet doer"

Corporate position   President, China Construction Bank

Corporate revenue   RMB 112.1 billion (US$13.5 billion)

"The biggest challenge we're going to have is in changing the way our employees think and in improving the quality of their work."
Mr Zhang Enzhao, when he first took charge of the CCB

Mr Zhang Enzhao became president of China's third largest commercial lender, the state-owned China Construction Bank, after his predecessor Mr Wang Xuehua[1] resigned on 18th January 2002 after the New York branch of the Bank of China corruption fiasco[2].

As a result, the quiet and down-to-earth 58-year-old career banker was thrown into limelight. He was tasked with cleaning up the large portfolio of bad loans at the top property bank to prepare it for a US$5 billion public flotation that would rank as one of the China's largest since Unicom's US$5.7 billion IPO in 2000.

A graduate of the prestigious Fudan University, he rose through the ranks to become head of the bank's operations in Shanghai in 1987. For the next decade or so, Mr Zhang helped led reforms in the bank and installed tighter lending practices. His role as an advocate of banking reform is well known and he is well aware of the dimensions of his own powerful position. "I am the bank's president, its party chief as well as the owner and operator of its assets - each of these roles, however, has different goals."

Although often overshadowed by the Bank of China, the nation's top foreign-exchange bank, Mr Zhang has set ambitious objectives for the Construction Bank when he first started. He promised to bring down the bank's bad loan ratio to less than 10% within two years.

The life-long employee[3] and former vice president in charge of the bank's credit management department immediately established a monitoring system to oversee the disposal of its non-performing loans, a major obstacle for the planned IPO of the bank. He held several auctions to sell off the bank's non-performing loans. In addition, he helped the bank enter into an agreement with Morgan Stanley, a United States-based investment bank, to further dispose of non-performing loans worth about US$482 million in 2003. In addition, he streamlined the operations of the bank at a cost of nearly RMB 2 billion (US$240 million).

As a result of his painstaking efforts, the Construction Bank reported profits of nearly RMB 4.3 billion (US$520 million) in 2002 and brought down its bad loan ratio to 11%, the lowest in China where the national average is usually above 20%.

---

[1] Mr Wang was subsequently convicted of bribery charges and is currently serving a 12-year term in prison
[2] Mr Wang was at that time the top executive in the Bank of China
[3] He joined the Shanghai branch of the China Construction Bank, aged 18

LEADERS OF CHINA'S LARGEST COMPANIES WHO'S WHO IN CHINA

In 2003, the China Construction Bank was one of two banks chosen for a RMB 186 billion[1] (US$22.5 billion) recapitalisation for each bank by the government as part of the initiative to list all the big four state-owned banks starting 2004. Given its healthy loan portfolio, it is expected to be the first of the big four state-owned commercial banks in the country to be listed, reflecting the tremendous contributions Mr Wang has made to a sector which is often seen as a weak link in China's booming economy.

Birth date	December 1946
Hometown	Shandong Province
Education	Bachelor of Arts, majoring in Finance, Fudan University
Professional qualifications	Senior accountant

Background

1984-1986	Deputy manager of China Bank of Investment, Shanghai Branch
1986-1987	Deputy manager of China Construction Bank, Shanghai Branch
1987-1999	General manager of China Construction Bank, Shanghai Branch
1999-2002	Vice president of China Construction Bank
2002-	President of China Construction Bank

Other titles and memberships

Director of Human Resource Management Committee

Chairman of China International Capital Corporation

CPC Secretary of Cinda Asset Management Company

Deputy president of the China Banking Association

Corporate structure of China Construction Bank

Contact information

Address China Construction Bank, 25 Finance Street, Beijing, China, 100032
Telephone 86-10-6759 7114   Website www.ccb.com.cn

---

[1] In late 2003, the government provided a total of RMB 372 billion (US$45 billion), representing nearly 10% of China's foreign reserves, to recapitalise two banks, namely the Bank of China and the China Construction Bank

Yang Mingsheng — Agricultural Bank of China

"Success as simple as ABC"

Corporate position   President, Agricultural Bank of China

Corporate revenue   RMB 96.5 billion (US$11.7 billion)

Mr Yang Minsheng was appointed the president of the Agricultural Bank of China, the smallest of the big four state-owned bank, in 2003 after working there for over two decades. He first joined the bank in 1980 as a manager in its credit department and has since slowly worked his way up rank-and-file to the No. 1 position in the bank. The loyal employee was chosen to replace Mr Shang Fulin when the former head of the bank was headhunted for the position of the chairman of China Securities Regulatory Commission, the country's stock market regulator.

As the top executive at one of the big four state-owned commercial banks in China, Mr Yang is charged with ensuring the Agricultural Bank of China play a key role in the remaking of China's financial system. Originally established to provide finance for the agriculture sector, the institution now has over 50,000 branches in cities as well as in the rural areas.

China's plan to develop its western region has entrusted the Agriculture Bank of China with an important role, given its extensive branch network in that part of country.

According to Mr Yang, "There are still 20 million poverty-stricken people in the western areas," He adds, "The bank manages 65% of poverty-relief loans and will continue to grant more poverty-relief loans but it must monitor the disbursement of these loans closely to avoid unnecessary losses."

Under his leadership, the bank has also begun diversifying into more financial products. Today, it has 931 units dealing in foreign exchange and has established partnerships and custodian relationships with over 328 banking head offices in 49 other countries.

The Agriculture Bank of China is also beginning to spread its wings overseas and has begun establishing offices in Hong Kong and Singapore as well as representative offices in New York, London and Tokyo.

With total assets of over RMB 2 trillion (US$240 billion), the Agriculture Bank of China is one of the 500 largest banks in the world. Given its reach into the rural areas of China, Mr Wang is charged with the delicate task of overseeing over 500,000 employees and modernising the bank.

Background

1980-2003	Manager of Credit Department, Agriculture Bank of China
	Managing director of Tianjin Branch, Agriculture Bank of China
	Vice president of Agriculture Bank of China
2003-	President of Agriculture Bank of China

Contact information

Address 23 Fu Xin Jia Road, Beijing, China, 1000
Telephone 86-10-6821 1610   Website www.abchina.com

Spectacularly positioned on the upper floors of the landmark Jin Mao Tower. The city's most luxurious accommodation with views to take your breath away.

FEEL THE HYATT TOUCH®

www.hyatt.com

LEADERS OF CHINA'S LARGEST COMPANIES WHO'S WHO IN CHINA

Ma Mingzhe — China Ping An Insurance Co Ltd
"Adversity breeds character - moral from the fable of a frog"

Corporate position President, China Ping An Insurance Co Ltd

Corporate revenue RMB 62 billion (US$7.5 billion)

"I am willing to dedicate my entire life to the insurance industry."

Mr Ma Mingzhe

Far from being averse to the idea of hiring foreign talent, Mr Ma Mingzhe is a firm believer in attracting only the best to work in Ping An – an insurance company which has grown to become the second largest insurer in China and Asia's 23rd largest since it was set up in 1988.

Under his leadership, Ping An hired a number of foreign talents including the director of one of the largest United States IT company to head its computing department, a former deputy president of Lincoln Finance Group as its chief accountant, a partner from one of the largest accounting firms as its financial controller, a former partner of McKinsey & Company as the director-in-charge of its e-commerce department.

Mr Ma's reasoning was simple – the contribution of these individuals far outstrips the costs of bringing them into the company.

And it would seem that he is right. In 2002, the total policy income of Ping An was RMB 62 billion (US$7.5 billion) while its total capital asset increased to RMB 144.8 billion (US$17.4 billion).

Inspite of Ping An's achievements, Mr Ma believes that complacency is often fatal. With his close associates, he is known to always share his favourite fable of the "the frog which did not react while being slowly boiled to death". The moral of the story, he often reminds them, is that companies must remain vigilant lest they are oblivious of the gradual changes in their operating environment that may later prove detrimental to their survival.

An insightful manager, Mr Ma comments, "Between being reactive and proactive, Ping An has to be constantly proactive and the best defence is attack - Ping An has a company saying that we strive to own when others have none, we strive to innovate when others own, we strive to specialise when others innovate, we strive for longevity when others innovate."

Ping An's product innovation is best illustrated in year 2002, when together with the Chubb Group of Insurance Companies, it launched an insurance product to cover the risks to companies when they lose the services of their senior executives, the first of its kind in China. When commenting on the product, Mr Ma said, "Following China's WTO entry, we feel the need to upgrade management, products and services in the insurance sector. "

Mr Ma is also a big believer in training his employees. He elucidates this point with a borrowed saying from the late Chairman Deng Xiao Peng, "In the process of building a market economy, we should be extremely cautious and cross the river by feeling the way through the stones on the riverbed," Mr Ma adds, "We need not face the same risks as a blind man crossing the bridge - if we pay some toll, there should be no reason why we cannot use the bridge to cross the river. " And the toll, Mr Ma paid, amounted to 6.9% of its annual revenue that year. To implement staff training, Ping An partnered with Peking University to set up an executive MBA program where he sent more than 600 of its employees for further education. In 2003, it invested close to RMB 300 million (US$36 million) and founded the Ping An Finance Institute.

Although Mr Ma stepped down as general manager of Ping An in 2003, he remains an influential figure as its president, a position he has held since the company was established.

Friends and associates of Mr Ma describe him as energetic, with a never say die attitude and a penchant for continual lifelong learning. A director of another China insurance company once said, "Mr Ma is my idol - he has already done what I have thought of doing and he has already thought of what I have never considered before."

Background

1988-1994	General manager and president of Ping An Insurance
1994-	General manager and president of Ping An Insurance Co Ltd (listed on the Shenzhen Stock Exchange)

Other titles and memberships

Guest lecturer at Nankai University

Director of Central Advanced Technology Insurance Ltd, USA

Contact information
Address Ping An Building, Baguasan Road, Bagualing District, Shenzhen City, Guangdong, China, 518029
Telephone 86-755-8226 2888   Facsimile 86-755-8243 1019   Website www.paic.com.cn

Fang Chengguo   Bank of Communications
"Head of the first joint-stock bank"

Corporate position	President and Vice Chairman, Bank of Communications
Corporate revenue	RMB 24.6 billion (US$3.0 billion)

Considered as one of China's authorities in banking and finance, Mr Fang Chengguo was appointed the president of China's first joint-stock bank in 2000. Prior to his appointment, Mr Fang served as the vice president of the Shanghai based fifth largest bank in China and the deputy head of the Party Branch from 1996 to 2000.

When he first took the office of chairman in 2000, Mr Fang placed utmost priority on increasing the bank branch network as well as the bank's move towards electronic banking. He took to the tasks like fish to water – setting up 28 new branches within three years of his appointment while improving the bank's electronic and online banking system at the same time.

Mr Fang's reputation as a progressive banker is best illustrated in 2001 when he was one of the first few bankers to explore plans to sell 15% of the bank to foreign banks in order to strengthen its position in the market. "Foreign involvement in the operations of our bank is a priority in any merger," Mr Fang remarked. He believes that leading foreign banks inject technological and management expertise to the Bank of Communications and commented, "Foreign involvement would help bring the bank on par with its foreign counterparts."

Although it has only been established for about 15 years as a result of the amalgamation of several state-owned enterprises, the Bank of Communications is among the world's 100 largest banks today as well as the leading joint-stock bank and one of China's top five commercial banks. It has been ranked by *The Banker* magazine as 94th largest bank in terms of asset value – a testimony of Mr Fang's ability.

Background

1996-2000	Vice president and the deputy head of CPC Party Commission, Bank of Communications
2000-	President of Bank of Communications
	Head of CPC Party Commission, Bank of Communications

Political affiliation

Member of the CPPCC

Contact information

Address No. 188 Yin Cheng Zhong Road, Shanghai, China, 200120
Telephone 86-21-5878 1234   Website www.bankcomm.com

Power and Natural Resources

LEADERS OF CHINA'S LARGEST COMPANIES WHO'S WHO IN CHINA

Chen Geng China National Petroleum Corporation
"China's new oil sheikh"

Corporate position	President, China National Petroleum Corporation Director and president, PetroChina
Corporate revenue	RMB 379.2 billion (US$45.8 billion)

"From this year, we give our overseas business greater prominence. We will reinforce oil exploration and production, develop the high-quality refinery assets, and tap the foreign trading business."

Mr Chen Geng

In a sentence, Mr Chen Geng is all about oil and gas.

As president of China National Petroleum Corporation (CNPC) and director and president of its listed subsidiary, PetroChina, Mr Chen heads China's largest corporation and producer of crude oil and natural gas. He was appointed on 13 April 2004 after the ex-president of CNPC, Mr Ma Fucai resigned to take responsibility for the gas well explosion in December 2003. The blast at a CNPC facility near Chongqing is thought to be one of China's worst industrial accidents since 1949. It released a cloud of toxic gases that killed 243 people, poisoned thousands more and forced the evacuation of about 60,000 nearby villagers.

A senior economist and graduate of Beijing Economics Institute[1], Mr Chen has over 30 years' of experience in China's oil and gas industry. Mr Chen was deputy director of Changqing Petroleum Exploration Bureau, deputy director of the Labour Department under the Ministry of Petroleum Industry, director of the Labour Bureau of CNPC, assistant president of CNPC, vice president of CNPC and deputy director of the State Petroleum and Chemical Industry Bureau successively from 1983 to 2001. He was appointed the president of PetroChina on December 2002.

As a member of the senior management team, Mr Chen was involved in one of the largest restructuring in China in which PetroChina was formed in 1999 to hold selected assets of CNPC, a prelude to its eventual US$2.9 billion listing on both the New York and Hong Kong stock exchanges in April 2000. During the restructuring, CNPC shed more than a million workers. This efficiency drive has since become a continuing theme as PetroChina continues its bid to becoming a world-class player. In the last three years, PetroChina has further trimmed its workforce by another 50,000 since its listing.

As a result of these efforts, the Beijing-based company is a highly successful and profitable business and is ranked the fourth-largest oil and gas company in the world based on output and proven reserves. Its market capitalisation of RMB 289.8 billion (US$35 billion) is about one-eighth that of ExxonMobil Corporation. PetroChina today operates 13 large oil and gas fields, 29 refinery plants, nine petrochemical companies, 19 petrochemical marketing companies and 12,102 gas stations. It is also the de facto gas company of China, with 95.0% of the gas pipeline market. Its market share of China's domestic oil market is close to 70.0% while it has a 40.0% market share of the domestic refinery oil products retail pie. Such is his contribution to China's efforts to turn state owned enterprises into world-class businesses.

---

[1] Beijing Economics Institute is currently named the Capital University of Economics and Business.

A very driven executive, Mr Chen is not contented with the current achievements of the company. He is currently leading the effort to double PetroChina's revenue to US$83 billion by 2010 and to ensure PetroChina become one of the top 10 oil companies globally. As domestic oil production is predicted to remain constant, Mr Chen has set targets to ensure its overseas revenue contribute up to one-quarter of its total revenues by 2010, making sure PetroChina stay true to its mission. Another challenge faced by Mr Chen is to ensure that accidents such as the gas well explosion in 2003 do not happen again.

Birth date	1947
Education	Bachelor degree, Beijing Economics Institute
Professional qualifications	Senior Economist

Background

1983-1985	Deputy director of Changqing Petroleum Exploration Bureau
1985-1993	Deputy director of the Labour Department under the Ministry of Petroleum Industry, Director of the Labour Bureau of CNPC
1993-1996	Assistant president of CNPC
1997-1998	Vice president of CNPC
1998-2001	Deputy director of the State Petroleum and Chemical Industry Bureau
2001-2004	Vice president of CNPC
2001-	Director of PetroChina
2002-	President of PetroChina
2004-	President of CNPC

Contact information
Address 6 Liu Pu Kang Street, Xi Cheng District, Beijing, China, 100724
Telephone 86-10-6209 4114 Facsimile 86-10-6209 4806 Website www.cnpc.com

LEADERS OF CHINA'S LARGEST COMPANIES WHO'S WHO IN CHINA

Chen Tonghai Sinopec Group
"Rising young star in China's petrochemical industry"

Corporate position	Chairman, Sinopec Corporation President, Sinopec Group
Corporate revenue	RMB 378 billion (US$45.7 billion)

> *"Rather than dance with wolves, Sinopec should itself become a big strong wolf."*
> Mr Chen Tonghai, commenting on potential competition from foreign companies entering the China market

What Mr Chen achieved in five years at China's second-largest oil conglomerate would probably take his peers more than two decades to achieve.

When he first joined China Petrochemical Corporation (Sinopec Group) in 1998, he was a vice president five levels down in the management ladder. But the former mayor of Ningbo City in Zhejiang Province rose quickly through the ranks, becoming vice chairman in 2000, before taking the top executive position in Sinopec Group as its president in 2003. Mr Chen is also the chairman of its flagship subsidiary, China Petroleum and Chemical Corporation (Sinopec Corporation).

Although the son of the former Party Chief, Chen Weida of Tianjin, his meteoric rise was not totally due to his privileged background but rather, as some industry observers have noted, "more due to his youthful energy and the lack of competing talent at his level".

As with most state owned enterprises, Sinopec Corporation was formed on February 28, 2000 by its parent company, Sinopec Group which is in line with the principle of "separation of core business from the ancillary, performing assets from non-performing assets, and enterprise functions from the social", restructured its business portfolio and hived down selected assets, liabilities and personnel to Sinopec Corporation.

Under Mr Chen's nurturing, Sinopec Corporation, has grown into a vertically integrated energy and chemical conglomerate. It is China's largest producer and marketer of oil products including gasoline, diesel, and jet fuel. It is also the country's largest supplier of major petrochemical products such as synthetic resin, synthetic fiber, synthetic rubber and fertilizer. Sinopec Corporation's visibility in China can be seen by its staggering 29,425 petrol stations on top of over 5,200 franchised stations. This network of businesses help Sinopec Corporation make a net profit in 2002 of RMB 14.1 billion (US$1.7 billion) and for its achievements under Mr Chen's stewardship, the company has won many accolades in corporate governance and management.

Sinopec Corporation listed its shares on the Hong Kong, New York and London Stock Exchanges in October 2000 and later on the Shanghai Stock Exchange in July 2001. Today, Sinopec is still majority owned by the Chinese government as with most state owned enterprises. Close to 55% of its shares are held by the state, 23% by banks and assets management companies, 19% by foreign investors such as ExxonMobil, Shell, and British Petroleum with the remaining 3% by retail investors.

Birth date	1949
Education	Bachelor of Engineering, majoring in Oil Production, Northeastern Petroleum Institute
Professional qualifications	Senior economist

Background

1983-1986	Head, Sinopec Zhenhai General Petrochemical Works
1986-1994	Deputy mayor, acting mayor and mayor of Ningbo City, Zhejiang Province
1994-1998	Vice minister, State Planning Commission
1998-2003	Vice president, Sinopec Group
2000-2003	Vice chairman, Sinopec Corp
2003-	President, Sinopec Group, chairman, Sinopec Corporation

Contact information
Address No. A6 Hui Xin East Street, Chao Yang District, Beijing, China, 100029
Telephone 86-10-6499 8828   Website www.sinopec.com

LEADERS OF CHINA'S LARGEST COMPANIES WHO'S WHO IN CHINA

Liu Deshu SinoChem Corporation
"Captain of China's flagship international trading company"

Corporate position   President, SinoChem Corporation

Corporate revenue   RMB 155.3 billion (US$18.8 billion)

"In today's fast-changing world, only reformation will create certainty for success."
Mr Liu Deshu

Mr Liu Deshu was appointed Sinochem Corporation's (SinoChem) president in March 1998 and subsequently the secretary of SinoChem's Chinese Communist Party Committee in June 2000.

Prior to his current appointment, he was the deputy general manager for another trading organisation, the China National Machinery Import & Export Corporation. In total, Mr Liu has been involved in world trade for more than 20 years, all in a professional capacity and as a result he is highly respected for his deep understanding of China's macroeconomic and world trade policies and also for his insights as a progressive manager. He places a high emphasis on knowledge and training within SinoChem. Mr Liu himself graduated from the prestigious Tsinghua University's department of precision instrumentation and later went on to obtain an executive MBA from the China-Europe International Business School while working as a senior executive.

Today, Mr Liu is at the helm of China's leading international company, ranked 11th among the world's largest trading companies by *Fortune* magazine in 2003. Founded in 1950, SinoChem is China's largest trading company and its first truly multinational conglomerate. Originally named China National Chemicals Import and Export Corporation, SinoChem is the first national trading enterprise to change its name with the approval of the Commission for Supervision and Management of State-owned Properties under the State Council.

SinoChem trades chemicals, primarily in the petroleum industry. It operates more than a hundred subsidiaries in China and abroad which deal in businesses that range from petroleum trading, chemicals, rubber, plastics, fertilizer, technology, finance, information businesses to real estate. SinoChem is one of only a few Chinese companies to make it to *Fortune* magazine's Global 500 and it has done so for the last 14 years. Mr Liu has ambitious plans for the company and he once said that, "the only way for SinoChem to remain evergreen and vibrant in a competitive industry is to constantly be creative and adapt to the changing environment. " To fulfill his goals for SinoChem, Mr Liu has been raising capital and nurturing the growth of the group. In 2003, SinoChem's only listed subsidiary, the Shanghai-listed SinoChem International issued 135,000 new shares to the public to raise RMB 1.7 billion (US$205 million), for the acquisition of 90% of SinoChem International Fertilizer Trading Corporation and 100% of SinoChem Bahama, two sister companies within the group. The transaction created the largest fertilizer company in China with a 60% domestic market share.

Mr Liu's reputation as a decisive and ethical executive who is not averse to making tough calls is reflected by the London incident which involved the audit of a subsidiary. During a routine internal audit, the auditors were thwarted from performing their duties despite his personal intervention. In addition, Mr Liu received an anonymous threat whereby he was asked to stop the investigation. With the help of the British police, Mr Liu and the auditors were escorted to audit the subsidiary whereby they uncovered embezzlement involving millions of dollars.

LEADERS OF CHINA'S LARGEST COMPANIES WHO'S WHO IN CHINA

Birth date	November 1952
Education	Bachelor of Engineering, majoring in Precision Instrumentation, Tsinghua University
	Master of Business Administration, China-Europe International Business School

Background

Before 1998	Deputy general manager, China National Machinery Import & Export Corporation
1998-	President, SinoChem Corporation
2000-	Secretary, SinoChem Corporation's Chinese Communist Party Committee

Corporate structure of SinoChem Corporation

Categories	Subsidiaries
The Oil Group	Sinochem International Oil Co
	Sinochem Petroleum Exploration and Development Co Ltd
	Sinochem International Industries Co
	Sinochem Shenzhen Industry Co Ltd
	Dalian West Pacific Petro-Chemical Co Ltd
	Sinochem Pudong Trading Co Ltd
	Sinochem - Xingzhong Oil Staging (Zhoushan) Co Ltd
	Shanghai Orient Terminal Co Ltd
	Sinochem International Oil (Hong Kong) Co Ltd
	Sinochem International Oil (Singapore) Pte Ltd
	Atlantis Holding Norway AS
	Sinochem International Oil (London) Co Ltd
The Fertilizer Group	Sinochem International Fertilizer Trading Corporation
	Sinochem Sierte (Ningguo) Co Ltd
	Yunnan Three Circles - Sinochem - Cargill Fertilizers Co Ltd
	Hubei Sinochem & Orient Fertilizer Co Ltd
	Fujian Sinochem Zhisheng Fertilizer Co Ltd
	Dohigh Trading LimitedSinochem (United Kingdom) Ltd
	U.S. Agri-Chemicals Corporation
	U.S. Chem Resources Inc

LEADERS OF CHINA'S LARGEST COMPANIES WHO'S WHO IN CHINA

Sinochem International	Sinochem International Co Ltd
	Sinochem Trading Development Ltd
	Sinochem Liaoning Import & Export Corporation
	Sinochem Tianjin Import & Export Corporation
	Sinochem Hebei Import & Export Co Ltd
	Sinochem Shandong Import & Export Group Corporation
	Sinochem Shanghai Import & Export Corporation
	Sinochem Jiangsu Import & Export Corporation
	Sinochem Ningbo Import & Export Co Ltd
	Sinochem Guangdong Import & Export Co
	Sinochem International Chemicals (Hong Kong) Co Ltd
	Sinochem Trading (Singapore) Pte Ltd
	Sinochem Japan Co LtdSinochem (USA) Inc
The Domestic Group	Sinochem Ningbo Import & Export Co Ltd
	Sinochem Guangdong Import & Export Co
	Sinochem Jiangsu Import & Export Corporation
	Sinochem Shanghai Import & Export Corporation
	Sinochem Shandong Import & Export Group Corporation
	Sinochem Hebei Import & Export Co Ltd
	Sinochem Tianjin Imp & Exp Corporation
	Sinochem Liaoning Import & Export Corporation
	Sinochem Trading Development Ltd
	Sinochem Electronics Information Technology Co
	Sinochem International Tendering Co Ltd
Property and Hotel Group	Sinochem International Property & Hotels Management Co Ltd
	Beijing Yishengyuan International Conference Centre
	Wangfujing Grand Hotel
China Foreign Economy and Trade Trust & Investment Co Ltd / International Far Eastern Leasing Co Ltd	China Trust And Investment Corporation For Foreign Economic Relations & Trade
	International Far Eastern Leasing Co Ltd
	Manulife-Sinochem Life Insurance Co Ltd
	Baoying Fund Management Co Ltd
	Jiangtai Insurance Brokering Co Ltd
Overseas Enterprises	Sinochem Asia Holdings Co Ltd
	Sinochem International Oil (Singapore) Pte Ltd
	Sinochem Trading (Singapore) Pte Ltd
	Sinochem Investment (Singapore) Co Ltd
	Sinochem Japan Co Ltd
	Yu Hua Loong Trading SdnBhd
	Chemiforward Trading Co
	Sinochem Europe Holdings Plc

LEADERS OF CHINA'S LARGEST COMPANIES WHO'S WHO IN CHINA

	Sinochem International Oil (London) Co Ltd
	Sinochem (United Kingdom) Ltd
	Sinochem Trading Hamburg Gmbh
	Sinochem American Holdings Inc
	Sinochem (US) Inc
	U. S. Agri-Chemicals Corporation
	U. S. Chem Resources Inc
	Sinochem Hong Kong (Holdings) Co Ltd
	Sinochem International Oil (Hong Kong) Co Ltd
	Slnochem Internatlonal Chemicals (Hong Kong) Co Ltd
	Dohigh Trading Ltd
	Rillfung Company Ltd
	Sinochem Japan Co Ltd
	Sinochem Trading (Singapore) Pte Ltd
Overseas Representative Offices	Sinochem representative office in Singapore
	Sinochem representative office in Moscow
	Sinochem representative office in Iraq

Contact information

Address A2 Sinochem Tower, Fu Xing Men Wai Street, Beijing, China, 100045
Telephone 86-10-8849 4210 / 8849 4218 / 8849 4366   Facsimile 86-10-8831 6017   Website www.sinochem.com

Zhou Mingchen
China National Cereals, Oils and Foodstuffs Import & Export Corporation
"Feeding the world"

Corporate position President, China National Cereals, Oils and Foodstuffs Import & Export Corporation (COFCO)

Corporate revenue RMB 109.7 billion (US$13.3 billion)

#11

"COFCO can re-invent itself in five years time."
— Mr Zhou Mingchen

A veteran in international trade with over 30 years of experience, Mr Zhou Mingchen is commonly regarded as a peer of Mr Liu Deshu of SinoChem as both stem from similiar international trading backgrounds. Previously the vice president of China National Metals & Minerals Import & Export Corporation and the president of China National Instrument Import & Export Corporation, Mr Zhou became the president of China National Cereals, Oils and Foodstuffs Import & Export Corporation (COFCO) in 1992.

A graduate of Beijing Institute of Foreign Trade[1], Mr Zhou landed COFCO a mention in *Fortune's* Top 500 Companies in 1994 and has continued to do so every year since. One of the largest import and export companies in China, Beijing-based COFCO was established in 1952. It is one of 44 state-owned enterprises under the central government's administration and has long been primarily engaged in the import and export business of cereals, oils and food. In 2002, the total import and export values handled by COFCO reached a record RMB 1.2 trillion (US$143.5 billion).

Under his leadership, COFCO has organised its business under four major profit-centres and companies namely, COFCO Grain and Oil Import and Export Corporation, COFCO International, Top Glory International and COFCO Development.

COFCO Grain and Oil Import and Export Corporation is mainly involved in the business of trading raw agri-product materials for China. COFCO International, listed on the Hong Kong Exchange, holds the group's processed food business and deals in leading products and brand names such as Fortune (edible oil), Great Wall (wine), Le Conte (chocolate) and Ma Ling (canned food). Top Glory International, another subsidiary listed on the Hong Kong Stock Exchange manages most of

[1] *Later renamed the University of International Business and Economics.*

the group's property development and hotel management activities while COFCO Development holds the other businesses of the conglomerate including asset management, shipping, packaging and the poultry and meat businesses. COFCO's other diverse business activities include operating one of the key bottling plants for Coca-Cola in China.

In an interview, Mr Zhou once commented that trading cereals, oil and foods is a tough business whereby, "on a good day, one tonne of corn would at best fetch US$120, at worst, US$90, barely enough to cover the export and import taxes."

Still, COFCO, he said, will continue the trading business division for three major reasons. Firstly, trading will continue to contribute to COFCO growth. Secondly, it will also give COFCO access to raw foods material and enable it to develop its processed food business. And lastly, through its trading activities, COFCO can diversify into the food-related areas such as futures and financial derivatives business. Mr Zhou cited General Electric as a model for COFCO, and his strategy is to create a "new" COFCO by 2010.

Education	Bachelor of Arts, majoring in Japanese Language Study, Beijing Institute of Foreign Trading

Background

1970-1992	Deputy chief, chief, vice president, China National Metal & Minerals Import & Export Corporation
	President, China National Instruments Import & Export Corporation
1992-	President, China National Cereals, Oils and Foodstuffs Import & Export Corporation

Corporate structure of COFCO

LEADERS OF CHINA'S LARGEST COMPANIES WHO'S WHO IN CHINA

Corporate structure of COFCO International Ltd (Listed in Hong Kong)

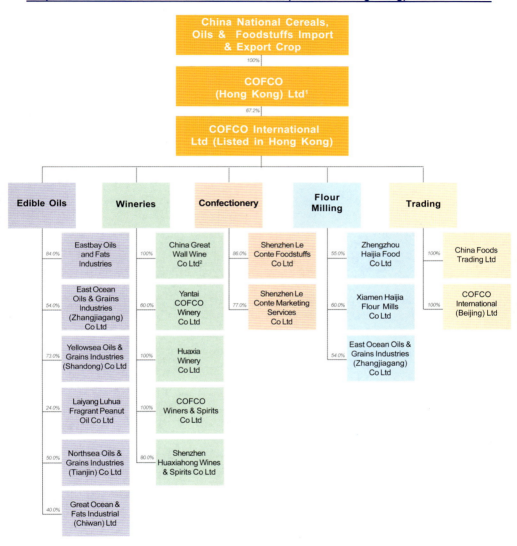

[1] Top Glory sold its equity in COFCO International (21.5%) to COFCO Hong Kong
[2] Shareholding increased from 50% to 100% during 2003

Contact information

Address Zhongliang Square, No. 8 Jiannei Street, Beijing, China, 100005
Telephone 86-10-6526 8888 x2715   Facsimile 86-10-6527 8613   Website www.cofco.com

LEADERS OF CHINA'S LARGEST COMPANIES WHO'S WHO IN CHINA

Corporate structure of Top Glory International Holdings Ltd (Listed in Hong Kong)

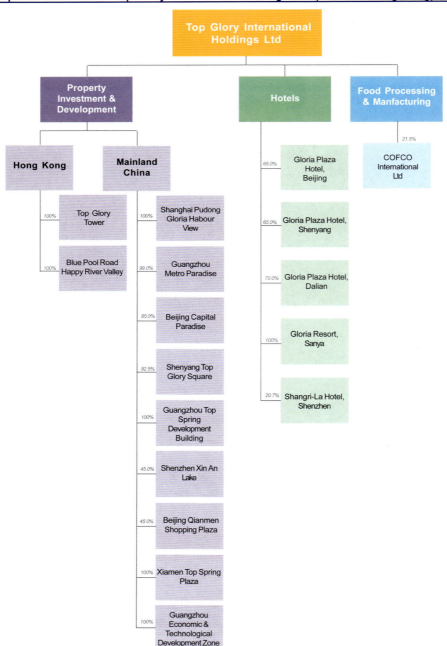

LEADERS OF CHINA'S LARGEST COMPANIES WHO'S WHO IN CHINA

Xie Qihua Shanghai Baosteel Group
"The iron lady of China"

Corporate position   Chairman and President, Shanghai Baosteel Group Corporation

Corporate revenue   RMB 77.7 billion (US$9.4 billion)

Literally the lady of steel, the chairman of Shanghai Baosteel Group Corporation, China's largest steelmaker. Indeed, Ms Xie Qihua is a rare face in a world dominated by men. Toughened by her nearly 36 years in the steel industry, she earned the reputation of being a tough but fair and flexible manager.

Ms Xie's success has not been by chance. She graduated with a degree in engineering from the prestigious Tsinghua University and joined Shanghai Baosteel Group when it was formed in 1978. In the only company she has ever worked for, Ms Xie worked her way through the rank-and-file until 1994, when she became the president of Shanghai Baosteel Group's flagship company, Baoshan Iron and Steel. When she was finally appointed the chairman in 2002, she immediately set her sights on becoming the best steel maker in the world and one of the largest 500 companies globally.

A progressive manager with her own unique style of management, she introduced a number of unconventional measures within the Shanghai Baosteel Group, luring top talent to join the company by paying annual salaries as high as RMB 600,000 (US$72,500) and implementing flexible working hours, unusual in most state-owned enterprises.

As the chairman, Ms Xie has also been steering Shanghai Baosteel Group to look for partners to break into new markets. Agreements have been concluded with the chinese partners of General Motors, Volkswagen, and Nissan to develop steel products for the automotive market and it has also signed an agreement with Arcelor and Nippon Steel Corporation in 2003 to build a RMB 6.5 billion (US$785 million) plant in Shanghai. The new plant will provide 1.7 million tonnes of cold-rolled strips and hot-dipped galvanized steel sheets every year to the country's automotive industry. Ms Xie's believes that, "partnering with international steelmakers allows the company to learn more about new steel products and its technology."

Her methods seemed to work. In year 2003, sales jumped 48% to RMB 116 billion (US$14 billion), while profits soared 89% to US$1.6 billion. "We have been growing with China's economy for the past 20 years," remarked Ms Xie.

For her achievements, *Fortune* magazine ranked her 16th among the Top 50 Businesswomen with the most business influence outside the United States in 2003.

Birth date	June 1943
Hometown	Yin County, Zhejiang Province
Education	Bachelor of Engineering, major in construction engineering, Tsinghua University, 1968
Professional qualifications	Senior engineer (Professor ranking)

LEADERS OF CHINA'S LARGEST COMPANIES WHO'S WHO IN CHINA

Background

1961-1968	Tsinghua University
1968-1978	Shanxi Steel Factory, technician and deputy director of Engineering Design Group
1978-1984	Deputy director and director of the Beijing Construction Department, Baosteel Engineering Headquarter; director of the Planning Department, Baosteel Engineering Headquarter
1984-1986	Assistant director, Baosteel Engineering Headquarter
1986-1990	Assistant director, Baosteel Engineering Headquarter and director, Planning Department, Baosteel Engineering Headquarter
1990-1994	Associate director, Baosteel Engineering Headquarter; director, Planning and Development Department, Shanghai Baosteel Group
1994-2000	President and vice chairman, Shanghai Baosteel Group
2000-	President and chairman, Shanghai Baosteel Group

Other titles and membership

Businessman of the Year, China Central TV Station, 2002

Ranked 16th and 18th, Top 50 Businesswoman with the most business influence outside the United States, *Fortune* magazine, 2003 and 2002

Corporate Structure of Baosteel Co Ltd (listed in Shanghai)

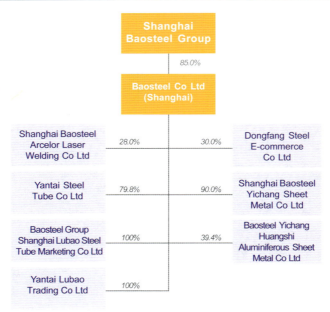

Subsidiaries of Shanghai Baosteel Group

Categories	Subsidiaries
Steel	Baosteel Co Ltd (listed in Shanghai) **(85.0%)**
	Baosteel Group Shanghai Pudong Steel Co Ltd
	Baosteel Group Shanghai Meishan Co Ltd
	Baosteel Group Shanghai Steel Tube Co Ltd
	Ningbo Baosteel Stainless Steel Co Ltd
	Baosteel Group Nanjing Steel Rolling Factory
	Baosteel Group Shanghai First Steel Co Ltd
	Baosteel Group Shanghai Fifth Steel Co Ltd
	Shanghai Baosteel Yichang Sheet Metal Co Ltd
	Nantong Baosteel Xinri Steel Co Ltd
	Nanjing Baori Steel Wire Co Ltd
Manufacturing	Shanghai Baosteel Industrial Development Co Ltd
	Shanghai Baosteel Engineering Technology Co Ltd
	Baosteel Group People's Machine Factory
International trade	Shanghai Baosteel International Trading Co Ltd
Finance	Baosteel Group Financial Co Ltd
	Huabao Trust Investment Co Ltd
IT	Shanghai Baoxin Software Co Ltd
Real Estate	Shanghai Baosteel Real Estate Co Ltd
Chemical	Shanghai Baosteel Chemical Industry Co Ltd
Construction	Shanghai Baosteel Construction Co Ltd
Services	Nantong Baonan Enterprise Co Ltd
	Shanghai Baosteel Equipment Repairing Co Ltd
	Baosteel Enterprise Development Co Ltd
Overseas	Baosteel Australia Mining Co Ltd
	Baohe Commerce Limited
	Baosteel America Trading Co Ltd
	Baosteel Europe Trading Co Ltd
	Baosteel France Trading Co Ltd
	Baosteel Brazil Trading Co Ltd
	Baosteel Singapore Trading Co Ltd
	Baohuarui Mining Co Ltd
	Baoyun Enterprise Co Ltd
	Baojin Enterprise Co Ltd
	Baodao Trading Co Ltd

Contact information

Address Guo Yuan, Fu Jin Road, Baoshan District, Shanghai, China, 201900
Telephone 86-21-5678 4567   Facsimile 86-21-2664 8046   Website www.baosteel.com

LEADERS OF CHINA'S LARGEST COMPANIES WHO'S WHO IN CHINA

Li Xiaopeng   China Huaneng Group
"China's power king"

Corporate positions   President and Director, China Huaneng Group
Chairman, Huaneng Power International
Chairman and General Manager, Huaneng International Power Development Corporation

Corporate revenue   RMB 37 billion (US$4.5 billion)

#34

Xiaopeng is a common Chinese name but China Huaneng Group's president is no ordinary person. To understand Mr Li's position in the company, it is important to understand his lineage and background. As the scion of former Chinese Prime Minister Li Peng, the younger Li undoubtedly harks from an influential background.

The chairman of Huaneng Power International, which is listed on the Hong Kong, New York and Shanghai Stock Exchange, is often referred to as "China's Power King", as he controls China's power industry. Together with his mother, Madam Zhu Lin, who heads Huaneng International Power Development Corporation (the parent company of Mr Li's Huaneng Power International), it is widely known in the industry that the younger Li is the "tiller" of the ship while Madam Zhu is the "captain".

Power lies in the young Mr Li's blood and he has always had an interest in power plants and systems. His first posting was at the Electric Power Research Institute, shortly after graduating from the North China Institute of Electric Power in 1982.

An engineer by profession, he moved to Asia's largest independent power generator Huaneng Power International in 1991 and never looked back since. His star shone when his father was made China's prime minister and he rose quickly to become the company's chairman in 1999. "Our ultimate goal is to make Huaneng an internationally competitive company", Mr Li stating his goal for the group as the chairman.

Under his leadership the power giant is diversifying into other businesses. In 2004, Mr Li announced that the Huaneng Group is expanding into financial services and revealed that it is "preparing for the launch of an insurance company and a fund management joint-venture".

Birth date	June 1959
Hometown	Chengdu City, Sichuan Province
Education	Bachelor of Engineering, majoring in Power Plants and Power Systems, North China Institute of Electric Power, 1982.
Professional qualifications	Senior engineer

Background

1978-1982	North China Institute of Electric Power
1982-1991	Assistant engineer and engineer, Power System Research Division, Deputy director and director, Power Technology and Economic Research Division, Electric Power Research Institute

1985-	Joined the CPC
1991-1999	Assistant to general manager, associate general manager, general manager, board director, vice chairman, and chairman, Huaneng Power International and Huaneng International Power Development Corp
1999-	Director and general manager, China Huaneng Group
	Chairman and general manager, Huaneng International Power Development Corp
	Chairman, Huaneng Power International

Corporate structure of China Huaneng Group

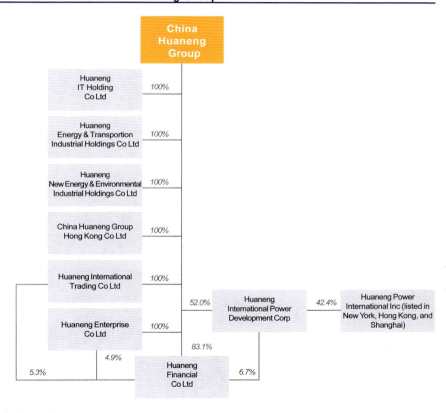

Other information

Mr Li's sister, a major in electronics engineering in university, is one of the member of the senior management of a power investment company in China.

Contact information

Address No. 40 South Xue Yuan Road, Hai Dian District, Beijing, China, 100088
Telephone 86-10-6229 1888 Facsimile 86-10-6229 1899 Website www.chng.com

Telecommunications and Postal Services

Zhang Ligui — China Mobile Communication Corporation
"Connecting China and the world"

Corporate position President, China Mobile Communication Corporation

Corporate revenue RMB 163.7 billion (US$19.8 billion)

"Let everyone enjoy being connected"
Mr Zhang Ligui

Mr Zhang Ligui has been with China Mobile Communication Corporation (China Mobile) since its formation on 20 April 2000 when the mobile business of the country's telecommunication monopoly, China Telecom, was hived off to create one of the world's largest mobile service providers.

Prior to being appointed the top man at China Mobile, Mr Zhang was the minister in charge of the Ministry of Information Industry and its predecessor, the Ministry of Posts and Telecommunications for two consecutive terms. As such, he is considered to be highly appropriate for the position, given his comprehensive understanding of the Chinese telecommunication markets. He oversaw the most important period of the industry where between 1995 and 2000, the country's telecommunication network expanded rapidly and China's analog network began to give way to digital systems. He was also involved in the introduction of multiple service providers into the industry.

As a legislator, Mr Zhang was behind many of the industry's bills. He is a firm believer that a sound legal infrastructure, complete with effective policing and enforcement must be firmly in place when the industry opens up, as without an effective legal framework, the telecommunications market would become chaotic and inefficient, much to the detriment of the telecommunication service providers and their consumers.

Under his management, China Mobile is today one of the central government's most valuable companies with a registered capital of RMB 51.8 billion (US$6.2 billion), assets of over RMB 320 billion (US$38.6 billion) and 120,800 employees. The mobile player is ranked the 287th largest company globally by *Fortune* magazine in 2003. It is also the No. 1 GSM network operator in the world with roaming services in 116 countries and regions. In 2002, it registered 138 million subscribers for its services.

LEADERS OF CHINA'S LARGEST COMPANIES WHO'S WHO IN CHINA

Its key subsidiary, China Mobile (HK) Limited, is listed on both the Hong Kong and New York Stock Exchanges and has one of the largest market capitalisation among the overseas listed Chinese companies.

Mr Zhang, who believes that the industry must constantly adapt itself to changing consumer patterns and demands, points to Charles Darwin's Theory of Evolution. "The survivors are not the strongest nor the most intelligent, but those who are quickest to adapt, " He adds, "Times are changing, as is society. And adapting to the changes is essential for survival, be it for a country or a company. "

"If you remain stagnant in the midst of these changes, you will be left behind," he stressed[1].

Birth date	1943
Professional qualifications	Senior engineer

Background

1965-1995	Deputy director, director of Telecommunication Bureau, Lanzhou City
	Director of Telecommunication Bureau, Gansu Province
	Deputy director, director of Ministry of Communication, Telecommunication Department, director of Beijing Telecommunications Bureau
1995-2000	Director of General Bureau of Posts and Telecommunications (predecessor to the Ministry of Posts and Telecommunications)
2000-	Director of Ministry of Telecommunication
	President of China Mobile Communication Corporation

Corporate structure of China Mobile

[1] Xinhua News Agency: 13 October 2002

Subsidiaries of China Mobile (Hong Kong) Limited

Subsidiaries of China Mobile (Hong Kong) Limited	Pecentage
Hainan Mobile Communication Company Limited	100%
Beijing Mobile (BVI)	100%
Beijing Mobile Communication Company Limited	100%
Shanghai Mobile (BVI) Limited	100%
Shanghai Mobile Communication Company Limited	100%
Tianjin Mobile (BVI) Limited	100%
Tianjin Mobile Communication Company Limited	100%
Hebei Mobile (BVI) Limited	100%
Hebei Mobile Communication Company Limited	100%
Liaoning Mobile (BVI) Limited	100%
Liaoning Mobile Communication Company Limited	100%
Shandong Mobile (BVI) Limited	100%
Shandong Mobile Communication Company Limited	100%
Guangxi Mobile (BVI) Limited	100%
Guangxi Mobile Communication Company Limited	100%
Anhui Mobile BVI	100%
Anhui Mobile	100%
Jiangxi Mobile BVI	100%
Jiangxi Mobile	100%
Chongqing Mobile BVI	100%
Chongqing Mobile	100%
Sichuan Mobile BVI	100%
Sichuan Mobile	100%
Hubei Mobile BVI	100%
Hubei Mobile	100%
Hunan Mobile BVI	100%
Hunan Mobile	100%
Shaanxi Mobile BVI	100%
Shaanxi Mobile	100%
Shanxi Mobile BVI	100%
Shanxi Mobile	100%
China Mobile (Shenzhen) Limited	100%
Aspire Holdings Limited	66.4%
Aspire (BVI) Limited	100%
Aspire Technologies (Shenzhen) Limited	100%
Aspire Information Network (Shenzhen) Limited	100%
China Motion United Telecom Limited	30.0%
Shenzhen China Motion Telecom United Limited	30.0%
Fujian Nokia Mobile Communication Technology Co Limited	50.0%

Contact information

Address No. 29 Finance Street, West District, Beijing, China
Website www.chinamobile.com

LEADERS OF CHINA'S LARGEST COMPANIES WHO'S WHO IN CHINA

Zhou Deqiang
China Telecommunications Corporation
"No price wars please, we're Chinese"

#6

Corporate position	Chairman and CEO, China Telecommunications Corporation
Corporate revenue	RMB 149.1 billion (US$18 billion)

 "My target is to lead the development of China Telecommunications Corporation into a world-class telecommunications company in five years."

Mr Zhou Deqiang

With more than 34 years of experience in China's telecommunications industry, the Chairman and CEO of China Telecommunications Corporation (China Telecom), Mr Zhou Deqiang is another industry veteran. Prior to joining the company in May 2000, he was the vice minister at the Ministry of Information Industry, the powerful ministry which oversees the telecommunication industry.

His biggest challenge came when the telecommunication industry in China was restructured in 1999. As a result of the reforms which swept through the industry, the former state-monopoly, China Telecom was sized down in 2000 when China Mobile was spun off. The company was subsequently split in 2002 into China Telecom Corporation, which caters to the fixed-line telecommunications market in southern China and China Netcom, which caters to the fixed-line market in northern China.

After the restructuring and split, China Telecom Corporation is made up of 21 provincial corporations with 70% of the national trunk-line transmission network assets previously owned by the former state-monopoly. The company was reorganised into what is now China Telecom and listed on both the Hong Kong and New York stock exchanges in 2002.

Despite a much sized down company, Mr Zhou, a graduate of Nanjing Institute of Posts and Telecommunications, started to search for new business opportunities to grow the revenue of China Telecom including providing services such as multimedia information services and international telecom accounts settlement. These ventures soon became new sources of revenue for the company. In 2002, China Telecom reported revenues of RMB 149 billion (US$18 billion) and was ranked sixth largest among all companies in China.

The success of China Telecom is a reflection of Mr Zhou's leadership qualities. This is best depicted by his business philosophy. Mr Zhou is a strong believer that competing in China's telecommunications industry is more than just lowering prices. "Competition," he said, "is not about competing to offer the lowest pricing for services to consumers." Having worked with consultants and advisors, he concluded that, "The consequence of a price war will be bad not only for the company and its shareholders, but for the customers as well in the longer run," he asserted.

Mr Zhou is also an advocate of high quality and strongly believes that, "If we are criticised by only one or two of our customers, that may be just an isolated incident, however, if the majority of the customers find fault with us, we must be introspective and try to get to the root of problem when customers are dissatisfied."

Mr Zhou is also a believer in making his company more efficient. "The development of every company implies a mathematical relationship, a relationship between numerator and denominator. In the last 10 years, China Telecom tried to increase the numerator by increasing the number of customers. However, it is now more important for us to reduce the denominator, thereby achieving higher efficiency," he asserted.

In 2004, China Telecom, filed to raise some RMB 24.8 billion (US$3 billion) of capital for purchasing 10 provincial phone networks from its parent company as part of its strategy to continue its revenue growth amidst growing competition from China's mobile service operators.

Birth date	September 1941
Education	Bachelor of Engineering, majoring in Telecommunication Engineering, Nanjing Institute of Posts and Telecommunications, 1968
Professional qualifications	Senior engineer (professor rank)

Background

1969	Joined the CPC
Before 1994	Deputy chief engineer of Beijing Long Distance Telephone Bureau, deputy director of Posts and Telecommunications Administration, Anhui Province
1994-2000	Vice minister of Posts and Telecommunications and vice minister of Information Industry
2000-	Chairman of Board of Directors, CEO of China Telecommunications Corporation

Political affiliation

Member of the Political Bureau of CPC Central Committee

Subsidiaries of China Telecommunications Corporation

Anhui Telecommunications Corporation	Jiangxi Telecommunications Corporation
Chongqing Telecommunications Corporation	Ningxia Telecommunications Corporation
Fujian Telecommunications Corporation	Qinghai Telecommunications Corporation
Gansu Telecommunications Corporation	Shanghai Telecommunications Corporation
Guangdong Telecommunications Corporation	Shaanxi Telecommunications Corporation
Guangxi Telecommunications Corporation	Sichuan Telecommunications Corporation
Guizhou Telecommunications Corporation	Tibet Telecommunications Corporation
Hainan Telecommunications Corporation	Xinjiang Telecommunications Corporation
Hunan Telecommunications Corporation	Yunnan Telecommunications Corporation
Hubei Telecommunications Corporation	Zhejiang Telecommunications Corporation
Jiangsu Telecommunications Corporation	China Telecom Corporation Limited Research Institute

Contact information

Address 31 Jin Rong Avenue, Beijing, China, 100032
Telephone 86-10-6602 7188   Website www.chinatelecom.com.cn

China Franchise Consulting

Develop your expansion strategy through the power of franchising in China. Franchising is a genuine route to rapid wealth creation. By utilising the power of synergy, you will be able to develop the true potential of your business. We will help you develop your franchising system and assist in recruiting potential franchisees in China.

Corporate Training

To improve your strategic, tactical and operational processes through the training of executives, managers, sales or staff. We assess, design and deliver highly customised executive training.

Brand Consulting

Assess, develop, and re-launch your corporate strategy using your most valuable asset: your brand. First Link International will help you discover your corporate identity, develop your business strategy to reach out and communicate to your customers in China.

CHINA BUSINESS INTELLIGENCE & CORPORATE SERVICES
5 Shenton Way
#37-02 UIC Building
Singapore 068808
Tel: (65) 6358 2289
www.1st-link.com

Zhang Chunjiang
China Network Communications Group Corporation
"Banking on youth"

Corporate position	President, China Network Communications Group Corporation
Corporate revenue	RMB 66 billion (US$8 billion)

Another alumni of the Ministry of Information Industry, the former deputy minister did not feel entirely out of place when he was appointed in 2003 as the president of China Network Communications Group Corporation (China Netcom), China's second largest fixed-line operator. Faced with a new business environment and given the leadership role, Mr Zhang Chunjiang met the challenge with flying-colours and has since earned himself the reputation of being a tough manager who has turned China Netcom, a very large organisation even by state-owned enterprise standards, into an aggressive player.

Under his leadership, China Netcom, has become a vibrant, forward-looking and young organisation – the average age of employees coming up to only a sprightly 34 years, highly unusual among state-owned enterprises.

The telecom giant with the responsibility for northern China, is a major corporation, with more than RMB 220 billion (US$26.6 billion) of assets and 230,000 employees. China Netcom's major investor and shareholder remains the state government. The company has direct control of telecommunication companies in 10 provinces, and telecommunication holding companies in eight provinces, including China Network Communication (Holding) Ltd, Jitong Communication Ltd and various other holding companies, subsidiaries and affiliations.

China Netcom, the only major Chinese telecom operator which is still unlisted, started off as the major provider of fixed-line services to northern China. It has since under Mr Zhang's direction expanded its product offerings to include voice, data, image and multimedia services and system integration.

Given its steady progress since it was formed in 2002, China Netcom's public listing is widely anticipated to be by mid-2004. "We haven't reached any specific plans," Mr Zhang told *China Daily* in Beijing in January 2004, during an interview on the establishment of China Netcom Northern Communications Co Ltd (Netcom North), a subsidiary of China Netcom. However, Mr Zhang revealed that the setup of Netcom North signalled that China Netcom is nearing its goal to get listed.

According to Mr Zhang's blueprint, the next step is to establish China Netcom Shareholding Co Ltd, as a prelude to the company going public in mid-2004. The listed company is then expected to purchase assets from its parent company in stages. "All the purchases are expected to be completed before the end of 2006," Mr Zhang said.

Birth date	1958

LEADERS OF CHINA'S LARGEST COMPANIES WHO'S WHO IN CHINA

Background

1995-2000	Deputy director-general of Post Bureau, Liaoning Province
	Director of Office Management Department, Ministry of Information Industry
2000-2003	Deputy minister of Ministry of Information Industry
2003-	President of China Network Communications Group Corporation

Corporate structure of China Network Communications Group Corporation

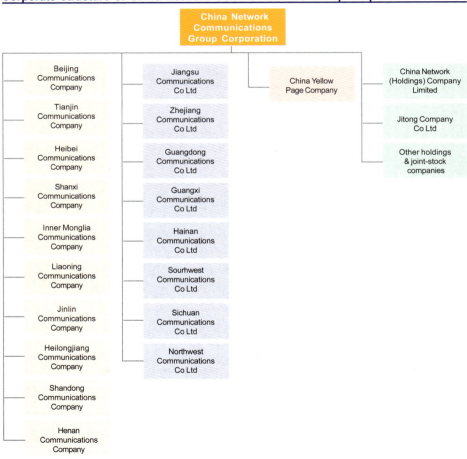

Contact information

Address   156 Fuxingmennei Avenue, Tower C, International Finance Building, West District, Beijing, China, 100031
Telephone 86-10-6611 0006   Facsimile 86-10-6611 0009   Website www.chinanetcom.com.cn

Liu Andong State Post Bureau
"Posting to the world"

Corporate position	Postmaster General, State Post Bureau
Corporate revenue	RMB 51 billion (US$6.2 billion)

> *"China will make extra effort to promote its postal service so that it becomes more market-oriented while ensuring universal postal service obligations."*
>
> Mr Liu Andong, speaking at the 2002 Strategic Conference of Universal Postal Union

The State Post Bureau (SPB), China's regulatory authority for the national postal industry as well as postal enterprise management, was created after the Government's move to restructure to merge two Chinese ministries, the Ministry of Posts and Telecommunications and the Ministry of Electronics Industry in 1998 to form the Ministry of Information Industry.

Under the restructuring the SPB comes under the administration of the Ministry of Information Industry. The SPB, as the local postal bureau, has the authority and responsibility to manage its local post industry and is able to act independently as a public enterprise. The SPB also oversees the operation of both the domestic and international postal network.

Mr Liu Andong, previously the deputy postmaster-director general and the No. 2 executive at the SPB was chosen to become the postmaster-general in 2003 after his predecessor retired. His ascent to the top executive position is partly due to his abilities and partly due to his international outlook. Mr Liu, with over 20 years experience in dealing with foreign investments, was largely credited for SPB's strong growth with annual revenue increasing some 78% over five years, from RMB 28.7 billion (US$3.5 billion) in 1998 to RMB 51 billion (US$6.2 billion) in 2003. With Mr Liu at the helm, there is suggestion that the postal powerhouse may wish to go for a public listing as part of its strategic development.

As a symbolic gesture of the SPB emergence as a key postal player and state-owned enterprise, and also China's growing economic clout on the global stage, SPB announced that China will donate US$250,000 to the Asian-Pacific Postal Union (APPU) to support its efforts to improve postal services in impoverished member states. "China is ready to support and participate in APPU activities and would strive for the common development of postal businesses in the Asian-Pacific region," Mr Liu said at the opening of the 2003 annual conference of the APPU executive council in Boao, south China's Hainan Province.

Birth date	September 1946
Education	Bachelor of Engineering, majoring in Wireless Communication, Beijing Institute of Post and Communication
Professional qualifications	Engineer

Background

1966-	Joined the CPC
1970-1973	Staff member of Broadcasting Instruments Factory, Baise County, Guangxi Autonomous regions
1973-1978	Technical specialist at Petrochemistry Research Institute, Ministry of Energy
1978-1984	Associate engineer of Computing Bureau, Ministry of Commerce, Department of Foreign Trade
1984-1985	Staff member of City Development Group, National Development Zone Office, State Council
1985-1986	Deputy chief of City Development Group, National Development Zone Office, State Council
1986-1988	Deputy head of Foreign Investment Group, National Development Zone Office, State Council
1988-1990	Deputy department head of City Development Department, National Development Zone Office, State Council
1990-1993	Deputy department head of Development Zone Department, National Development Zone Office, State Council
1993-1998	Head of department of Coastal Development Zone Department, National Development Zone Office, State Council
1998-2003	Deputy postmaster-general of China State Post Bureau
2003-	Postmaster-general of China State Post Bureau

Subsidiaries of State Post Bureau

Postal Savings and Remittance Bureau
Information and Technology Bureau
Postage Stamp Printing Bureau
China National Philately Corporation
China Postal Courier/EMS Corporation Ltd
National Postal news Publicity Centre
China Postal Academy
Shijiazhuang Postal College (Shijiazhuang Training Center of State Post Bureau)
China Postal Airlines Corporation Ltd
China Postal Advertising Corporation Ltd
Postal Culture and History Centre
Zhongyu Postal Code Information Service Corporation Ltd
Beijing P & T Sanatorium
Postal Culture and History Centre
All-China Philatelic Federation (related unit of SPB)

LEADERS OF CHINA'S LARGEST COMPANIES WHO'S WHO IN CHINA

Yang Xianzu
China United Communications Corporation
"Sole provider of CDMA network"

Corporate position   President, China United Communications Corporation

Corporate revenue   RMB 50.3 billion (US$6.1 billion)

 "Today, the world's communications market is undergoing a networking revolution."

Mr Yang Xianzu

Mr Yang Xianzu was appointed the president of China United Communications Corporation (China Unicom) in 1999 and is recognised as the main force behind China Unicom's transformation into a key player in the China telecommunications market.

Another vice minister from the Ministry of Information Industry with a long history of involvement in China's telecommunication industry, he joined the Yichang City Posts and Telecom Office in Hubei province just after graduation and served from 1966 to 1983 as chief of the Carrier Wave Section and a director. In 1983, he was promoted to be the deputy director of the Hubei Provincial Posts and Telecom Administration, where he spent another three years. In 1986, he was promoted again to become the director of the Henan Provincial Posts and Telecom Bureau, where he served until 1990. He was subsequently appointed a vice minister of the Ministry of Posts and Telecommunications in 1990.

While at the Ministry of Posts and Telecommunications, Mr Yang worked closely with Mr Wu Jichuan, the minister of the Ministry of Posts and Telecommunications who had also earlier worked with Mr Yang in Henan. Mr Yang, a believer in building national champions once said that, "companies involved in infrastructure development projects should buy domestically produced telecom goods to promote local industry". In 1999, with the blessings of Mr Wu, Mr Yang was appointed the chairman and CEO of China Unicom to fulfil his dream of building a national champion.

At the time of the 30-year telecommunications veteran's appointment, China Unicom was facing a number of challenges. The appointment was intended to turn China Unicom into a competitor to China Telecom as part of the government's plan to improve service and reduce end-user costs. In addition, they also needed someone to raise funds and end the over 40 Chinese-Chinese-Foreign (CCF) joint venture contracts worth RMB 8.3 billion (US$1 billion) which were declared "irregular" by the State Council.

Despite difficulties, Mr Yang was able to make progress in terminating the contracts and by June 2000 and within a year of his appointment, China Unicom was one of the largest public offerings in Asia, on the New York Stock Exchange, Shanghai Stock Exchange and Hong Kong Stock Exchange.

Under his stewardship, China Unicom has transformed itself into an integrated telecom service operator. Its infrastructure and services include a broadband fibre transmission network, CDMA mobile network, long distance network, data communications network, paging network and internet with nationwide coverage and worldwide connectivity. In addition, the company has acquired a broad base of blue-chip shareholders including China International Trust and Investment Corporation (CITIC), China Everbright International Trust and Investment Corporation, and China Resources Group.

LEADERS OF CHINA'S LARGEST COMPANIES WHO'S WHO IN CHINA

China Unicom is currently the only supplier of both GSM and Code Division Multiple Access (CDMA) based mobile communications services in China and launched its CDMA service network, U-Max, in March 2003. As one of the largest CDMA network providers in the world, China Unicom's CDMA network currently caters to 20 million users as at February 2004 and its service capacity is expected to more than doubly increase over the next three years. China Unicom also has 74 million GSM subscribers.

China Unicom has gone a long way since Mr Zhang assumed the top executive position in 1999. A tribute to the man's determination and abilities.

Birth date	August 1939
Education	Bachelor of Engineering, majoring in Communication, Wuhan Telecommunication Institute

Background

1965-1990	Director, Post Bureau Yichang City, Sichuan Province
	Deputy director, Post Bureau Hubei Province
	Director, Post Bureau Henan Province
1990-1998	Deputy minister, Ministry of Posts and Telecommunication
1998-1999	Deputy minister, Ministry of Information Industry
1999-	President, China United Communications Corporation

Corporate structure of China United Communications Corporation

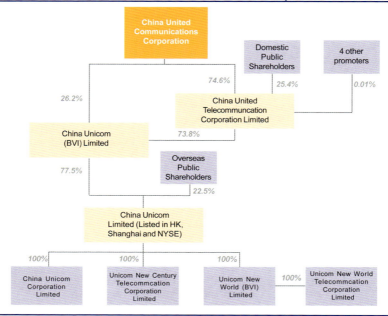

Contact information
Address 18 Jiannei Avenue, 12th Floor, Tower 1, Hengji Building, China, 100005
Telephone 86-10-6518 1800   Facsimile 86-10-6518 3405   Website www.chinaunicom.com.cn

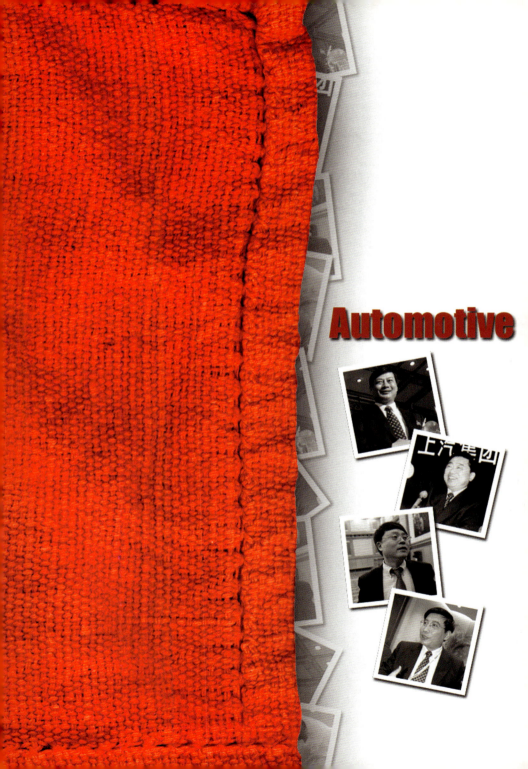
Automotive

LEADERS OF CHINA'S LARGEST COMPANIES WHO'S WHO IN CHINA

Zhu Yanfeng
China First Automobile Works Group Corporation
"First in line for First Automobile Works"

#7

Corporate position	President, China First Automobile Works Group Corporation
Corporate revenue	RMB 127.2 billion (US$15.4 billions)

 "You must be patient for at least another 20 years with the Chinese automobile industry."
Mr Zhu Yanfeng

Born into a family with a long tradition in the automotive industry, Mr Zhu Yanfeng followed in his father's footstep. In 1983, at the age of 23, he started working as a technician in same company his father worked in when he joined Changchun First Automobile Works, the predecessor of China First Automobile Works Group Corporation (FAW).

Changchun First Automobile Works started in 1953. In 1956, it produced China's first locally produced truck. Two years later, it followed that feat with the first locally manufactured sedan and on 15 July 1991, the business was reorganised as FAW. By 1999, at the young age of 38, Mr Zhu has worked his way through the rank-and-file to take over the reins of an automobile empire, FAW.

Well known for his patience, he often reminded that, "One has to be patient for at least 20 years." However, Mr Zhu is a fast-worker when required. In 2002 he spearheaded FAW's bid to become China's largest automotive player. In that short period of time, he successfully concluded joint ventures with Toyota, Volkswagen and Mazda turning FAW into the country's leading automotive company.

Under Mr Zhu's guidance, FAW continues to perform beyond expectations. It quickly became the largest automobile manufacturer in China and the first automotive company in China to be able to produce over 500,000 cars a year.

In year 2003, FAW's joint venture with Volkswagen sold 694,000 cars in China, up from 510,000 units in 2002. By the beginning of 2003, FAW has 29 wholly owned subsidiaries, 14 affiliated companies, including three listed companies namely, First Automobile, First Xiali and First Sihuan. FAW's total vehicle output grew by 33.2% to 900,000 units in 2003, controlling 21% of China's total vehicle market. The company aims to increase its annual output to 2.07 million units by 2008. In the next five years, FAW will invest RMB20 billion (US$2.4 billion) in its headquarters at Changchun, Northeast China's Jilin Province, to double its annual auto output in the city alone.

Mr Zhu says, "I believe there will be a ceremony when the production capacity of FAW Volkswagen exceeds the millionth car per year in the near future with the completion of its second car plant."

Birth date	March 1961
Education	Zhejiang Province
	Bachelor of Engineering, Zhejiang University
Professional qualifications	Senior engineer, research fellow

Background

1983-1986	Technician at Instruments Workshop, Thermoelectricity Factory, FAW Group
1986-1992	Technician at Measurement Section, FAW Group
	Assistant engineer at Measurement Section, FAW Group
	Engineer at Measurement Section, FAW Group
	Senior engineer at Measurement Section, FAW Group
1992-1994	Deputy head of Research Section, FAW Group
1994-1997	Head of Marketing Division, FAW Group
1997-1998	Deputy manager, FAW Group
	Manager, FAW Group
1998-1999	Vice president, FAW Group
1999-	President, FAW Group
2000-	Chairman of the Board of Directors, Tianjin Automobile

Other titles and memberships

Vice president of National Youth Association

Political affiliations

Elected member of CPC Central Committee for Discipline Inspection at the 16th National Congress of the CPC, November 2002

Contact information
Address Yingchun Road, Lvyuan District, Changchun City, China, 130011
Telephone 86-431-7666 666   Facsimile 86-431-5909 771   Website www.faw.com.cn

Corporate structure of China First Automobile Works Group Corporation

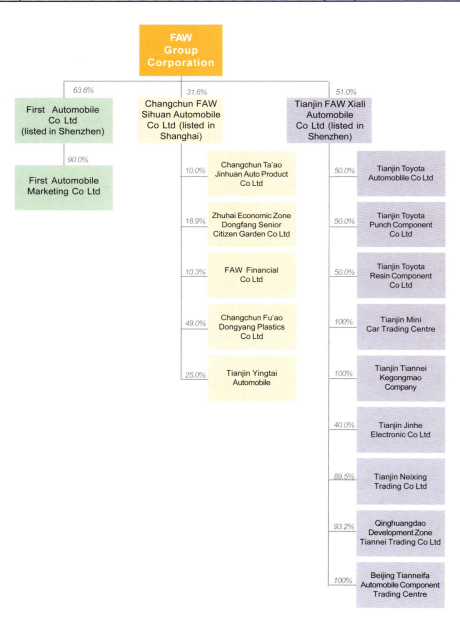

Hu Maoyuan — Shanghai Automotive Industry Corporation

"Rival looking out to be No. 1"

Corporate position — President and Director, Shanghai Automotive Industry Corporation

Corporate revenue — RMB 71.2 billion (US$8.6 billion)

#15

"We strongly support the development of a healthy automotive industry in which major players consolidate their resources and increase their economies of scale so as to avoid repetitive and uncoordinated building of capacity."

Mr Hu Maoyuan

Mr Hu Maoyuan's Shanghai Automotive Industry Corporation (SAIC) is one of the top three automobile manufacturers in China with some 60,000 employees and it stands as a worthy competitor to Mr Zhu Yanfeng's First Automobile Works (FAW). It is a key manufacturer and distributor of passenger cars, buses, tractors, motorcycles, heavy-duty trucks, auto parts and components and has diversified into various auto-related businesses including the servicing of vehicles.

Perhaps the clearest indication of SAIC's success in the Chinese automotive industry lies in it being ranked first in the list of top 500 biggest domestic industrial enterprises, despite lacking the same level of state support as FAW.

The world marvels at the ease in how Mr Hu engages world-renowned automobile companies in joint-ventures. During the Forbes Global CEO Conference 2003, Mr Hu attracted the attention of many established business leaders who admired at how one of China's state-owned enterprises managed to set up major joint ventures with six different foreign enterprises in a very short period of time. "Exports are important to us," said Mr Hu, illustrating the point with one of the joint ventures with SAIC. "We hope Shanghai Volkswagen (a 50-50 joint venture between SAIC and Volkswagen AG) will be an export base for Volkswagen in the Asia Pacific." Shanghai Volkswagen exports the Santana, Santana 2000 and Passat sedans.

SAIC has so far set up 57 joint ventures with world-renowned automotive groups from Germany, United States, Japan, United Kingdom, France, Italy and many other countries. SAIC achieved an

LEADERS OF CHINA'S LARGEST COMPANIES WHO'S WHO IN CHINA

annual production capacity of 400,000 sedans in 2002. Mr Hu says his company is seeking to stay astride of industry restructuring by leading the way in mergers and consolidations.

In 2001, SAIC reached a sales volume of its passenger cars exceeding 300,000 units and a market share of 43% in the domestic market.

Birth date	April 1951
Education	Bachelor of Engineering, Tongji University
Professional qualifications	Senior engineer, senior economist

Background

1983-1985	Managing director of Shanghai Tractor Manufacturing Company
1985-1990	Deputy manager of Shanghai Tractor Industry Affiliated Company
1990-1995	Assistant manager of Shanghai Automobile Industry Company
	Deputy manager of Shanghai Automobile Industry Company
	Vice president of Shanghai Automobile Industry Company
1995-1999	Vice president of Shanghai Automotive Industry Corporation
	Managing director of Shanghai General Motors Pte Ltd
1999-	President and director of Shanghai Automotive Industry Corporation

Corporate structure of Shanghai Automotive Industry Corporation

Shanghai Automotive Industry Corporation has more than 58 subsidiaries, including one listed company, Shanghai Automobile Co Ltd (listed in Shanghai: 600104). The corporate structure of Shanghai Automobile Co Ltd:

Contact information

Address # 489 Weihai Road, Shanghai, China, 200041
Telephone 86-21-2201 1888   Facsimile 86-21-2201 1777   Website www.saicgroup.com

Jiang Mianheng
Shanghai Automotive Industry Corporation
"China's automotive princeling"

Corporate position	Board Director, Shanghai Automotive Industry Corporation
Corporate revenue	RMB 71.2 billion (US$8.6 billion)

It is quite difficult not to compare Dr Jiang Mianheng, board director of the Shanghai Automotive Industry Corporation, with Mr Li Xiaopeng, chairman of Huaneng Power International.

Both share a similar background, being the scions of powerful, political families in China. Mr Li is the son of former Premier Li Peng, while Dr Jiang is the eldest son of former President Jiang Zemin. But the similarities stop there. While Mr Li is dubbed "Asia's Power King" for his clout in China's power industry, it would be next to impossible to pigeon-hole Dr Jiang into a specific domain.

The "Digital Prince of China", who is also vice president of the Chinese Academy of Sciences (CAS) and deputy director of China Manned Spaceflight Project, has his fingers in many pies.

He is the director of several large and influential companies with interests ranging from automobile, aeronautics, telecommunications to electronics. These include China Netcom, Shanghai Automotive Industry Corporation, Shanghai Airport Group and Grace Semiconductor Manufacturing Corporation.

A graduate of China's renowned Fudan University in electronic engineering, Dr Jiang first worked for the Shanghai Institute of Metallurgy before he left China to pursue his doctorate's degree at Drexel University in Philadelphia and even worked for a spell at Hewlett-Packard Company in Palo Alto, California. After his return, he was appointed to various seats of power in the academic and military fields.

Rich, savvy and well connected, he is involved in some of China's highest-profile IT ventures. Amongst other things, he is chairman of state-run China Netcom, which is wiring the country for high-speed internet access. He is also in partnership with Taiwanese tycoon Mr Winston Wong to build a US$1.6 billion semiconductor plant in Shanghai.

Birth date	April 1951
Hometown	Shanghai
Education	Bachelor of Engineering, majoring in Electronic Engineering, Fudan University, 1977
	Master of Science, Institute of Semiconductor Research, CAS, 1982
	Ph.D. majoring in Electronic Engineering, Drexel University, Philadelphia, USA, 1991
Professional qualifications	Professor

LEADERS OF CHINA'S LARGEST COMPANIES WHO'S WHO IN CHINA

Background

1977	Graduated from Fudan University
1977-1979	Worked for a semiconductor device research institute in Shanghai
1979-1982	Graduated from the Institute of Semiconductor Research, the Chinese Academy of Sciences
1982-1986	Worked at the Shanghai Institute of Metallurgy
1986-1991	Ph.D. student at Drexel University, Philadelphia, USA
1991-1993	Worked in Hewlett-Packard company in Palo Alto, California, USA
1993-1997	Worked at the Shanghai Institute of Metallurgy
1997-	President of Shanghai Institute of Metallurgy
1999-	Vice president of CAS, board director of China Netcom Company, Shanghai Automotive Industry Corporation, Shanghai Airport Group, Grace Semiconductor Manufacturing Corp, deputy director of China manned spaceflight project

Contact information
Address Chinese Academy of Sciences, No. 52 San Li He Road, Xi Cheng District, Beijing, China, 100864

Be part of Asia's first, world's largest and most sucessful e-Learning service provider ourside of the USA

PurpleTrain.com Pte Ltd
5 International Business Park Tel: (65) 6568 0807 Email: licensing@purpletrain.com
Singapore 609914 Fax: (65) 6569 7060 Website: www.purpletrain.com/licensing
24 x 7 Hotline Cher (65) 9698 4237 Josephine (65) 9698 4257

"Passenger cars will be the major growth engine for China's auto market."

Mr Miao Wei

Miao Wei Dong Feng Automobile Co
"Reversal of fortunes"

#23

Corporate position	President, Dong Feng Automobile Co
Corporate revenue	RMB 53.4 billion (US$6.4 billion)

When Mr Miao Wei took over Dong Feng Automobile Co (Dong Feng), the company was on its last leg. Plagued by various problems over the years, Dong Feng was in shambles. Compounded by its low sales, poor credit rating, heavy debts and wage deductions, it was on the brink of collapse. In 1998, Dong Feng's balance sheet showed a debt of over RMB 500 million (US$60.4 million).

Despite these difficulties, Mr Miao reshuffled the entire management team, created a new management strategy and new product lines. Just one short year later, Dong Feng's fortunes turned around. It recorded profits of RMB 16 million (US$1.9 million), which increased to an astonishing RMB 2.5 billion (US$302 million) in 2001.

Dong Feng, originally founded in 1969 as a major state-owned automobile corporation, has more than 120 subsidiaries and more than 120,000 employees. It manufactures include heavy trucks, mini vans, buses and business sedans.

Mr Miao believes that human resource is the key asset for a company and the basis of core competence.

His objective is to lead Dong Feng to become one of the Fortune 500 companies by the end of 2005, with the annual sales of more than RMB 100 billion (US$12.1 billion) and a market share of 18%. In early 2004, in line with this objective, Dong Feng and French partner PSA Peugeot Citroen revealed their plans to invest 600 million euros (US$759 million) to double the production capacity of their joint venture and introduce new models in the years leading to 2006.

In addition, Dong Feng also entered a joint venture with Nissan in June 2003 to launch a US$2 billion joint venture. It is the largest Sino-foreign auto joint venture in terms of investment – to produce 620,000 passenger cars and trucks annually by 2007. Other partnerships in the pipeline include foreign car makers like Renault.

Birth date	May 1955
Hometown	Changli County, Hebei Province
Professional qualifications	Senior engineer

LEADERS OF CHINA'S LARGEST COMPANIES WHO'S WHO IN CHINA

Background

1982-1989	Deputy manger of China Automobile Sales & Services Company
1989-1993	Deputy director of Production Department, China Automobile Company
1993-1995	Deputy director of Automobile Department, former Ministry of Machine & Industry
1995-1997	Deputy chief engineer of former Ministry of Machine & Industry
1997-1999	General secretary of CPC Committee, Dong Feng Automobile Co
1999-	President of Dong Feng Automobile Co

Corporate structure of Dong Feng Automobile Co

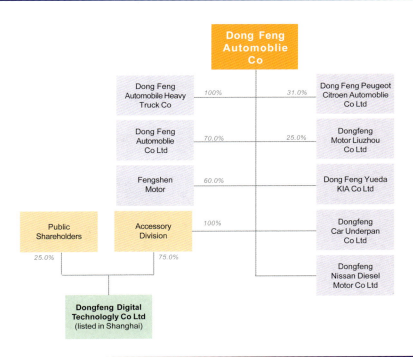

Contact information
Address 29 Bai Ye Raod, Wuhan Economic & Tehcnological Development Zone, Wuhan City, Hubei Province, China, 442000
Telephone 86-719-8201 255   Facsimile 86-719-8217 393   Website www.dfmc.com.cn

COSCO CORPORATION (SINGAPORE) LIMITED
中远投资（新加坡）有限公司

9 Temasek Boulevard, #07-00 Suntec Tower Two, Singapore 038989
Tel: (65) 6885 0888 Fax: (65) 6336 9006 Website: www.cosco.com.sg

COSCO Corporation (Singapore) Limited ("The Company"), a member of the Straits Times Index effective 1 March 2004, is a subsidiary of **COSCO** Holdings (Singapore) Pte Ltd, which in turn is the wholly owned subsidiary of China Ocean Shipping Group Companies (COSCO Group), headquartered in Beijing.

As part of the largest shipping conglomerate in China, **COSCO** Corporation conducts business in three distinct segments: shipping, shipping-related and onshore business. The Company's shipping segment owns and operates ships, while the shipping-related segment provides support services such as ship agency service, marine engineering, ship repairs and container depots.

COSCO Corporation is strongly focused in its core businesses and is also set to expand further in the region by seeking out synergistic alliances and strategic acquisitions, to complement its core shipping and shipping-related businesses.

Wei Jiafu COSCO
"Undisputed captain of shipping"

Corporate position   President and CEO, China Ocean Shipping (Group) Company

Corporate revenue   RMB 59.5 billion (US$7.2 billion)

"Security effort is a constant work in progress. Our combined efforts to ensure a safe and secure international commerce will eventually push supply chain management to a seamless level."

Mr Wei Jiafu, during the 2003 Liners CEO Forum in Boston

As the president and CEO of China Ocean Shipping (Group) Company (COSCO Group), Mr Wei Jiafu is the standard bearer of the largest international shipping conglomerate in China.

Mr Wei, who has spent over 35 years in COSCO, holds a doctorate's degree in naval architecture. Since his appointment in 1998, Mr Wei has been working aggressively to extend the global reach of COSCO. He has also overhauled and modernised COSCO by procuring advanced systems and equipment.

COSCO's fleet includes 600 modern and multifunctional vessels and it runs regular liners and tramp services which extend to more than 1,100 ports in 150 countries. Its entry into the shipping industry began over 40 years ago on 27 April 1961 when the S.S. Guanghua vessel sailed for Indonesia from Guangzhou.

Its transnational operational network covers major ports in areas such as Hong Kong, Japan, Singapore, America and Europe.

It has more than 70 wholly-owned companies, joint ventures and representative offices abroad and the strength of its foreign employees hovers around 4,500. The figures echo Mr Wei's conviction that the employees form the most crucial aspect in the organisation. The company's philosophy is not just about making sure the employees are well-fed and well looked after, he says. It is about allowing them the space they need to evolve within the organisation – the same way COSCO had allowed him to develop his career from an officer to its CEO.

He revealed that his criteria in his selection of people is based on their ability to speak (English), their drive and their understanding of the business.

Keeping the employees satisfied figures much in Mr Wei's mind. Although the shipping industry has long forbidden women on board ships, Mr Wei has plans to allow its ship officers to bring their families on board. "A crew with his family on board will be a happy crew," he explains.

Together with Bank of China and Tsingtao Brewery, COSCO was valued by the School of Management at Tsinghua University as the top three Chinese brands.

The September 11 attacks on the United States left a profound impact on COSCO's operations. During the 2003 Liners CEO Forum in Boston, Mr Wei said, "The events of September 11 will continue to transform our industry. These changes will be embedded into the routine of doing business and will involve closer cooperation and communication among everyone. The interest of better security in transportation is vested in all of us."

He added that although compliance and closer cooperation add cost to the transportation chain, it also has a positive effect on China's efforts to work closer with other governments, shippers, carriers, terminal operators and port authorities worldwide. "After everything is digested, our international supply chain will be better and more efficient," he concluded.

Mr Wei also reminded that the effort to enhance security is a constant work-in-progress. "Our efforts to promote a safe and more secured international commerce will eventually push supply chain management to a seamless level, a level of service efficiency, information transparency and technological advancements. A sound security system requires good standards and procedures, precise execution and practical government regulations. When the supply chain is international in nature, the requirements for cooperation become even more challenging and important. We need a highly coordinated effort to make the international supply chain secured."

Birth date	1950
Hometown	Jiangsu Province
Education	Bachelor in Engineering, Wuhan Marine College
	Masters of Engineering, majoring in Shipping Management Engineering, Dalian Maritime University
	Ph. D., majoring in Ship Building and Marine Architectural Design, Tianjin University

Background

1967-1992	Guangzhou Ocean Shipping Company
1992-1993	General manager of Chinese-Tanzanian Joint Shipping Company, Tanzania
1993-1995	President of COSCO Holdings (Singapore) Pte Ltd
1995-1997	General manager and CEO of Tianjin Ocean Shipping Company
1997-1998	General manager and CEO of COSCO Bulk Carriers Co Ltd
1998-	President and CEO of COSCO Group

Other titles and memberships

Chairman of China Ship-owners Association
Vice chairman of China Enterprise Confederation
Vice chairman of China Entrepreneurs' Association
Co-chairman of China Federation of Industrial Economics
Chairman of China Grouping Companies Promotion Association
Chairman of the Board of Directors, China Ship-owners Mutual Assurance Association
Vice chairman of China Merchants Bank
Member of the Board of Directors, Bo'ao Forum for Asia
Member of Asia-Pacific Advisory Board, Harvard Business School
Member of Executive Committee, Baltic and International Maritime Council (BIMCO)
Member of International Committee of Distinguished Shipping Personages of the American Bureau of Shipping (ABS)
Member of Advisory Board of Panama Canal Authority
Member of International Advisory Council of PSA
World Economic Forum Knowledge Navigator

Political affiliations

Member of the CPC Central Committee for Discipline Inspection at the 16th National Congress of the Communist Party of China, 14 November 2003.

Corporate structure of COSCO Group

Listed Companies	Code	Place	Percentage of ownership
COSCO Shipping Co Ltd	600428	Shanghai	63.9%
COSCO Pacific Ltd	1199HK	Hong Kong	54.0%
COSCO Corporation (Singapore) Ltd	COSINV	Singapore	63.8%
China International Marine Containers (Group) Co Ltd	000039	Shenzhen	20.1%
COSCO International Holdings Ltd	517HK	Hong Kong	60.0%
COSCO Development Ltd	600641	Shanghai	68.4%
China International Marine Containers (Group) Co Ltd[1]	200039	Shenzhen	20.1%

[1] B-shares in HK$

Contact information
Address Ocean Plaza, 158 Fuxingmennei Street, Beijing, China, 100031
Telephone 86-10-6649 3388   Facsimile 86-10-6649 2266   Website www.cosco.com

Yan Zhiqing China Southern Airlines Co Ltd
"Largest fleet, largest revenue"

Corporate position	Chairman, China Southern Airlines Co Ltd President and Deputy Party Head, China Southern Airlines Group
Corporate revenue	RMB 26.9 billion (US$3.3 billion)

As the chairman of China Southern Airlines Co Ltd as well as the president and deputy Party Head of China Southern Airlines Group, Mr Yang Zhiqing is known to be both an astute businessman and a savvy deal maker. He was involved in the merger of China Northern Airlines and Xinjiang Airlines, to create China Southern Airlines Group in 2002.

When he took over the reins at China Southern Airlines, he restructured the company by eliminating all non-airline related ventures, choosing to focus only on its core business. At present, it is the largest airline company in China in terms of the number of airplanes, routes, and revenue. China Southern Airlines' assets total RMB 50.1 billion (US$6 billion). The company employs 34,000 staff and has a fleet of 180 airplanes and 666 routes. China Southern Airlines went public and listed on the Shanghai Stock Exchange in early July 2003, and raised RMB 2.7 billion (US$325.3 million) on China's A shares market for the expansion of the company's aircraft fleet.

In a conference in July 2003 when commenting on how China Southern Airlines can stay competitive, Mr Yan said, "The world is becoming smaller. As national economies continue to cross boarders and embrace globalisation, state-of-the-art logistics will pace the future development of air cargo. China Southern should speed up the construction of its network and logistics hub, participate more in the provision of a more integrated air-ground-sea transportation services, and build a brand new logistics concept for the future while continuing to acquire more international management experience. And without question, domestic cargo service standards should be enhanced."

By the end of 2002, China Southern Airlines has 349 airlines including 286 domestic airlines and 63 international airlines.

China Southern Airlines is headquartered in Guangzhou, which is the communication and economic centre of southern China.[1]

Birth date	Huarong County, Hunan Province
Education	Bachelor degree, Civil Aviation and Flight Administration College, 1962

---

[1] Su Dong, *Southern China Daily*, 2002-10-13

LEADERS OF CHINA'S LARGEST COMPANIES WHO'S WHO IN CHINA

Background

1962-1996   Started working and acted as manager of Flying Department at Hunan Civil Aviation Administration Bureau

Director of Guangxi Civil Aviation Administration Bureau and director of Middle South China Civil Aviation Administration and bureau director of Political Department at Civil Aviation Administration of China successively

1996-   Joined China Southern Airlines, acted as Party head, president, chairman of China Southern Airlines Co Ltd

President and deputy Party head of China Southern Airlines Group successively

Political affiliations

Member of the National People's Congress of China

Corporate structure of China Southern Airlines Co Ltd

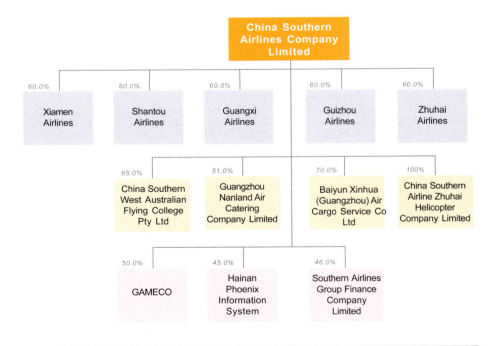

Contact information

Address   China Southern Airlines, Baiyun International Airport, 278 Airport Road, Guangzhou, China, 510406
Telephone 86-20- 8612 4738   Facsimile 86-20- 8612 4739   Website www.cs-air.com

"*After the regrouping, the overall competitiveness of China's civil aviation industry can be enhanced. Competition between companies will be carried out in an orderly manner.*"

Mr Ye Yigan

Ye Yigan — China Eastern Airlines Co Ltd
"From regional flights to international routes"

Corporate position Chairman, China Eastern Airlines Co Ltd
President, China Eastern Airlines Group

Corporate revenue RMB 20.5 billion (US$2.5 billion)

#23

With nearly 40 years of experience in civil aviation, Mr Ye Yigan was appointed the chairman of China Eastern Airlines Co Ltd and president of China Eastern Airlines Group.

Taking charge of the third largest airline company in China is not as easy task for the China Civil Aviation College graduate who majored in airplane instrument maintenance. He spent his early career as a senior engineer in airplane instrument maintenance under the Shanghai Civil Aviation Administration Bureau until he was appointed the director in 1985 before he was assigned to China Eastern Airlines in 2001.

Based in Shanghai, China Eastern Airlines was set up on 25 June 1988. In 15 years, China Eastern Airlines has developed into an international airline. As one of the three largest airlines in China, China Eastern Airlines has subsidiaries and branches in Shandong, Shaanxi, Hebei, Tianjin, Jiangxi, Jiangsu, Anhui and Ningbo. It is also the holding company of China Cargo Limited, China Eastern Jiangsu Limited and China Eastern Wuhan Limited.

Its fleet includes 89 wide and medium-sized aircraft. Its more than 300 international and domestic routes serve 100 cities inside and outside China. China Eastern Airlines has a hub-and-spoke network of airline routes centered around Shanghai, and the rest of China. The airline has routes to several parts of Asia, Europe, America and Australia.

In 1997, China Eastern Airlines was successfully listed on the New York, Hong Kong and Shanghai Stock Exchanges. It was also honoured with the Five Star Diamond Award given by the American Academy of Hospitality Sciences in 2001.

In 2002, China Eastern Airlines was restructured and merged with two other airlines in China namely, Yunnan Airlines and Northwestern Airlines. Currently, the "Oriental Swallow" is ranked No. 40 worldwide.[1]

Birth date	Senior engineer
Education	Bachelor of Engineering, majoring in Airplane Instrument Maintenance, China Civil Aviation College, Tianjin

Background

1965-	Joined the civil aviation industry
1983-1985	Deputy general engineer of Airplane Instrument Maintenance Factory, Shanghai Civil Aviation Administration Bureau

[1] Liu Zhenhua, *Xin Min Evening News*, 13 October 2002

LEADERS OF CHINA'S LARGEST COMPANIES WHO'S WHO IN CHINA

1985-1987	Director of Airplane Instrument Maintenance Factory, Shanghai Civil Aviation Administration Bureau
1987-1992	Deputy director of Eastern China Administration Bureau, Civil Aviation Administration of China
1992-1996	President and Party head of China Airline Equipment Corp
1996-2001	Director and Party head of Eastern China
2001-	Chairman of China Eastern Airlines Co Ltd and president of China Eastern Airlines Group

Corporate structure of China Eastern Airlines Co Ltd

233

As at 31 December 2002, the 10 largest shareholders of China Eastern Airlines and their respective shareholdings are as follows:

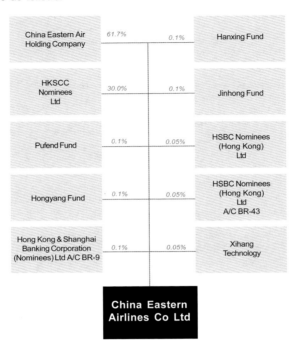

Contact information

Address No. 66 Airport Street, Pudong International Airport, Shanghai, China, 201202
Telephone 86-21-6268 6268   Facsimile 86-21-6268 6116   Website www.ce-air.com

LEADERS OF CHINA'S LARGEST COMPANIES WHO'S WHO IN CHINA

Li Jiaxiang Air China Group Corp
"Bringing a touch of the military"

Corporate position President, Air China Group Corp
CPC Party head of Air China Group Corp

Corporate revenue RMB 23.2 billion (US$2.8 billion)

"The global aviation industry is growing from competition to cooperation, so airlines can boost their development only on the basis of sound partnerships."
Mr Li Jiaxiang, when China Airlines and ANA signed a code sharing agreement

For over 30 years, Mr Li Jiaxiang was a military serviceman. He was in the People's Liberation Army (PLA), serving the air force before rising up the ranks to become a major-general. So when he was appointed to head Air China, China's largest transportation company in terms of assets in 2002, he decided to do what he does best, whipping the company into shape by focusing on improving its efficiency.

Mr Li re-engineered the inefficient traditional practices within the company. He introduced a reward management system based on merits and established tough criteria when selecting managers. These internal reforms turned out to be an inspiration for employees of this huge state-owned airline company, resulting in the company reporting profits from 2001 onwards.

Following the success of the initial reforms, Air China made plans to be listed in overseas stock markets. "Air China can be listed and the plan is in the pipeline," Mr Li said in February 2004, although he declined to give the exact listing date and venue.

The aviation power house is likely to be listed in Hong Kong in 2004, according to some sources "As a top ranking airline in the air transportation industry in China, Air China has a good brand in the civil aviation sector and can therefore tap the capital markets," Mr Li says.

Forming partnerships with other foreign airlines has long been an Air China strategy, according to Mr Li. He says, "The global aviation industry is growing from competition to cooperation, so airlines must boost their development through sound partnerships."

Currently Air China's fleet consists of 69 airplanes and it operates 114 flight routes around the world. Air China reported revenues of RMB 23.2 billion (US$2.8 billion) and profits of RMB 500 million (US$60.4 million) in 2002.

Birth date	November 1949
Hometown	Zaozhuang City, Shandong Province
Military rank	Major-general of Air Force

LEADERS OF CHINA'S LARGEST COMPANIES WHO'S WHO IN CHINA

Background

1969-2000	Joined the PLA, starting from the rank of monitor, director, colonel, division director to deputy Party head of the Air Force, Shenyang Army Base
1970-	Joined the CPC
2000-2002	Party head of Air China
2002-	President of Air China and Party head, Air China Group Corp

Honours and awards

Appraised as an outstanding political director in the PLA.

Political affiliations

Member of the Chinese People's Political Consultative Conference.

Other information

Hobbies: sports and literature.

Corporate structure of Air China Group Corp

Contact information

Address No. 15, West Chang An Street, Beijing, China
Telephone 86-10-6601 3336   Website www.airchina.com.cn

Others

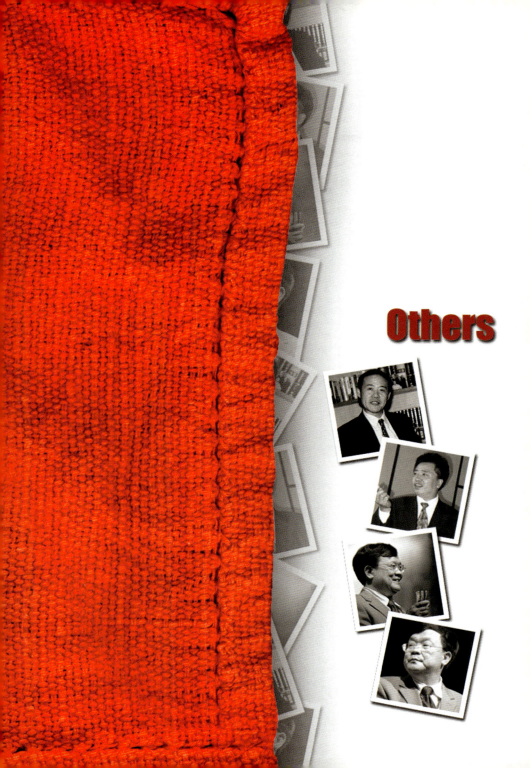

LEADERS OF CHINA'S LARGEST COMPANIES WHO'S WHO IN CHINA

Liu Wandong Hongta Group
"Building a famous trademark for tobacco"

Corporate position   Chairman, Hongta Group

Corporate revenue   RMB 33.6 billion (US$4.1 billion)

Although a physics graduate from Jilin University majoring in metal physics, Mr Liu Wandong's business acumen was unmistakable to those around him.

In 1995, Mr Liu was promoted to head the Yunnan Administration of Industry and Commerce. He was also assigned to help CPC members develop the economy of Yunnan Province.

From administrative work, he soon found himself back in the commercial world in 2002. He was appointed chairman of Hongta Group when its former head, Mr Zi Guorui, was dismissed after allegations of corruption, involving the misuse of company funds.

As chairman of Hongta Group, Mr Liu presides over the leading tobacco company in China. The Hongtashan brand has won many accolades including the national gold medal as a famous brand in China. The Chinese are the world's most enthusiastic smokers, consuming up to 1.7 trillion cigarettes a year. More than 60% of men over the age of 15 are smokers.

To prepare for increasing competition following China's entry in WTO, the group has invested RMB 300 million (US$36.2 million) to establish a technology centre which is staffed by highly qualified researchers. The national-level technology centre, which includes seven research institutes, is aimed at improving the group's capability to compete internationally.

In 2001, the brand value of Hongtashan was estimated at RMB 46 billion (US$5.5 billion). Other famous brands of Hongta Group include Yuxi, Ashima, Hongmei, and Gonghexinxi. Since tobacco joint ventures are not yet permitted in China, Hongta Group has started a loose collaborations with the Imperial Tobacco Group and has started producing the "West" brand of cigarettes since 2003.

The challenge for Mr Liu is to lead Hongta to become a Top 500 Global company in the near future.

Education	Bachelor of Science, majoring in Metal Physics, Jilin University

Background

Before 1995	Worked at Yuntianhua Group
1995-2002	Worked as head of Yunnan Administration of Industry and Commerce
	Deputy head of Organisation Department, CPC Yunnan Province Committee
2002-	Chairman of Hongta Group

Political affiliations

Member of 16th National Congress of the Communist Party of China.

Contact information

Address Upper Phoenix Rd, Yuxi High-tech Development Park,
Yuxi City, Yunnan Province, China, 653100
Telephone 86-877-2968 395   Facsimile 86-877-2968 732   Website www.hongta.com

Wang Shi China Vanke Co Ltd
"China's land broker"

Corporate position Founder and Chairman, China Vanke Co Ltd

Corporate revenue RMB 4.6 billion (US$551.9 million)

"Five years ago, no foreigners could bother about pleasing the Chinese. Now I feel like the world realises we matter."
Mr Wang Shi, commenting on the growing affluence of Chinese

An avid mountain climber, Mr Wang Shi is also an authority on real estate in China. Always one to embrace life, he also has a penchant for hiking and flying. Mr Wang can easily be spotted in a Motorola advertisement poster descending in a hot-air balloon. At 53, he is an embodiment of a successful individual who enjoys a balanced life.

Prior to founding China Vanke Co Ltd (China Vanke), Mr Wang worked at the Shenzhen Special Economic Zone Development Company until 1983. A year later, he formed the Shenzhen Exhibition Centre of Modern Science and Education Equipment and became its general manager. In 1988, he restructured the company to form China Vanke.

Mr Wang was appointed chairman and general manager of the company which focuses on China's real estate business. He stepped down from the post of general manager on 8 February 1999, while remaining as chairman. China Vanke is one of the first companies to list on the Shenzhen Stock Exchange. And although its headquarters is in Shenzhen, the company has many projects and offices in all the major cities of China.

Mr Wang won the coveted title of 'Master Sportsman', an award by the National Physical Culture Bureau for his achievement in mountaineering in 2001. He was also elected the deputy chairman of China Mountaineering Association in 2002. As a team member of China Mountaineering Team, Mr Wang Shi climbed the summit of Mount Everest on 22 May 2003 and made history for being "the oldest person in China to scale the summit of Mount Everest". On 30 May 2003, Mr Wang was awarded 'Athletic Sports Glory', a top honour issued by National Physical Culture Bureau.

LEADERS OF CHINA'S LARGEST COMPANIES WHO'S WHO IN CHINA

Birth date	January 1951
Hometown	Liuzhou City, Guangxi Province
Education	Bachelor of Engineering, majoring in Water Supply and Drainage, Lanzhou Railway College
Professional qualifications	Engineer

Background

1983-1984	Worked at the Shenzhen Special Economic Zone Development Co
1984-1988	Founded Shenzhen Exhibition Centre of Modern Science and Education Equipment (predecessor of Vanke), acting as general manager
1988-1999	Reorganised Shenzhen Exhibition Centre of Modern Science and Education Equipment into China Vanke Co Ltd, acting as the chairman and general manager
1999-	Chairman of China Vanke Co Ltd

Corporate structure of China Vanke Co Ltd

Contact information

Address No.27, Shuibei 2 Road, Luohu District, Shenzhen City, China, 266101
Telephone 86-755-5606 666 Facsimile 86-755-5601 764 Website www.vanke.com.cn

LEADERS OF CHINA'S LARGEST COMPANIES WHO'S WHO IN CHINA

Jin Zhiguo Tsingtao Brewery Co Ltd[1]
"Quenching the people's thirst"

Corporate position   President, Tsingtao Brewery Co Ltd

Corporate revenue   RMB 1.5 billion (US$181.2 million)

 "Half of the brand is culture."
                      Mr Jin Zhiguo

After the sudden death of Mr Peng Zuoyi, the legendary chief of Tsingtao Brewery Co Ltd (Tsingtao) in July 2001, Mr Jin Zhiguo took over the presidency. On the first day of his work, he asked all personnel of Tsingtao to turn their tables to face the sea. His point to them was rather clear. He not only needed Tsingtao to maintain its market position, he also wanted the employees to be forward-looking visionaries.

Mr Jin joined Tsingtao Brewery Factory, the predecessor of Tsingtao Brewery Co Ltd, in 1957. In 1996, Mr Jin was appointed general manager of Tsingtao Xi'an Hansi Brewery Company. At that time, Hansi Brewery was in a financial crisis. Within two years, Mr Jin had reversed the company's fortune and turned Hansi Brewery around to be profitable by rebuilding its brand and revamping its sales and marketing plans.

By 2003, brewery consumption in China has reached 24 million tonnes, and China has replaced the United States as the biggest market for beer. Mr Jin observed that seven key brewery companies control 95% of the market in the United States, while four companies control 99% of the market in Japan. And he concluded that a monopoly is very unlikely in China. He decided to cooperate with foreign breweries and entered a joint venture with Anheuser-Busch Corporation. This gave Tsingtao the distribution infrastructure to expand overseas.

Tsingtao Brewery was founded in 1903. In 1993, it went public and listed on the Hong Kong Stock Exchange. In the same year, it listed on the Shanghai Stock Exchange. Tsingtao has 17 brewery manufacturing lines in China with an annual production of more than 3 million tonnes. Tsingtao is the leading brewery in China, based on annual production, turnover, tax contribution, market share and export volume.

In 2003, Tsingtao started manufacturing lines in Southeast Asia. In November 2003, Tsingtao passed the Hazard Analysis and Critical Control Point (HACCP) test conducted by China Quality Certification Center (CQC), the first brewery in China to have done so. In August 2003, Tsingtao spent RMB 103 million (US$12.5 million) to buy a 45% stake in Huashi Beer Group Co, the largest brewer in Central China's Hunan Province.

"With more foreign direct investments pouring in, Chinese beer producers will witness another round of acquisitions," Mr Jin predicts.

---

1 Although Tsingtao Brewery does not rank as China's top 100 companies in terms of sales, it is included in Who's Who in China because it is the most famour beer in China.

Despite good performance in the past, Mr Jin believes Tsingtao still has much to do after China's accession into WTO. "Tsingtao must seize the opportunity to strengthen its popularity and brand name worldwide."

Under Mr Jin, Tsingtao Brewery aims to become one of world's top 10 breweries.

Birth date	1956
Hometown	Shandong Province

Background

1957-1996	General manager of Tsingtao Brewery Factory
1996-2001	General manager of Tsingtao Brewery Company, northern division
2001-	President of Tsingtao Brewery Co Ltd

Contact information
Address Tsingtao Brewery Building, Wusi Square, Hong Kong Central Road, Qingdao, China
Telephone 86-532-5711 119   Facsimile 86-532-5714 719   Website www.tsingtaobeer.com.cn

We plant the flags for you

Business Intelligence and Company Setup

Entering the China market could prove an important decision for your company and provide the next stage of growth or it could tie up precious time and money.

The rewards are real but so are the risks.

First Link International provides tailored market intelligence and research through our comprehensive network of research analysts stationed in over 70 cities in China. We aim to provide the critical intelligence and information that will help you make those tough decisions required for your ventures to succeed in China.

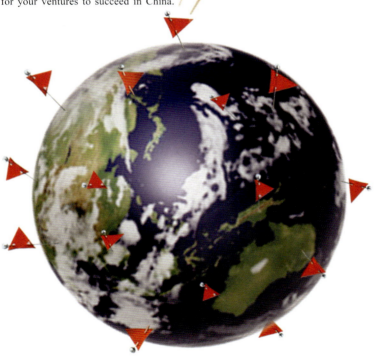

CHINA BUSINESS INTELLIGENCE & CORPORATE SERVICES
5 Shenton Way
#37-02 UIC Building
Singapore 068808
Tel: (65) 6358 2289
www.1st-link.com

China's Political Figures

Great men are seldom made, but often shaped by their hardship and struggles. Some find greatness after they are thrust in the limelight; others are bestowed greatness because of the body of work they become associated with.

These accounts of the most important people in the political arena of modern China will shed some light on how they become who they are today.

Like how General Secretary Hu Jintao toiled in the western provinces of China before ascending the pinnacle of power.

Or how Premier Wen Jiabao remained unshaken through three successions of Chinese leadership and witnessed some of the most tumultuous changes in modern China's history.

But above all, it is their dedication to improving the quality of lives of the millions in their country that will perhaps help carve their names in Chinese history.

CHINA'S POLITICAL FIGURES WHO'S WHO IN CHINA

State Organs of People's Republic of China (PRC)

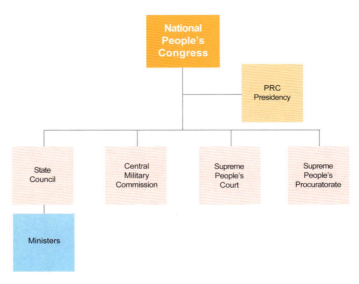

The Constitution of the People's Republic of China stipulates that Chinese central state organs should comprise of six key components:

- The National People's Congress (NPC)
- The President of the People's Republic of China
- The State Council
- The Central Military Commission
- The Supreme People's Court
- The Supreme People's Procuratorate (China's judicial supervisory organ)

The five organs, namely, the President of the People's Republic of China, the State Council, the Central Military Commission, the Supreme People's Court and the Supreme People's Procuratorate, are all created by the governing authority - National People's Congress – and these five organs will be held responsible to the National People's Congress and its Standing Committee.

Central Committee of the Communist Party of China (CPC)

General Secretary: Hu Jintao

Members of the Standing Committee of the Political Bureau: Hu Jintao, Wu Bangguo, Wen Jiabao, Jia Qinglin, Zeng Qinghong, Huang Ju, Wu Guanzheng, Li Changchun, Luo Gan

Other Members of the Political Bureau: Wang Lequan, Wang Zhaoguo, Hui Liangyu, Liu Qi, Liu Yunshan, Wu Yi, Zhang Lichang, Zhang Dejiang, Chen Liangyu, Zhou Yongkang, Yu Zhengsheng, He Guoqiang, Guo Boxiong, Cao Gangchuan, Zeng Peiyan

Alternate Members of the Political Bureau: Wang Gang

CHINA'S POLITICAL FIGURES WHO'S WHO IN CHINA

List of Members of the 16th CPC Central Committee

Abul'ahat Abdurixit (Uygur)	Jin Renqing	Niu Maosheng (Manchu)	Wu Shuangzhan
Bai Enpei	Jing Zhiyuan	Pu Haiqing	Wu Yi (f.)
Bai Keming	Legqog (Tibetan)	Qian Guoliang	Xi Jinping
Bai Lichen (Hui)	Lei Mingqiu	Qian Shugen	Xiang Huaicheng
Bai Zhijian	Li Andong	Qian Yunlu	Xiao Yang
Bo Xilai	Li Changchun	Qiao Qingchen	Xu Kuangdi
Cao Bochun	Li Changjiang	Raidi (Tibetan)	Xu Qiliang
Cao Gangchuan	Li Dezhu (Korean)	Shen Binyi	Xie Zhenhua
Chai Songyue	Li Dongheng	Shi Xiushi	Xu Caihou
Chang Wanquan	Li Guixian	Shi Yunsheng	Xu Guangchun
Chen Bingde	Li Jianguo	Shi Zongyuan (Hui)	Xu Guanhua
Chen Chuankuo	Li Jinai	Song Defu	Xu Rongkai
Chen Fujin	Li Jinhua	Song Fatang	Xu Yongyue
Chen Jianguo	Li Keqiang	Song Zhaosu	Xu Youfang
Chen Kuiyuan	Li Qianyuan	Su Rong	Yan Haiwang
Chen Liangyu	Li Rongrong	Sui Mingtai	Yang Deqing
Chen Yunlin	Li Shenglin	Sun Jiazheng	Yang Huaiqing
Chen Zhili (f.)	Li Tielin	Sun Zhiqiang	Yang Yuanyuan
Chi Wanchun	Li Yizhong	Tang Jiaxuan	Yang Zhengwu (Tujia)
Chu Bo	Li Zhaozhuo (Zhuang)	Tang Tianbiao	Yu Yunyao
Dai Bingguo (Tujia)	Li Zhilun	Teng Wensheng	
Dai Xianglong	Liang Guanglie	Tian Chengping	
Deng Changyou	Liao Hui	Tian Congming	
Doje Cering (Tibetan)	Liao Xilong	Tian Fengshan	
Du Qinglin	Liu Dongdong	Uyunqimg (f.,Mongolian)	
Fu Tinggui	Liu Huaqiu	Wang Chen	
Gao Siren	Liu Jing	Wang Gang	
Ge Zhenfeng	Liu Qi	Wang Guangtao	
Guo Boxiong	Liu Shutian	Wang Hongju	
Guo Jinlong	Liu Yandong (f.)	Wang Qishan	
Han Zheng	Liu Yongzhi	Wang Huning	
He Guoqiang	Liu Yunshan	Wang Jianmin	
He Yong	Liu Zhenhua	Wang Jinshan	
Hong Hu	Liu Zhenwu	Wang Lequan	
Hu Jintao	Liu Zhijun	Wang Shengjun	
Hua Jianmin	Lu Fuyuan	Wang Shucheng	
Huang Huahua	Lu Hao	Wang Taihua	
Huang Ju	Lu Yongxiang	Wang Xiaofeng	
Huang Qingyi (f.)	Lu Zhangong	Wang Xudong	
Huang Zhendong	Luo Gan	Wang Yunkun	
Huang Zhiquan	Luo Qingquan	Wang Yunlong	
Hui Liangyu (Hui)	Ma Kai	Wang Zhaoguo	
Ismail Amat (Uygur)	Ma Qizhi (Hui)	Wang Zhongfu	
Ji Yunshi	Ma Xiaotian	Wei Liqun	
Jia Chunwang	Meng Jianzhu	Wen Jiabao	
Jia Qinglin	Meng Jinxi	Wen Shizhen	
Jia Zhibang	Meng Xuenong	Wen Zongren	
Jiang Futang	Mou Xinsheng	Wu Bangguo	

The Presidency of People's Republic of China

President: Hu Jintao

Vice President: Zeng Qinghong

The president of the People's Republic of China is the Head of State, as well as the supreme representative of China both internally and externally.

The State presidency is an independent State apparatus and a component part of China's State organisation.

According to international practice, the Chinese president, like most heads of state in the world, has the power to promulgate statutes and holds supreme diplomatic and ceremonial rights.

Under the current Constitution, the president has the power to promulgate statutes adopted by the NPC; appoint and remove members of the State Council; confer State medals and titles of honour in line with the decisions of the NPC and its Standing Committee; issue orders for special pardons; proclaim martial law; declare a state of war and issue orders of mobilisation; accept letters of credential offered by foreign diplomatic representatives on behalf of the People's Republic of China; appoint and recall China's diplomatic envoys stationed abroad; and ratify and abrogate treaties and important agreements signed with foreign states.

China's system of the head of state is a system of collective leadership. The president is subordinate to the NPC and directly receives instructions from the supreme organ of State power. To date, six men have held the office of the president of the People's Republic of China, Mao Zedong, Liu Shaoqi, Li Xiannian, Yang Shangkun, Jiang Zemin, and the current president, Hu Jintao.

CHINA'S POLITICAL FIGURES WHO'S WHO IN CHINA

The State Council

Premier:	Wen Jiabao
Vice Premiers:	Huang Ju, Wu Yi, Zeng Peiyan, Hui Liangyu
State Councillors:	Zhou Yongkang, Cao Gangchuan, Tang Jiaxuan, Hua Jianmin, Chen Zhili
State Council Secretary General:	Hua Jianmin (concurrently)

The State Council of the People's Republic of China, namely the Central People's Government, is the highest executive organ of State power, as well as the highest organ of State administration.

The State Council is composed of a premier, vice premiers, State councillors, ministers in charge of ministries and commissions, the auditor-general and the secretary-general. The premier of the State Council is nominated by the president, reviewed by the NPC, and appointed and removed by the president. Other members of the State Council are nominated by the premier, reviewed by the NPC or its Standing Committee, and appointed and removed by the president.

In the State Council, a single term of each office is five years, and incumbents cannot be reappointed after two successive terms.

The State Council follows the system of premier responsibility in work while various ministries and commissions under the State Council follow the system of ministerial responsibility. In dealing with foreign affairs, State councillors can conduct important activities on behalf the premier after being entrusted by the premier of the State Council.

The auditor-general is the head of the State Auditing Administration, in charge of auditing and supervising State finances. The secretary-general, under the premier, is responsible for the day-to-day work of the State Council and is in charge of the general office of the State Council.

The State Council is responsible for carrying out the principles and policies of the Communist Party of China as well as the regulations and laws adopted by the NPC, and dealing with such affairs as China's internal politics, diplomacy, national defence, finance, economy, culture and education.

Under the current Constitution, the State Council exercises the power of administrative legislation, the power to submit proposals, the power of administrative leadership, the power of economic management, the power of diplomatic administration, the power of social administration, and other powers granted by the NPC and its Standing Committee.

CHINA'S POLITICAL FIGURES WHO'S WHO IN CHINA

Ministries and Commissions under the State Council

Ministry of Foreign Affairs:	Minister Li Zhaoxing
Ministry of National Defence:	Minister Cao Gangchuan (concurrently)
State Development and Reform Commission:	Minister in Charge: Ma Kai
Ministry of Education:	Minister Zhou Ji
Ministry of Science and Technology:	Minister Xu Guanhua
State Commission of Science, Technology and Industry for National Defence:	Minister in Charge: Zhang Yunchuan
State Ethnic Affairs Commission:	Minister in Charge: Li Dek Su (Korean)
Ministry of Public Security:	Minister Zhou Yongkang
Ministry of State Security:	Minister Xu Yongyue
Ministry of Supervision:	Minister Li Zhilun
Ministry of Civil Affairs:	Minister Li Xueju
Ministry of Justice:	Minister Zhang Fusen
Ministry of Finance:	Minister Jin Renqing
Ministry of Personnel:	Minister Zhang Bolin
Ministry of Labour and Social Security:	Minister Zheng Silin
Ministry of Land and Resources:	Minister Sun Wensheng
Ministry of Construction:	Minister Wang Guangtao
Ministry of Railways:	Minister Liu Zhijun
Ministry of Communications:	Minister Zhang Chunxian
Ministry of Information Industry:	Minister Wang Xudong
Ministry of Water Resources:	Minister Wang Shucheng
Ministry of Agriculture:	Minister Du Qinglin
Ministry of Commerce:	Minister Bo Xilai
Ministry of Culture:	Minister Sun Jiazheng
Ministry of Health:	Minister Wu Yi (concurrently)
State Population and Family Planning Commission:	Minister in Charge Zhang Weiqing
People's Bank of China:	Governor Zhou Xiaochuan
National Audit Office:	Auditor-General Li Jinhua

CHINA'S POLITICAL FIGURES WHO'S WHO IN CHINA

Special Organisation directly under the State Council

Commission of the State-owned Assets Supervision and Administration:	Chairman Li Rongrong

Organisation directly under the State Council

General Administration of Customs:	Director Mou Xinsheng
State Bureau of Taxation:	Director Xie Xuren
State Environmental Protection Administration:	Director Xie Zhenhua
Civil Aviation Administration of China:	Director Yang Yuanyuan
State Administration of Radio, Film and Television:	Director Xu Guangchun
State Sports General Administration:	Director Yuan Weimin
State Statistics Bureau:	Director Zhu Zhixin
State Administration for Industry and Commerce:	Director Wang Zhongfu
State Press and Publication Administration:	Director Shi Zongyuan
State Forestry Bureau:	Director Zhou Shengxian
General Administration of Quality Supervision, Inspection and Quarantine:	Director Li Changjiang
State Drugs Administration:	Director Zheng Xiaoyu
State Intellectual Property Office:	Director Wang Jingchuan
National Tourism Administration:	Director He Guangwei
State Administration for Religious Affairs:	Director Ye Xiaowen
Counsellor's Office under the State Council:	Director Cui Zhanfu
Bureau of Government Offices Administration:	Director Jiao Huancheng
State Administration of Work Safety:	Director Wang Xianzheng

Offices

Office of Overseas Chinese Affairs:	Director Chen Yujie
Taiwan Affairs Office:	Director Chen Yunlin
Hong Kong and Macao Affairs Office:	Director Liao Hui
Legislative Affairs Office:	Director Cao Kangtai
Information Office:	Director Zhao Qizheng
Research Office:	Director Wei Liqun

CHINA'S POLITICAL FIGURES WHO'S WHO IN CHINA

Institutions

Xinhua News Agency:	President Tian Congming
Chinese Academy of Sciences:	President Lu Yongxiang
Chinese Academy of Social Sciences:	President Chen Kuiyuan
Chinese Academy of Engineering:	President Xu Kuangdi
Development Research Centre:	Director Wang Mengkui
National School of Administration:	President Hua Jianmin (concurrently)
State Seismological Bureau:	Director Song Ruixiang
China Meteorological Administration:	Director Qin Dahe
China Banking Regulatory Commission (CBRC):	Chairman Liu Mingkang
China Securities Regulatory Commission:	Chairman Shang Fulin
China Insurance Regulatory Commission:	Chairman Wu Dingfu
State Electricity Regulatory Commission (SERC):	Chairman Chai Songyue
National Council for Social Security Fund:	President Xiang Huaicheng
National Natural Science Foundation:	Chairman Chen Jiaer

Administrations and Bureaus under the Ministries & Commissions

State Grain Bureau:	Director Nie Zhenbang
State Tobacco Monopoly Industry Bureau:	Director Jiang Chengkang
State Bureau of Foreign Experts Affairs:	Director Wan Xueyuan
State Oceanography Bureau:	Director Wang Shuguang
State Bureau of Surveying & Mapping:	Director Chen Bangzhu
State Postal Bureau:	Director Liu Andong
State Bureau of Cultural Relics:	Director Shan Jixiang
State Administration of Traditional Chinese Medicine:	Director She Jing(concurrently)
State Administration of Foreign Exchange:	Director Guo Shuqing(concurrently)

CHINA'S POLITICAL FIGURES WHO'S WHO IN CHINA

The Central Military Commission

Chairman:	Jiang Zemin
Vice Chairman:	Hu Jintao, Guo Boxiong, Cao Gangchuan
Other Central Military Commission Members:	Xu Caihou, Liang Guanglie, Liao Xilong, Li Jinai

The Central Military Commission (CMC) is the supreme leading organ of the armed forces of the People's Republic of China. It directs and commands the national armed forces.

The chairman of the CMC is elected by the NPC, and the NPC and its Standing Committee on the basis of the nomination by the chairman decide the selection of other members. The State CMC follows the system of Chairman responsibility in work, while the chairman is responsible to the NPC and has the right to make final decisions on affairs within its functions and powers.

Under the leadership of CMC, the Chinese army has been reformed, streamlined and reorganised in recent years. Now a three million-strong armed force is heading towards normalisation and modernisation, becoming an important force devoted to safeguarding national sovereignty, territorial integrity and world peace.

The Supreme People's Court

President: Xiao Yang

The Supreme People's Court is the highest judicial organ in China and is responsible to the NPC and its Standing Committee.

It independently exercises the highest judicial right according to the law and without any interruption by administrative organs, social organisations or individuals.

Its structure comprises of a judicial committee, or the highest judicial organisation, and courts or the No. 1 Criminal Tribunal, the No. 2 Criminal Tribunal, the Civil Tribunal, the Economic Tribunal, the Administrative Tribunal, the Complaint and Appeal Tribunal and the Communication and Transportation Tribunal.

According to the Constitution and statutes, the Supreme People's Court is charged with three responsibilities:

First, trying cases that have the greatest influence in China, hearing appeals against the legal decisions of higher courts, and trying the cases the Supreme People's Court claims are within its original jurisdiction.

Second, supervising the work of local courts and special courts at every level, overruling wrong judgements they might have made, and deciding interrogations and reviewing cases tried by the lower courts.

Third, giving judicial explanations of the specific utilisation of laws in the judicial process that must be carried out nationwide.

The president of the Supreme People's Court is elected by the NPC and remains in office for no more than two successive terms with each term of five years.

The deputy presidents of the Supreme People's Court, members of the judicial committee, presiding judges of affiliated courts and their deputies, and judicial officers are appointed and recalled by the Standing Committee of the NPC.

CHINA'S POLITICAL FIGURES WHO'S WHO IN CHINA

The Supreme People's Procuratorate

President: Jia Chunwang

The people's procuratorates are State organs for legal supervision.

The Supreme People's Procuratorate is the highest procuratorial organ. It is mainly responsible for supervising regional procuratorates and special procuratorates to perform legal supervision by law and protecting the unified and proper enforcement of State laws.

The Supreme People's Procuratorate has to report its work to the NPC and its Standing Committee, to whom it is responsible, and accept their supervision.

According to the Constitution and statutes, the Supreme People's Procuratorate is primarily in charge of: leading the procuratorial work of regional and special procuratorates at all levels; accepting and hearing cases of corruption, bribery, tort to citizen's democratic rights and misconduct in office, and placing them on file for investigation and prosecution; performing legal supervision of the judicial process of courts and investigation of criminal cases; deciding arrest and prosecution concerning severe criminal cases; performing legal supervision of the trying of criminal cases; lodging protests against effective but wrong judgements and rulings made by various courts to the Supreme People's Court according to law; exercising legal supervision of activities conducted in prisons and reform through labour institutions; providing legal explanations of the application of laws in practical procuratorial works; formulating regulations and by laws concerning procuratorial works; leading and administrating public procurators according to law; organising and guiding the education and training of officials with the procuratorial departments; sponsoring negotiations with foreign procuratorial departments; and developing judicial assistance.

Structure of the Communist Party of China (CPC) Leadership

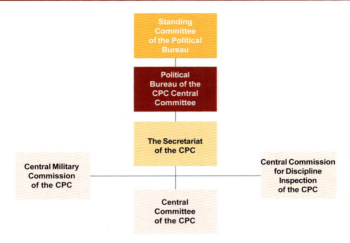

The party constitution lists out the primary organs of power in the CPC. These include:

- The Politburo Standing Committee, which currently consists of nine members;
- The Politburo, consisting of 24 full members (including the members of the Politburo Standing Committee) and one alternate member;
- The Secretariat, the principal administrative mechanism of the CPC, headed by the General Secretary of the Communist Party of China;
- The Central Military Commission, a parallel organisation of the government institution also named the Central Military Commission (*Please refer to the previous chart*);
- The Discipline Inspection Commission, which is charged with rooting out corruption and misconduct among party cadres.

Every five years, the CPC holds a National Congress. Formally, the National Congress serves two functions: to approve changes to the Party constitution and to elect a Central Committee, which is about 300 strong. The Central Committee in turn elects the Politburo. In practice, positions within the Central Committee and Politburo are determined before a National Congress, and the main purpose of the Congress is to announce the party policies and the vision for the direction of China in the following five years.

The party's central locus of power is the nine-member Politburo Standing Committee. The process for selecting Standing Committee members, as well as Politburo members, occurs behind the scenes in a process parallel to the National Congress

Business Process Outsourcing

No matter what industry, every company has non-core functions that take resources and focus away from core strategic goals. That's where business process outsourcing can make the biggest cost and time savings for your new China venture.

Conferences & Event Management

First Link Event Services is uniquely qualified to support your conference & event management needs in China. We have the technical skills and resource capability that enables us to build your China event into a successful experience for your customers.

From planning the foundation of your event, to promotion and post-event activities, our dedicated team will oversee the entire event from start to finish.

Translation Services

First Link Translation provides English to Chinese or Chinese to English translation services to meet your multilingual needs. We solve the 'language barrier' that may otherwise hinder your business in China, enabling you to communicate successfully with your customers, prospects and partners China-wide.

Be it a simple document translation or a complex localisation project, we strive to achieve total client satisfaction through our high quality professional services.

CHINA BUSINESS INTELLIGENCE & CORPORATE SERVICES
5 Shenton Way
#37-02 UIC Building
Singapore 068808
Tel: (65) 6358 2289
www.1st-link.com

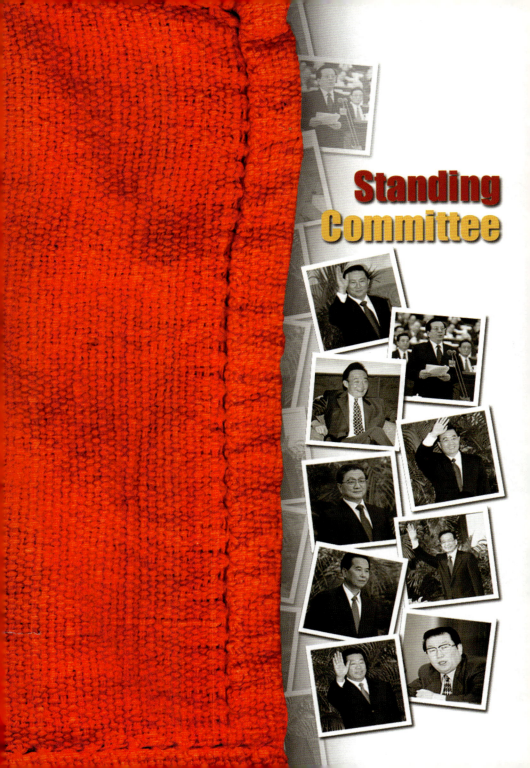

Standing Committee

Hu Jintao
"Proponent of transparency and reforms"

Titles and positions	General Secretary, CPC Central Committee President, PRC Vice Chairman, CPC Central Military Commission Vice Chairman, Central Military Commission of the PRC
Political influence	Number 1 member, Standing Committee of the Political Bureau of the CPC Central Committee

Mr Hu, the General Secretary of the Communist Party of China (CPC) Central Committee, was handpicked by China's stalwart Deng Xiaoping as a member of the 4th Leading Generation of CPC - the innermost assembly of leaders in CPC from which members are groomed for leadership posts.

There is, hence, very little surprise that Mr Hu eventually succeeded former China President Jiang Zemin in March 2003 when he was elected president of the People's Republic of China at the First Session of the 10th National People's Congress, becoming the new head of state of a country with a population of approximately 1.3 billion.

It had not always been plain sailing for Mr Hu, who spent 22 years working in China's harsher western areas, including Gansu, Guizhou, and Tibet.

Still, his experiences there coupled with that in his work at the top echelons within the central committees have developed his thorough understanding of the overall political, economic and social structure of China.

It reinforced his conviction that China must speed up economic development, and promote reforms and open its economy.

Mr Hu has also cultivated an approach with an emphasis on fairness, honesty, exemplary role, cutting-edge research, concern for people's welfare, integrity and pragmatism, all geared towards encouraging a pioneering spirit.

Birth date	21 December 1942
Hometown	Jixi County, Anhui Province
Education	Bachelor of Engineering, majoring in Hub Hydropower Stations, Water Conservancy Engineering Department, Tsinghua University, 1965
Professional qualifications	Engineer

CHINA'S POLITICAL FIGURES WHO'S WHO IN CHINA

Background

1959-1964	Undergraduate studies, Water Conservancy Engineering Department, Tsinghua University
1964-	Joined the CPC
1964-1965	Postgraduate and political instructor, Water Conservancy Engineering Department, Tsinghua University
1965-1968	Participated in R&D at the Water Conservancy Engineering Department, Tsinghua University and served as political instructor before the start of the "Cultural Revolution"
1968-1969	Worked with the housing construction team of Liujia Gorge Engineering Bureau, Ministry of Water Conservancy
1969-1974	Technician and secretary, of No. 813 Sub-Bureau, Fourth Engineering Bureau, Ministry of Water Conservancy and deputy secretary, general Party branch of the sub-bureau's head office
1974-1975	Secretary, Gansu Provincial Construction Committee (GPCC)
1975-1980	Deputy director of design management division, GPCC
1980-1982	Vice chairman of GPCC and Secretary, Gansu Provincial Committee of the Communist Youth League (September 1982 – December 1982)
1982-1984	Secretary, secretariat of the Central Committee of the Communist Youth League of China, Chairman, All-China Youth Federation
1984-1985	First secretary, secretariat of the Central Committee of the Communist Youth League of China
1985-1988	Secretary of Guizhou Provincial Party Committee
1988-1992	Secretary of Party Committee of Tibet Autonomous Region
1992-1993	Member of Standing Committee of the Political Bureau of the CPC Central Committee, and member of secretariat of CPC Central Committee
1993-1998	Member, Standing Committee of the Political Bureau of the CPC Central Committee, member of, secretariat of CPC Central Committee, President, Party School of CPC Central Committee
1998-1999	Member, Standing Committee of the Political Bureau of the CPC Central Committee, member of secretariat of CPC Central Committee, vice president of PRC, president of Party School of the CPC Central Committee
1999-2002	Member, Standing Committee of the Political Bureau of the CPC Central Committee, member, of secretariat of CPC Central Committee, vice chairman of CPC Central Military Commission, vice president of PRC, vice chairman, Central Military Commission of PRC, president of Party School of the CPC Central Committee

2002-2003	General secretary of CPC Central Committee, vice chairman of Central Military Commission and vice president of PRC
2003-	General secretary of CPC Central Committee, president of the PRC, vice chairman of CPC Central Military Commission, vice chairman of Central Military Commission of the PRC

Other titles and memberships

Mr Hu started as an alternate member and was subsequently appointed a full member of the 12th, 13th, 14th and 15th CPC Central Committees and is a currently a full member of the 16th CPC Central Committee. He was a member of the Political Bureau and its Standing Committee, and member of the Secretariat of the 14th and 15th CPC Central Committees and is currently a member of the Political Bureau and its Standing Committee as well as General Secretary of the 16th CPC Central Committee. He was made an additional vice chairman of the CPC Central Military Commission at the Fourth Plenary Session of the 15th CPC Central Committee. He was a member of the Standing Committee of the 16th National Committee of the Chinese People's Political Consultative Conference.

Other information

Mr Hu and his wife Ms Liu Yongqing were schoolmates at Tsinghua University. The couple has a son and a daughter, who are also graduates of Tsinghua University.

Ms Hu Haiqing, the only daughter of Mr Hu, is married to Mr Mao Daolin, the CEO of Sina.com in 2003.

CHINA'S POLITICAL FIGURES WHO'S WHO IN CHINA

Wu Bangguo
"Leader of the common people"

Title and position   Chairman, Standing Committee of the 10th National People's Congress (NPC)
Political influence   Number 2 member, Standing Committee of the Political Bureau of the CPC Central Committee

"Development is the most important task for the Communist Party of China."
— Mr Wu Bangguo

A brilliant economist with the "people's touch" would be what is best to describe Mr Wu Bangguo, the No. 2 man within the CPC's hierarchy.

After eight years as vice premier, he was elected chairman of the Standing Committee of the NPC on March 15, 2003 to succeed former Chairman Li Peng as leader of China's supreme state power.

But his path had been arduous to say the least.

Born into a common family, Mr Wu started out as a technician in a state-owned enterprise (SOE), rising steadily through the ranks as first, a factory director, then a manager, before becoming a provincial, municipal and state leader.

The hard work he put in during his youth afforded him a precious perspective which enabled him to handle situations and problems in a down-to-earth manner, earning him the unofficial title of "secretary of the common people" when he was secretary of the CPC Municipal Committee of Shanghai.

However, his greatest efforts were spent on reforming the state-owned enterprises. It was during the most difficult period for China's SOEs that Mr Wu faced one of his greatest challenges.

He left his mark with more than 80% of China's major SOEs. After his painstaking efforts, aggregate profits of state-owned and state-controlled enterprises rose four-fold over three years, reaching a record high of RMB 263.6 billion in 2002.

CHINA'S POLITICAL FIGURES WHO'S WHO IN CHINA

Birth date	July 1941
Hometown	Feidong County, Anhui Province
Education	Bachelor of Engineering, majoring in Electron Tube, Department of Radio Electronics, Tsinghua University, 1966
Professional qualifications	Engineer

Background

1960-1967	Bachelor of Engineering majoring in Electron Tube, Department of Radio Electronics Tsinghua University
1964-	Joined the CPC
1967-1976	Worker, technician, deputy chief of technical section, and chief of technical section, Shanghai Number 3 Electronic Tube Factory
1976-1978	Deputy secretary of Party Committee of Shanghai Number 3 Electronic Tube Factory, deputy director of its revolutionary committee, deputy factory director, deputy secretary of Party Committee of the factory, and director of the factory
1978-1979	Deputy manager of Shanghai Electronic Elements Company
1979-1981	Deputy manager of Shanghai Electron Tube Company
1981-1983	Deputy secretary of Party Committee of Shanghai Meters, Instruments and Telecommunications Bureau
1983-1985	Member of Standing Committee of CPC Shanghai Municipal Committee, secretary of CPC Municipal Committee in charge of Science and Technology
1985-1991	Deputy secretary of CPC Shanghai Municipal Committee
1991-1992	Secretary of CPC Shanghai Municipal Committee
1992-1994	Member of Political Bureau of CPC Central Committee, secretary of CPC Shanghai Municipal Committee
1994-1995	Member of Political Bureau of CPC Central Committee and member of secretariat of CPC Central Committee
1995-1997	Member of Political Bureau of CPC Central Committee and member of secretariat of CPC Central Committee and vice premier of State Council
1997-1998	Member of Political Bureau of CPC Central Committee, vice premier of State Council
1998-1999	Member of Political Bureau of CPC Central Committee, vice premier of State Council and secretary of Work Committee of Large Enterprises of CPC Central Committee
1999-2002	Member of Political Bureau of CPC Central Committee, vice premier of State Council, member of its Leading Party Member Group and secretary of Central Work Committee of Large Enterprises

CHINA'S POLITICAL FIGURES WHO'S WHO IN CHINA

2002- Member of Standing Committee of Political Bureau of CPC Central Committee, vice premier of State Council, member of Leading Party Member Group and secretary of Work Committee of Large Enterprises of CPC Central Committee

Other titles and memberships

Mr Wu was an alternate member of the 12th and 13th CPC Central Committees and a full member of the 14th and 15th CPC Central Committee. He was also a member of the Political Bureau of the CPC Central Committee, and elected as additional member of the Secretariat of the CPC Central Committee at the 4th Plenary Session of the 14th CPC Central Committee. He is currently a member of the 16th CPC Central Committee, a member of its Political Bureau and Standing Committee member of the Political Bureau.

Other information

Married, with one son and one daughter. Mr Wu's hobbies include tennis and calligraphy.

CHINA'S POLITICAL FIGURES WHO'S WHO IN CHINA

Wen Jiabao
"Pragmatic and prudent leader"

Title and position Premier of the State Council

Political influence Number 3 member, Standing Committee of the Political Bureau of the CPC Central Committee

"I will do whatever it takes to serve my country even at the cost of my own life regardless of fortune or misfortune to myself."
Mr Wen Jiabao at his first public speech as China's new Premier (March 23, 2003)

China's Premier Wen Jiabao is one of only a few top-ranking officials who had served through three successions of leadership within the CPC – from Hu Yaobang, Zhao Ziyang to Jiang Zemin.

He witnessed the critical and tumultuous events in recent Chinese history such as the student political procession in 1986 and the Tiananmen demonstrations in 1989.

Mr Wen was born into a family with deeply entrenched values of Confucianism, one that is both revered and well known in academia.

He graduated with a master's degree in geological structures after eight years of study and started his career as a technician in the remote Gansu province.

That was where he began developing a name for himself as "pragmatic, prudent and all-competent".

Party officials sat up and took notice and Mr Wen was soon sent to Beijing, first serving in the Ministry of Geology and Mineral Resources and then his subsequent appointment to the General Office of the CPC Central Committee for 10 years.

Because of his accomplishments, he was selected as one of the vice premiers in former Premier Zhu Rongji's cabinet for five consecutive years, where he took charge of issues relating to agriculture, rural areas, development planning and finance.

As Vice Premier, he successfully promoted agricultural development and rural economic restructuring, and also experimented with tax reforms in China's rural areas.

Widely known as an affable and down-to-earth person, Mr Wen is equally at home analysing political and economic theories as he is chatting amiably and cordially with local folks and commoners in villages or disaster-afflicted areas, clad usually in a casual jacket and sneakers.

CHINA'S POLITICAL FIGURES WHO'S WHO IN CHINA

Birth date	September 1942
Hometown	Tianjin City
Education	Bachelor, majoring in Geological Structure, Beijing Institute of Geology, 1965
	Postgraduate diploma, majoring in Geological Structure, Beijing Institute of Geology, 1968
Professional qualifications	Engineer

Background

1960-1965	Bachelor of Engineering Studies majoring in Geological Surveying and Prospecting of the Number 1 Department of Geology and Minerals, Beijing Institute of Geology
1965-	Joined the CPC
1965-1968	Postgraduate majoring in Geological Structure, Beijing Institute of Geology
1968-1978	Technician and political instructor as part of Geomechanics Survey Team, Gansu Provincial Geological Bureau and head of its political section
1978-1979	Member of Standing Committee, Party Committee of the Geomechanics Survey Team, Gansu Provincial Geological Bureau and deputy head of the team
1979-1981	Deputy section head and engineer, Gansu Provincial Geological Bureau
1981-1982	Deputy director-general of Gansu Provincial Geological Bureau.
1982-1983	Director of Policy and Law Research Office, Ministry of Geology and Mineral Resources and member of its Leading Party Member Group
1983-1985	Vice minister of Geology and Mineral Resources, member and deputy secretary of Leading Party Member Group and director of its Political Department
1985-1986	Deputy director of General Office of CPC Central Committee
1986-1987	Director of General Office of CPC Central Committee
1987-1992	Alternate member, secretariat of CPC Central Committee, director of General Office of CPC Central Committee and secretary of Work Committee of Departments under CPC Central Committee
1992-1993	Alternate member of Political Bureau of CPC Central Committee, member of secretariat of CPC Central Committee, director of General Office of the CPC Central Committee and secretary of Work Committee of Departments under CPC Central Committee
1993-1997	Alternate Member of Political Bureau of CPC Central Committee, member of secretariat of CPC Central Committee
1997-1998	Member of Political Bureau of CPC Central Committee, member of secretariat of CPC Central Committee

1998-2002	Member of Political Bureau of CPC Central Committee, member of secretariat of CPC Central Committee, vice premier of State Council, member of Leading Party Member Group and secretary of Financial Work Committee of CPC Central Committee
2002-2003	Member of Standing Committee of Political Bureau of CPC Central Committee, vice premier of State Council, member of Leading Party Members' Group and secretary of Financial Work Committee of CPC Central Committee
2003-	Member of Standing Committee of Political Bureau of CPC Central Committee and premier of State Council

Other titles and memberships

Mr Wen was a full member of the 13th, 14th, and 15th CPC Central Committee, an alternate member of the Secretariat of the CPC Central Committee and an alternate member of the Political Bureau of the CPC Central Committee.

He is currently a full member of the 16th CPC Central Committee, a full member of the Political Bureau and its Standing Committee of the 16th CPC Central Committee.

Other information

Mr Wen's wife, Ms Zhang Peili, is the vice chairman of China Jewellery Association. They have a son and a daughter. Their daughter is studying in the United States.

CHINA'S POLITICAL FIGURES WHO'S WHO IN CHINA

Jia Qinglin
"Man behind Beijing's 2008 Olympic bid"

Title and position   Chairman, Chinese People's Political Consultative Conference (CPPCC) National Committee

Political influence   Number 4 member, Standing Committee of the Political Bureau of the CPC Central Committee

 "We must firmly count on the wisdom and strength of the broad masses of the people, and count on the joint efforts of all political parties and organisations, all ethnic groups and people from all walks of life."

Mr Jia Qinglin, at the CPPCC Session, Closing Ceremony (March 14, 2003)

The former mayor of Beijing started off as a technician in the former First Ministry of Machine-Building Industry and for over two decades devoted himself to the development of China's machine-building industry.

His first major assignment was in China's southeast coastal province of Fujian, the ancestral home of numerous Taiwan residents and overseas Chinese, and spent 11 years dedicating him to its local economic development.

One of his more notable successes whilst at Fujian was the sale of state-owned enterprises in Quanzhou City to a Hong Kong businessman in 1992.

He returned to Beijing as its mayor in 1995 and has since risen to the No. 4 ranking in the top decision-making body of the CPC.

He was also selected as the new head of China's political advisory body, the Chinese People's Political Consultative Conference (CPPCC), in March 2003.

As mayor of China's capital city, Mr Jia put forth a high-tech-based "capital economy" concept and development strategy for Beijing. He also led Beijing's successful 2008 Olympic bid.

Mr Jia is seen as a person of northern China origin and is said to be a popular and charismatic figure in both political and social circles.

Birth date	March 1940
Hometown	Botou City, Hebei Province
Education	Bachelor of Engineering, majoring in Electric Motor and Appliance Design and Manufacture, Department of Electric Power, Hebei Engineering College, 1962
Professional qualifications	Engineer

CHINA'S POLITICAL FIGURES WHO'S WHO IN CHINA

Background

1956-1958	Majoring in Industrial Enterprise Planning, Shijiazhuang Industrial Management School
1958-1962	Bachelor of Engineering Studies majoring in Electric motor and Appliance Design and Manufacture, Department of Electric Power, Hebei Engineering College
1959-	Joined the CPC
1962-1969	Technician at Complete Plant Bureau of the First Machine-Building Industry Ministry and deputy secretary of its CYLC organisation
1969-1971	Was assigned to work, as a result of the Cultural Revolution, in the May 7th Cadre School of the First Machine-Building Industry Ministry in Fengxin County, Jiangxi Province
1971-1973	Technician at Policy Research Office of the General Office at the First Machine-Building Industry Ministry
1973-1978	Chief of Product Management Bureau, First Ministry of Machine-building Industry
1978-1983	General manager of China National Machinery and Equipment Import and Export Corporation
1983-1985	Director of Taiyuan Heavy Machinery Plant and Secretary of its Party committee
1985-1986	Member of Standing Committee of CPC and deputy secretary of Fujian Provincial Committee
1986-1988	Deputy secretary of CPC Fujian Provincial Committee and head of Organisation Department, CPC Fujian Provincial Committee
1988-1990	Deputy secretary of CPC Fujian Provincial Committee, president of Party School of the CPC Fujian Provincial Committee and secretary of Work Committee of Departments, CPC Fujian Provincial Committee
1990-1991	Deputy secretary of CPC Fujian Provincial Committee, deputy governor and acting governor of Fujian Province
1991-1993	Deputy secretary of CPC Fujian Provincial Committee and governor of Fujian Province
1993-1994	Secretary of CPC Fujian Provincial Committee and governor of Fujian Province
1994-1996	Secretary of CPC Fujian Provincial Committee and chairman of Standing Committee of Fujian Provincial People's Congress
1996-1997	Deputy secretary of CPC Beijing Municipal Committee, vice mayor, acting mayor and mayor of Beijing
1997-1999	Member of Political Bureau of CPC Central Committee, secretary of CPC Beijing Municipal Committee and mayor of Beijing
1999-2002	Member of Political Bureau of CPC Central Committee and secretary of CPC Beijing Municipal Committee

CHINA'S POLITICAL FIGURES WHO'S WHO IN CHINA

2002- Member of Standing Committee of Political Bureau of CPC Central Committee
2003- Elected chairman of the 10th National Committee of Chinese People's Political Consultative Conference

Other titles and memberships

Mr Jia was a full member of the 14th and 15th CPC Central Committees and a member of the Political Bureau of the 15th CPC Central Committee. He is also currently a member of the 16th CPC Central Committee and a member of the Standing Committee of the Political Bureau of the 16th CPC Central Committee.

Other information

Mr Jia and his wife Ms Lin Youfang were classmates in college. Ms Lin is a returned overseas Chinese from Malaysia. They have a son and a daughter.

CHINA'S POLITICAL FIGURES WHO'S WHO IN CHINA

Zeng Qinghong
"Politics is in his blood"

Titles and positions Vice President of the PRC
President, Party School of the CPC Central Committee

Political influence Number 5 member, Standing Committee of the Political Bureau of the CPC Central Committee

"Gold or silver prizes are not as good as compliments from China's citizens."
Mr Zeng's comment on the achievement of cadres

Vice president of the People's Republic of China aside, Mr Zeng also stands as one of the nine members at the Standing Committee of Political Bureau of the CPC Central Committee.

Ranked fifth in the hierarchy, the engineer was born into a senior CPC cadre family and spent the early years of his illustrious career as a technician in the People Liberation Army after he graduated from the Beijing Institute of Technology.

After several years in the machine building and oil industry, gathering rich fundamental work experience, his political career took off when he was transferred to China's largest city, Shanghai, in 1984.

It was there that he met Mr Jiang Zemin, the former No. 1 leader in the CPC who was the mayor of Shanghai at that time.

When Mr Jiang was promoted as general secretary of the CPC centre commission in 1989, Mr Zeng was transferred from Shanghai to Beijing along with him.

Since then, Mr Zeng has remained by his side, playing a significant role as a trusted adviser and offering supervision and coordination in the CPC.

He was behind the reformation of CPC's personnel system and played an important role in the selection of honest and competent officials in what was probably the most significant change in Chinese politics in recent years.

According to political observers, Mr Zeng is seen to be someone with both clarity of thought and a predilection for creativity. He is also far-sighted in his thinking, having demonstrated strategic foresight in planning and handling issues.

Birth date	July 1939
Hometown	Ji'an City, Jiangxi Province
Education	Bachelor of Engineering, Automatic Control Department, Beijing Institute of Technology, 1963
Professional qualifications	Engineer

CHINA'S POLITICAL FIGURES WHO'S WHO IN CHINA

Background

1958-1963	Bachelor of Engineering Studies, Automatic Control Department, Beijing Institute of Technology
1960-	Joined the CPC
1963-1965	Technician, Number 743 Army Unit, the People's Liberation Army
1965-1969	Technician, Number 6 Office, Number 2 Department of the Second Academy, the Seventh Machine-Building Industry Ministry
1969-1970	Did manual work at the Chikan base of the Guangzhou troops and at the Xihu production base in Hunan Province
1970-1973	Technician at Number 2 Department of the Second Academy, the Seventh Machine-Building Industry Ministry
1973-1979	Technician at Production Division and Science and Technology Division, Beijing Office of National Defence Industry
1979-1981	Secretary of General Office of the State Planning Commission
1981-1982	Deputy division director of General Office of the State Energy Commission
1982-1983	Worked at the Liaison Department, Foreign Affairs Bureau of the Ministry of Petroleum Industry
1983-1984	Deputy manager of Liaison Department of China National Offshore Oil Corporation, deputy director of Foreign Affairs Bureau of the Ministry of Petroleum Industry, secretary of Party Committee of the South and Yellow Seas Petroleum Corporation
1984-1986	Deputy head and head of Organisation Department, member of Standing Committee of CPC Shanghai Municipal Committee and secretary-general of CPC Shanghai Municipal Committee
1986-1989	Deputy secretary of CPC Shanghai Municipal Committee
1989-1993	Deputy director of General Office of CPC Central Committee
1993-1997	Director of General Office, CPC Central Committee and secretary of Work Committee for offices directly under CPC Central Committee
1997-1999	Alternate member of Political Bureau of CPC Central Committee, member of secretariat of CPC Central Committee, director of General Office of the CPC Central Committee, secretary of Work Committee for offices directly under CPC Central Committee
1999-2002	Alternate member of Political Bureau of CPC Central Committee, member of secretariat of CPC Central Committee and head of Organisation Department of the CPC Central Committee
2002-	Member, Standing Committee of the Political Bureau of the CPC Central Committee and Member, the Secretariat of the CPC Central Committee
2003-	Vice president of PRC

Other titles and memberships

Mr Zeng was a member of the 15th CPC Central Committee, an alternate member of its political bureau and a member of its Secretariat. He is currently a member of the 16th CPC Central Committee, a member of the Standing Committee of its Political Bureau, and a member of the Secretariat of the CPC Central Committee.

Other information

Mr Zeng's father, Mr Zeng Shan, was a revolutionary veteran who had served as the Minister of Internal Affairs after the founding of PRC in 1949. His mother, Ms Deng Liujin, was one of the few women soldiers in the Red Army which at that time was made up of Chinese workers and peasants who survived the famous Long March during the 1930s.

Mr Zeng's wife, Ms Wang Fengqing, works in the State Administration of Quality Supervision and Quarantine. The couple has a son.

CHINA'S POLITICAL FIGURES WHO'S WHO IN CHINA

Huang Ju
"Overseer of economy"

Title and position   Vice Premier of the State Council

Political influence   Number 6 member, Standing Committee of the Political Bureau of the CPC Central Committee

 "China will take more effective ways to develop the state-owned sectors, improve the efficiency of managing state-owned assets and add impetus to economic growth."

Mr Huang Ju at the Forum of State-Owned Assets Supervision and Administration Commission of China

The former mayor of Shanghai is ranked sixth among the Standing Committee members of the CPC Central Committee, and as one of the vice premiers of the State Council, he holds an important portfolio overseeing the management of the economy and state-owned enterprises.

Mr Huang graduated from the prestigious Tsinghua University and began his career like many of his cohorts amidst the backdrop of a solid technical background.

In the 1980s, he entered into the political arena as one of the governors in China's largest city, Shanghai. Like Mr Zeng Qinghong, Mr Huang met Mr Jiang Zemin there.

The association blossomed and Mr Huang soon emerged as one of Mr Jiang's most trusted and loyal associates, paving a steady path in his political career.

He became the mayor of Shanghai in 1991 and the city's CPC party chief in 1994. He relinquished the positions in Shanghai and was elevated to become a member of the Political Bureau of the CPC Central Committee in October 2002.

Birth date	September 1938
Hometown	Jiashan County, Zhejiang Province
Education	Bachelor of Engineering, Department of Electrical Machinery Engineering, Tsinghua University, May 1963
Professional qualifications	Engineer

Background

1956-1963	Bachelor of Engineering Studies majoring in Electrical Machinery Manufacturing, Department of Electrical Machinery Engineering, Tsinghua University
1963-	Joined the CPC

1963-1967	Technician at Power Workshop and Cast Steel Workshop of Shanghai Artificial Board-Making Machinery Plant, secretary of the plant director
1967-1977	Technician at Power Workshop of Zhonghua Metallurgical Plant in Shanghai, deputy secretary of the workshop's CPC branch
1977-1980	Deputy chairman of Revolutionary Committee of Shanghai Zhonghua Metallurgical Plant, deputy director and engineer of the plant
1980-1982	Deputy manager of Shanghai Petrochemical General Machinery Manufacturers Company
1982-1983	Deputy director of Shanghai First Bureau of Electrical and Machinery Industry
1983-1984	Member of Standing Committee of the CPC Shanghai Municipal Committee, secretary of CPC Shanghai Municipal Committee for Industrial Work
1984-1985	Member of Standing Committee and secretary-general of CPC Shanghai Municipal Committee
1985-1986	Deputy secretary of CPC Shanghai Municipal Committee
1986-1991	Deputy secretary of CPC Shanghai Municipal Committee and vice mayor of Shanghai
1991-1994	Deputy secretary of CPC Shanghai Municipal Committee and mayor of Shanghai
1994-1995	Member of Political Bureau of CPC Central Committee, secretary of CPC Shanghai Municipal Committee and mayor of Shanghai
1995-2002	Member of Political Bureau of CPC Central Committee, secretary of CPC Shanghai Municipal Committee
2002-	Member of Standing Committee of Political Bureau of CPC Central Committee
2003-	Vice premier of State Council

Other titles and memberships

Mr Huang was an alternate member of the 13th CPC Central Committee and a full member of the 14th and 15th CPC Central Committees. He was elected an additional member of the Political Bureau of the CPC Central Committee at the Fourth Plenary Session of the 14th CPC Central Committee. He was a member of the Political Bureau of the 15th CPC Central Committee. He is currently a member of the 16th CPC Central Committee and a member of the Standing Committee of its Political Bureau.

Other information

Married with Ms Yu Huiwen. His daughter, Ms Huang Fan, married the son of a pro-Taiwan politician in San Francisco in 1995. Karaoke is one of Mr Huang's hobbies.

"The anti-corruption legal systems as well as the clean and honest work style of the CPC will guarantee the fight for anti-corruption."

Mr Wu Guanzheng at the CPC working conference on disciplinary inspection

Wu Guanzheng
"Relentless graft buster"

Titles and positions	Secretary, Central Commission for Discipline Inspection Secretary, Shandong Provincial Party Committee President, Party School of Shandong Provincial Committee of CPC
Political influence	Number 7 member, Standing Committee of Political Bureau of CPC Central Committee

He is the de facto graft buster in China, having held appointment as the head of the Central Commission for Disciplinary Inspection, the anti-corruption body of the CPC which carries considerable weight as anti-corruption has become a major focus of China's leaders.

Mr Wu, party chief of Shandong province in eastern China, graduated from the prestigious Tsinghua University and was trained as an engineer, similar to many other senior officials in the CPC.

After several years as a technician and an expert in the technology field, he made his political debut in Wuhan, where he was appointed the industrial town's mayor from 1983 to 1986.

Mr Wu moved to Shandong Province in 1997 and was made a full member of the Political Bureau in the same year.

He is said to wield considerable influence in the CPC as not only is he seen to be close friends with former President Jiang Zemin, he is also said to have close links with China's new leader Mr Hu Jintao himself.

Birth date	August 1938
Hometown	Yugan County, Jiangxi Province
Education	Postgraduate diploma, majoring in Thermal Measurement and Automatic Control, Power Department, Tsinghua University, April 1968
Professional qualifications	Engineer

CHINA'S POLITICAL FIGURES WHO'S WHO IN CHINA

Background

1959-1965	Tsinghua University and secretary of the branch of Communist Youth League of the university
1962-	Joined the CPC
1965-1968	Postgraduate majoring in Thermal Measurement and Automatic Control at Power Department of Tsinghua University, deputy secretary of the Party branch
1968-1975	Technician at Gedian Chemical Plant in Wuhan, Hubei Province, deputy chief of the plant's technology section, head of its workshop, member of the plant's Party Committee, and deputy chairman of the plant's revolutionary committee
1975-1982	Deputy director of Wuhan Municipal Science and Technology Committee at Hubei Province, member of its Leading Party Members' Group, vice chairman of Wuhan Municipal of Science and Technology Association, member of its Leading Party Members' Group, deputy chief of Wuhan Municipal Innovation, Transformation and Potential Tapping Headquarters and head of the office of the headquarters, chairman of Wuhan Municipal Centre for Engineering Science and Technology and secretary of its Party Committee
1982-1983	Member of Standing Committee of Wuhan Municipal Committee of CPC at Hubei Province
1983-1986	Party secretary and mayor of Wuhan, Hubei Province
1986-1995	Deputy party secretary, deputy governor, acting governor and governor of Jiangxi Province
1995-1997	Secretary of Jiangxi Provincial Committee of CPC
1997-2002	Member of Political Bureau of CPC Central Committee, secretary of Shandong Provincial Committee of CPC and president of Party School of the Shandong Provincial Party Committee
2002-	Member of Standing Committee of Political Bureau of CPC Central Committee, secretary of Central Commission for Discipline Inspection, secretary of Shandong Provincial Committee of CPC and president of Party School of Shandong Provincial Committee of CPC

Other titles and memberships

Mr Wu was an alternate member of the 12th CPC Central Committee, a full member of the 13th, 14th and 15th CPC Central Committees and a member of the Political Bureau of the 15th CPC Central Committee. He is currently a member of the 16th CPC Central Committee and Standing Committee member of its Political Bureau. He is also a member of the Standing Committee of and secretary of the Central Commission for Discipline Inspection at the 16th National Congress of CPC.

Be a builder of dreams.

* Awarded World's 200 Best Small Companies by Forbes Global Magazine
* Awarded Singapore Brand Award 2003
* Awarded Singapore Brand Award 2002
* Awarded Singapore Franchise Mark
* Awarded International Franchise Excellence Award

You can when you partner with us to build the education industry in the Middle East, South Africa, South America and Central America.

Informatics Holdings Ltd is one of the global leaders in providing award-winning, quality and lifelong learning services. Through our international franchising system and strategic acquisitions, we have a global network of over 647 centres spanning more than 50 countries.

With over twenty years' experience, a proven high business margin, profitable model and internationally acclaimed support, Informatics will help position you as the education partner of choice.

Depending on the location, you can start your own franchise centre for as little as US$250,000. If you are entrepreneurial and have an interest in education and training, we invite you to build your success with us.

Unique Business Propositions

* Internationally recognized brand name
* Worldwide business network
* International affiliations and partnerships with over 40 esteemed universities and institutions
* Immediate links with strategic partners
* Advertising and PR advisory
* Over 20 years of experience and expertise
* Global leader in training and IT education
* Attractive profit margins and returns
* Continuous and innovative product and research development
* Comprehensive franchise support services
* Multilevel training level for partners and internal staff
* Informatics Group Corporate University for internal training
* e-Informatics University
* Computerised operations
* Established systems and processes
* Financial model and feasibility studies
* Progressive franchise business models
* Immediate access and share of multi-million dollar proprietary IT systems

Our award winning international higher education franchise brands

INFORMATICS INSTITUTE

Offers a complete range of IT training and education programmes validated and awarded by reputable examination bodies leading to degree programmes in over 40 universities worldwide.

 **THAMES**

Offers a complete range of management and business programmes validated and awarded by reputable examination bodies leading to degree programmes in over 40 universities worldwide.

 **PurpleTrain.com**

Asia's first, world's largest and most successful e-Learning service provider outside of the USA offers a one-stop e-Learning solution for business, IT education and Health Sciences programmes, corporate training courses and education related services. With over 700 courses available, ranging from certificate level to master degree, our online learning community now stands at over 72,000 e-users.

Informatics Holdings Ltd
Informatics Building, 5 International Business Park, Singapore 609914
24x7 Hotline : Josephine Lee (65) 9698 4257 / Cher Lim (65) 9698 4237

Tel : (65) 6568 0808 • Fax : (65) 6665 3605
Email : franchise@informaticsgroup.com
Website : www.informaticsgroup.com/franchise

CHINA'S POLITICAL FIGURES WHO'S WHO IN CHINA

Li Changchun
"Youngest member of CPC's Standing Committee"

Title and position Number 8 member, Standing Committee of Political Bureau of CPC Central Committee

"The top priority for Hong Kong is to maintain social stability. Only with social stability, could it be possible for Hong Kong to create favourable conditions for rapid economic recovery and continued development."

Mr Li Changchun

When he was appointed a member of the Standing Committee of the Political Bureau of CPC Central Committee in 1997, Mr Li made history of sorts by being the youngest ever member to be appointed in the highest echelon of the CPC at the age of 53.

Mr Li, previously the CPC's party chief in the southern province of Guangdong, China's richest province, was also the youngest mayor and party chief of a major city when he was appointed to these two positions in Shenyang, the capital of Liaoning province, in 1983.

He was only 39, and since then, he had been party chief of the Henan province, an important agricultural province in China.

His rapid rise is due to his strong record in economic reforms which was noticed by former President Jiang Zemin.

CHINA'S POLITICAL FIGURES WHO'S WHO IN CHINA

Birth date	February 1944
Hometown	Dalian City, Liaoning Province
Education	Postgraduate diploma, majoring in Industrial Enterprise Automation, Department of Electric Machinery, Harbin Institute of Technology, September 1966
Professional qualifications	Engineer

Background

1961-1966	Postgraduate studies, Industrial Enterprise Automation of the Department of Electric Machinery, Harbin Institute of Technology
1965-	Joined the CPC
1966-1968	Stationed at Harbin Institute of Technology
1968-1975	Technician at Shenyang Switchgear Plant in Liaoning Province
1975-1980	Vice chairman of Revolutionary Committee of Shenyang Electrical Equipment Company in Liaoning Province, member of Standing Committee of CPC Committee of the company and deputy manager and manager of Shenyang Electrical Control Equipment Company and deputy secretary of the company's CPC Committee
1980-1981	Deputy director of Shenyang Bureau of Mechanical and Electrical Industry and deputy secretary of the bureau's CPC Committee
1981-1982	Deputy secretary-general of Shenyang Municipal Committee of the CPC in Liaoning Province
1982-1983	Vice mayor of Shenyang, Liaoning Province and chairman of Shenyang Municipal Economic Committee
1983-1985	Secretary of Shenyang Municipal Committee of CPC in Liaoning Province and mayor of Shenyang
1985-1986	Deputy secretary of Liaoning Provincial Committee of CPC and secretary of Shenyang Municipal Committee of CPC
1986-1987	Deputy secretary of Liaoning Provincial Committee of CPC, vice governor and acting governor of Liaoning Province
1987-1990	Deputy secretary of Liaoning Provincial Committee of CPC and governor of Liaoning Province
1990-1991	Deputy secretary of Henan Provincial Committee of CPC, vice governor and acting governor of Henan Province
1991-1992	Deputy secretary of Henan Provincial Committee of CPC and governor of Henan Province
1992-1993	Secretary of Henan Provincial Committee of CPC

1993-1997	Secretary of Henan Provincial Committee of CPC and chairman of Standing Committee of Henan Provincial People's Congress (attended the workshop on theory held by the Party School of CPC Central Committee for cadres at the provincial and ministerial level from October 1993 to November 1993)
1997-1998	Member of Political Bureau of CPC Central Committee, secretary of Henan Provincial Committee of CPC and chairman of Standing Committee of Henan Provincial People's Congress
1998-2002	Member of Political Bureau of CPC Central Committee and secretary of Guangdong Provincial Committee of CPC
2002-	Member of Standing Committee of Political Bureau of CPC Central Committee

Other titles and memberships

Mr Li was an alternate member of the 12th CPC Central Committee and a member of the 13th, 14th and 15th CPC Central Committees and is currently a member of the 16th CPC Central Committee. He was a member of the Political Bureau of the 15th CPC Central Committee and is a member of the Political Bureau and a member of the Political Bureau's Standing Committee of the 16th CPC Central Committee.

"To keep stability and improve public security, we must exert the political advantage of the CPC and try to resolve social-economic disparity starting from the grass roots level."

Mr Luo Gan

CHINA'S POLITICAL FIGURES WHO'S WHO IN CHINA

Luo Gan
"Legal expert of China"

Titles and positions	State councillor Member, Leading Party Members' Group of the State Council Secretary, Political and Legislative Affairs Committee of the CPC Central Committee
Political influence	Number 9 member, Standing Committee of the Political Bureau of the CPC Central Committee

#9

A close associate of former Prime Minister Li Peng, Mr Luo holds considerable influence in the CPC as head of the Committee of Political and Legislative Affairs under the CPC Central Committee.

His appointment means he is effectively CPC's legal and security guardian.

The son of a senior-ranking CPC official, Mr Luo spent six years studying in the former Democratic Republic of Germany as a research engineer.

He established his career as a researcher and then research director before moving into the political arena in 1980, eventually becoming the vice governor of Henan Province at age 46.

Hiis star continued to shine as he went on to become deputy secretary of the Central Political Science and Law Committee in 1993 and subsequently, secretary of the Committee of Political Science and Law in 1998, making him the chief personnel in CPC's legal and security organisation.

Birth date	July 1935
Hometown	Jinan City, Shandong Province
Education	Bachelor, majoring in Machine Casting, Freiburg Institute of Mining and Metallurgy, Democratic Republic of Germany, May 1962
Professional qualifications	Senior engineer

Background

1953-1954	Studied at Pressure Processing Department, Beijing Institute of Iron and Steel Engineering
1954-1955	Studied at Karl Marx University, Leipzig, Democratic Republic of Germany
1955-1956	Field practice, Leipzig Iron and Steel Plant and Leipzig Metal Casting Plant, Democratic Republic of Germany
1956-1962	Bachelor of Engineering Studies, majoring in Machine Casting, Freiburg Institute of Mining and Metallurgy, Democratic Republic of Germany
1960-	Joined the CPC

1962-1969	Project group leader and technician at Mechanical Engineering Research Institute under the First Ministry of Machine-Building Industry
1969-1970	Was assigned to work, as a result of the Cultural Revolution at the May 7th Cadre School Under the First Ministry of Machine-Building Industry
1970-1980	Director of Luohe Preparatory Office at Mechanical Engineering Academy under the First Ministry of Machine-Building Industry and deputy director of Zhengzhou Mechanical Engineering Research Institute under the First Ministry of Machine-Building Industry
1980-1981	Vice chairman of Henan Provincial Import and Export Committee and chairman of Henan Provincial Science and Technology Committee
1981-1983	Vice governor of Henan Province and secretary of CPC Henan Provincial Committee
1983-1988	Vice chairman of All-China Federation of Trade Unions, member of secretariat of the Federation and deputy secretary of Leading Party Members' Group of the federation
1988-1993	Minister of Labour (April-December 1988), secretary-general of State Council, secretary of Leading Party Members' Group of the Government Offices of the State Council and secretary of State Organs Work Committee of CPC
1993-1997	State councillor and secretary-general of State Council, secretary of Leading Party Members' Group of Government Offices of State Council, secretary of State Organs Work Committee of CPC and deputy secretary of Political and Legislative Affairs Committee of CPC Central Committee
1997-1998	Member of Political Bureau of CPC Central Committee, member of secretariat of CPC Central Committee, state councillor and concurrently secretary-general of State Council, secretary of Leading Party Members' Group of Government Offices of State Council, secretary of State Organs Work Committee of CPC and deputy secretary of Political and Legislative Affairs Committee of the CPC Central Committee
1998-2002	Member of Political Bureau of CPC Central Committee, member of secretariat of CPC Central Committee, state councillor and member of Leading Party Members' Group of State Council and secretary of Political and Legislative Affairs Committee of CPC Central Committee
2002-	Member of Standing Committee of the Political Bureau of CPC Central Committee, state councillor and member of Leading Party Members' Group of State Council, secretary of Political and Legislative Affairs Committee of CPC Central Committee

CHINA'S POLITICAL FIGURES WHO'S WHO IN CHINA

Other titles and memberships

Mr Luo was an alternate member of the 12th CPC Central Committee and a member of the 13th, 14th and 15th CPC Central Committees and is currently a member of the 16th CPC Central Committee. He was a member of the Political Bureau of the 15th CPC Central Committee and a member of the Secretariat of the CPC Central Committee. He is a member of the Political Bureau of the 16th CPC Central Committee and a member of its Standing Committee.

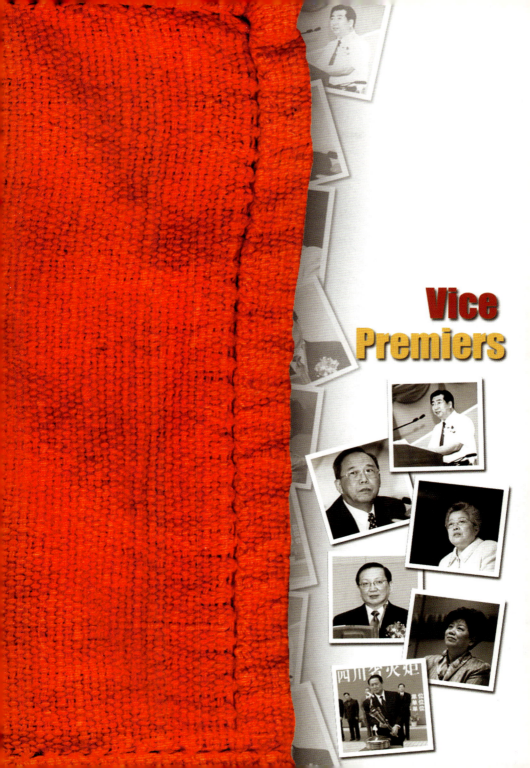

Vice Premiers

CHINA'S POLITICAL FIGURES WHO'S WHO IN CHINA

Wu Yi
"The rose among the thorns"

Titles and positions Vice Premier, State Council
Minister of Health

Political influence Member, Political Bureau of the CPC Central Committee

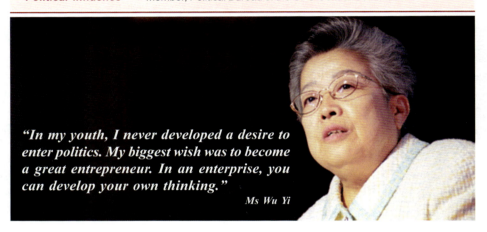

"In my youth, I never developed a desire to enter politics. My biggest wish was to become a great entrepreneur. In an enterprise, you can develop your own thinking."
— Ms Wu Yi

China's "Iron Lady" is the only female among all the vice premiers in the State Council.

Considered the most powerful woman in China, she became China's Minister of Health after the dismissal of her predecessor, Mr Zhou Yongkang, in May 2003 because of his breach of duty during the severe acute respiratory syndrome (SARS) crisis.

Although she has built up a sound reputation from her work in foreign trade and industrial development, it was not until 1993 when trade tensions between China and the United States were at a peak that she came into her own.

Ms Wu impressed party delegates with the way she handled the rounds of talks and negotiations with US delegates Mickey Kantor and Charlene Barshefsky.

As Minister of the former Ministry of Foreign Trade and Economic Cooperation, Ms Wu demonstrated her exemplary negotiating skills, toughness and intelligence.

After a sterling performance, she was appointed as one of China's five state councillors in 1998.

Born into a family of intellectuals, Ms Wu was trained as an engineer and she had paid her dues after graduation, working first as a technician, and then technology section chief and deputy chief engineer before becoming the deputy director at the Beijing Dongfanghong Refinery.

CHINA'S POLITICAL FIGURES WHO'S WHO IN CHINA

But it was her reputation as a tough but flexible negotiator, which caught the attention of the CPC.

A close associate of former Premier Zhu Rongji, Ms Wu is associated with current government efforts to promote the development of China's neighbours via increased foreign trade and economic cooperation.

She is also tasked with the expansion of China's cooperation with the World Intellectual Property Organisation and the push to promote the growth of high-tech China exports.

As a further sign of her influence, she is behind China's drive to attract foreign direct investment through policies and laws more favourable for foreign investors as well as to encourage Chinese firms to invest in overseas assembly plants.

Birth date	November 1938
Hometown	Wuhan City, Hubei Province
Education	Bachelor of Engineering, majoring in Oil Refinery Engineering, Oil Refinery Department, Beijing Petroleum Institute, 1962
Professional qualifications	Senior engineer

Background

1956-1962	Bachelor of Engineering Studies at the National Defence Department, Northwest Polytechnic Institute and the Oil Refinery Department, Beijing Petroleum Institute majoring in Oil Refinery Engineering
1962-	Joined the CPC
1962-1965	Workshop technician and staff member of Political Department of the Lanzhou Oil Refinery
1965-1967	Technician at production division of Production and Technology Department, Ministry of Petroleum Industry
1967-1983	Technician, deputy chief and chief of technology section, deputy chief engineer and deputy director of Beijing Dongfanghong Refinery
1983-1988	Deputy general manager and CPC committee secretary of Yanshan Petrochemical Corporation
1988-1991	Vice mayor of Beijing
1991-1993	Vice minister of Foreign Economic Relations and Trade and deputy secretary of the ministry's Leading Party Members' Group
1993-1997	Minister of Foreign Trade and Economic Cooperation and secretary of the ministry's Leading Party Members' Group
1997-1998	Alternate member of Political Bureau of CPC Central Committee, Minister of Foreign Trade and Economic Cooperation and secretary of the ministry's Leading Party Members' Group

CHINA'S POLITICAL FIGURES WHO'S WHO IN CHINA

1998-2002   Alternate member of Political Bureau of CPC Central Committee, state councillor and member of Leading Party Members' Group of the State Council
2002-   Member of Political Bureau of CPC Central Committee, state councillor and member of Leading Party Members' Group of the State Council
2003-   Minister of Health

Other titles and positions

Ms Wu was the alternate member of the 13th CPC Central Committee, a full member of the 14th, 15th and 16th CPC Central Committee, an alternate member of the Political Bureau of the 15th Central Committee, and a member of the Political Bureau of 16th CPC Central Committee.

Other information

Ms Wu is single. She maintains, "I'm not committed to celibacy. In my youth, I had an ideal image of a man, but he doesn't exist in real life. I had wanted to establish a career before starting a family. I spent 20 years in the backwoods. When I got out, I was already too old. Plus work was hectic. So I gave up."

CHINA'S POLITICAL FIGURES WHO'S WHO IN CHINA

Hui Liangyu
"Minority with a major portfolio"

Titles and positions	Vice Premier, State Council
	Deputy Head, Central Rural Work Leading Group
Political influence	Member, Political Bureau of the CPC Central Committee

 "The Chinese government pays close attention to the steady growth of agriculture and well-coordinated economic and social development in rural areas. After decades of hard struggle, China has accomplished a historic transition from chronic shortages in major agricultural products to a general balance between overall supply and demand, with surpluses during years of good harvest."

Mr Hui Liangyu

As one of China's four vice premiers in the State Council, Mr Hui stands out from his cohorts on two counts.

He is of Hui nationality, one of the ethnic minorities in China, and unlike most of the other high-ranking officials, he did not receive a university education.

However, his lack of academic qualifications is more than made up by his vast political experience. His current portfolio covers the agricultural and rural affairs of China due to his extensive experience in such areas.

His political career started in his hometown, Jilin province, where he was promoted from a clerk to the vice governor of the province. Later on, he was transferred as provincial level governor to various rural provinces such as Hubei, Anhui, and Jiangsu.

With more than 10 years experience in rural provinces such as Jilin, Hubei, and Anhui, Mr Hui is a natural leader in dealing with agricultural and rural issues.

Birth date	October 1944
Hometown	Yushu City, Jilin Province
Education	Junior college education, Jilin Provincial Party School
Professional qualifications	Economist

CHINA'S POLITICAL FIGURES WHO'S WHO IN CHINA

Background

1961-1964	Student at the Agricultural School of Jilin Province
1964-1968	Clerk at Agricultural Bureau and Personnel Supervision Bureau of Yushu County
1966-	Joined the CPC
1968-1969	Was assigned to work, as a result of the Cultural Revolution, in May 7th Cadre School of Yushu County, Jilin Province
1969-1972	Clerk and deputy head at office of Political Department of the Revolutionary Committee of Yushu County, Jilin Province
1972-1974	Deputy director of Organisation Department of the CPC Yushu County Committee, Jilin Province, secretary of CPC Yujia People's Commune Committee
1974-1977	Deputy secretary of CPC Yushu County Committee, Jilin Province
1977-1984	Deputy director-general of Jilin Provincial Agricultural Department, deputy director-general and deputy secretary of Leading Party Members' Group of Jilin Provincial Agricultural and Animal Husbandry Department
1984-1985	Deputy secretary of CPC Baicheng Prefecture Committee, Jilin Province, commissioner of Baicheng Prefecture Administrative Office
1985-1987	Member of Standing Committee of Jilin Provincial Party Committee and concurrently head of Rural Policy Research Office and director of Rural Work Department, CPC Jilin Provincial Committee (took correspondence courses at the Provincial Party School, majoring in basic knowledge for Party and government officials from August 1984 to July 1987)
1987-1990	Vice governor of Jilin Province
1990-1992	Deputy head of Policy Research Office of CPC Central Committee
1992-1993	Deputy secretary of CPC Hubei Provincial Committee
1993-1994	Deputy secretary of CPC Hubei Provincial Committee, chairman of Hubei Provincial Committee at the Chinese People's Political Consultative Conference
1994-1995	Deputy secretary of CPC Anhui Provincial Committee, vice governor and acting governor of Anhui Province
1995-1998	Deputy secretary of CPC Anhui Provincial Committee and governor of Anhui Province
1998-1998	Secretary of CPC Anhui Provincial Committee and governor of Anhui Province
1998-1999	Secretary of CPC Anhui Provincial Committee
1999-2002	Secretary of CPC Jiangsu Provincial Committee
2002-	Member of Political Bureau of CPC Central Committee and secretary of CPC Jiangsu Provincial Committee
2003-	Member of Political Bureau of the CPC Centre Committee, Deputy head of Central Rural Work Leading Group, and vice premier of the State Council

Other titles and positions

Mr Hui was an alternate member of the 14th CPC Central Committee and a member of the 15th CPC Central Committee and is currently a member of the 16th CPC Central Committee and a member of the Political Bureau of the 16th CPC Central Committee.

CHINA'S POLITICAL FIGURES WHO'S WHO IN CHINA

Zeng Peiyan
"China's master planner"

Title and position Vice Premier, State Council

Political influence Member, Political Bureau of the CPC Central Committee

"As entrusted by the State Council, I now report to this session the implementation of the 2002 Plan for National Economic and Social Development and on the 2003 Draft Plan for National Economic and Social Development. I present these to you for your examination and approval and also for comments and suggestions from members of the National People's Congress."

Mr Zeng Peiyan presenting a report of National Economic and Social Development every year since the 1990s

In the eyes of the foreign media, Vice Premier Zeng Peiyun is the man with the plan.

China's top planner, who is the mastermind behind the economic and development planning of China, is responsible for managing the economy, finance, IT, construction, and the development of western China.

A Tsinghua University graduate, Mr Zeng was trained as an engineer and in research, and was considered an expert in electronics in the early years of his career.

But it was in the political arena where he clearly shone, especially after meeting former President Jiang Zemin and forging a close friendship with him at the former Minister of Electronics Industry where he used to work.

He cemented his reputation when he was appointed to the Ministry of the State Planning Commission, where he became involved with China's 8th, 9th and 10th "Five Year Plan", which coincided with the period of most rapid development in China's economy.

Mr Zeng is seen by many as the best economic mind in China and an important assistant to former President Jiang Zemin. Due to his close relationship with Mr Jiang, as well as his vast experience in economic planning, he was promoted to vice premier of the State Council in 2003, further extending his responsibilities in taking charge of China's economic planning.

Birth date	December 1938
Hometown	Shaoxing City, Zhejiang Province
Education	Bachelor in Engineering, majoring in Electronics, Radio and Electronics Department, Tsinghua University, 1962
Professional qualifications	Senior engineer and research fellow

Background

1956-1962	Bachelor of Engineering Studies majoring in Electronics, Radio and Electronics Department, Tsinghua University
1962-1964	Technician at Shanghai Electrical Appliances Institute of the First Ministry of Machine-Building Industry and chief of the Research Project Group of the Institute
1964-1965	Technician and group leader of Rectifier Research Office, Xi'an Switch and Rectifier Factory under the First Ministry of Machine-Building Industry
1965-1982	Group leader, deputy head of office and deputy chief engineer of Xi'an Rectifier Institute under the First Ministry of Machine-Building Industry
1978-	Joined the CPC
1982-1984	Second secretary and first secretary of Commercial Counsellor's Office of the Chinese Embassy in the United States
1984-1987	Head of General Office and concurrently director-general of Planning and Construction Department of the Ministry of Electronics Industry
1987-1988	Vice minister of Electronics Industry, member of Ministry's Leading Party Members' Group and concurrently director-general of Ministry's Planning and Construction Department
1988-1991	Vice minister of Machine-Building and Electronics Industry and member of Ministry's Leading Party Members' Group (Studied at the Central Party School from September 1989 to November 1989)
1991-1992	Vice minister of Machine-Building and Electronics Industry, deputy secretary of Ministry's Leading Party Members' Group and concurrently member of Leading Party Members' Group of the China Electronics Industrial Corporation
1992-1993	Deputy secretary-general (ministerial rank) of Central Economic and Financial Leading Group and vice minister of State Planning Commission
1993-1994	Deputy secretary-general of Central Economic and Financial Leading Group and vice minister of State Planning Commission and deputy secretary of Commission's Leading Party Members' Group
1994-1998	Deputy secretary-general of Central Economic and Financial Leading Group, minister-in-charge of State Planning Commission and deputy secretary of Commission's Leading Party Members' Group
1998-2001	Deputy secretary-general of Central Economic and Financial Leading Group, minister in charge of State Development Planning Commission, secretary of Commission's Leading Party Members' Group, deputy director of Three Gorges Project Construction Committee under the State Council (May 1998) and director of office of State Council Leading Group for Western China Development (January 2000)

CHINA'S POLITICAL FIGURES WHO'S WHO IN CHINA

2001-2002 Deputy secretary-general of Central Economic and Financial Leading Group, minister in charge of State Development Planning Commission, secretary of Commission's Leading Party Members' Group, deputy leader of State Council Leading Group for Information Development, head of office of State Council Leading Group for Information Development, secretary of Office's Leading Party Members' Group (October 2001), deputy director of Three Gorges Project Construction Committee under State Council and head of office of State Council Leading Group for Western China Development

2002-2003 Minister in charge of State Development Planning Commission

2002 - Member of Political Bureau of CPC Central Committee, deputy secretary-general of Central Economic and Financial Leading Group, secretary of Commission's Leading Party Members' Group, deputy leader of State Council Leading Group for Information Development, head of office of State Council Leading Group for Information Development, secretary of Office's Leading Party Members' Group (October 2001), deputy director of Three Gorges Project Construction Committee under State Council and head of office of State Council Leading Group for Western China Development

2003- Vice premier of State Council

Other titles and positions

Mr Zeng also served as an alternate member of the 14th and 15th CPC Central Committees and is a member of the 16th CPC Central Committee and member of the Political Bureau of the 16th CPC Central Committee.

Other information

Mr Zeng is said to be a man with immense intellect. He is known to be armed with a deep understanding of the computing and the IT industry. One of Mr Zeng's main hobbies is cooking.

"China's public security system should launch a profound revolution in the philosophy of law enforcement and police officers must demonstrate through their own performance that they are executing the law for the people."

Mr Zhou Yongkang

CHINA'S POLITICAL FIGURES WHO'S WHO IN CHINA

Zhou Yongkang
"Public security is his business"

Titles and positions	State Councillor
	Member, Secretariat of the CPC Central Committee
	Minister of Public Security
Political influence	Member, Political Bureau of the CPC Central Committee

Taking charge of public security in China, a country with an immense 1.3 billion population, is an extermely challenging task and Mr Zhou's job is made no simpler by the gulf between income levels in the population as a result of economic reforms.

Still, the minister of Public Security is coping well, even though he was trained as an engineer and was previously a specialist in petroleum and geological surveying.

Some of the solutions he had implemented included monitoring the activities of the police force, refining law enforcement and improving the image of China's police force.

His political career started at the Ministry of Petroleum Industry. Having been appointed as the general manager of China National Petroleum Corporation, he developed extensive experience in managing large state-owned enterprises.

His political career also included working in at the Ministry of Land and Resources and as the party chief of Sichuan Province, China's most populaous province.

Birth date	December 1942
Hometown	Wuxi City, Jiangsu Province
Education	Bachelor, majoring in Geophysical Survey and Exploration, Survey and Exploration Department, Beijing Petroleum Institute, 1966
Professional qualifications	Senior engineer (professor rank)

Background

1961-1966	Studied geophysical survey and exploration, Survey and Exploration Department, Beijing Petroleum Institute
1964-	Joined the CPC
1966-1967	Remained at the Institute, awaiting for job assignment
1967-1970	Internship as a technician, geological survey team of No. 673 Factory, Daqing Oilfield
1970-1973	Technician, party branch secretary and brigade leader of regional office at Geological Survey Regiment, Liaohe Oil Exploration Campaign Headquarters Regiment, Liaohe Oil Exploration Campaign Headquarters

1973-1976	Director of Geophysical Survey Division, Liaohe Oil Exploration Bureau (LOEB)
1976-1979	Deputy director of Political Department, LOEB
1979-1983	Deputy director-general of LOEB and concurrently Party secretary of LOEB Drilling Headquarters, Party secretary and commander of LOEB Geophysical Survey Headquarters
1983-1985	Director-general and deputy Party secretary of LOEB, deputy Party secretary and mayor of Panjin City, Liaoning Province
1985-1988	Vice minister of petroleum industry and member of Ministry's Leading Party Member Group
1988-1996	Deputy general manager and deputy secretary of Leading Party Member Group of China National Petroleum Corporation, concurrently commander of Tarim Oil Exploration Campaign Headquarters and secretary of its ad hoc Party Committee from March 1989 to September 1990, Party secretary and director-general of Shengli Petroleum Administration and Party secretary of Dongying, Shandong Province
1996-1998	General manager of China National Petroleum Corporation and secretary of its Leading Party Member Group
1998-1999	Minister of Land and Recourses, secretary of Leading Party Member Group, Ministry of Land and Resources
1999-2002	Secretary of Sichuan Provincial Party Committee
2002-	Member of Political Bureau and member of Secretariat of CPC Central Committee, deputy secretary of Committee of Political and Legislative Affairs under CPC Central Committee and minister of Public Security
2003-	State councillor

Other titles and positions

Mr Zhou was an alternate member of the 14th CPC Central Committee and a member of the 15th CPC Central Committee. He is a member of the 16th CPC Central Committee and of its Political Bureau and Secretariat.

CHINA'S POLITICAL FIGURES WHO'S WHO IN CHINA

Tang Jiaxuan
"Diplomat with the special touch"

Title and position State Councillor

Political influence Member, CPC Central Committee

 "The mission of China's diplomatic work is to safeguard world peace and promote global development."

Mr Tang Jiaxuan in a press conference at the First Session of the 10th National People's Congress

As the state councillor in charge of foreign affairs, an appointment he held since March 2003, Mr Tang has made diplomacy a lifelong profession.

A graduate from the foreign language departments of Fudan University and Beijing University majoring in Japanese and English, Mr Tang's formative years as a diplomat were spent dealing with Japan, starting as a junior staff to becoming the minister of the Chinese Embassy in Japan in 1988.

He was promoted to vice minister of Foreign Affairs in 1993 and subsequently headed the ministry in 1998 because of his extensive experience in foreign affairs and his close relationship with former President Jiang Zemin.

Birth date	January 1938
Hometown	Zhenjiang City, Jiangsu Province
Education	Diploma, majoring in English Language, Foreign Languages Department, Fudan University, 1958
	Bachelor in Arts, majoring in Japanese Language, Oriental Languages Department, Beijing University, 1962

Background

1955-1958	Foreign Languages Department, Fudan University, majoring in English language
1958-1962	Oriental Languages Department, Beijing University, majoring in Japanese language
1962-1964	Staff member of Japanese division in Overseas Service Department, Bureau of Broadcasting Undertakings
1964-1969	Staff member of interpreters' team of Ministry of Foreign Affairs
1969-1970	Sent to work in the May 7th cadre school of Ministry of Foreign Affairs
1970-1978	Deputy division chief of Chinese People's Association for Friendship with Foreign Countries and council member of Sino-Japanese Friendship Association

1973-	Joined the CPC
1978-1983	2nd secretary, then 1st secretary of Chinese Embassy in Japan
1983-1985	Deputy director of Office of directing group for Party organisation rectification in foreign affairs departments of the central authorities
1985-1988	Deputy director of Asian Affairs Department of Ministry of Foreign Affairs
1988-1991	Minister-counsellor and minister of Chinese Embassy in Japan
1991-1993	Assistant minister of Foreign Affairs, member of Party committee of Ministry of Foreign Affairs
1993-1994	Vice minister of Foreign Affairs, member of Party committee of Ministry of Foreign Affairs
1994-1997	Vice minister of Foreign Affairs, deputy secretary of Party committee of Ministry of Foreign Affairs
1997-1998	Party secretary of Ministry of Foreign Affairs and vice minister of Foreign Affairs
1998-2000	Minister of Foreign Affairs and Party secretary of Ministry of Foreign Affairs
2000-2003	Minister of Foreign Affairs and member of Party committee of Ministry of Foreign Affairs
2003-	State councillor

Other titles and positions

Mr Tang is a member of the 15th and 16th CPC Central Committees.

Hua Jianmin
"Trusted lieutenant to Jiang Zemin"

Titles and positions	State Councillor General Secretary, State Council
Political influence	Member, CPC Central Committee

Mr Hua Jianmin was one of two people from Shanghai whom former President Jiang Zemin took with him to Beijing when he become the president of PRC.

State Councillor Hua is also the general secretary of the State Council and a member of the CPC Central Committee.

Trained as an engineer in China's famous Tsinghua University, Mr Hua has spent over 20 years in various research institutes, starting as a technician, eventually progressing to become the deputy director and to his eventual appointment as head of research for a Shanghai engineering institute.

He cut his teeth in politics in Shanghai after attending a training class in the Party School of the CPC Central Committee in 1984, first in the power industry and then in the planning commission.

Birth date	January 1940
Hometown	Wuxi City, Jiangsu Province
Education	Bachelor in Engineering, majoring in Gas Turbine, from the Power and Dynamics Department of Tsinghua University, 1963
Professional qualifications	Senior engineer

Background

1957-1963	Power and Dynamics Department, Tsinghua University, majoring in Gas Turbine
1961-	Joined the CPC
1963-1969	Technician and deputy secretary of Party branch of Automatic Control Division of Shanghai Air Turbines and Boilers Research Institute
1969-1975	Technician at Research Institute of Shanghai Air Turbine Factory
1975-1979	Deputy director of Research Institute of Shanghai Air Turbine Factory
1979-1983	Head of scientific research office at Shanghai Design and Research Institute for Whole-Set Power Generating Equipment (concurrently received technical training on air turbines in the United States from June to September 1982)
1983-1984	Deputy director of Shanghai Design and Research Institute for Whole Set Power Generating Equipment

1984-1986	Studied in a training class run by the Training Department of Party School, CPC Central Committee
1986-1987	Official at General Office of CPC Central Committee
1987-1991	General manager of Shanghai Shenneng Power Development Corporation
1991-1992	Deputy director of Shanghai Municipal Planning Commission, general manager of Shenneng Corporation
1992-1993	Executive deputy director and deputy secretary of Leading Party Members' Group of Shanghai Municipal Planning Commission
1993-1994	Director and secretary of Leading Party Members' Group of Shanghai Municipal Planning Commission, deputy secretary of Shanghai Municipal Committee on Comprehensive Economic Work and director of Shanghai Municipal Planning Commission
1994-1996	Member of Standing Committee of CPC Shanghai Municipal Committee, vice mayor of Shanghai
1996-1998	Deputy director of office of Financial and Economic Leading Group of CPC Central Committee
1998-2003	Vice secretary and office director of Financial and Economic Leading Group of CPC Central Committee
2002-	Member of CPC Central Committee
2003-	State councillor and general secretary of State Council

"In the next few years, the implementation of the nine-year compulsory education program will target mountainous, rural, remote and border areas with underdeveloped economies."

Ms Chen Zhili

Chen Zhili
"The only lady state councillor"

Title and position   State Councillor

Political influence   Member, CPC Central Committee

A rare sight among the CPC, former Education Minister Chen Zhili is the only woman among the five state councillors. She was also the country's first female education minister and her current portfolio now covers education, science and technology, making her one of the most influential women in the country.

A graduate from Fudan University where she was trained as a science researcher, her political career blossomed after she met Mr Jiang Zemin and Mr Zhu Rongji.

Her ambitious plan to eliminate illiteracy in China was unveiled almost immediately after she was appointed the education minister.

Towards this end, she established the goal of eliminating illiteracy among those aged 15 to 50 by the end of the year 2000.

She also pushed for the reform of China's higher education system, under which universities and institutions are to be run jointly by central and local governments, with the latter assuming greater responsibility.

Birth date	November 1942
Hometown	Xianyou County, Fujian Province
Education	Bachelor in Science, majoring in Solid-state Physics, Physics Department, Fudan University, 1964
	Postgraduate Diploma, Shanghai Institute of Silicate, China Academy of Sciences (CAS), 1968
Professional qualifications	Associate research fellow

Background

1959-1964	Physics Department, Fudan University, majoring in Solid-State Physics
1961-	Joined the CPC
1964-1968	Postgraduate studies, Shanghai Institute of Silicate, China Academy of Sciences (CAS) (joined the "four clean-up" work team from August 1965 to January 1967)
1968-1970	Assigned to the Danyang Lake Farm affiliated to the No 6409 Army Unit of the PLA
1970-1980	Intern and associate research fellow under Shanghai Institute of Silicate, CAS
1980-1982	Visiting scholar at Material Research Institute, University of Pennsylvania, United States

1982-1984	Associate research fellow at Shanghai Institute of Silicate, CAS, and deputy secretary of CPC Committee of the institute
1984-1988	Deputy secretary and secretary of Science and Technology Work Committee of CPC Shanghai Municipal Committee, head of Publicity Department of CPC Shanghai Municipal Committee
1988-1989	Member of Standing Committee and head of Publicity Department of CPC Shanghai Municipal Committee
1989-1991	Deputy secretary and head of Publicity Department in CPC Shanghai Municipal Committee
1991-1997	Deputy secretary of CPC Shanghai Municipal Committee
1997-1998	Secretary of Leading Party Members' Group and vice minister of State Education Commission
1998-2003	Minister of Education and secretary of Leading Party Members' Group of the Ministry of Education (studied at the CPC Central Committee Party School in September-November 2001)
2003-	State councillor

Other titles and positions

Ms Chen was an alternate member of the 13th and 14th CPC Central Committees, and is a member of the 15th and 16th CPC Central Committees.

Other information

Ms Chen is married. She was also amongst the first group of Chinese scholars to visit the United States.

Military

"The (CPC) Party must always represent the development trend of China's advanced productive forces, the orientation of China's advanced culture and the fundamental interests of the overwhelming majority of the Chinese people."

Theory of Three Representations
Mr Jiang Zemin

CHINA'S POLITICAL FIGURES WHO'S WHO IN CHINA

Jiang Zemin
"The man holding the military might"

Titles and positions	Chairman, CPC Central Military Commission
	Chairman, Central Military Commission of the PRC
Political influence	Former number 1 member, Standing Committee of the Political Bureau of the CPC Central Committee

Although he has since stepped down as the president of the People's Republic of China and retired from the Standing Committee of the Political Bureau of the CPC Central Committee in 2002, Mr Jiang has lost none of his clout.

He still stands as the chairman of CPC Central Military Commission and the chairman of Central Military Commission of PRC.

Mr Jiang, who was born into a family of intellectuals and in his youth he aspired to be an engineer. However, his calling has always been in politics. He began his political career in Shanghai and became its mayor in 1985.

But his greatest political opportunity came four years later in 1989 when he was selected by Mr Deng Xiaoping, then the leader of CPC, to become a core member of the second leading generation of CPC.

He was groomed to eventually succeed and become the new leader of the party and the country.

During his leadership, Mr Jiang highlighted the theory of "three representations", which was put into the CPC's basic constitution in 2003.

Despite his laid-back demeanour, many observers note that Mr Jiang has a steely edge which belies his affable appearance.

Behind the scenes, he is known as "a shrewd survivor", "a veteran of the epic leadership battles in the CPC" and an economic reformer intent on "shaking up China's massive state-run industries".

His influence did not appear to have waned since his heydays in the 1990s when he was the most influential person in China even though he has retired from several official positions. He can still rely on his position in the army and association with the current Standing Committee of CPC's Political Bureau.

Birth date	17 August 1926
Hometown	Yangzhou City, Jiangsu Province
Education	Bachelor of Engineering, majoring in Electrical Machinery, Shanghai Jiaotong University, 1947
Professional qualifications	Engineer

[1] Mr Jiang Zemin remains the number 1 influence in the PLA while Mr Hu Jintao is seen as the number 2 power behind the PLA.

CHINA'S POLITICAL FIGURES WHO'S WHO IN CHINA

Background

1943-1947	Electrical Machinery Department, Shanghai Jiaotong University
1946	Joined the CPC
1947-1955	Deputy engineer and chief of Works section and concurrently head of power workshop, party branch secretary and first deputy director of Shanghai Yimin Number 1 Foodstuff Factory, first deputy director of Shanghai Soap Factory, chief of electrical machinery section of Shanghai Number 2 Design Division of the First Machine-Building Industry Ministry
1955-1956	Trainee under Stalin Automobile Works in Moscow
1956-1962	Deputy chief of dynamic mechanics division, deputy chief engineer for dynamic mechanics, the First Automobile Plant in Changchun and director of power factory in the plant
1962-1980	Deputy director of Shanghai Electrical Equipment Research Institute under the First Machine-Building Industry Ministry, director and acting party committee secretary of Wuhan Heat-Power Machinery Institute under the ministry, deputy director-general and director-general of Foreign Affairs Bureau of the First Ministry of Machine-Building Industry
1980-1982	Vice chairman and concurrently secretary-general of State Administration Commission on Import and Export Affairs and the State Administration Commission on Foreign Investment and a member of the Leading Party Member Group of the two commissions
1982-1985	First vice minister and deputy secretary of Leading Party Member Group, Ministry of Electronics Industry, minister and secretary of Leading Party Members' Group of the Ministry
1985-1987	Mayor of Shanghai and deputy secretary and secretary of Shanghai Municipal Party Committee, member of CPC Central Committee
1987-1989	Member of Political Bureau of CPC Central Committee at the First Plenary Session of the 13th CPC Central Committee
1989-2002	Member of Standing Committee of Political Bureau and general secretary of CPC Central Committee during the Fourth Plenary Session of the 13th CPC Central Committee.
1989-	Chairman of CPC Central Military Commission
1990-	Chairman of Central Military Commission of PRC
1993-2003	President of PRC

Other information

Mr Jiang is married to Ms Wang Yeping with two sons, Mr Jiang Mianheng and Mr Jiang Miankang.

Cao Gangchuan
"Leading weapons official"

Titles and positions	State Councillor Minister of National Defence Vice Chairman, CPC Central Military Commission Vice Chairman, Central Military Commission of PRC Director and Secretary of Party committee, PLA General Armament Department
Political influence	Member, Political Bureau of the CPC Central Committee

"We will defend the Taiwan island even when not a single blade of grass remains on the island."

General Cao Gangchuan's reply to a CNN reporter's question about the independence of Taiwan (October 29, 2003)

A no-nonsense leader in the People's Liberation Army (PLA), General Cao Gangchuan is the first Asian defence minister to have a personal meeting with the President of the United States at the Oval Office.

General Cao started off as a general staff member at the PLA in the late 1970s and worked his way up to become the chief of PLA's Office of Military Trade in charge of arms sales by the early 1990s.

From then on, with patronage from Mr Deng Xiaoping's family and a close relationship with Mr Jiang Zemin, his career took off and he became PLA's leading weapons and armaments official ever since.

Currently, he is ranked third in the hierarchy of PLA behind Mr Hu Jintao and he is also the National Defence Minister.

He is concurrently a member of the Political Bureau of the CPC Central Committee and a vice chairman of CPC Central Military Commission.

Birth date	December 1935
Hometown	Wugang County, Henan Province
Education	Military Engineering School, Artillery Corps of the Soviet Union, 1963
Military rank	General

CHINA'S POLITICAL FIGURES WHO'S WHO IN CHINA

Background

1954-1956	Nanjing No. 3 Artillery Ordnance Technical School and No 1 Ordnance Technical School and taught at No. 1 Ordnance Technical School in 1956
1956-	Joined the CPC
1956-1957	PLA Dalian Russian-Language School
1957-1963	Military Engineering School, Artillery Corps of the Soviet Union
1963-1969	Assistant of Ammunition Division of Ordnance Department, PLA General Logistics Department
1969-1975	Assistant of Munitions Division of Military Equipment Department, PLA General Logistics Department
1975-1982	Staff officer and deputy director of General Planning Division of Military Equipment Department of PLA Headquarters of the General Staff
1982-1989	Deputy director of Military Equipment Department of PLA Headquarters of the General Staff
1989-1990	Director of Military Affairs Department of PLA Headquarters of the General Staff
1990-1992	Director of Office of Military Trade of Central Military Commission
1992-1996	Deputy chief of General Staff of PLA
1996-1998	Minister of Commission of Science, Technology and Industry for National Defence
1998-1998	Director of PLA General Armament Department
1998-2002	Member of CPC Central Military Commission, director and secretary of Party Committee of PLA General Armament Department
2002-	Member of Political Bureau of CPC Central Committee, vice chairman of CPC Central Military Commission, director and secretary of Party Committee of PLA General Armament Department
2003-	State Councillor, Minister of National Defence and vice chairman of Central Military Commission of PRC

Other titles and positions

General Cao was a member of the 15th CPC Central Committee. He is currently a member of the 16th CPC Central Committee and member of the Political Bureau of the 16th CPC Central Committee.

Guo Boxiong
"PLA's General Staff Commander"

Titles and positions	Vice Chairman, CPC Central Military Commission Vice Chairman, Central Military Commission of the PRC Executive Deputy Chief, Headquarters of the General Staff of the Chinese People's Liberation Army (PLA) Deputy Secretary, Party Committee of the Headquarters of the General Staff of the PLA
Political influence	Member, Political Bureau of the CPC Central Committee

A 50-year veteran in the PLA, General Guo is ranked No. 4 in PLA and is regarded as the main authority in PLA's General Staff.

General Guo, who is a member of the Political Bureau of the CPC Central Committee and a vice chairman of CPC Central Military Commission, began life in the military back in the 1950s.

He worked his way up from a platoon commander to become the commander of Lanzhou Military Area Command, one of China's largest military bases.

His military and political career took off due to his close relationship with Mr Jiang Zemin, and he rose to become the top figure within the PLA General Staff.

Birth date	July 1942
Hometown	Liquan County, Shanxi Province
Education	PLA Military Academy of the Chinese People's Liberation Army, 1963
Military rank	General

Background

1958-1961	Staff, No. 408 Factory of Xingping County, Shaanxi Province
1961-1964	Soldier, deputy squad leader and then squad leader, Eighth Company, 164th Regiment, 55th Division, 19th Army, PLA Ground Force
1963-	Joined the CPC
1964-1965	Platoon commander of Eighth Company of 164th Regiment, 55th Division, 19th Army, PLA Ground Force
1965-1966	Staff member of Propaganda Group of the Political Section, 164th Regiment, 55th Division, 19th Army, PLA Ground Force
1966-1970	Staff of Combat Training Group, Headquarters, 164th Regiment, 55th Division, 19th Army, PLA Ground Force

CHINA'S POLITICAL FIGURES WHO'S WHO IN CHINA

1970-1971	Leader of Combat Training Group, Headquarters, 164th Regiment, 55th Division, 19th Army, PLA Ground Force
1971-1981	Staff officer, deputy head and head of Combat Training Section, Headquarters of the 19th Army, PLA Ground Force
1981-1982	Chief of Staff, 55th Division, 19th Army, PLA Ground Force (studied at the Military Academy of the Chinese PLA from September 1981 to July 1983)
1982-1983	Deputy director of Combat Department, Headquarters of the Lanzhou Military Area Command
1983-1985	Chief of Staff, 19th Army, PLA Ground Force
1985-1990	Deputy chief of Staff, Lanzhou Military Area Command
1990-1993	Commander, 47th Group Army, PLA Ground Force
1993-1997	Deputy commander, Beijing Military Area Command
1997-1999	Commander, Lanzhou Military Area Command
1999-2002	Member of Central Military Commission, executive deputy general chief of staff, PLA and deputy secretary of Party Committee of PLA General Staff
2002-	Member of Political Bureau of CPC Central Committee, vice chairman of CPC Central Military Commission, vice chairman of the Central Military Commission of the PRC, executive deputy chief of PLA Headquarters of General Staff and deputy secretary of Party Committee of the PLA Headquarters of General Staff

Other titles and positions

General Guo was a member of the 15th CPC Central Committee and is now a member of the 16th CPC Central Committee and member of the Political Bureau of the 16th CPC Central Committee.

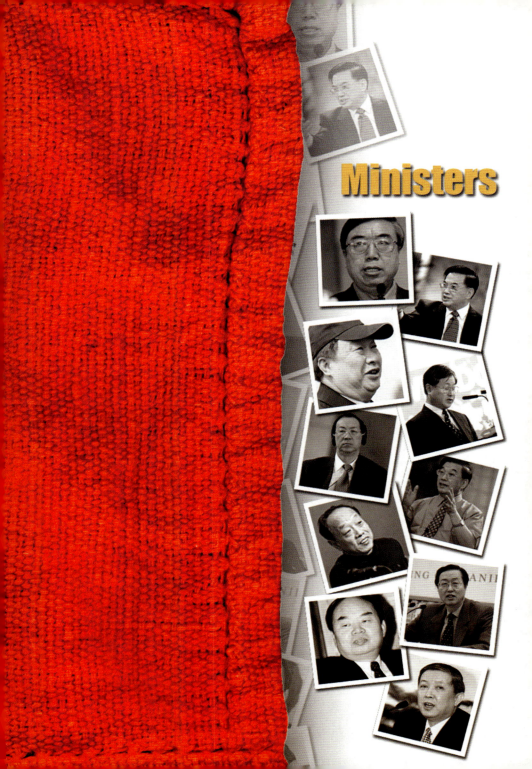
Ministers

CHINA'S POLITICAL FIGURES WHO'S WHO IN CHINA

Li Zhaoxing
"Diplomat with dreams of flight"

Title and position	Minister of Foreign Affairs
Political influence	Member, CPC Central Committee

As a youth, Foreign Affairs Minister Li Zhaoxing harboured dreams of becoming a pilot, writer or a journalist. But he eventually answered his calling as a diplomat and never faltered, as he became first a lecturer at the Chinese People's Institute of Foreign Affairs and then distinguishing himself as a diplomat on the world stage.

Born in Shandong, Mr Li has been involved in foreign affairs since completing his degree and postgraduate education in Beijing University and Beijing Institute of Foreign Languages respectively.

He started as a diplomat in 1970, when he was appointed a staff member and attaché of the Chinese Embassy in Kenya. Other postings included spells at the Chinese Embassy in the Kingdom of Lesotho and the Information Department of the Chinese Ministry of Foreign Affairs.

As one of the assistant ministers of Foreign Affairs, Mr Li was appointed the Permanent Representative, Ambassador Extraordinary and Plenipotentiary of the PRC to the United Nations in 1993.

He was later promoted to be the vice minister of Foreign Affairs where he distinguished himself in advancing Sino-America relationship as the Ambassador Extraordinary and Plenipotentiary of the PRC to the United States and eventually the Minister of Foreign Affairs in 2003.

Birth date	October 1940
Hometown	Shandong Province
Education	Bachelor's degree, Peking University, 1964
	Postgraduate, Peking Institute of Foreign Languages, 1967

Background

1967-1968	Staff member of Chinese People's Institute of Foreign Affairs
1968-1970	Worked in cadres' schools in Lishi, Shanxi Province, Shanggao, Jiangxi Province, Niutianyang Farm, Shantou, and Guangzhou Military Area Command
1970-1977	Staff member and attaché of the Chinese Embassy in Kenya
1977-1983	Third secretary, second secretary and deputy division chief of Information Department of the Chinese Ministry of Foreign Affairs
1983-1985	First secretary of the Chinese Embassy in the Kingdom of Lesotho

CHINA'S POLITICAL FIGURES WHO'S WHO IN CHINA

1985-1990	Deputy director-general and director-general of Information Department of the Chinese Ministry of Foreign Affairs, spokesman of Chinese Ministry of Foreign Affairs
1990-1993	Assistant minister of Foreign Affairs
1993-1995	Permanent Representative and Ambassador Extraordinary and Plenipotentiary of PRC to the United Nations
1995-1998	Vice minister of Foreign Affairs
1998-2001	Ambassador Extraordinary and Plenipotentiary of PRC to the United States
2001-2003	Vice minister of Foreign Affairs
2003-	Minister of Foreign Affairs

Other titles and positions

1993   Guest professor, Peking University and Nankai University

Other information

Mr Li is married with one son.

Hobbies: Playing table tennis, listening to choir, and occasionally writing poems

Favourite books: Atlas, biographies, classic tragedies and comics

Foreign languages: English, basic French and Swahili

Contact information
Address No. 2, Chaoyangmen Nandajie, Chaoyang District, Beijing, 100701
Telephone 86-10-6596 1114

Ma Kai
"Top economic theorist"

Title and position Minister in charge, State Development and Reform Commission

 "China must persist with a measurable pace of economic development."
Mr Ma Kai

Considered the top economic theorist on commodity pricing in Premier Wen Jiabao's cabinet, Mr Ma was appointed the minister in charge of State Development and Reform Commission in March 2003.

His expertise on the topic of pricing mechanisms, as well as his practical experience with implementing both price reforms and central government pricing guidelines made him the most influential pricing economist in China's leadership.

In practice, he strived to meld Marxist theory along with free market policies.

The son of a legendary first generation Chinese minister, Mr Ma is a member of the "princelings", sons and daughters of top communist party leaders, but has cultivated a reputation for honesty, affability, diligence, and above all, intellect.

Mr Ma was amongst the first group of graduate students in China in the post-Cultural Revolution period. He graduated with a masters in political economics from China's prestigious People's University in Beijing.

He started his career as a researcher in the State Commodity Pricing Bureau's Research Office in 1982 and was behind the early drafts of a strategy to implement China's new "Price Reform Plans".

Birth date	June 1946
Hometown	Jinshan County, Shanghai
Education	Masters in Economics, majoring in Politics and Economy, People's University of China, 1982

CHINA'S POLITICAL FIGURES WHO'S WHO IN CHINA

Background

1965-1970	Instructor, Beijing's Fourth Boys' Middle School
1965-	Joined the CPC
1971-1973	Sent to the May Seventh Cadre School in outer Beijing as a result of the Cultural Revolution
1973-1979	Instructor at CPC Party School of Beijing West District
1979-1982	Studied at the Political Economics department of Chinese People's University in Beijing, focusing in Questions of Pricing in Socialism
1982-1989	Researcher at State Commodity Pricing Bureau's Research Office
1989-1993	Deputy director of State Commodity Pricing Bureau
1993-1994	Vice director of State Commission of Reform for Economic System
1994-1998	Vice chairman of China Society of Youth Research
1995-1998	Vice director of State Planning Commission
1997-	Member of CPC Central Commission for Discipline Inspection
1998-2003	Vice secretary general of State Council of China
2003-	Minister in charge of State Development and Reform Commission

Other titles and positions

Mr Ma was elected as a delegate to the 15th CPC National Congress in 1997 and in the same year was made a member of the CPC Central Commission for Discipline Inspection.

Books and articles

In 1982, Mr Ma completed his highly regarded dissertation entitled *An Analysis of Factors Included in Planned Pricing.*

Mr Ma has written a number of books, including one entitled *The Collected Works of Ma Kai* (Heilongjiang Education Publishers, 1991).

Other information

Mr Ma Kai is the son of Mr Ma Mingfang, who had a distinguished career. The elder Ma was the deputy political commissar in Marshall Peng Dehuai's First Field Army. He was also part of the pre-Long March Shanxi Soviet, and later a student in the USSR. At the beginning of the Chinese Civil War (1946-1949), Mr Ma was arrested by Nationalists in the far western city Xinjiang, but was quickly rescued by Red Army commandos. In 1946, Mr Ma was named party secretary and governor of Shanxi province, and deputy political commissar of Marshall Peng Dehuai's First Field Army. In the 1950s, the Mr Ma was vice minister of the Party Central Organisation, and was later appointed deputy secretary-general of CCP Central Office and eventually, as minister of Finance and Trade.

Sell Your Events, Facilities & Services
Expand Your Market

Be at the Global Marketplace
Where Buyers Meet Sellers

22 - 24 September 2004 • Singapore Expo

Concurrent Events
Exhibition • Regional Meetings • Award Presentations • Professional Training Courses • Golf Competition

Exhibitor Profile

» Organisers
Exhibitions, Conventions, Meetings, Special Events, Festivals, Entertainment,

» Facility Operators
Exhibition & Convention Centers, Hotels, Hospitality & Tourism Facilities

» Suppliers, Contractors & Service Providers
Designers & Contractors, Equipment Rentals, Logistics, Gifts, Publications Tour Operators, Publishers, PR Agencies

Visitor Profile

» Government Agencies
Export Promotion Agencies, Chambers of Commerce and Industry, Embassies / High Commissions, National Trade Offices

» Industry & Trade Associations
Professional Societies, Marketing / Research Institutions

» Multinationals and SMEs, Importers, Exporters

» Media / Publishing Companies

» Suppliers, Contractors & Service Providers

» Travel Agencies

ROI: Save on multiple marketing trips, here's one event to meet them all!

Contact us today for more details and space bookings!
Special exhibiting privileges for association members like SACEOS and ICCA.

#13-01 Fook Hai Building
South Bridge Road, Singapore 058727
Tel: +65 6339 7383   Fax: +65 6339 2318
Email: iecm@saceos.org.sg
Website: www.saceos.org.sg

Supported by

Global Industry Associations Support

The Official Airline
SINGAPORE AIRLINES

www.iecm2004.com   Exhibition space enquiries: interfama@pacific.net.sg

"China's Ministry of Education has set three goals to promote education reforms in China's rural areas. The goals include: to promote a nine-year compulsory education and to eradicate illiteracy among the young and middle-aged people in the west; to improve the educational quality and reduce the number of dropout students in rural junior middle schools; and to cultivate rural schools into training bases to help peasants find or create jobs and to become more affluent through compulsory, professional and adult education."

Professor Zhou Ji

Zhou Ji
"Education minister and computer expert"

Title and position Minister of Education

Professor Zhou was a beneficiary of the CPC's new policy to appoint younger, more knowledgeable people to manage the country.

However, that did not detract from his sterling accomplishment in the academic field where he developed a name for himself as an expert in Computer-Aided Design (CAD) and numerical controls.

He received his bachelor and masters degrees from China's prestigious Tsinghua University and Huazhong University of Science and Technology respectively.

He also spent four years in the United States to obtain his Ph.D. From 1984, he spent 15 years in Huazhong University of Science and Technology, rising from a junior staff to becoming the president of the university.

His standing rose dramatically from year 2000, spending just two years to move from a city level official to become minister of Education in March 2003, effectively changing his role from an academic researcher and educator to become China's chief education administrator.

Birth date	August 1946
Hometown	Shanghai
Education	Bachelor of Science in Mechanical Engineering, Tsinghua University, 1970
	Masters, Huazhong University of Science and Technology (HUST), 1980
	Ph.D. State University of New York at Buffalo, USA, 1984
Professional qualifications	Professor

Background

1965-1970	Tsinghua University
1970-1978	Staff at Xinjiang Institute of Technology
1978-1980	Postgraduate studies at Huazhong University of Science and Technology (HUST)
1980-1984	Ph.D. student/candidate at State University of New York at Buffalo, USA
1984-2000	Staff and director of CAD centre / CIMS centre / Research Institute of Numerical Control, dean of School of Mechanical Engineering, vice president and president of HUST
1999-	Member of Chinese Academy of Engineering

2000-2001	Member of Standing Committee of CCP Hubei Commission, director of Hubei Bureau of Science and Technology, and general secretary of General Party Branch of Hubei Bureau of Science and Technology
2001-2002	Member of Standing Committee of CCP Hubei Commission and deputy secretary of CCP Wuhan Commission
2002-	Member of Standing Committee of CCP Hubei Commission and mayor of Wuhan City Deputy secretary of General Party branch of Ministry of Education and vice minister of Education
2003-	Minister of Education

Other titles and positions

Representative of the Ninth National People Congress of China

Chairman of Mechanical Basic Education Instructing Committee of Education Ministry in China

Commissioner of Education Committee of Chinese Engineering Academy

Books and articles

Professor Zhou's research fields include Computer Aided Design (CAD), Optimisation Design, Intelligent Design and Computer Integrated Manufacturing.

Professor Zhou is the director of more than 30 projects sponsored by the National Science Funds, National 863 Hi-Tech Program and Ph.D. Special Scientific Research Funds of the State Ministry of Education. He has also clinched four National Awards.

The CIMS Centre of HUST led by Professor Zhou is the recipient of the '1999 CACA/SME University Lead Awards'.

Professor Zhou is the author / co-author of 11 books and more than 200 academic papers.

Xu Guanhua
"Research in satellites lauded"

Title and position Minister of Science and Technology

Political influence Member, CPC Centre Committee

The minister of Science and Technology is a renowned scientist in remote sensing, after spending several years as an academic at the Chinese Academy of Sciences prior to his present appointment.

Mr Xu Guanhua was the beneficiary of a special government allowance after he was recognised by authorities as a national scientist with outstanding contributions to China. He successfully developed the earliest digital image processing system for remote sensor satellites in China.

After graduating from the Beijing Forestry University in 1963, Mr Xu went to study abroad in Stockholm, Sweden in 1979 and came back to China in 1981.

He was appointed the minister of Science and Technology in February 2001.

Birth date	December 1941
Hometown	Shanghai
Education	Bachelor degree, Beijing Institute of Forestry, 1963
Professional qualification	Research fellow

Background

1958-1963	Beijing Institute of Forestry
1963-2001	Research fellow, research professor and director of Institute of Remote Sensing Application, Beijing Institute of Forestry, vice president of Chinese Academy of Sciences, vice commissioner of State Science and Technology Commission
1979-1981	Visiting scholar at Stockholm University, Sweden
2001-	Minister of Science and Technology

Other titles and positions

Mr Xu is a member of Chinese Academy of Sciences since 1991. Mr Xu is also the director of Division of Geography Study of Chinese Academy of Sciences, director of Academic Committee of National Key Laboratory of Resource and Environmental Information System, director of Academic Committee of National Key Laboratory of Remote Sensors and Aerial Survey, deputy director of China GIS Association and editor-in-chief of *Transaction of Remote Sensors*.

Other information

Mr Xu has been engaged in resource remote sensors and geographical information system for a long time. He successfully developed the earliest digital image processing system for remote sensor satellites in China. He has also developed theories and methodologies for remote sensors integrated survey and relevant geographical mapping technologies.

He has led the formulation of the first technological regulation of remote sensing integrated survey and mapping for regenerative resources. His lead in the remote sensors integrated survey for the "Three North" protective forests project was at the forefront of remote sensor technology application. His efforts in this particular project resulted in him being awarded the first prize of National Scientific and Technological Progress by the Ministry of Forestry in 1989 and the third prize of National Scientific and Technological Progress in 1991.

"Since the eruption of the 1997 Asian financial crisis, the stability of the RMB exchange rate has not only enhanced China's economic and financial stability, but also contributed to the financial and economic stability in the Asian region and the world."

Mr Jin Renqing

Jin Renqing
"Expanded tax revenue despite lean years"

Title and position   Minister of Finance

After chalking up a list of impressive credentials over two decades of leadership in southern China's multi ethnic Yunnan Province, Mr Jin was awarded with the position of vice minister of China's powerful Ministry of Finance in 1991 at the age of 47.

He became deputy secretary general of the State Council, China's cabinet in 1995, before he was appointed the minister of Finance in March 2003. Prior to that Mr Jin was appointed to the post of vice mayor of Beijing in 1995 for a short period before Mr Liu Qi replaced him. He was also elected the honourary chairman of the 9th and 10th executive committees of the Beijing Federation of Industry and Commerce in 1996 and 1997. Also on his list of accomplishments was the deputy directorship of the Beijing Planning and Construction Committee.

Having been involved in China's tax administration for about 10 years, Mr Jin has spared no effort in raising tax revenues to keep pace with increasing government expenditure arising from efforts to stimulate economic growth and domestic demand, and to develop China's infrastructure.

Despite slow economic growth in 1998, Mr Jin and his agencies managed to expand tax revenues by 13% over the previous year. Tax collection and auditing have been further beefed up in 1999 to meet the 6.4% increase in taxation. Mr Jin urged a crack down on tax evasion and fraud in export refunding, and called for redoubled efforts to penalise corruption and clear tax arrears.

After 23 years of Chinese Communist Party membership, Mr Jin was made a standing committee member of the CPC Beijing Municipal Committee, a position to which he returned in 1997, with the added title of deputy secretary. In 1997, Mr Jin was elected an alternate member of the 15th CPC Central Committee.

Birth date	1944
Hometown	Suzhou City, Jiangsu Province
Education	Bachelor in Economics, Financial Department, Central Institute of Finance and Banking, Beijing, 1966

Background

1968-1980	Deputy director of Grain Bureau and deputy director of Financial Office of Yongsheng County, Yunnan Province
1982-	Joined the CPC
1980-1983	Magistrate of Yongsheng County, Yunnan Province
1983-1985	Deputy commissioner of Lijiang Administrative Office, Yunnan Province
1985-1991	Vice governor of Yunnan Province

1991-1995	Vice minister of Finance
1995-	Deputy secretary-general of State Council
1995-1998	Vice mayor of Beijing
1996-1997	Honourary chairman of the 9th and 10th Executive Committee of Beijing Federation of Industry and Commerce
1997-	Elected as deputy secretary of CPC Beijing Municipal Committee, elected as alternate member of the 15th CPC Central Committee
1998-	Director of State Administration of Taxation
2003-	Minister of Finance

Wang Guangtao
"Dedicated to the under-privileged"

Title and position   Minister of Construction

Political influence   Member, CPC Central Committee

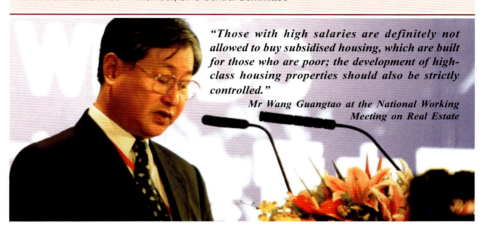

"Those with high salaries are definitely not allowed to buy subsidised housing, which are built for those who are poor; the development of high-class housing properties should also be strictly controlled."

Mr Wang Guangtao at the National Working Meeting on Real Estate

Once a vice mayor of Beijing, he was appointed the post of minister of Construction in December 2001 – a post which he has since held on to.

Armed with a masters degree from Tongji University, regarded as China's top university in construction studies, Mr Wang Guangtao's early career saw him as an engineer before he was promoted to become the deputy director of construction commission in Xuzhou, Jiangsu Province.

After joining the CPC in 1983, he was selected a vice mayor of the city of Xuzhou.

In 1989, he moved to the Ministry of Construction as a department chief. From 1998, his political career saw him become first the acting mayor of Harbin, the capital of Heilongjiang Province, and then later the vice mayor of China's capital, Beijing.

An engineer by profession, Mr Wang devoted his career to construction. In particular, Mr Wang is dedicated to advancing the infrastructure of China's city development and to improving the living conditions of the under-privileged in society.

Birth date	1943
Hometown	Shanghai
Education	Bachelor's degree, Department of Urban Construction, Tongji University, 1965
	Master's degree, Department of Road Bridge, Tongji University, 1981
Professional qualifications	Engineer

CHINA'S POLITICAL FIGURES WHO'S WHO IN CHINA

Background

1960-1965	Department of Urban Construction, Tongji University
1965-1978	Technician at Xuzhou urban construction bureau, Jiangsu Province
1978-1981	Postgraduate studies at Department of Road Bridge, Tongji University
1981-1984	Engineer, section chief, vice chief engineer and deputy director of Urban and Rural Construction Commission of Xuzhou, Jiangsu Province
1983-	Joined the CPC
1984-1989	Vice mayor of Xuzhou, Jiangsu Province
1989-1995	Department chief, chief engineer in the urban construction department of Ministry of Construction
1995-1998	Deputy secretary of CPC Harbin Committee, acting mayor, mayor of Harbin, Heilongjiang Province
1998-2001	Vice mayor of Beijing
2001-	Secretary of Leading Party Members Group of Ministry of Construction
2001-	Minister of Construction

Other titles and positions

Mr Wang is a member of the 16th CPC Central Committee.

Liu Zhijun
"On the fast track"

Title and position   Minister of Railways

Political influence   Member, CPC Central Committee

 "Communications must be improved first, only then can the country develop. This is the general rule."

Mr Liu Zhijun

As minister of Railways, Mr Liu holds considerable influence in a country where the railway is considered an important and essential mode of transport.

For close to 30 years, Mr Liu has been involved with the administration of China's railway system, first in major railway bureaus including Wuhan, Guangzhou, Zhengzhou and Shenyang, and then taking charge of the operations of railways across the whole of China in 1994.

Two years later, he was selected the vice minister of Railways before he was picked to head the ministry in March 2003.

With extensive experience in railway administration, Mr Liu was awarded the 'Outstanding entrepreneur in Liaoning Province'. His major challenge is to improve the speed and efficiency of railways across China.

Birth date	January 1953
Hometown	Ezhou City, Hubei Province

Background

1972-1994	Party secretary and director of Wuhan Railway Branch Bureau, deputy director of Political Department of Guangzhou Railway Bureau, deputy director of Zhengzhou Railway Bureau, party secretary of Hubei Provincial National Defence Commission, director and deputy party secretary of Shenyang Railway Bureau
1994-1996	Member of CPC Standing Committee of Ministry of Railways and general dispatcher
1996-2002	Vice minister of Railways
2002-2003	Party secretary of Ministry of Railways and vice minister of Railways
2003-	Minister of Railways

Other titles and positions

Mr Liu is a member of the 16th CPC Central Committee.

Honours and awards

Mr Liu was awarded the 'Outstanding entrepreneur in Liaoning Province' in 1994.

CHINA'S POLITICAL FIGURES WHO'S WHO IN CHINA

Zhang Chunxian
"Young minister"

Title and position   Minister of Communications

Political influence   Member, CPC Central Committee

 "As world communications progresses towards higher technology, technological innovations will lead China's information highway development in the 21st century."

Mr Zhang Chunxian

Very little is known about China's Minister of Communications Zhang Chunxian who received his appointment in October 2002 at the age of 49, suffice to note that he is one the youngest ministers in the country.

Mr Zhang, who graduated with a master's degree in management, was the deputy minister of Communications before he assumed his current position. Prior to that, he had several spells working in state-owned enterprises and the local government.

Birth date	1953
Hometown	Yuzhou City, Henan Province

Background

1998-2002	Deputy minister of Communications
2002-	Minister of Communications

Other titles and positions

Mr Zhang is now a member of 16th Central Committee of the CPC.

"We shall not fail, in this era of globalisation and the information age - where there is an increasing disparity between the rich and poor, the developed and developing countries, and the IT have and have-nots."

Mr Wang Xudong

CHINA'S POLITICAL FIGURES WHO'S WHO IN CHINA

Wang Xudong
"Regulating telcos is his greatest challenge"

Title and position   Minister of Information Industry

Political influence   Member, CPC Central Committee

As the minister of Information, Mr Wang Xudong's biggest task will be to supervise and regulate China's IT and telecommunications industry.

Although Mr Wang has limited experience in the information industry, he has taken on the challenge of overseeing the development of this important sector in China. Heading the ministry will be a new ball game for Mr Wang in a challenging era as foreign players slashed prices to gain market share, muscling their way into the world's largest mobile telephone market.

Mr Wang formerly worked as secretary of the Chinese Communist Youth League Committee. In October 1991, he began serving as the deputy secretary of the CPC Tianjin Municipal Committee.

In May 1993, he was re-elected the deputy secretary of the CPC Tianjin Municipal Committee. He was later transferred to the post of deputy director of the Organisation Department of the CPC Central Committee.

Since June 2000, Wang has been working as a member of the Standing Committee and secretary of the CPC Hebei Provincial Committee.

In November 2002 he became vice minister of the Information Industry. Two months later, he was promoted to the post of minister.

He is an alternate member of the 15th CPC Central Committee and member of the 16th CPC Central Committee.

Birth date   January 1946
Hometown   Yancheng City, Jiangsu Province
Education   Diploma, majoring in Systems Engineering, Tianjin Institute of Science and Technology, 1982

Background

1972-	Joined the CPC
Pre-1983	Secretary of Chinese Communist Youth League Committee and deputy secretary of CPC Committee of No. 1418 Research Institute of the Chinese PLA, director of No. 18 Research Institute of the Ministry of Electronics Industry
1983-1991	Member of Standing Committee of CPC Tianjin Municipal Committee and director of its Organisation Department
1991-1993	Deputy secretary of CPC Tianjin Municipal Committee
1993-2000	Deputy director of Organisation Department of CPC Central Committee
2000-2002	Member of Standing Committee and secretary of CPC Hebei Provincial Committee
2002-2003	Vice minister of Information Industry and secretary of CPC Committee of Ministry of Information Industry
2003-	Minister of Information Industry

Other titles and positions

Mr Wang was an alternate member of the 15th CPC Central Committee and is now a member of the 16th CPC Central Committee.

Contact information

Address #13 West Chang An Street, Beijing, China, 100804

"Another point I want to emphasise is that a well-off Chinese society and its quadrupled GDP by 2020 based on the level of 2000, first and foremost, means that China's marketplace can be quadrupled in size and total demand. Subsequently, China will then become the world's second biggest market."

Mr Lv Fuyuan's speech at the fifth WTO Ministerial Conference in Mexico

Lv Fuyuan
"Foreign trade, his concern"

Title and position   Minister of Commerce

Political influence   Member, CPC Central Committee

As the minister of the newly created Ministry of Commerce, Mr Lv Fuyuan shoulders a heavy responsibility.

The ministry was created due to China's entry into the World Trade Organisation. With his extensive market experience and training in Montreal, Canada, Mr Lv is expected to introduce policies and reform plans related to China's foreign trade, economic cooperation and foreign investments.

Mr Lv, who graduated from Jilin University, began his career in a township housing management office in Jilin Province in northeast China.

For nearly 10 years beginning from 1972, he worked as a technician for leading Chinese automaker, the Changchun First Automobile Works (FAW) Group Corporation. After his working spell there, he went on to attend a research and training course as a visiting scholar at the Ecole Polytechnic of Montreal University in Canada for two years.

When he returned, he was promoted to vice president and chief economist for FAW in 1985 and became the vice president of the China National Automobile Industrial Company in 1990.

Following his appointment in the Ministry of Education as deputy minister, in 1998, Mr Lv became deputy minister of Foreign Trade and Economic Cooperation in 2002 and remained there until he was appointed to lead the newly created Ministry of Commerce in 2003.

Birth date	October 1945
Hometown	Suihua County, Heilongjiang Province
Education	Bachelor of Science, Department of Physics, Jilin University, 1970
Professional qualifications	Senior engineer

CHINA'S POLITICAL FIGURES WHO'S WHO IN CHINA

Background

1964-1970	Studied in the Department of Physics of Jilin University
1970-1972	Worked in the Housing Management Office of Guojiadian Town, Lishu County, Jilin Province
1972-1981	Technician at Changchun First Automobile Works Manufacturing Plant
1981-1983	Attended a research and training course as a visiting scholar at the Ecole Polytechnic of Montreal University in Canada
1983-1985	Continued to engage in technical and management work of Changchun First Automobile Manufacturing Plant, serving consecutively as engineer, deputy section chief and vice director of a factory branch
1985-1990	Vice president and chief economist for Changchun First Automobile Works Manufacturing Plant
1990-1993	Vice president of China National Automobile Industrial Company
1993-1994	Member of Party Committee and director-general of Department of Automobile Industry under the Ministry of Machinery Industry
1994-1998	Vice minister of Machinery Industry
1998-2002	Deputy secretary of Party Committee and deputy minister of Ministry of Education
2002-2003	Deputy secretary of Party Committee and deputy minister of Ministry of Foreign Trade and Economic Cooperation
2003-	Minister of Commerce

Titles and positions

Mr Lv is now a member of 16th Central Committee of the CPC.

Zhou Xiaochuan
"China's bank regulator"

Title and position   Governor, People's Bank of China

Political influence   Member, CPC Central Committee

"It is our main objective to protect the interest of investors."   Mr Zhou Xiaochuan

Mr Zhou's magic in the finance industry is well-documented and felt in the "bull run" on China's stock market on the second day that Xinhua News Agency announced his posting as the chairman of the China Securities Regulatory Commission in 2000.

China's 11th governor of the People's Bank of China is highly respected by investors and those in the financial circles. He is also its first governor with a Ph.D. degree.

The Tsinghua University graduate introduced a series of reforms during his two-year tenure in the commission. These measures, which drew international praises, included the implementation of international accounting guidelines and the setting of strict guidelines in upholding China's financial regulation.

These measures greatly improved the standards of China's securities market and Mr Zhou was singled out as one of the star performers in Asian markets by *BusinessWeek* magazine.

The scholarly Mr Zhou brings with him an abundance of experience in China's banking industry. He was formerly the deputy governor of the Bank of China in 1991 and later worked at the State Administration of Foreign Exchange, the China Construction Bank, and then at the People's Bank of China.

Birth date	January 1948
Hometown	Yancheng City, Jiangsu Province
Education	Bachelor degree, Beijing Chemical Engineering Institute, 1975
	Ph.D. in Systems Engineering, Tsinghua University, 1985

CHINA'S POLITICAL FIGURES WHO'S WHO IN CHINA

Background

1986-1991	Commission member of State Commission for Restructuring Economic System
1986-1989	Assistant minister of Ministry of Foreign Trade and Economic Cooperation
1991-1995	Deputy governor, Bank of China
1995-1996	Director-general of State Administration of Foreign Exchange
1996-1998	Deputy governor, People's Bank of China
1998-2000	President and CEO, China Construction Bank
2000-2002	Chairman of China Securities Regulatory Commission
2002-	Governor of the People's Bank of China

Other titles and positions

Guest professor at Tsinghua University and the Postgraduate Faculty of the People's Bank of China

Honours and awards

Sun Yefan Award in Economic Science (the highest honour in China's Economics arena), 1994 and 1997

Asian Star by *BusinessWeek*, 2001

Li Jinhua
"Corruption buster"

Title and position   Auditor-General, National Audit Office

"The objective of the 'auditing storm' is to be responsible to the people."
Mr Li Jinhua, said during the interview on Half Hour about Economy program aired by CCTV

Mr Li Jinhua, the auditor-general of the National Audit Office, is also known as "Mr Graft Buster" for his dogged attempts in clamping down corruption. He has been given free rein to create a new auditing regime, complete with new auditing principles, regulations on incentives for auditors and rules of responsibility.

An expert in finance, Mr Li assigned 50,000 accountants to examine the records of government-controlled grain markets across the country soon after his appointment in 1998.

The results cut a swathe of fear across all levels in all government bodies.

Corruption was rampant among officials who were found to have defrauded the government of RMB 214 billion (US$25.8 billion) since 1992.

Mr Li promptly made the findings public and followed up with 14 major audit campaigns.

He turned his attention to the customs officials in the Guangdong Province, who were responsible for China's biggest smuggling network. 23 of the country's largest state-owned enterprises were also targeted.

To further ensure a sound financial system, Mr Li tightened supervision of financial institutions, subjecting the activities of the Industrial and Commercial Bank of China (ICBC) and the China Construction Bank to particular scrutiny.

The State Auditing Administration has also cracked down on the misrepresentation of fiscal accounts to ensure a reliable operation of the country's fiscal system.

CHINA'S POLITICAL FIGURES WHO'S WHO IN CHINA

Mr Li is firmly behind the opinion that false accounts and deception in the handling of budgetary revenue and expenditure are the major causes of China's current economic disorder.

His office has also tackled irregularities in the use of public funds by government departments and institutions. Such abuses include misappropriation of funds, fraudulent applications and claims, unlawful money lending and off-the-records businesses.

Not contented with simply exposing corruption, Mr Li has taken a giant step forward in calling for a revamped system that will determine managers' culpability in order to mete out the appropriate punishment.

Birth date	July 1943
Hometown	Rudong County, Jiangsu Province
Education	Postgraduate diploma, from the Banking Department of Central Institute of Finance and Banking, Beijing, 1966
Professional qualifications	Senior auditor

Background

1965-	Joined the CPC
1968-1971	Served as teacher at the Northwest China Institute of Finance and Banking
1975-1980	Deputy director of Political Department, at the No. 575 factory under Ministry of Aeronautics Industry
1980-1983	Deputy secretary of CPC Committee at the No. 575 factory under Ministry of Aeronautics Industry
1983-1985	Director of No. 575 factory under Ministry of Aeronautics Industry, director of Economic and Trade Department of Shanxi Province
1985-1998	Appointed deputy auditor-general
1998-	Auditor-general of National Audit Office

Other titles and positions

Mr Li was a delegate to the 14th CPC National Congress and a member of CPC Central Commission for Discipline Inspection. He was also elected as member of 15th CPC Central Committee in 1997.

CHINA'S POLITICAL FIGURES WHO'S WHO IN CHINA

Wu Dingfu
"Warden of China's insurance industry"

Title and position Chairman, China Insurance Regulatory Commission (CIRC)

Political influence Alternate member of CPC Central Committee

> "*We have to be wise when developing the insurance industry. Development is not merely to increase business, but also to create better business environment and quality.*"
>
> Mr Wu Dingfu

Born in a small county in Hubei Province, Mr Wu Dingfu started his career in his hometown as a teacher and the secretary-general of the China Communist Youth League (CCYL) at Wuxu Middle School in Guangji County. After several years in education, Mr Wu was promoted to be the head of Guangji County in the mid-1980s. Due to his outstanding performance in the county's developing economy, he was soon promoted to assume the position of deputy head in charge of economy and trading at Huanggang Administration Office[1], Hubei Province.

In 1990, Mr Hu was appointed the deputy director of the Audit Office, Hubei Province. Five years later, Mr Wu was promoted from local audit office to be a key member of the National Audit Office. The focus of his job scope shifted to discipline inspection.

Mr Wu entered China's insurance industry in 1998 when he was appointed the lead vice chairman of China Insurance Regulatory Commission. During the years 2000 to 2002, he left the insurance industry provisionally and worked in the Central Discipline Inspection Commission of CPC. He was one of the key members who investigated the corruption allegations in the Xiamen Yuanhua case in which several high level officials were eventually convicted and sentenced to death.

After the notorious Yuanhua case, Mr Wu returned to the insurance industry and was promoted to the chairman of China Insurance Regulatory Commission (CIRC) in November 2002. Founded in 18 November 1998, CIRC is the highest administrative and supervision department of China's insurance industry. CIRC was elevated to a ministry level in March 2003.

As the head of CIRC, Mr Wu faces four challenges to China's insurance industry. Firstly, the reform of state-owned insurance companies must be expedited. Secondly, the restrictions for foreign insurance companies have to be eased. Thirdly, optimisation of structure for China's insurance industry and the development of more insurance products and services must be achieved. Lastly, CIRC has to tackle the mammoth task of supervising insurance companies to ensure that they have good solvency levels and can pay out future claims. Mr Wu believes that a rational development of the insurance industry is the key to facing the challenges.

Mr Wu conceives that China's insurance market needs faster growth to support the nation's economic and social development, and joint-stock reforms are a major way to achieve that. "We encourage and support all qualified insurance companies to list, either abroad or at home," he says.

CHINA'S POLITICAL FIGURES WHO'S WHO IN CHINA

Mr Wu says that CIRC will selectively approve new Chinese-funded insurance companies in 2004 to bring in fresh blood, especially in the areas of health, annuities and agricultural insurance. The commission stopped approving new Chinese insurance firms a few years ago. According to him, "The number of applications to set up new firms has has capped at 20."

Other changes in the pipeline include a long-awaited proposal by the State Council to let insurers invest directly in the stock markets. "We are talking about a step-by-step approach in allowing insurance funds to enter the capital markets," Mr Wu explains.

Birth date	1946
Hometown	Guangji County, Hubei Province
Education	Bachelor of Arts, majoring in Chinese, Hubei University

Background

1967-1972	Teacher and secretary-general of the China Communist Youth League (CCYL) at Wuxu Middle School at Guangji County, Hubei Province
1972-1980	Director at the Guangji Traditional Drama Troupe
1980-1983	Deputy director at the Culture and Education Bureau, Guangji County, Hubei Province
1983-1987	Deputy head and head of Guangji County, Hubei Province
1987-1990	Deputy head of Huanggang Administration Office, Hubei Province
1990-1995	Deputy director and director of Audit Office, Hubei Province
1995-1998	Member of the CPC Party Committee of National Audit Office and director of the Discipline Inspection Department, National Audit Office
1998-2000	The lead vice chairman of China Insurance Regulatory Commission
2000-2002	Standing committee and secretary-general of the Central Discipline Inspection Commission of CPC
2002-	Chairman of China Insurance Regulatory Commission

Contact information

Address 410 Fu Cheng Men Nei Street, Xi Cheng District, Beijing, China, 100034
Telephone 86-10-6601 6688   Website www.circ.gov.cn

Shang Fulin
"Stock market maestro"

Title and position   Chairman, China Securities Regulatory Commission (CSRC)

Political influence   Alternate member of the CPC Central Committee

"The CSRC will change its style of supervision, to have a more balanced and even approach. CSRC will focus on better procedures for supervision as the stock market recovers."

Dr Shang Fulin

Born in November 1951, Dr Shang Fulin holds a Ph.D. in finance from Southwestern University of Finance and Economics, Chengdu. He was appointed the chairman of China Securities Regulatory Commission (CSRC) and a member of Monetary Policy Committee of the People's Bank of China (PBOC), China's Central Bank, in December 2002.

Dr Shang spent most of his career as a central banker at PBOC. His photographic memory for numbers left a lasting impression with Mr Zhu Rongji, then China's vice premier in 1994. In addition, Dr Shang is "well-liked figure who exudes much trustworthiness," says one of his ex-colleagues. With Mr Zhu's commendations, Dr Shang rose to become deputy governor of the central bank. While working in PBOC, he steadily rose through the ranks and served successively as deputy division chief, division chief, deputy director and director of the Planning and Budgeting Department (now Monetary Policy Department).

From 1996 to 1999, he took charge of monetary policy making and was at the helm of the design and construction of the bank's clearing and settlement system. From 1998 to 2000, he headed China's nation-wide taskforce to prepare for the Y2K in the banking industry and his effective leadership was widely lauded with the successful completion of the Y2K task. Then, after 18 years with the PBOC, he left in January 2000 to run the Agricultural Bank of China as its president for two years.

Dr Shang is well known for his theoretical research and publications on the practice of monetary policy and related areas. His major publications include *The Situational Analysis on State-owned Commercial Banks* (2002), *A Study on the Transmission Mechanism of Monetary Policy* (2000), *Encyclopedia of Financial Guarantees* (1999), *China's Success in Controlling Inflation and Its Future Policy Orientation* (1997), *The Operation, Efficiency and Development of Central Banks* (1996) and *China's Monetary Policy and Credit System of China* (1995).

The rapid development of the securities markets in China has led to the establishment of the State Council Securities Commission (SCSC) and the CSRC in October 1992. The SCSC is the State authority responsible for exercising centralised market regulations. The CSRC is the SCSC's executive branch responsible for conducting supervision and regulation of the securities markets in accordance with the law. During his first year at CSRC, Dr Shang spent his early months investigating the stock exchanges in Shanghai and Shenzhen. As opposed to the more forceful style of his predecessor, Mr Zhou Xiaochuan, Dr Shang conducted investigations and quiet reforms.

CHINA'S POLITICAL FIGURES WHO'S WHO IN CHINA

Dr Shang commented that CSRC will adjust its regulatory policies according changes in the environment - ensuring the protection of the lawful rights of investors while giving securities companies more leeway in financing and business expansion.

Birth date	3 November 1948
Hometown	Jinan City, Shandong Province
Education	Ph.D. in Finance, Southwestern University of Finance and Economics

Background

1969-1973	Services in the PLA
1973-1982	Worked in People's Bank of China, Beijing Taoyuan Branch
1982-1990	Deputy division chief and division chief at the Planning division, the Planning and Budgeting Department, People's Bank of China
1990-1993	Deputy director and director of the Planning and Budgeting Department, People's Bank of China
1993-2000	Assistant governor and deputy governor of People's Bank of China
2000-2002	President of Agricultural Bank of China
2002-	Chairman of China Securities Regulatory Commission

Contact information
Address Jin Yang Plaza 16, Jin Rong Street, Xi Cheng District, Beijing, China, 100032
Telephone 86-10-8806 1700 Website www.csrc.gov.cn

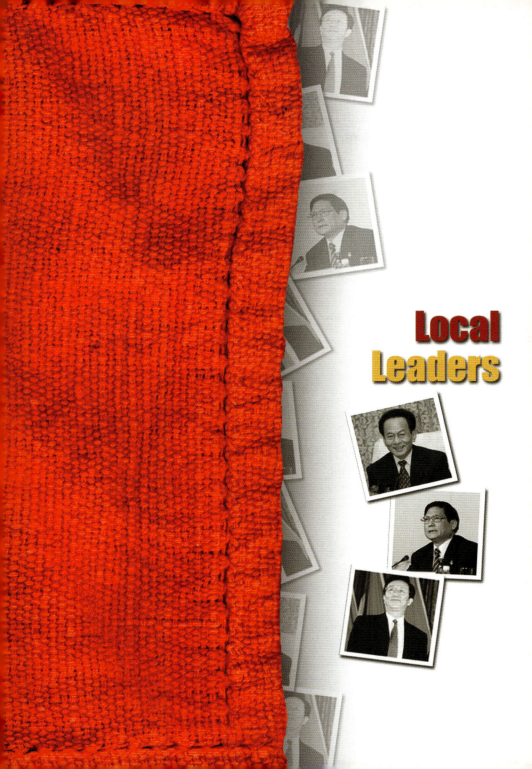

Local Leaders

"There will be no more traffic jams in Beijing in 2008."
Mr Liu Qi pledged during an interview on the Half an hour about Economy program aired by CCTV Station

CHINA'S POLITICAL FIGURES WHO'S WHO IN CHINA

Liu Qi
"Fighter and survivor"

Titles and positions	Mayor of Beijing
	Secretary, CPC Beijing Municipal Committee
Political influence	Member, Political Bureau of the CPC Central Committee

The mayor of Beijing caught the public eye in 2003 when he found himself in the centre stage for things both good and bad – Beijing's successful bid for the 2008 Olympics and then the severe acute respiratory syndrome (SARS) which plagued the world.

An engineer by profession, Mr Liu Qi went through the ranks from a technician to becoming a manager of Wuhan Iron and Steel Company, one of the most important state-owned enterprises (SOE) in China.

He was promoted to become the minister of Metallurgy in 1993. Five years later, he was given charge of China's political and cultural capital, Beijing where he has been waging a battle to solve the transportation woes in the capital city. Mr Liu faces strong expectations to prepare the 2008 Beijing Olympics in a few short years.

Birth date	November 1942
Hometown	Wujin City, Jiangsu Province
Education	Bachelor in Engineering, majoring in Iron Smelting, from the Metallurgical Department of Beijing Institute of Iron and Steel Engineering, 1964
	Postgraduate Diploma, majoring in Iron Smelting, from the Metallurgical Department of Beijing Institute of Iron and Steel Engineering, 1968
Professional qualifications	Senior engineer (Professor rank)

Background

1959-1964	Student at the Metallurgical Department of Beijing Institute of Iron and Steel Engineering, majoring in Iron Smelting
1964-1968	Postgraduate of the Metallurgical Department of Beijing Institute of Iron and Steel Engineering, majoring in Iron Smelting
1968-1978	Gas controller, furnace-man and founder of No. 2 blast furnace, Wuhan Iron and Steel Company
1975-	Joined the CPC
1978-1983	Technician and deputy head of No. 3 blast furnace, Wuhan Iron and Steel Company Committee

CHINA'S POLITICAL FIGURES WHO'S WHO IN CHINA

1983-1985	Deputy director of Steel Works and Head, Production Department, Wuhan Iron and Steel Company
1985-1990	First deputy manager of Wuhan Iron and Steel Company, member of Standing Committee of the company's CPC Committee
1990-1993	Manager of Wuhan Iron and Steel Company, member of Standing Committee of the Company's CPC Committee
1993-1998	Minister of Metallurgy, secretary of Leading Party Members' Group of the Ministry of Metallurgical Industry
1998-1998	Deputy secretary of CPC Beijing Municipal Committee and a candidate for the mayor of Beijing
1998-1999	Deputy secretary of CPC Beijing Municipal Committee and vice mayor of Beijing
1999-2002	Deputy secretary of CPC Beijing Municipal Committee and mayor of Beijing
2002-2002	Secretary of CPC Beijing Municipal Committee and mayor of Beijing
2002-	Member of Political Bureau of CPC Central Committee, secretary of CPC Beijing Municipal Committee and mayor of Beijing

Other titles and positions

Mr Liu was an alternate member of the 14th CPC Central Committee and member of the 15th CPC Central Committee. He is now a member of the 16th CPC Central Committee and a member of the Political Bureau of the 16th CPC Central Committee.

"In the next eight years, Tianjin will develop quickly through a 'three-step' strategy. The first step is to realise an average GDP of US$3,000 at the end of 2003. The second step is to double the GDP and personnel income of the year 2000. The third step is to realise an average GDP of US$6,000 by the end of 2010."

Mr Zhang Lichang at the third meeting of the eighth Tianjin Municipal People's Congress

CHINA'S POLITICAL FIGURES WHO'S WHO IN CHINA

Zhang Lichang
"Bringing in the dough"

Titles and positions	Mayor of Tianjin
	Secretary, CPC Tianjin Municipal Committee
	Chairman, Standing Committee of the Tianjin Municipal People's Congress
Political influence	Member, Political Bureau of the CPC Central Committee

The mayor of Tianjin, has been in the hot seat since 1993. But the feisty mayor is going all out to revitalise the old city by developing it into an international port with an average GDP of US$6,000 by 2010.

Mr Zhang is the head and the CPC's party chief of Tianjin, a key city in north China and one of China's municipal cities.

Although he is a Hebei native, Mr Zhang has spent much time in Tianjin, having first studied at the Tianjin Metallurgical Industry School and then kicking off his political career in the same city.

He joined the Communist Youth League Committee (CYLC) of Tianjin Seamless Steel Tube Mill where he got to know President Hu Jintao. Due to his experience at CYLC, Mr Zhang is thought to be closely associated to President Mr Hu Jintao.

Mr Zhang was later promoted to take charge first of the Metallurgical Industry of Tianjin, and then the Tianjin Economic Commission.

Birth date	July 1939
Hometown	Nanpi County, Hebei Province
Education	Junior college education, majoring in Economic Management, from Beijing Economic Correspondence University, 1968

Background

1958-1960	Student and teacher at the Tianjin Metallurgical Industry School
1960-1966	Deputy secretary of committee and CYLC, head of power section at Tianjin Seamless Steel Tube Mill
1966-	Joined the CPC
1966-1968	Deputy director of Tianjin Seamless Steel Tube Mill (Sent to do manual labour for a period during this time)
1968-1972	Workshop director and construction section chief of Tianjin Seamless Steel Tube Mill
1972-1980	Deputy secretary of Party Committee of Tianjin Seamless Steel Tube Mill and director of the Mill
1980-1983	Member of Standing Committee of the Party Committee and deputy director-general of Tianjin Municipal Metallurgical Industry Bureau

1983-1985	Deputy secretary of Party Committee and director-general of Tianjin Municipal Metallurgical Industry Bureau, deputy director-general and director-general of Tianjin Municipal Economic Commission
1985-1986	Vice mayor of Tianjin and director-general of Tianjin Municipal Economic Commission
1986-1989	Vice mayor of Tianjin and concurrently secretary of Industrial Working Committee of CPC Tianjin Municipal Committee (studied at Beijing Economic Correspondence University, majoring in Economic Management as a part-time student from January 1987 to January 1989)
1989-1993	Deputy secretary of CPC Tianjin Municipal Committee, vice mayor of Tianjin and director-general of Tianjin Port Committee
1993-1997	Deputy secretary of CPC Tianjin Municipal Committee and mayor of Tianjin
1997-1998	Secretary of CPC Tianjin Municipal Committee and mayor of Tianjin
1998-2002	Secretary of CPC Tianjin Municipal Committee and chairman of Standing Committee of Tianjin Municipal People's Congress
2002-	Member of Political Bureau of CPC Central Committee, secretary of CPC Tianjin Municipal Committee and chairman of Standing Committee of Tianjin Municipal People's Congress

Other titles and positions

Mr Zhang was an alternate member of the 12th and 13th CPC Central Committees and a member of the 14th and 15th CPC Central Committees. He is now a member of the 16th CPC Central Committee and a member of its Political Bureau.

"Another immediate measure to ensure Shanghai becomes an international financial centre is to convince multinational companies to shift their regional headquarters to the city."

Mr Chen Liangyu

Chen Liangyu
"Coming into his own"

Titles and positions	Mayor of Shanghai
	Secretary, CPC Shanghai Municipal Committee
Political influence	Member, Political Bureau of the CPC Central Committee

The new mayor of Shanghai, China's largest city and economic centre is said to have a close relationship with former President Jiang Zemin. Mr Chen Liangyu is also a member of the Political Bureau of the CPC Central Committee.

As the new head of China's economic centre, Mr Chen envisions Shanghai as a world-class city and has on more than one occasion voiced his ambitions for the city to become an international economic, financial, trading and shipping centre.

After graduating from a military college, Mr Chen studied to become an architectural specialist in the army. He spent his early years in a machinery factory in Shanghai, joining the CPC in 1980. He started his political career in Shanghai, spending much of his time on the management of state-owned enterprises.

Birth date	October 1946
Hometown	Ningbo City, Zhejiang Province
Education	Bachelor in Engineering, majoring in Architectural Structure from the Architecture Department of the PLA Institute of Logistics Engineering, 1968
Professional qualifications	Engineer

Background

1963-1968	Student at Architecture Department of the PLA Institute of Logistics Engineering majoring in Architectural Structure
1968-1970	Soldier in the PLA army unit No. 6716
1970-1983	Worker, designer and deputy section chief of infrastructure in Shanghai Pengpu Machinery Factory (studied at the Engineering Structure Department of Tongji University from February 1979 to January 1980)
1980-	Joined the CPC
1983-1984	Deputy director of Shanghai Pengpu Machinery Factory and deputy secretary of CPC Committee of Shanghai Metallurgical and Mining Machinery Corporation (studied in a cadres' training program at the Party School of the First Bureau of Electrical Machinery from September 1982 to April 1983)

CHINA'S POLITICAL FIGURES WHO'S WHO IN CHINA

1984-1985	Secretary of CPC Committee of Shanghai Electrical Appliances Corporation
1985-1987	Deputy director of Retired Cadre Bureau of the CPC Shanghai Municipal Committee
1987-1992	Deputy party secretary and head of Huangpu District, Shanghai (studied in the College of Public Policies, Birmingham University, UK, from January 1992 and September 1992)
1992-1992	Deputy secretary-general of CPC Shanghai Municipal Committee
1992-1996	Deputy secretary of CPC Shanghai Municipal Committee
1996-2001	Deputy secretary of CPC Shanghai Municipal Committee and vice mayor of Shanghai
2001-2002	Deputy secretary of CPC Shanghai Municipal Committee and acting mayor of Shanghai
2002-	Deputy secretary of CPC Shanghai Municipal Committee, secretary of CPC Shanghai Municipal Committee, member of the Political Bureau of CPC Central Committee and Mayor of Shanghai

Other titles and positions

Mr Chen was an alternate member of the 15th CPC Central Committee and is currently a member of the 16th CPC Central Committee and of its Political Bureau.

Zhang Dejiang
"Chief of Guangdong province"

Title and position   Secretary, Guangdong Provincial Party Committee

Political influence   Member, Political Bureau of the CPC Central Committee

 "Entrepreneurs should aim to make history in helping China's economic development."

Mr Zhang Dejiang at the Forum of Guangdong Entrepreneurs (April 21, 2003)

His position as the party chief in the Guangdong Province, one of China's most important and strategic economic centres, is an indication of the influence this man wields.

Mr Zhang's education was in the social sciences. He first studied Korean language at Yanbian University in the Jilin province. Later, he left for North Korea to pursue economics at the Kim Il Sung Comprehensive University of Democratic People's Republic of Korea (DPRK).

He was eventually made a vice minister of Civil Affairs, where he stayed for five years before he was appointed party chief of his hometown province, Jilin, an impoverished province in northeast China for a period of eight years.

His big break came in 1998 when he became secretary of the Zhejiang Provincial Party Committee. Zhejiang happened to be the most "capitalistic" province in China, with close to 70% of its GDP coming from state-owned enterprises.

At the end of 2002, his experience in Zhejiang was sought when he was assigned to become party chief of Guangdong, a province with a strong economy driven mainly by private enterprises.

He has stated that his objective for Guangdong is to become not just an economic powerhouse but a cultural centre as well.

Birth date	November 1946
Hometown	Tai'an County, Liaoning Province
Education	Diploma, majoring in the Korean language, from the Yanbian University, Jilin Province, China, 1975
	Bachelor in Economics, from the Economics Department of the Kim Il Sung Comprehensive University, DPRK, 1980
Professional qualifications	Lecturer

CHINA'S POLITICAL FIGURES WHO'S WHO IN CHINA

Background

1968-1970	Sent to the Taiping Brigade of Luozigou Commune of Wangqing County, Jilin Province, to work in the fields as a young intellectual
1970-1972	Secretary of Propaganda Group and Communist Youth League Branch, secretary of the Wangqing County Revolutionary Committee of Jilin Province
1971-	Joined the CPC
1972-1975	Student of Yanbian University, majoring in the Korean language
1975-1978	Deputy secretary of General Party Branch of the Korean Language Department of Yanbian University, member of Standing Committee of its Party Committee and vice chairman of its revolutionary committee.
1978-1980	Student at the Economics Department of the Kim Il Sung Comprehensive University of the DPRK and secretary of Party branch of the Chinese students studying in the university
1980-1983	Member of Standing Committee of Yanbian University's Party Committee and vice president of university
1983-1985	Member of Standing Committee of the Yanbian Prefecture's Party Committee and concurrently deputy secretary of Yanji city's Party Committee
	Deputy secretary of Yanbian Prefectural Party Committee, Jilin Province
1985-1986	Vice minister of Civil Affairs and deputy secretary, Ministry's Leading Party Members' Group
1986-1990	Deputy secretary of Jilin Provincial Party Committee and concurrently secretary of Yanbian Prefectural Party Committee
1990-1995	Secretary of Jilin Provincial Party Committee
1995-1998	Secretary of Jilin Provincial Party Committee and chairman of Standing Committee of the Jilin Provincial People's Congress
1998-1998	Secretary of Zhejiang Provincial Party Committee
1998-2002	Member of Political Bureau of CPC Central Committee and secretary of Guangdong Provincial Party Committee

Other titles and positions

Mr Zhang was an alternate member of the 14th CPC Central Committee and member of the 15th CPC Central Committee. He is now a member of the 16th CPC Central Committee and member of its Political Bureau.

Sheraton Grand Tai Ping Yang Hotel Shanghai, an Int'l 5-star hotel sits strategically between downtown and Hongqiao Int'l Airport (12mins), and the new citywide freeway which provides easy access to Pudong Int'l Airport (45mins) and SNIEC Pudong (35mins). Shanghai Intex, Shanghai Int'l Trade Center, Shanghaimart, and nearby shopping centers are all within walking distance. The Sheraton Grand offers 496 elegant and comfortable guestrooms including suites with 9 restaurant & lounge/bar. It also boasts a Grand Ballroom and 13 meeting rooms with total space area of 1,452sqm.

A GREAT HOTEL BECAME GRAND
(Formerly The Westin Tai Ping Yang)

5 Zunyi Nan Road
Shanghai 200336 P.R. China
Tel: 86 21 6275 8888
Fax: 86 21 6275 5420
EMAIL: sheratongrand@uninet.com.cn
WEB: www.sheratongrand-shanghai.com

Other Influential People

While they may not necessary be the wealthiest in China, the contributions of this group of economists, educators, attorneys and artists' cannot be underestimated.

China holds deep respect for its intellectual and professional class. Its' economists are influential in shaping the country's policies, and guiding China's financial systems.

Its academia are widely consulted on major policies in the country and are highly respected for their contributions to the prestigious universities and research institutions they lead.

China's professional class especially the legal professionals are major contributors to a legal system that promotes China's economic growth.

China is not all work and no play. Its culture and arts are widely appreciated. The arts, entertainment and media scenes appear to be the few realms where freedom of expression has taken root. Films, performances and music by some of China's finest are basking in the international limelight. The foreknowledge, insight and artistry mapped out by these people are providing China with the catalytic elements towards an even greater civilisation.

Li Yining Peking University
"Leading China's radical economic reforms"

Titles and positions
Professor and Dean of Guanghua School of Management, Peking University (PKU)
Vice chairman of the Financial and Economic Committee of National People's Congress
Science adviser to the Environmental Protection Commission of the State Council
Adviser to the National Environmental Protection Agency
Member of the China Council for International Cooperation on Environment and Development
Vice president of Chinese Association for International Understanding
Member of the Standing Committee of National People's Congress
Vice chairman of the China Democratic League
Vice chairman of the China Association
Vice chairman of the China Association for International Exchange
Member (on behalf of China) of the China Environment and Development International Cooperation Commission

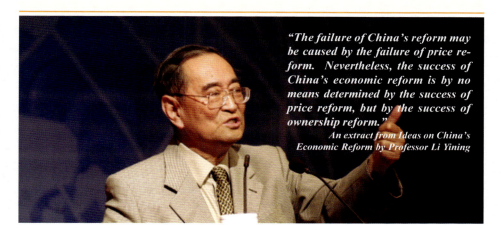

"The failure of China's reform may be caused by the failure of price reform. Nevertheless, the success of China's economic reform is by no means determined by the success of price reform, but by the success of ownership reform."
An extract from Ideas on China's Economic Reform by Professor Li Yining

Acclaimed to be the most famous and influential economist in China, Professor Li also sits as the vice chairman of the Financial and Economic Committee in the National People's Congress. He has been widely lauded for introducing moves that were pivotal in China's economic reform.

Born in November 1933, Professor Li Yining graduated from China's prestigious Peking University in 1955 and has held the posts of assistant professor, associate professor, professor, and dean successively.

Professor Li's major contributions to China's economic reform and development can be highlighted in three aspects.

Firstly, through comparative studies between China and western countries, Professor Li developed the theory of disequilibrium in economics and applied it to illuminate the functions of China's economy.

Next, Professor Li pointed out that the primary task for China's economy reform lies in the reform of ownership, emphasising on corporate ownership transparency. This viewpoint is embodied in his book, *Ideas on China's Economic Reform*. Since this notable revelation, China has been paying more attention to the growth of non-state owned economies.

Finally, Professor Li developed the share-holding theory and made relevant policy proposals which have helped propel the reform and growth of China's economy. Because of his advocacy in the share-holding theory, he is also known both in China and overseas as the distinguished "Mr Stock Market Li".

Professor Li has not only contributed significantly to China's economic policies, but has also emphasised the role of ethics in China's economy. He pointed out, "There are two foundations on which efficiency is built – one is the material and the other moral. With material foundation alone, people can only get ordinary efficiency, whereas with moral foundation, they can obtain extraordinary efficiency."

Because of his insights in economics and exceptional contribution to China's economic landscape, Professor Li has been awarded many prizes, including the highest award of economics in China named after the notable economist Sun Yefan and International Academic Prize of the Fukuoka Asian Cultural Prizes.

Birth date	22 November 1930
Hometown	Yizheng City, Jiangsu Province
Education	Bachelor of Arts, majoring in Economics, Peking University, 1955
	Honourary Doctorate, Hong Kong Polytechnic University, 1998

Background

1951-1955	Student at the Department of Economics, Peking University
1955-1983	Assistant professor, lecturer, associate professor at Peking University
1983-	Professor at Peking University
1985-1992	Dean of the Department of Economic Management, Peking University
1988-	Science adviser to the Environmental Protection Commission of the State Council
1988-	Member of the Standing Committee of National People's Congress
1991-	Member of the China Council for International Cooperation on Environment and Development
1992-1997	Vice chairman of the Law Committee of National People's Congress
1993-1994	Dean of College of Business and Management, Peking University
1993-	Vice president of Chinese Association for International Understanding
1993-	Adviser to the National Environmental Protection Agency
1994-	Dean of Guanghua School of Management, Peking University
1998-	Vice chairman of the Financial and Economic Committee of National People's Congress

Honours and awards

National expert with outstanding devotion, 1984

Golden Triangle Prize, 1987

Sun Yefan Award for Economics, "Outline of Mid-Term Economic Restructuring in China", 1989

First-class award for Philosophy and Social Sciences given by the Beijing Municipality, "Major Contemporary Schools of Economics in the West", 1987

First-class award for Scientific Achievement given by the State Commission for Education, "Research on Educational Economics", 1990

First-class award for Philosophy and Social Sciences given by the Beijing Municipality, "Modern Economic Theories in the West", 1991

First-class award for Philosophy and Social Sciences given by the Beijing Municipality, "Economic Growth and Fluctuation in China", 1995

Other information

Married to Ms He Yuchun, a senior engineer at Architectural Design and Research Institute of Peking University. They have a son and a daughter.

Contact information

Address Guanghua School of Management,
No.504, Building 47, Zhongguan Yuan, Peking University, Beijing, China, 100871
Telephone 86-10-6275 1664 / 6275 2967   Facsimile 86-10-6275 1463

OTHER INFLUENTIAL PEOPLE WHO'S WHO IN CHINA

Lin Yifu (Justin) Peking University
"Shaping the economic landscape of China"

Titles and positions Founder and Director, China Centre for Economic Research, Peking University

 "We will realise 'Xiao Kang' (a Chinese term referring to the status of simple prosperity) only if the common citizen has realised Xiao Kang."

Professor Lin Yifu

Professor Lin Yifu is the founder and director of China Centre for Economic Research at Peking University, China's most famous economic research institute and a free market think tank.

Born in Taiwan, Professor Lin received his MBA degree in 1978 from the National Chengchi University. Following this, Professor Lin embarked on a journey that will forever change his life.

So intense was his belief in the emergence of 'Great China' that he fled Taiwan and swam across the Taiwan Straits to Mainland China in 1979. He was banned from returning to Taiwan. "If I stayed in Taiwan, I could serve only 20 million people. But by coming to the Mainland, I can serve both one billion people here and 20 million people in Taiwan," Professor Lin said in explanation of his famous swim many years ago.

Despite this tumultuous phase of his life, he completed his masters in economic studies in China's prestigious Peking University in 1982.

Professor Lin then continued his Ph.D. studies at the Department of Economics in the University of Chicago, making him one of the first Chinese from Mainland China to receive a western Ph.D. in China after the Cultural Revolution.

Under the supervision of Professor Theodore W. Schultz, (1979 Nobel Laureate), his research interests centred on institutional economics and agricultural economics. After receiving his doctorate in 1986, he spent another year as a post-doctoral researcher in Yale University before returning to China in 1987.

Professor Lin's contributions to China's agricultural economic reform and development are truly commendable. As one of China's most dignified economists, he is the principal behind the drafting of many important regulations relating to China's economic reform.

Recently in March 2004, while giving a joint seminar with Mr Wang Yifu, vice governor of Fujian Province, on the Taiwan issue, Professor Lin shared his views that the best way to develop Taiwan in the future would be to combine Taiwin's capital and technology with the low cost labour and resources of Mainland China.

He has received numerous accolades, including the highest award of economics in China named after the eminent economist Sun Yefan.

OTHER INFLUENTIAL PEOPLE WHO'S WHO IN CHINA

Birth date	15 October 1952
Hometown	Yilan City, Taiwan
Education	MBA, National Chengchi University, Taiwan, 1978
	MA, Political Economy, Beijing University, 1982
	Ph.D., Economics, University of Chicago, 1986

Background

1984-1986	Research assistant, Economics Department, University of Chicago
1986-1987	Postdoctoral fellow, Economic Growth Centre, Yale University
1987-1989	Head of Department of Economic Growth Studies, Development Institute, Research Centre for Rural Development (RCRD)
	Deputy director of Development Institute, RCRD of the State Council
1987-1993	Associate professor at Peking University
1989-1993	Visiting associate professor at Department of Economics and Centre for Chinese
1990-1994	Studies, University of California, Los Angeles
	Deputy director of Department of Rural Economic Development, Development Research Centre of the State Council
1990-	Adjunct professor at Australian National University
1993-	Professor at Peking University
1994-	Fellow at Centre for International Food and Agricultural Policy, University of Minnesota
	Founder and director of China Centre for Economic Research, Peking University
1994	Visiting professor at Department of Economics, Duke University
1996	Programme director of 21st SEANZA (South East Asia, New Zealand, and Australia) Central Banking Course in Kunming and Beijing, China
1997-	Professor at Hong Kong University of Science and Technology

Memberships

American Economics Association

American Agricultural Economics Association

Chinese Economists Society (USA)

East Asian Economic Association

Econometric Society

International Association of Agricultural Economists

Royal Economic Society

Association for Comparative Economic Studies

Economic History Association

OTHER INFLUENTIAL PEOPLE WHO'S WHO IN CHINA

Fellowships

Postdoctoral Fellowship, Rockefeller Foundation, 1986-1987

Prince Fellowship, 1982-1986

Other information

Married with two children

Contact information

Address: China Centre for Economic Research, Langrun Park, Peking University, Beijing, China, 100871
Department of Economics, School of Business and Management,
Hong Kong University of Science and Technology, Clear Water Bay, Kowloon, Hong Kong
Telephone 86-10-6275-1475; 852-2358-7608   Facsimile 86-10-6275-1474; 852-2358-2084
Email jlin@ccer.pku.edu.cn

Wu Jinglian
Development Research Centre of the State Council
"The knight who liberated China's financial markets"

Titles and positions
Senior Research Fellow, Development Research Centre of the State Council of P. R. China
Professor of Economics, Graduate School of Chinese Academy of Social Sciences
Baosteel Chair Professor of Economics and member of the Academic Council, China Europe International Business School (CEIBS)
Chairman of Committee of Academy and Management, Shanghai Institute of Law and Economics
Member of Standing Committee of the Chinese People's Political Consultative Conference
Deputy Director of Economic Committee, CPPCC

 "In the market economy, we should diminish the role of government, allowing enterprises and the private sector to become the backbone of investment." Professor Wu Jinglian, expressing his view that the private sector should play a more prominent role in China's economic development (November 2003)

Professor Wu Jinglian is probably best known for being the first intellectual to advocate the idea of a market economy in China.

Way back in 1992, Professor Wu held a discussion with the former President Jiang Zemin and former Prime Minister Zhu Rongji to broach the topic of "Socialism Market Economy." This concept has since formed the basis of China's economic reform.

During his speech on "The analysis and prospective outlook of China's Economy - How to achieve stable and efficient economic growth" in 30 November 2003, Professor Wu argued that in the short-term, China's economic development will go well with possible annual growth exceeding 8.5%; but in the mid and longer-term, economic growth will encounter setbacks due to the conflicts, problems and risks derived from low economic efficiency. The key to reducing such risks, according to Professor Wu, lies in sustainable and efficient growth. The way to achieve higher efficiency would be to establish a sound economic system.

Professor Wu Jinglian has been the senior research fellow at Development Research Centre of the State Council since 1984. He also serves as the professor of economics at the graduate school of the Chinese Academy of Social Sciences, and also holds the Baosteel chair for professor of economics at China Europe International Business School (CEIBS).

As the chief economist of China International Capital Co Ltd (CICC), Professor Wu is also invited to serve as an independent director at the boards of several key Chinese companies.

Professor Wu graduated from China's prestigious Fudan University with a major in economics in 1954.

OTHER INFLUENTIAL PEOPLE WHO'S WHO IN CHINA

He was a visiting fellow at Yale University between 1983 and 1984. His other research fellowships include spending time in the Massachusetts Institute of Technology, Stanford University and Oxford University.

His main research interests are focused on the areas of theoretical economics, comparative institutional analysis, and theory and policy of China's economic reform.

He is the author of several books, including *Reform: Now at a Critical Point in 2001* and *Fifteen Critical Issues of the Reform of SOEs in 1999*.

Due to his distinguished contributions to China's market economy, Professor Wu is widely revered as "Mr Market Wu".

Birth date	24 January 1930
Hometown	Nanjing City, Jiangsu Province
Education	Bachelor in Arts, majoring in Economics, Fudan University, 1954

Background

1954-1983	Assistant research fellow, associate research fellow and research fellow at Chinese Academy of Sciences (subsequently name changed to Chinese Academy of Social Sciences)
1983-1984	Visiting fellow at the Department of Economics, Yale University, USA
1984-	Professor of economics at the graduate school of Chinese Academy of Sciences
	Senior research fellow at Development Research Centre of the State Council, China
1996-	Baosteel chair professor of economics and member of the Academic Council of CEIBS

Memberships

Member of International Academy of Management
Chairman of Committee of Academy and Management, Shanghai Institute of Law and Economics
Member of Standing Committee of the Chinese People's Political Consultative Conference (CPPCC)
Deputy director of Economic Committee, CPPCC

Contact information
Address 225 Chaoyang Men Internal Street, Dongcheng District, Beijing, China, 100010
Telephone 86-10-6527 0900 Email wjlian@ceibs.edu

Zhang Weiying Peking University
"The awakening of a new Chinese economy"

Titles and positions
Professor of Economics and Executive Associate Dean, Guanghua School of Management, Peking University
Director of the Institute of Business Research, Peking University

 "The motivating force behind the development of economy came from the efficiency of two aspects: allocation and production."
Professor Zhang at the 4th annual conference of Chinese Enterprisers Forum held in Yabuli, Heilongjiang province (5 February 2004)

Professor Zhang Weiying is the first associate dean at Guanghua School of Management of Peking University and the director of Institute of Business Research at Peking University. As a Ph.D. graduate in economics from Oxford University, he is a widely recognised authority on the theory of firm and ownership reforms in China, in particular, his theory of "capital-hiring-labour", "management selection" and the relationship between "ownership and reputation".

During the fourth annual conference of the Chinese Enterprises Forum on 5 February 2004, Professor Zhang pointed out that the future of Chinese enterprises depends on whether they can seize the opportunity to harness high technology. Furthermore, the future of the Chinese economy will depend on whether China's enterprises can become global multi-national corporations. Professor Zhang also warned that its enterprises will be placed in a precarious position if no efforts were made to boost research and development.

Professor Zhang graduated from the Northwestern University at the Xi'an province of China with a bachelor degree in 1982 and a masters degree two years later. From 1984 to 1990, Professor Zhang worked at the Economic System Reform Institute of China (ESRIC), under the State Commission for Restructuring Economic System and published several influential articles.

In 1984, he became the first Chinese economist to propose the "dual-tracking price system reform". He is also known for his contributions to macro-control policies, ownership reforms and entrepreneurship studies. Having published five books and numerous academic articles, Professor Zhang has been the most cited economist in Chinese academic journals since 1995.

Between 1990 and 1994, Professor Zhang pursued his Ph.D. studies at Oxford University under the supervision of Professor James Mirrlees (1996 Nobel Laureate) and Professor Donald Hay. Subsequently, he co-founded the China Centre for Economic Research at Peking University in 1994. He stayed with the centre for another three years before moving to the Guanghua School of Management. There, he focused on the research of industrial organisation, corporate governance and information economics.

Professor Zhang's theories have been instrumental to the progress of enterprise reforms and economic development in China. With involvement in government and the private sector, Professor Zhang is indisputably one of the most esteemed economists in China.

OTHER INFLUENTIAL PEOPLE WHO'S WHO IN CHINA

Birth date	10 January 1959
Hometown	Wubao County, Shaanxi Province
Education	Bachelor in Arts, majoring in Economics, Northwestern University, China, 1982
	Masters of Arts, majoring in Economics, Northwestern University, China, 1984
	M. Phil., majoring in Economics, New College, Oxford University, 1992
	D. Phil., majoring in Economics, Nuffield College, Oxford University, 1994

Background

1984-1985	Research assistant at The Economic System Reform Institute of China (ESRIC) (under the State Commission for Restructuring Economic System), Beijing
1986-1988	Research fellow at ESRIC, Beijing
1988-1990	Senior research fellow (equivalent to associate professor) and division chief at ESRIC, Beijing
1990-1994	Student at Oxford University, England.
1994-1997	Professor of economics at China Centre for Economic Research, Peking University

Memberships

Member of the advisory board on Enterprise Reform to the State Commission for Restructuring Economic system

Consultant to the Department of Enterprises of the State Economic and Trade Commission

Local consultant to the World Bank Project on Chinese State-owned Enterprises Reform

Member of the advisory board for the State Informatisation Committee

Member of the advisory board for Telecommunication Law Drafting

Honours and awards

The Man of the Year in Chinese Economy, by China Centre TV Station, 2002

The National Science Fund for Distinguished Young Scholars, by Natural Science Foundation of China, 2000

The George Webb Medley Prize for the best thesis, Oxford University, 1992

The Lionel Robbins Memorial Scholarship (offered by LSE), 1992-1994

Nuffield Funded Studentship, 1992-1994

The World Bank Graduate Scholarship, 1990-1992

The Excellent Paper Prizes (two papers) by the Editorial Board of China: Reform and Development, Beijing, China, 1988

The National Young Economists Prize for the best thesis, China, 1985

The National Young Economists Prize for the best thesis, China, 1984

Contact information

Address Guanghua School of Management, Peking University, Beijing, China, 100871
Telephone 86-10-6275 1664 / 6275 6257   Facsimile 86-10-6275 1470   Email wyzhang@pku.edu.cn

Striking a deal with Confidence

Credit Checks

Need to check out the background, credit and history of your competitors, distributors, suppliers and potential partners in China? First Link International's Credit Investigation Service covers all cities across China - both public and private companies - helping you minimise your risk when collaborating with a new partner.

Business matching

Finding good partners and building strong business networks in China are the most vital element in business in China. As such, the right partners will determine the success of your venture in China. First Link International's specialised partner sourcing service will ensure you find the right partner - be it a supplier, buyer, or a long term strategic partner.

First Link International

CHINA BUSINESS INTELLIGENCE & CORPORATE SERVICES
5 Shenton Way
#37-02 UIC Building
Singapore 068808
Tel: (65) 6358 2289
www.1st-link.com

Hu Angang Tsinghua University
"The birth of a modern Chinese household"

Titles and positions	Professor and director, Development Research Academy for the 21st Century, Tsinghua University
	Director, Centre for China Studies, Chinese Academy of Sciences

Professor Hu Angang is currently the director of Development Research Academy for the 21st Century at Tsinghua University and the director of Centre for China Studies at Chinese Academy of Sciences. He is hailed as one of China's most revered economists and is widely perceived as an expert on China studies, owing to his much quoted *Report on China Studies*.

These reports provide deep insights on the plight of the masses and China's provincial and higher level officials are known to look to the reports to provide guidance for their decision-making.

Professor Hu sees five big challenges for China: the widening gap between rural and urban areas; the increasing disparity between different regions; unbalanced economic and social development; over-exploitation of resources and environment, and increasing unemployment figures.

"The new concept of people-centred development should focus on improving the quality of people's lives, instead of just increasing the per capita gross domestic product (GDP)," Professor Hu says, "The relentless push for per capita GDP growth usually overlook problems such as the increasing gap between the rich and the poor, unbalanced regional development and unfair social distribution," he adds.

After his graduation from middle school, he was sent to work at Beidahuang farm at Hei Long Jiang province. Subsequently, he became part of the North China Geology team during the Cultural Revolution.

In 1978, he was admitted by Tangshan Institute of Technology, becoming China's first batch of university students after the Cultural Revolution. He then completed his postgraduate studies in Beijing and was awarded his Ph.D. in 1988.

Holding a Ph.D. in engineering, Professor Hu focused on China Studies as early as 1985, when he joined the Group for China Study at the Chinese Academy of Sciences. As one of the pioneers in this field, Professor Hu's primary interest is China's economic reform and development. With his research background as a visiting scholar in major western universities (including Massachusetts Institute of Technology and Harvard University), Professor Hu is able to apply western economic theories to his work in China Studies.

Professor Hu founded the Centre for China Studies at the Chinese Academy of Sciences in 1999. Since its inauguration, Professor Hu and his team have published more than 500 editions of the *Report on China Studies*.

Professor Hu's painstaking efforts culminated into a number of reforms aimed at addressing the predicaments of China's underprivileged. "China must handle three reforms, in the social, state-owned enterprises and finance sectors," he mentioned in an interview back in year 2000.

OTHER INFLUENTIAL PEOPLE WHO'S WHO IN CHINA

Professor Hu is a frequent speaker at forums on national issues. On 13 April 2003, Professor Hu submitted a report, *Coping with SARS disease positively and in an all-round manner* to the State Council. His nine noteworthy suggestions on battling the SARS epidemic were all adopted.

Birth date	27 April 1953
Hometown	Anshan City, Liaoning Province
Education	Bachelor of Engineering, Department of Metallurgy, Tangshan Institute of Technology, 1982
	Masters of Engineering, Department of Metal Forming, Beijing University of Science and Technology, 1984
	Ph.D., Institute of Automation, Chinese Academy of Sciences, 1988

Background

1969-1976	Worked at Beidahuang Farm, Heilongjiang province and was part of the North China Geology Team successively during the Culture Revolution
1978-1988	Student at Tangshan Institute of Technology, Beijing University of Science and Technology, and Chinese Academy of Sciences successively
1986-2000	Member of the Group for China Study, Chinese Academy of Sciences
1991-1992	Post-doctoral work at the Department of Economics, Yale University, USA
1992-1993	Visiting scholars at the Department of Economics and Finance, Murray State University, USA
1996-	Director at the Centre for China Study, Chinese Academy of Sciences
1997-1998	Research fellow at the Centre for International Studies, Massachusetts Institute of Technology, USA
1998-	Research fellow at the Department of Economics, Chinese University of Hong Kong
1999-	Professor at the Development Research Academy for the 21st Century, Tsinghua University, Beijing
2000-2001	Visiting professor at the School of Media and Governance SFC, Keio University of Japan
2000-	Commissioner at the Experts Commission on Territory Resources, Chinese Academy of Sciences
	Member of academic committee at Centre for Crossed Science Study, Chinese Academy of Sciences
	Guest professor at School of Economics and Management, Tongji University, Shanghai
2001-2001	Visiting professor at JFK School of Government, Harvard University, USA

Contact information

Address 5th floor, Min-Li Building, Tsinghua University, Beijing, China, 100084
Telephone 86-10-6277 3826   Facsimile 86-10-6278 2605   Email anganghu@tsinghua.edu.cn

Educators

OTHER INFLUENTIAL PEOPLE WHO'S WHO IN CHINA

Ranking of China's top universities

Rank	Name
1	Tsinghua University
2	Peking University
3	Zhejiang University
4	Fudan University
5	Huazhong University of Science and Technology
6	Nanjing University
7	Wuhan University
8	Jilin University
9	Shanghai Jiaotong University
10	Sichuan University
11	Zhongshan University
12	Xi'an Jiaotong University
13	Harbin Insitute of Technology
14	Shandong University
15	University of Science and Technology of China
16	Tianjin University
17	Central South University
18	Peking Union Medical College
19	Nankai University
20	Southeast University

Source: Wu Shulian, Lv Jia and Guo Shilin, *Ranking of China Universities* 2004

Xu Zhihong Peking University
"Nurturer, botanist and schoolmaster"

Titles and positions   President of Peking University
Vice President of Chinese Academy of Sciences

Professor Xu Zhihong was appointed 30th President of Peking University in December 1999. He is concurrently the vice president of the Chinese Academy of Sciences.

Born in 1942, he majored in botany studies at Peking University. After graduating in 1965, he joined the Shanghai Institute of Plant Physiology of the Chinese Academy of Sciences. It was there that his passion for biology germinated into his lifelong career choice

As a famed botanist, Professor Xu has conducted researches in plant physiology, plant tissue, cell culture, protoplast manipulation, DNA transformation and plant biotechnology.

His work invariably placed China at the forefront of biology research and he has been awarded the 'First Prize in Natural Science' by the Chinese Academy of Sciences in 1990 and the 'Third Prize in National Natural Sciences' in 1991. In 1998, he was given the 'Young/Middle-Aged Scientist with Outstanding Contribution' award by the State Council in 1988.

Years of being in the academia has also established Professor Xu's adroitness as an education administrator. Since 1983, he has been appointed as the deputy director and director of Shanghai Institute of Plant Physiology of the Chinese Academy of Sciences and director of the National Laboratory of Plant Molecular Genetics in concurrence.

In 1992, he was appointed the vice president of the Chinese Academy of Sciences. Couple of years later, he landed the position of director at the Shanghai Research Centre of Life Sciences.

OTHER INFLUENTIAL PEOPLE WHO'S WHO IN CHINA

Today, he is at the helm of China's top university with over 60,000 students and staff. Against its backdrop of a rich and colourful history, Peking University stands as the oldest university in China. It has also been intimately linked throughout the resurgence of China as a powerful economy. The tertiary institution continues to play a core role in nurturing new talents for the country. Of all the famous educators in the world, the present president of Peking University Professor Xu says he admires Cai Yuanpei (1868-1940) most, because by proposing a reform programme, Cai was boldly challenging the status quo.

As president of Peking University, Professor Xu proudly upholds the traditions and roots of the institution while striking new bold directions for its future development. He envisions Peking University as a leading world-class university.

When delivering a speech on "The social responsibilities of a scientist and the issues of ethics and morality in scientific research" to nearly 400 postgraduates of the College of Chemistry and Molecular Engineering on 8 March 2004, Professor Xu highlighted, "The introduction of western science and technology has brought prosperity to our economy. Regrettably, we have neglected to inculcate academic ethics in our academic programmes."

Birth date	October 1942
Hometown	Wuxi City, Jiangsu Province
Education	Bachelor of Science, majoring in Botany, Department of Biology, Peking University, 1965 Masters of Science, Shanghai Institute of Plant Physiology, China Academy of Sciences, 1969

Background

1959-1965	Undergraduate student at the Department of Biology, Peking University
1965-1969	Masters student at Shanghai Institute of Plant Physiology, CAS
1969-1983	Worked at Shanghai Institute of Plant Physiology, CAS
1979-1980	Visiting scientist at John Innes Institute, UK
1980-1981	Visiting scientist at the Department of Botany, University of Nottingham, UK
1983-1991	Deputy director of Shanghai Institute of Plant Physiology, CAS
1988-1993	Professor at Shanghai Institute of Plant Physiology, CAS
1988-1994	Director of National Laboratory of Plant Molecular Genetics
1989-1992	Visiting professor at the Institute of Molecular and Cell Biology, National University of Singapore (for a period of three months every year)
1991-1994	Director of Shanghai Institute of Plant Physiology, CAS
1992-	Vice president of Chinese Academy of Sciences
1993-	Professor of College of Life Sciences, Peking University
1995-	Elected member of Third World Academy of Sciences
1997-	Elected member of Chinese Academy of Sciences
1999-	President of Peking University

Memberships and professional affiliations

Vice chairman of China National Committee of UNESCO, 1994-2000
Chairman of Chinese Society of Plant Physiology, 1990-1993
Vice chairman of Chinese Society of Biotechnology, 1998-2001
Vice chairman of Chinese Society of Botany, 1998-present
Chairman of Chinese Society of Cell Biology, 1999-present
Council member of UNESCO-International Cell Research Organisation, 1989-present
Member of UNESCO-Biotechnology Action Council, 1990-1998
National Correspondent of International Association of Plant Tissue Culture and Biotechnology 1988-present and member of Executive Committee, 1998-present
Member of China National Committee of MAB (Man and Biosphere)
Chairman of UNESCO, 1993

Contact information

Address President's Office, Peking University, Beijing, China
Telephone 86-10-6275 1200   Email xuzh@pku.edu.cn

OTHER INFLUENTIAL PEOPLE WHO'S WHO IN CHINA

Gu Binglin Tsinghua University
"At the zenith of teaching"

Title and position President of Tsinghua University

Professor Gu Binglin was officially appointed as the 17th president of Tsinghua University since 2003. Before his presidency, this professor of physics stood as the chairman overseeing the department of physics, the dean of graduate school and vice president of Tsinghua University.

Professor Gu was a student at the department of engineering physics of Tsinghua University from 1965 to 1970. After graduation, he joined the alumni and worked as a teacher. He enrolled in his postgraduate course at the same university until 1979 when he left for Aarhus University in Denmark to further his studies in physics. A short three years later, he received his doctorate degree of natural science.

His career is replete with cross-cultural experiences. He was previously a visiting scholar at the University of Notre Dame in the United States. He has also been requested to be a guest professor at Tohoku University in Japan. The major awards he has been granted include the second-class prize by China's National Natural Science Award and the first-class prize by Natural Science Award for Chinese universities.

Professor Gu has long been engaged in the research field of condensed matter physics. Besides his finesse in research, he also exhibited his aptitude in education and academic administration. In 1999, he was elected a member of the Chinese Academy of Sciences. As the new head of a university with a rich history, dating back to 1891, Professor Gu aims to lead the 7,100 strong faculty and over 100,000 students to build Tsinghua University into a world-class university in the 21st century.

When delivering his speech to kick-off the academic year in 2004, Professor Gu declared, "Let's keep in mind the philosophies of Self Discipline and Social Commitment, Patriotism, Devotion and Pursuit of Perfection and Action Speaks Louder Than Words. In our quest for comprehensive improvement, we must standardise management, encourage creativity, achieve significant development in 2004 and write another great page in the progress towards becoming a world-class university."

Birth date	October 1945
Hometown	Dehui County, Jilin Province
Education	Bachelor of Science, majoring in Physics, Tsinghua University, 1970
	Ph.D., majoring in Physics, Aarhus University of Denmark, 1982

Background

1965-1970	Student at Tsinghua University
1970-1979	Taught at the Department of Engineering Physics, Tsinghua University
1979-1982	Working on Ph.D. at the Aarhus University of Denmark
1982-1988	Taught at the Department of Engineering Physics, Tsinghua University
1985-1986	Visiting scholar at University of Notre Dame, USA
1988-	Professor at the Tsinghua University
2000-2001	Dean of the Graduate School, Tsinghua University
2001-2003	Vice president of Tsinghua University
2003-	President of Tsinghua University

Memberships

Member of China's National Academic Degree Appraisal Committee

Member of standing committee of Chinese Society of Physics

Board member of Chinese Society of Material Science

Director of the Steering Committee for Education of Physics and Astronomy under Ministry of Education

Honours and awards

Second-class Prize of China's National Natural Science Award

First-class Prize of Natural Science Award for Chinese universities

The Advancement of Science and Technology Award sponsored by Hong Kong Ho Leung Ho Lee Foundation

Including other awards granted by Beijing Municipal Government, Ministry of Education, State Science and Technology Commission and Ministry of Personnel of China.

Contact information

Address The President's Office, Tsinghua University, Beijing, China, 100084
Telephone 86-10-6278 2015   Facsimile 86-10-6277 0349

Wang Shenghong — Fudan University
"Taking to task the onus of educating"

Title and position — President of Fudan University

Professor Wang Shenghong was appointed president of one of China's most prestigious universities, Fudan University, since December 1998.

A graduate of Shanghai University of Science and Technology, Professor Wang's trove of experience stems from both studying and working at Purdue University, Arizona University and University of Texas at Austin in United States during the 1980s. He also received an honourary Ph.D. degree from Chonnam University of South Korea in June 2000.

Well versed in precision mechanical engineering, Professor Wang has made tremendous academic strides in this field. Approved by the State Education Ministry in 1984, he has been engaged in the groundbreaking work of structural design of precision radar tracking, radio telescopes and large scale antenna systems, as well as teaching and research in computation mechanics and other related fields.

Amongst Professor Wang's list of stellar appointments are executive vice president of Shanghai University of Science and Technology, director of Shanghai Municipal Education and Health Department, deputy chairman and secretary of the party committee of Shanghai Municipal Political Consultative Conference. Professor Wang was not only awarded for his accomplishments such as the First Prize of National Educational Achievement in Education (1990) but also for his excellent working attitude, including 'Excellent Staff Member of Shanghai University of Science and Technology' and 'Shanghai Model Worker'.

Founded in 1905, Fudan University is the most reputable university in Shanghai and has made a name internationally for academic excellence. "Fudan" literally means "a new morning" in Chinese, thus implying a new beginning. It was named after a quote from the Confucian classic, *Shang Shu*, compiled about 2,000 years ago. At present, Fudan University composes of 17 schools which offer an extensive range of disciplines. Student enrolment totals up to more than 36,000. Professor Wang aims to guide the development of Fudan University to turn it into one of the most influential universities in the world.

In October 2003, semiconductor player Novellus Systems Inc signed a partnership agreement with Fudan University to establish a semiconductor manufacturing technology research centre. The Fudan-Novellus Interconnect Research Centre, located in Fudan's Handan Road campus, will function as a regional research hub for copper interconnect technology, serving Fudan students, research groups at other universities and Novellus' regional customers.

Birth date	June 1942
Hometown	Shanghai
Education	Bachelor of Engineering, majoring in Precision Machinery, Mechanic Engineering Department of Shanghai University of Science and Technology, 1965

OTHER INFLUENTIAL PEOPLE WHO'S WHO IN CHINA

Background

1965-	Graduated from the Mechanic Engineering Department of Shanghai University of Science and Technology
1981-1982	Studied at the Civil Engineering Department and the Mechanical Engineering Department of Purdue University, USA
1982-1983	Studied at the Aeronautical Machinery Department of Arizona University, USA
1983-1983	Engaged in cooperative research at the Astronomical Department of The University of Texas at Austin, USA
1984-1995	Acted as executive vice president of Shanghai University of Science and Technology, and director of Shanghai Municipal Education and Health Department successively
1995-1998	Worked as the deputy chairman and secretary of the Party committee of Shanghai Municipal Political Consultative Conference
1998-	President of Fudan University

Political affiliations

Member of Chinese Communist Party

Delegate to the 15th National Congress of the Chinese Communist Party

Member of the ninth National People's Political Consultative Conference, the sixth and seventh Shanghai CPC

Member of the ninth Shanghai CPC Committee, the seventh and 10th National People's Congress of Shanghai

Member of the fifth National Youth Association

Deputy chairman of the fifth Shanghai Youth Association

Honours and awards

Third Prize for Shanghai Achievements in Scientific Research, 1978

Achievement Prize for Scientific and Technologic Breakthrough of the Sixth Five-Year Plan awarded by Chinese Academy of Sciences, 1986

First Prize for the National Science and Technology Progress Award, 1987

First Prize for Shanghai Science and Technology Progress Award, 1987

First Prize for National Educational Achievement in Education, 1990

Outstanding Young Staff Member of Shanghai

Excellent Staff Member of Shanghai University of Science and Technology

Excellent Staff Member Working on the Front of Science and Technology in Shanghai

Excellent Staff Member Working on the Front of Education in Shanghai

Shanghai Model Worker

Contact information

Address President's office, Fudan University, No. 220 Handan Road, Shanghai, China, 200433   Telephone 86-21-6564 2222

OTHER INFLUENTIAL PEOPLE WHO'S WHO IN CHINA

Xie Shengwu Shanghai Jiaotong University
"Fostering the keystone of China's academia"

Title and position   President of Shanghai Jiaotong University

   "We endeavour to develop Shanghai Jiaotong University into a world class university, serving the regional economic development and catering for the needs of faculty and staff."

Professor Xie Shengwu's main goals

Professor Xie Shengwu, one of the most famous physicists in China, took over as president of Shanghai Jiaotong University (SJTU) in 1997. "I would not run for the position if there was an election," said Professor Xie, who was appointed the position by the Ministry of Education four years ago. "I would choose to do research and teaching over an administration job." But he is determined to help build SJTU into a modern, world-class university and henceforth has been visiting top universities all over the world to find a country that would co-operate with each of the colleges in SJTU to boost communication and help eliminate the gap with the rest of the research world.

Back in 1966, Professor Xie graduated from SJTU with a bachelor's degree. He received his master's degree in applied physics in 1981. He joined the university as a faculty member in 1966, where he served at the department of physics for four years. Subsequently, he taught at the Institute of Laser before receiving his appointment as a lecturer. Just after two years, he became an associate professor and a professor in 1990. After four years, he rose to become a Ph.D. advisor, the next level of seniority.

Prior to being appointed the president of Shanghai Jiaotong University, Professor Xie served as a vice president of the university from 1991 to 1997, the dean of the graduate school from 1994 to 1998, and the chairman of the physics department from 1982 to 1991.

In more than 30 years of service at the university, Professor Xie has lent his expertise to various tasks such as the revision of undergraduate degree requirements, restructuring and expansion of graduate programs, and the promotion of the role of research and its review process.

An oxygen tank stands behind the sofa in his office. "I need it when I feel my brain is in short supply of oxygen. There is another one at home," he claims. A fervent map collector, Professor Xie is also an excellent bowling player. His wife, Ms Gu Meifeng is an expert in pre-school education. They have a 29-year-old son who is a graduate from the Department of Foreign Trade at SJTU.

Founded in 1896, SJTU is one of the top universities in China. The institution has churned out several eminent figures, including former President Jiang Zemin.

OTHER INFLUENTIAL PEOPLE WHO'S WHO IN CHINA

Today, the university boasts 21 academic schools, 60 undergraduate programs, 152 masters-degree programs, 93 Ph.D. programs, 21 post-doctorate programs, 16 State key doctorate programs, 16 State-supported doctorate programmes and 14 State-supported laboratories and national engineering centres in the university. As the leader of the university, Professor Xie's main charge includes international exchanges, faculty and curriculum development and graduate education.

Birth date	22 December 1943
Hometown	Shangyu County, Zhejiang Province
Education	Bachelor of Engineering, majoring in Nuclear Reactors, Shanghai Jiaotong University, 1966
	Masters of Engineering, Shanghai Jiaotong University, 1981

Background

1960-1966	Student at the Department of Engineering Physics, Shanghai Jiaotong University
1966-1978	Instructor at Shanghai Jiaotong University
1978-1981	Studied for the Master's degree at the Department of Applied Physics, Shanghai Jiaotong University
1981-1991	Worked at Shanghai Jiaotong University as a lecturer, associate professor, vice dean, dean and professor successively
1991-1997	Dean of the graduate school and vice president of Shanghai Jiaotong University
1997-	President of Shanghai Jiaotong University

Memberships

Member of Shanghai Chinese People's Political Consultative Conference

Member of Shanghai Municipal Government's Expert Committee for Science & Technology Progress

Chairman of Shanghai Laser Society

Council member of Chinese Society of Optics

Editorial Board of ACTA OPTICA SINICA

Chairman of the Editorial Board of *The Journal of Shanghai Jiaotong University*

Other information

Wide range of interests including collecting maps and bowling

Contact information

Address President's office, No. 1954 Huashan Road, Shanghai, China, 200030

Jiang Shusheng — Nanjing University
"The outstanding physicist"

Title and position President of Nanjing University

Professor Jiang Shusheng was selected the president of this prestigious university in 1997. His ties with Nanjing university can be traced back to as early as 1958 when he first enrolled as a student in the physics department.

Upon graduation, Professor Jiang remained to continue as a research assistant before becoming a lecturer. Thereafter, he rose to the position of associate professor before becoming a professor.

Professor Jiang's education administration career began in 1986, when he was appointed the director of crystal physics section at the physics department of Nanjing University. He then took over the running of the laboratory of Solid State Microstructure and the physics department at the university for another 10 years. His work shone and he became the vice president of Nanjing University in 1996 before assuming the post of president just a year later.

Nanjing University is one of China's oldest tertiary institutions. It is also come directly under the state education commission. Established at the turn of 20th century, the university comprises of 10 schools, 36 departments and a student body of 18,000. Nanjing University is known for providing stimulating, academic research, dynamic teaching, complete with well-bestowed infrastructure and resources. The university's guiding principle is to provide world class training, to nurture talent to stay relevant with the latest international development and the needs of society.

Under the leadership of Professor Jiang, Nanjing University is moulding itself into an influential, multi-disciplinary university.

Birth date	2 April 1940
Hometown	Jiangsu Province
Education	Bachelor of Science, Nanjing University, 1963

Background

1958-1963	Studied at Nanjing University
1963-1979	Research assistant and lecturer at Nanjing University
1979-1982	Research fellow, Bristol University, UK
1982-1990	Lecturer and associate professor at Nanjing University

1991-1992	Research fellow at Durham University, UK
1991-1993	Director of Crystal Physics Section at the Physics Department of Nanjing University
1993-1993	Professor at Nanjing University
1993-1996	Visiting professor at University of Sydney, Australia
1995-1995	Deputy director of Laboratory of Solid State Microstructure, Nanjing University
1996-1997	Visiting professor at University of Sydney, Australia
1997-	Chairman of Physics Department, Nanjing University
	Visiting professor at MASPEC, CNR, Italy
	Vice president of Nanjing University
	President of Nanjing University

Memberships

1964	Member of Chinese Physical Society
1993	Member of Chinese Crystal Society
1993	Editor of Chinese Physics
1993	Letters Editor of Modern Physics
1999	Member of the Standing Committee of Chinese Physical Society Commission

Honours and awards

1990	Second Class Prize in Science and Technology of the State Education Commission
1992	Nation's Young and Middle Aged Specialist with Outstanding Contributions
1992	Third Class Prize in Science and Technology of the State Education Commission
1994	First Class Prize in Science and Technology of Jiangsu Province
1995	Third Class National Prize in Natural Science
1997	First Class Prize in Science and Technology of Jiangsu Province

Contact information

Address Nanjing University, No. 22 Hankou Road, Nanjing, China, 210093
Telephone 86-25-3302 728 Email SSJiang@nju.edu.cn

Pan Yunhe Zhejiang University
"Irrefutable intelligence"

Title and position   President of Zhejiang University

Professor Pan Yunhe is the president of Zhejiang University, which merged with three other universities in 1998 to become the largest university in China.

Having excelled academically in computer graphics for industrial design, Professor Pan is the youngest member to be admitted into the Chinese Academy of Engineering. He is also one of the major founders of the international conference on computer aided industrial and conceptual design.

Born in Hangzhou city of Zhejiang province, Professor Pan obtained his degree from Tongji University in 1970. After graduation, he headed the Automation Research Institute and became vice director of the Science Commission at Xiangfan City in Hubei province. He went back to his hometown in 1978 and commenced his postgraduate studies at Zhejiang University.

In 1981, he graduated with a master's degree in science and remained in the university as an instructor. Professor Pan quickly polished his expertise both in academia and in administration. He was appointed the head of the Artificial Intelligence Institute and the head of the computer science department at Zhejiang University from 1990 to1994. Subsequently, he was promoted to become the vice president of Zhejiang University. From 1986 to 1988, he was a visiting scholar at University of California at Los Angeles (UCLA) and Carnegie Mellon University in the United States. From May 1995, he became the president of the largest university in China.

Professor Pan has over 70 publications to his credit and is the recipient of 10 state awards.

The new Zhejiang University was founded in 1998 with the amalgamation of the four former individual universities, namely Zhejiang University, Hangzhou University, Zhejiang Agricultural University and Zhejiang Medical University. Under the guidance of Professor Pan, the establishment of the new Zhejiang University was regarded as a momentous undertaking in the reform and progress of China's higher education. At present, Zhejiang University's fields of study span over 11 branches of learning. With 107 specialties, 225 masters programs and 138 doctorate programmes, the institution enrols more than 80,000 students.

Birth date	4 November 1946
Hometown	Hangzhou City, Zhejiang Province
Education	Bachelor of Science, majoring in Architecture, Tongji University, 1970
	Masters of Science, majoring in Computer Application, Zhejiang University, 1981

Background

1970-	Graduated from Tongji University with a bachelor's degree
1970-1978	Worked as the head of Automation Research Institute at Xiangfan, Hubei province
	Vice director of Science Commission, at Xiangfan, Hubei province successively
1978-1981	Studied at Zhejiang University as a postgraduate student
1981-1990	Instructor and associate professor at Zhejiang University successively
1986-1988	Visiting scholar at UCLA and Carnegie Mellon University, USA
1990-	Professor at Zhejiang University
1990-1994	Worked as the head of the Artificial Intelligence Institute and the head of Computer Science Department at Zhejiang University
1994-1995	Vice president of Zhejiang University
1995-	President of Zhejiang University

Memberships

Member of the Science and Technology Commission of State Education Commission
Member of Expert Group of State Climbing Plan
Director of China Computer Association
Director of China Artificial Intelligence Association
Editorial member of many journals, including *Journal of Science in China, Electronics (China), Pattern Recognition* and *Artificial Intelligence*

Contact information

Address President's office, No. 38 Zheda Road, Hangzhou, China, 310027
Telephone 86-571-8795 1248   Facsimile 86-571-8795 1358   Email panyh@sun.zju.edu.cn

Zhu Qingshi — University of Science and Technology of China
"For the love of imparting knowledge"

Title and position President of University of Science and Technology of China

In 1998, Professor Zhu Qingshi became the president of the University of Science and Technology of China (USTC), 30 years after he commenced his studies at this prestigious university.

Born in the Sichuan province, Professor Zhu has firmly established himself as one of China's experts in molecular spectroscopy and chemical physics. His spectroscopic studies on molecular local mode vibrations have vastly been regarded as major breakthroughs in the area of molecular local mode dynamics.

After graduating from the university in 1968, Professor Zhu worked at the Salt Lake Institute at Xining in Qinghai province until 1984. He was the director of the laser chemistry division at the Institute of Chemical Physics of Dalian in Liaoning province and was elected as a member of Chinese Academy of Sciences in 1991.

Professor Zhu returned to USTC in 1994 and became the vice president of the university in 1996.

With extensive experience at some of the foremost spectroscopic laboratories in the United States and Europe including Cambridge University, Oxford University and University of Nottingham, Professor Zhu excels not only in research areas but has proven to be equally adept as an administrator. Since being appointed the president of USTC, Professor Zhu has been engaged in the university's reforms on education, research and service.

To date, he has published three books and more than 140 articles and papers and has bagged awards such as the 'Award for Achievements in Asia' in 1994, and the 'Thompson Memorial Award'. When asked what his personal legacy would be as president of USTC, he says, "In recent years, USTC has somewhat lost its mission and vision. From administration to education, everybody does his or her own things. There are no coordinated plans, no world-class knowledge structure. In addition, USTC has many small research groups and small companies. There is nothing that exemplifies the vision a fine education institution such as USTC ought to have."

"In my current term, I would like to restore the mission and vision for USTC and put the administration back on the right track. It is very difficult to retrench people in China and old ways die hard. It is difficult to change things but I will try my best."

USTC was established by the Chinese Academy of Sciences in 1958. Aimed at fostering high-level personnel of science and technology, the university was relocated from Beijing to Hefei, the capital of Anhui province in 1970. Since then, the university has undertaken a number forward looking steps to instill an innovative spirit in the cohort. The university has nine schools, 23 departments and runs a special class to nurture the gifted young. Under the administration of Professor Zhu, the university is bent on becoming a first-class research based university globally.

OTHER INFLUENTIAL PEOPLE WHO'S WHO IN CHINA

Birth date	February 1946
Hometown	Chengdu City, Sichuan Province
Education	Bachelor of Science, majoring in Modern Physics, University of Science and Technology of China, 1968

Background

1963-1968	Studied at the University of Science and Technology of China
1968-1974	Technician at Shanchuan Machine Tool Factory, Xining, Qinghai Province
1974-1984	Research assistant at Salt Lake Institute, Xining, Qinghai Province
1984-1994	Project leader, associate research fellow, research fellow and director at the Laser Chemistry Division, Institute of Chemical Physics, Dalian, Liaoning Province
1991-	Elected as a member of Chinese Academy of Sciences
1994-1996	Worked at University of Science and Technology of China
1996-1998	Vice president of University of Science and Technology of China
1998-	President of University of Science and Technology of China

Contact information

Address President's office, No.96 Jinzhai Road, Hefei, China, 230026
Telephone 86-551-3602 184

Chen Luming King & Wood
"King's counsel"

Title and position Attorney and Partner of King & Wood

Dr Chen Luming is a partner at King & Wood, a leading law firm in China. As one of the recommended Chinese lawyers in the banking sector by *The Legal 500 Series*, his specialty lies in foreign direct investment, project finance, international mergers and acquisitions, energy, banking and international arbitration.

Dr Chen graduated from China's prestigious Fudan University with a bachelor's and a master's degree in 1983 and 1986 respectively. His highest degree, J. D., was awarded by the school of law at Harvard University in 1995. He also has extensive experience as a practicioner in the United States, where he was involved in securities offerings, project financing and banking transactions.

Fluent in both Mandarin and English, Dr Chen is well known for representing major foreign corporations in investment projects in China in diverse industries. Dr Chen also frequently represents foreign companies in arbitrations in the China International Economic and Trade Arbitration Commission. In the same strand, he also represents numerous Chinese companies in arbitrations before international arbitration institutions.

Founded in Beijing in 1993, King & Wood is one of the largest law firms in China with experienced practitioners in practically every major field of law. King & Wood has branched out of Shanghai and now has offices in Beijing, Shanghai, Shenzhen, Guangzhou, and Chengdu. The firm also opened two offices in San Francisco and the Silicon Valley in the United States to better serve its clients in the United States. Dr Chen is based in the Shanghai office of King & Wood.

Education
B. A., Fudan University, 1983
M. A., Fudan University, 1986
J. D., the School of Law, Harvard University, 1995

Background

Partner at King & Wood

Associate at O'Melveny & Myers, Shanghai

Associate at Vinson & Elkins, Beijing

Associate at Debevoise & Plimpton, New York

Arbitrator and section chief at China International Economic and Trade Arbitration Commission

Memberships

Member of New York Bar Association

Member of All-China Lawyers Association

Contact information
Address 21/F, Shui On Plaza, 333 Huai Hai Road (M), Shanghai, China, 200021
Telephone 86-21-6385 2299   Facsimile 86-21-6386 5660 / 6386 5770   Email lumingchen@kingandwood.com

Wang Zhilong Jun He Law Offices
"A pioneer in the Chinese legal profession"

Title and position   Founding partner of Jun He Law Offices

Professor Wang Zhilong is a founding partner of Jun He Law Offices, one of the prominent law firms in China. He is exalted for dealing with investments, general corporate matters and real estate cases. *The Legal 500 Series* places him amongst the top Chinese lawyers in the corporate, mergers and acquisitions, as well as the foreign direct investment sectors.

As the first group of certified lawyers in the China, Professor Wang graduated from Peking University School of Law with a LL. B. degree in 1951. During his early career, Professor Wang worked in several government departments and large state-owned enterprises, taking over the management of personnel, labour, planning, manufacturing and financial matters. He has also participated in the noteworthy negotiations and drafting of contracts for major Sino-foreign enterprises.

In 1980, Professor Wang went to Harvard Law School as a visiting scholar to carry out research. After he completed his research in 1982, he started teaching international business law at the Capital University of Economics and Business in Beijing. From 1986 to 1988, Professor Wang was invited to teach Chinese economic law and international business transactions at Suffolk University Law School in Boston, and comparative commercial law and international business transactions at the Law School of the State University of New York in Buffalo. During his stay in United States, Professor Wang also worked in the law firms of New York city with Hughes, Hubbard & Reed, as well as Donovan, Leisure, Newton & Irvine.

Being one of the first private law firms in China and the first in China to open branches in several Chinese cities and overseas, Jun He has grown into a leading Chinese law firm specialising in commercial legal practice with branches from the China provinces of Beijing, Shanghai, Shenzhen, Dalian, Haikou to New York city. Over the past few years, Jun He has been honoured several times including, the only law firm to be awarded 'National Model Unit in the Judicial System' by the Ministry of Justice and Ministry of Personnel of China and it was also ranked first among the top 20 Chinese law firms when selected as for the 'Outstanding Ministry Level Law Firms' award by the Ministry of Justice of China in 1998.

With a team of more than 80 well-trained lawyers, Jun He has become one of the largest and most established law firms in China. Professor Wang currently practises at the Beijing office of Jun He.

Education   LL. B., Peking University Law School, 1951
Professional qualification   Professor

Background

Before 1980	Worked in several government departments and large state-owned enterprises, responsible for the management of personnel, labour, planning, manufacturing and financial matters
1980-1982	Visiting scholar at Harvard Law School
1982-1986	Taught at the Capital University of Economics and Business, Beijing
1986-1988	Taught at Suffolk University Law School, Boston, and the Law School of the State University of New York at Buffalo, USA
1989-	Co-founded Jun He Law Offices

Memberships

Member of the All-China Bar Association

Contact information

Address The 20th Floor, China Resources Building, 8 Jianguomenbei Avenue, Beijing, China, 100005
Telephone **86-10-8519 1360**   Facsimile **86-10-8519 1350**   Email **wangzhl@junhe.com**   Website **www.junhe.com**

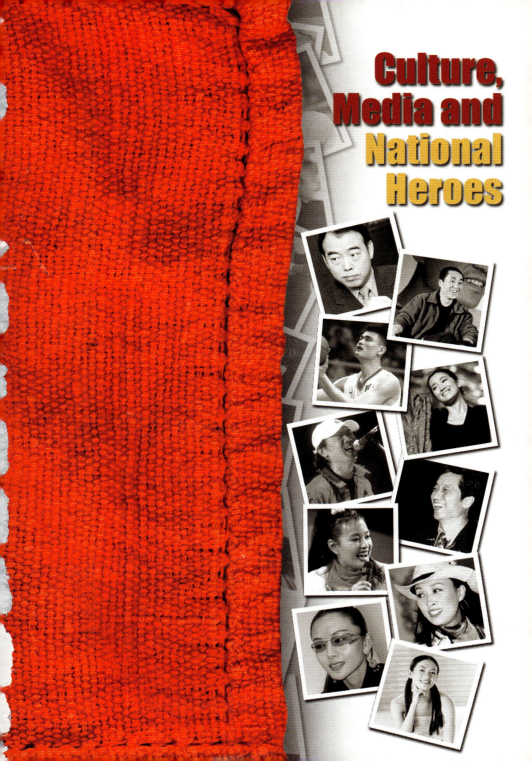

Culture, Media and National Heroes

Zhao Huayong CCTV
"Creating the new wave of virtual geographies"

Corporate position President of China Central Television (CCTV)

"Except for the news channel, CCTV's other channels will be reformed into commercial channels with specific sectors. These channels will also be managed by market economy; their survival will depend on how much advertisement revenue they get. This is to realize the commercial management of TV channels."

Mr Zhao Huayong

Zhao Huayong joined China Central Television (CCTV) after graduating from Fudan University in 1975. Having worked in the departments of current, special topics, social education, economy and in the Centre for Culture and Arts, he has been involved in the production of nearly 100 documentary films, numerous television contests and more than 10 arts performances and festival celebrations.

His *magnum opus* has been attributed to the phenomenal 25-episode documentary film *Hua Shuo Chang Jiang*. The production introduces the longest river in China, Chang Jiang, starting at its headstream and following it until it discharges in the sea. The film captures the mesmerising scenery and introduces its cultural landmarks. Juxtaposed with dramatic historical events of China, the film has stunned and moved much of its audience. The film has also been well received because of the collaboration with Japan's new-age musical guru Kitaro, giving it a universal appeal.

In 1989, Mr Zhao was promoted to lead the economy department of CCTV. Under his administration and directions, his *Economy 30 Minutes* and *Economic Information News* were hits and the viewership ratings soared. Throughout the years, he has been hailed for his brilliant work and he was appointed the president of CCTV in February 1999.

Founded in 1958, CCTV was formerly the Beijing Television Station before becoming China Central Television 20 years later. Today, the station has 14 channels and has grown into an enterprise offering multiple services such as television, movies, animation production, internet, print publications, teletext and advertising. It also produced China's first children's channel. Meanwhile, CCTV is looking for partners from abroad and has signed a co-operation contract with Nickelodeon, the No. 1 rated 24-hour children's channel in the United States.

CCTV programmes broadcast over 270 hours of television airtime daily. Its viewership exceeds a staggering 1.1 billion. By 2000, it has already become the most powerful media organisation in China. CCTV's capital surpasses RMB 5.4 billion (US$652.2 million) and in 2001, its turnover amounted to more than RMB 6 billion (US$724.6).

OTHER INFLUENTIAL PEOPLE WHO'S WHO IN CHINA

Birth date	1948
Hometown	Tongshan County, Jiangsu Province
Education	Bachelor in Journalism, Fudan University

Background

1975-1989	Editor at CCTV
1989-1992	Head of Economy Department, CCTV
1992-1993	Assistant to the President of CCTV
	Head of Economy Department, CCTV
1993-1995	Duty president of CCTV
	Manager at Centre for Culture and Arts
1995-1999	Duty president of CCTV
	Manager at Centre of Satellite Telecasting
1999-	President of CCTV

Contact information

Address 11B Fuxing Road, Media Centre, Beijing, China 100038
Telephone 86-10-6850 0378 Facsimile 86-10-6851 1134 Website www.cctv.com

"I always try to discover something from real life. Life is something that can always inspire me."

Mr Chen Kaige

Chen Kaige
"Breathing new life into Chinese cinematography"

Profession   Film director

This director's forage to redefine Chinese cinematography by challenging the visual aspects of film-making has catapulted him into one of the forerunners in the media industry.

Born in Beijing, Chen Kaige became a Red Guard during Mao Zedong's Cultural Revolution era. At 15 years of age, he had to publicly denounce his father, Chen Huaikai, the famous director who directed a number of popular films during the 1950s and 1960s. "What I remember most is coming home afterwards. I waited until everyone was asleep. I crept in and went through the three rooms in the apartment before reaching my bed. I was too ashamed to speak to anyone," he said, remorseful of what had happened in the past. "It took a long time for us to connect again," says Chen. "Yet, when it comes to making movies, my father can be considered as my mentor. Certain things never heal and I will have to live with that all my life."

Towards the end of the 1960s, he was assigned to labour in a rubber plantation in south western Yunnan province. When Chen returned to his hometown in 1975, he landed a job at the Beijing Film Processing Laboratory. His passion for the media compelled him to join Beijing Film Academy. In 1982, he graduated together with fellow renowned directors Zhang Yimou and Tian Zhuangzhuang. Chen Kaige represents the fifth generation filmmakers who attended Beijing's Film Academy after the Cultural Revolution.

One of his luminary projects also includes *Farewell to Yesterday* (1980) created for Fujian television. He has collaborated with classmates Zhang Yimou and Hu Qun to create *Yellow Earth* (1984), a film so riveting it astounded critics and audiences during its international debut at the Hong Kong Film Festival and cast international spotlight on the changing face of Chinese cinema.

In light of his life experiences, he was invited by Xi'an Film Studio to direct the *King of the Children* (1987), about children growing up during the Cultural Revolution. Despite missing out on the festival awards, the movie was thought to be insightful and provocative by critics.

In 1987, he received a filmmaking scholarship at New York University. During this period, he was granted funding to make *Life on a String* (1991), a piece of philosophical work revolving around two blind wandering musicians. His remarkable use of both visual and aural elements inevitably cast the movie into the *avant-garde* category and appealed only to a minority.

To date, he is best known for *Farewell My Concubine* (1992), Gong Li and the late Hong Kong actor Leslie Cheung. The movie was so highly acclaimed it bagged a joint *Palme d'Or* award along with *The Piano* at the 1993 Cannes Film Festival and was even nominated for an Academy award. Chen has been awarded top festival prizes in Tokyo, Cannes and Berlin.

Interestingly when asked why he feels the "need to do a contemporary story about China", he says, "It is a country that has no past," he avers. "Political regimes systematically robbed us of history and it's only now that we are beginning to get it back."

In the late 1990s, he made *The Emperor and the Assassin* (1999) which once again swept the box office and raked in millions. The film was also screened at the 1999 Cannes Film Festival.

Giving broad statements about the body of his work, "I'm trying to be sensitive about human nature. I'm curious to discover what it is to be human – it's in the nature of artists to be more in tune with our emotions. We can touch souls through expressions of art. The other thing I want to achieve through my films is to explore new elements of cinema language. Our job is to make sense of it all."

Birth date 12 August 1952
Hometown Beijing

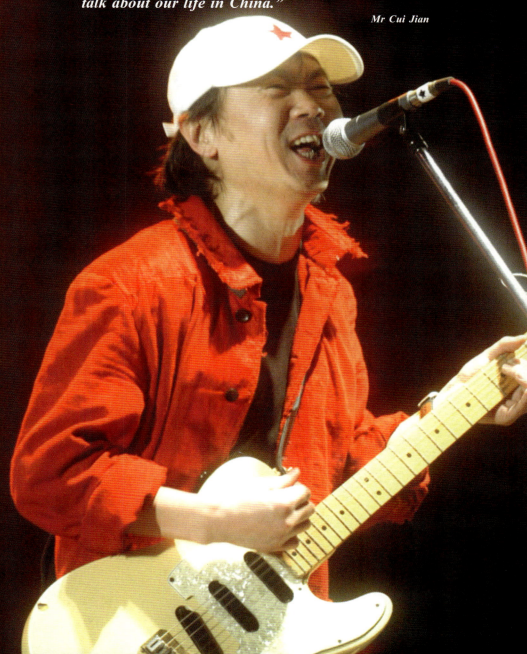

"I talk about serious things in my heart and people's lives, including, of course, love. But, mostly it's about Chinese culture, the modern culture. They're not political songs. It's just the truth, the modern truth. I talk about our life in China."

Mr Cui Jian

OTHER INFLUENTIAL PEOPLE WHO'S WHO IN CHINA

Cui Jian
"The man of unbridled spirituality"

Profession   Rock musician

This talented musician, who has enchanted millions with his euphonious music, hails from the northern part of China. Cui Jian not only plays the trumpet and guitar, he composes his own music as well.

Cui Jian's musical inclination was imbued in him since he was young by his Korean parents. His father is a professional trumpet player and his mother a member of a Korean minority dance troupe. His musical career took root when he was only 14 years old. While he began as part of a Chinese orchestra playing classical music, he soon experimented with western rock music.

In the early 1980s, he formed his first rock band. Since then, he has continued to explore new musical styles with the delivery of each album. His most recent album, for instance, has a distinct jazz presence. His compositions are viewed as one of the most unique and complex in China's musical scene.

Today, known to all as Lao Cui, he is recognised as the father of rock and roll in China and is perceived as the oriental equivalent of Elvis Presley, Bob Dylan and Bruce Springstein by the western media. However, to many of the younger generation, he remains relatively unknown. It is believed that his lack of recognition could be due to his lack of image and branding. Unlike many other singers, he does not succumb to aggressive marketing campaigns in a bid to attract mainstream music lovers.

One of his songs, *I have nothing,* inadvertently became the anthem for the pro-democracy movement in China during the famous Tiananmen Square protests of 1989. He would often perform the song at concerts with a red cloth wrapped around his eyes. Not surprisingly, the type of hardcore rock that Cui Jian performs is considered politically incorrect and has not swayed many of the music fans.

I have nothing comes across as a hauntingly sad and plaintive song that begins with a slow tempo culminating with an intense hard rock energy. This song was played repeatedly by students during the tragic Tiananmen Square clashes of 1989. He currently holds his performances worldwide including in Singapore, America, Europe, Cambodia, Korea and various cities in China.

Birth date   2 August 1961
Hometown   Beijing

"People keep pushing me to be the centre of attention... I would prefer to be on the sidelines, because that's where you see more."

Ms Gong Li

OTHER INFLUENTIAL PEOPLE WHO'S WHO IN CHINA

Gong Li
"Going with the wind of silver screen"

Profession   Movie actress

Gong Li is China's best known starlet in the west. On screen, she exerts such an alluring presence that audiences are spellbound by her performances time and again. Her timeless beauty has also graced countless magazines and books.

A daughter of an economics professor, she was born in Shenyang in 1965. She spent her childhood in Jinan. Music and acting came to her naturally and she has often dreamt of a singing career.

After failing to qualify for China's top music school in 1985, she enrolled in the Central Academy of Drama to study acting, graduating four years later. It was while she was still a drama student, she had her destiny sealed. In 1987, acclaimed director Zhang Yimou chanced upon her talented acting skills and cast her as the leading lady of his first film, *Red Sorghum*. This movie dazzled several of its critics and went on to bag the top award at the Berlin Film Festival. Since then, she continued working in several of his films.

Even beyond the shores of China, she has left behind an indelible mark in her international walk of fame. When the film *The Story Of Qiu Ju*, directed by Zhang Yimou, unveiled at the Venice Film Festival in 1992, Gong Li clinched the best actress award.

While the pair has worked together for much of her acting career, Gong Li has displayed her prolific acting skills in other Chinese co-productions and Hong Kong films as well. She is usually cast in epic dramas containing the martial arts genre. Most laudable of all is director Chen Kaige's *Farewell My Concubine* which clinched Gong Li an award as best supporting actress from the New York Film Critics circle.

She has also twice appeared in films directed by women - a contemporary drama by Taiwanese actress Sylvia Chang, *Mary from Beijing*, and *The Painter*, directed by Huang Shuqin, in which she portrays the woman painter Pao Yuliang, who was notorious for her portraits of nudes.

Off screen, Gong was known to have dated director Zhang Yimou for seven years. However, their relationship ended in 1994 when she decided to marry Singapore tobacco tycoon Ooi Hoe Soeng.

Commenting on the censorship in China of the 1993 film *Farewell My Concubine*, "No one's going to rebel or protest in front of the People's Congress after seeing this film. It's history. We should draw a lesson from it and not let it happen again. It's unreasonable to ban it," she said.

The 34-year-old said she had ambitions beyond the film industry. "I would be glad to work as an ambassador for the United Nations," she said.

Birth date   31 December 1965
Hometown   Shenyang city, Liaoning Province

OTHER INFLUENTIAL PEOPLE WHO'S WHO IN CHINA

Filmography

- *Red Sorghum* (1988)
- *The Empress Dowager* (1989)
- *Operation Cougar* (1989)
- *A Terracotta Warrior* (1989)
- *Ju Dou* (1990)
- *Raise the Red Lantern* (1991)
- *Back to Shanghai* (1991)
- *The Banquet* (1991)
- *Mary from Bejing* (1992)
- *The Story of Qiu Ju* (1992)
- *Farewell My Concubine* (1993)
- *The Painter* (1993)
- *The Flirting Scholar* (1993)
- *To Live* (1994)
- *The Great Conqueror's Concubine* (1994)
- *Demi-Gods and Semi-Devils* (1993)
- *Shanghai Triad* (1995)
- *Temptress Moon* (1995)
- *The Emperor and the Assassin* (1998)
- *Breaking the Silence* (1999)
- *Assassin* (1999)
- *Zhou Yu's Train* (2002)

Trivia

- Attended the Central Drama Academy, Beijing, China
- Awarded the French government's 'Officer des Arts et Lettres' for her contributions to the cinema, June 1998
- Included in *People* Magazine's '50 Most Beautiful People'
- Representative of the label, Shanghai Tang, line of clothing
- Beauty ambassador for L'Oreal cosmetics
- Received New York Film Critics award for *Farewell My Concubine*.
- Head juror of the 2000 Berlin International Film Festival
- Head juror of the 2002 Venice Film Festival
- Head juror of the 2003 Tokyo International Film Festival
- Personal favourite actor and actress - Dustin Hoffman and Meryl Streep

"I believe there are only three things in life that truly belong to myself: knowledge, health and family."

Ms Liu Xiaoqing

Liu Xiaoqing
"Regal screen presence"

Profession   Actress

Liu Xiaoqing was crowned China's movie queen in the 1980s. She is the only Chinese actress to have won the 'Baihua Best Actress' award twice.

In 1963, she enrolled with the Sichuan Music College Affiliated High. At age 18, she joined Chengdu's Army Performing Group. In 1973, Ms Liu landed a role in the movie, *Great Wall of South China Sea* (*Nanhai Changcheng*). The movie saw the tremendous rise of her popularity and her acting career swiftly took off.

Her role (as Zhang Lan) in the 1980 comedy *Look at this Family* (*Qiao Zhe Yi Jia Zi*) won her the top award as a Chinese actress.

With various roles that she took on during the 1980s, Ms Liu reinforced her reign as the movie queen of China. She gave vivid, natural and moving performances that endeared her to movie buffs and critics alike. She won one more 'Baihua Best Actress' for a role in *Town of Furong* (*Furong Zhen*), co-staring Jiang Wen, who later became her real life beau after her marriage collapsed. Ms Liu also appeared in classics such as *Hibiscus Town*, *Little Flowers*, *Cixi's Eunuch*, *Li Lianying* and *Ruling from Behind the Screen*.

In the 1990s however, Liu took a spin into the business world. Her investments reportedly fell foul due to several unfruitful deals and subsequent law-suits.

Despite her razed financial state, Ms Liu will remain one of the most unforgettable and enduring screen heroines that have ever been created in China's show business. Returning to acting after being released on bail in August 2003 for tax evasion, the actress says she hopes to push her acting career to a higher level.

Birth date   31 October 1951
Hometown   Peiling County, Sichuan Province

OTHER INFLUENTIAL PEOPLE WHO'S WHO IN CHINA

Filmography

Year	Title	Pinyin
2001	(TV)	Huo Feng Huang
2000	Tian Gui Hua (TV)	Huang Sao Tian Gui Hua
1998	(TV)	Huo Shao E Pang Gong
1995	(TV)	Wu Ze Tian
1991	Li Lianying, the Imperial Eunuch	Da Tai Jie Li Lian Ying
1989	Dream of Red Mansion 6	Hong Lou Meng 6
1989	Dream of Red Mansion 5	Hong Lou Meng 5
1989	Dream of Red Mansion 4	Hong Lou Meng 4
1989	Dream of Red Mansion 3	Hong Lou Meng 3
1988	Dream of Red Mansion 1	Hong Lou Meng 1
1988	Evil Empress	Yi Dai Yao Hou
1988	Woman For Two, A	Chun Tao
1988	Dream of Red Mansion 2	Hong Lou Meng 2
1987		Da Qing Pao Dui
1986	Hibiscus Town	Fu Rong Zhen
1986	Loveless Lover	Wu Qing de Qing Ren
1984		Bei Guo Hong Dou
1983		Chui Lian Ting Zheng
1983	Burning Down Yuan Ming Yuan	Huo Shao Yuan Ming Yuan
1982		Xin Ling Shen Chu
1981		Yuan Ye
1981		Qian Wang
1980		Shen Mi de Da Fo
1979	Look at This Family	Qiao Zhe Yi Jia Zi
1979	Little Flower	Xiao Hua
1979	Wedding	Hun Li
1978		Tong Zhi, Gan Xie Ni
1978	Spring Song	Chun Ge
1976	Great Wall of South China Sea	Nan Hai Chang Cheng

"Actually, a singer's vocal ability and overall personal strength are of the most importance. Many mainland singers have already proven their ability to hold solo concerts in the capital, but there is no hurry and no need to blindly follow this trend."

Ms Na Ying

OTHER INFLUENTIAL PEOPLE WHO'S WHO IN CHINA

Na Ying
"In tune with her records"

Profession   Singer

Na Ying is one of the most popular singers in China. She has swept numerous awards across Asia including the 10 Most Popular Singers in Asia at the MTV Asia Awards 2002.

Born in Shenyang in 1966, the songstress' father is a well known figure in the practice of traditional Chinese medicine.

At a tender age, Na Ying began to exhibit her flair and passion in singing. In 1980, Na Ying entered a local middle school and firmly decided that she would pursue singing as a career. Her parents, who wanted her to become a doctor, protested in vain.

Determined to become a professional singer someday, she joined the local Children's Palace and several other local arts group. She even found a part-time job to scrape enough money to buy her first cassette player.

When one of her father's friends chanced upon her singing potential, he urged her to join the Shenyang Arts Troupe. She needed no convincing. In 1987, she joined a singing competition held in Beijing.

She then decided to stay behind in Beijing to develop her singing career. Na Ying steadily expanded her singing repertoire by writing her own songs. She was soon invited to perform the theme song for the Asia Sports Games then held in Beijing.

With a silvery and outstanding voice, Na Ying soon rose to become one of the top singers in China. Throughout Hong Kong, Taiwan and Southeast Asia, she has gained firm ground with adoring fans everywhere.

Aside from stirring the entertainment industry with her songs, Na Ying is known in the entertainment circle for her quick and candid wit. Fellow celebrities could often find themselves the brunt of her sarcasm.

Her eight-year personal relationship with Chinese football star, Gao Feng has also ignited intense media publicity in China. The pair has often been nicknamed the David and Victoria Beckham of the East.

Birth date   27 November 1966
Hometown   Shenyang City, Liaoning Province

Trivia

English name:	La Yan
Favourite sports:	Swimming, skipping, jogging, basketball
Hobbies:	Shopping, collecting perfumes, antiques and old furniture pieces

"People limit the definition of dance. Dance is everywhere. Sitting here is a gesture and writing is a movement."

Ms Yang Liping

Yang Liping
"Donna of dance"

Profession   Dancer

Yang Liping is a dancer with the Bai Autonomous Prefecture in Yunnan Province.

Her exquisite choreography on stage during performances such as *The Soul of the Peacock*, *Two Trees*, and *Moonlight* are affirmative of the repute she enjoys both at home and abroad.

A descendent of the Bai ethnic group, she was born in Dali in 1958. At age nine, Ms Yang and her family relocated to Xishuangbanna. Due to her extraordinary gift of dance, she was picked to join the Xishuangbanna Song and Dance Troupe when she was 13 years old.

"Dancing has always been in my blood," says Ms Yang. "The Bai people believe nature is the essence of life. So we usually express our affection for nature and life through singing and dancing." Her unique choreography stems from compositions of silhouettes symbolising nature and movements with a tint of mystery and spirituality as depicted in the dance *Moonlight*.

Overnight, she became a sensation after delivering a captivating performance in the Dai dance drama, *The Peacock Princess*. "In the ethnic minority areas of Yunnan, the peacock is a totem. Our imitation comes out of respect and love towards peacocks and our source of inspiration comes from their movements." In 1988, she entered the China Central Song and Dance Ensemble of Nationalities. At the second national dance contest, her self-choreographed dance, *The Soul of the Peacock*, enthralled the judges so much she walked away with the top two prizes for choreography and performance of her piece.

Ms Yang once revealed during an interview, "The feeling of the body could come from farm work, such as planting rice seedlings, or turning a millstone; it could also come from anything in nature; clouds, a tree, a fish swimming." She has acted in a film *Sun Bird* which garnered her a prize at the Montreal International Film Festival.

Ms Yang is also regularly invited to perform on television programs. Through her lithe moves which are said to boast a lyrical touch, her performances deliver ingenious depictions of stories and tales. She has also appeared in a few movies that are mainly related to dancing that clinched her a few prizes.

Hometown   Xishuangbanna, Yunnan Province

Zhang Yimou
"Giving play to dreams, shadows and visions"

Profession　　　　　Film director

"I always adapt films from stories that I like."
Zhang Yimou

As a director in his own right, Zhang Yimou has become one of the most influential directors to graduate from the Beijing Film Academy in the 1980s.

Mr Zhang was born in Xi'an, Shaanxi province, in 1951. Like many Chinese youths during this period, Mr Zhang was dispatched to take on a blue-collar job during the Cultural Revolution. It was during this arduous period that he reportedly sold his own blood to buy his first camera when he cultivated a fervent interest in photography.

Despite being overaged, he managed to successfully enrol in the cinematography department of the Beijing Film Academy when he was 27.

Four years later, Mr Zhang graduated alongside with classmates, Chen Kaige and Tian Zhuangzhuang who would eventually emerge as distinguished Chinese film directors themselves. This graduating class formed a core of young filmmakers called the "Fifth Generation". Their artistry has been responsible for engendering a new wave of Chinese cinematography that torched across screens at home and overseas during the mid-80s.

After graduation, he worked as a cinematographer in small inland studios which often lacked the entrenched apprenticeship system of the big coastal studios.

Later in Guangxi Film Studio, Mr Zhang worked on the immensely popular *One and Eight* (co-directed with Zhang Junzhao, 1984) and *Yellow Earth* (co-directed with Chen Kaige, 1984).

He was then invited to Xi'an Film Studio where his "true vocation" as a director finally materialised. His directorial debut, *Red Sorghum* (1987), was incidentally the first "Fifth Generation" film to be

OTHER INFLUENTIAL PEOPLE WHO'S WHO IN CHINA

so well received by domestic mass audience. Mr Zhang and his star, Gong Li shot to local and international fame. Its thundering success brought international funding for his next two films, *Judou* (1990) and *Raise the Red Lantern* (1991).

His cinematic production versatility has been evident in the making of his movies. *The Story of Qiu Ju* (1992) was a communist party-approved documentary based on a contemporary theme. The stirring use of visuals was exemplified in movies such as *To Live* (1994) and film noir, *Shanghai Triad* (1995). Equally deemed poignant was the calendar art movie, *The Road Home* (1999) which starred Chinese actress Zhang Ziyi. His last film, *Hero* (2002), is a Chinese epic film that unifies the notion of the mythical with the most popular of all Chinese genres, martial arts. His acting skills are no less exceptional – Mr Zhang won a best actor award at Tokyo Film Festival in the film, *The Old Well*. He is also highly appraised by his crew for his team communication skills and openness.

Zhang Yimou's pieces typically cast strong female characters whose deepest desires challenge the very societal systems that threaten to engulf their growth and freedom. Hence, Mr Zhang's films personify one's eagerness for liberation and represents China's quest for collective liberation that is promised but has never really been actualised.

It has been unanimously conceded that Mr Zhang's approach in visual imagery enlarges the dimension of the politics of the Chinese individual and his identity. However, he claims his work documents a being's desire, not the country and its people. For whatever this legacy he has left behind, he is credited for weaving themes that are fraught with notions of reality, dreams and nightmares into his movies.

Birth date 14 November 1951
Hometown Xi'an city, Shaanxi Province

"In real life, she is the hidden dragon."

Crouching Tiger, Hidden Dragon director Ang Lee, on Zhang Ziyi

Zhang Ziyi
"Icon of stardom"

Profession　　　Movie actress

Born in Beijing, Zhang Ziyi is the daughter of an economist father and a kindergarten teacher. The now 25-year-old actress was originally interested in dance and gymnastics.

For four years, she trained in dancing when she signed up with a secondary school affiliated with Beijing Dancing College in 1991. She picked up a few awards, including one at National Young Dancer competition. By the time she was 15, she believed that a dance career would not hold much prospects for her and she decided to take up acting instead.

She enrolled with the Central Drama Academy in Beijing, where she received acting lessons. Ms Zhang was later talent-scouted for a shampoo commercial which was directed by a "Fifth Generation" director Zhang Yimou. Finding her screen demeanour perfect for the lead character in the *The Road Home* (*Wo de fuqin muqin* literally translated as My Parents), she was eventually cast as a young rural schoolgirl who fell in love with a school teacher in the movie released in 1999.

When *The Road Home* opened in China, Ms Zhang was nicknamed by the media as "Little Gong Li" in reference to the acclaimed Chinese actress, Gong Li, who also shot to stardom owing to director Zhang Yimou. *The Road Home* went on to clinch the Jury Grand Prix Silver Bear at the 2000 Berlin Film Festival.

Ms Zhang's performance in *The Road Home* impressed Taiwanese director Ang Lee immensely. When he began casting actors for his epic martial-arts film, *Crouching Tiger, Hidden Dragon* (*Wo hu cang long*), he knew she would be ideal for the role. The film went on to sweep the Oscar nominations, eventually picking up best foreign language film, as well as best director at the Golden Globes, and emerged the highest grossing foreign-language film ever released in America.

Her role garnered her the Toronto Film Critics Association Award for best supporting actress in 2000 as well as the MTV Movie Award for best fight scene in 2001. She was also picked as one of *People* magazine's 50 Most Beautiful People in the World 2001.

Hong Kong superstar Jackie Chan's *Rush Hour 2* marked her foray into the Hollywood movie blockbuster scene where she played a sexy villain.

She next played the role of Princess Bu Yong in an epic Korean period film *The Warriors* (Musa) by director Kim Sung-soo, *The Legend Of Zu*, a science fiction flick and another Zhang Yimou film *Hero*, co-starring kung-fu superstar Jet Li. She is set to star in her next movie, 2046, directed by Hong Kong director, Wong Kar-Wai.

Ms Zhang has expressed a slight bewilderment at her numerous action roles as she had not planned to venture in this direction. She is currently on a lookout for other serious dramatic roles. On her acting capability, she says, "I am very confident of myself. I give my utmost to the making of movies. To me, it is an honour and brings about a sense of achievement. If I can still be remembered 10 years later for a role in a particular movie, it means I have found my worth."

Ms Zhang later set an unprecedented record for the industry by demanding RMB 10 million (US$1.2 million) for any role in commercial advertisements in year 2000.

Birth date 9 February 1979
Hometown Beijing

Filmography

Year	Starring	Movie
2004	Jet Li, Zhang Ziyi, Tony Leung Chiu-Wai, Donnie Yen, Chen Dao Ming	Hero
2003	Jet Li, Sunny Deol, Preity Zinta, Zhang Ziyi, Priyanka Chopra	The Hero
2001	Zhang Ziyi	Musa: The Warrior
2001	Ekin Cheng, Louis Koo, Cecilia Cheung, Kelly Lin, Sammo Hung, Jacky Wu, Zhang Ziyi	The Legend of Zu
2001	Jackie Chan, Chris Tucker, John Lone, Zhang Ziyi, Roselyn Sanchez	Rush Hour 2
2000	Michelle Yeoh, Zhang Ziyi, Chang Chen, Chow Yun-Fat, Sihung Lung	Crouching Tiger, Hidden Dragon
1999	Zhang Ziyi, Sun Honglei, Zheng Hao, Zhao Yuelin, Li Bin	The Road Home

"I can't wait for people to attack me. I have to attack them."

Yao Ming - on how he didn't hesistate to shoot against the Orlando Magic on a night he scored a career high 37 points, 25 January 2004.

Yao Ming
"Courting fame"

Profession   Professional NBA basketball player, Houston Rockets

Yao Ming was selected in the first round (first overall) by the Houston Rockets of the National Basketball Association (NBA) in the United States in 2002 and became one of the stars of Houston Rockets. One of the most gifted players ever to join the NBA, Yao Ming has quickly made a name as one of the best and most dominant player in China. In the arena of sports, he is certainly the most sought-after and richest Chinese basketball player. He was recently ranked No. 1 on China's Top Celebrity Lists by *Forbes* in February 2004.

Born into a family where both his parents played for the national basketball teams, he has been encouraged to play the sport since he was little. At age 20, Yao started his professional career in Shanghai and became the dominant player in the Shanghai Sharks during the 2000-2001 China Basketball Association (CBA) season. Towering well above two metres in height, he was named the season's Most Valued Player (MVP). In the 2001-2002 CBA season, Yao Ming led the league in blocked shots (4.8 bpg), and ranked second in scoring (32.4 ppg) and rebounding (19.0 rpg). He was even more outstanding in the championship series, where he led the Sharks to a 3-1, earning Shanghai's first CBA championship.

When Yao Ming was selected in the first round by the Houston Rockets in the summer of 2002, he became the only foreigner to take home the first place overall draft in NBA history. Scouting reports note Yao Ming's agility and quickness for a player of his height. Possessing a soft shooting touch and a shooting range up to 15 feet, Yao Ming has improved his free throw shooting accuracy to above 75% and was selected as the first choice of the West Team in the NBA All Star in 2002-2003 and 2003-2004 seasons.

Spurred by a pure love for basketball, Yao Ming revels in his career of choice. The sport to him is a hobby and a profession he is completely devoted to. He contemplates, "Fame is a real big headache for me. I only want to play basketball, play it well and be happy about it. But with fame, comes a lot of expectations." Yao stated on his goal when he came to the NBA, "The idea when I came here to America was to fit and to play basketball at the highest level in the NBA. I am not comfortable being a symbol."

Yao Ming's prominence as one of the century's greatest players has been further entrenched with the world's largest fast food company, MacDonalds, signing him on as their global spokesman. The contract was signed in February 2004.

Birth date	12 September 1980
Hometown	Shanghai
Education	Shanghai Sports College
Past Team	Shanghai Sharks
NBA Team	Houston Rockets
NBA Position	Centre

OTHER INFLUENTIAL PEOPLE WHO'S WHO IN CHINA

Awards / Achievements

- Chinese Under 22 National Team, 1997
- World Championships Under 22, 1997
- Chinese Junior National Team, 1998- 1999
- Asian Junior Championships MVP, 1998
- Asian Championships 1999 (Champion), 2001 (Champion), 2002 (Champion)
- Asian Championships Winner, 1999 (12.3ppg, 6.7rpg), 2002
- World Championships for Juniors, 1999
- Chinese National Team, 1999- 2002
- Chinese League Finalist, 2000 - 2001
- Olympic Games (Sydney), 2000
- Chinese CBA All-Star Game, 2001- 2002
- Chinese CBA MVP, 2001
- CBA All-Playoff Team, 2001
- East Asia Games in Japan (Finalist), 2001
- Asian Championships MVP and Best Rebounder, 2001
- Chinese University National Team, 2001
- World University Games in Benjin (CHN) (Finalist), 2001
- Asian ABA 2001 Club Championships Tournament, 2001
- Chinese CBA Champion, 2002
- World Championships in Indianapolis (USA), 2002
- World Championships All-Star Team, 2002
- All-Asian Championships 1st Team, 2002
- Rookie of the Month, NBA, December 2002

Yang Liwei
"China's spaceflight hero"

Profession   Astronaut

 "Make peaceful use of the outer space to benefit all mankind."
Mr Yang Liwei's first words in space

Yang Liwei, a lieutenant colonel of China Air Force, is China's first astronaut to pilot a spacecraft. He was written into history books on 15 October 2003 when Yang piloted China's first successful manned spacecraft, Shenzhou 5, into outer space.

Born in Suizhong County of northeast China's Liaoning Province, Yang had always dreamt of flying during his childhood. When he was completing his secondary education at the Huanzhong County's Number 2 Secondary School, the Armed Forces visited the school to search for potential pilot trainees. Yang was one of the final shortlisted candidates. Due to his outstanding physical abilities, Yang was selected into the Air Force.

In September 1983 when he was only 18, Yang joined the Chinese People's Liberation Army (PLA). In the same year, Yang entered the Number 8 Aviation College of the PLA Air Force and became an Air Force pilot. Mr Yang graduated in 1987 with the equivalent of a bachelor degree. He became a fighter pilot, accumulating 1,350 flight-hours by the time of his first spaceflight in 2003.

In January 1998, Mr Yang came closer to his flying dream when he was selected as a member of the group of Chinese astronauts set to train to fly the "Project 921" (later renamed to "Shenzhou") spacecraft. He was one of 14 chosen from among 1,500 pilot candidates. The team underwent five years of vigorous physical, psychological and technical training at the Astronaut Training Base in Beijing.

"The study was much more difficult than that in college. The astronauts also had to learn survival skills under extreme conditions in case their capsule made an emergency landing anywhere on earth, land or sea." Yang revealed.

On 20 September 2003, the 14 shortlisted astronauts started training in the real Shenzhou 5 spacecraft at the Jiuquan Launch Centre. Yang was finally selected in October 2003 as one of three finalists to be China's first astronaut. It was estimated that the budget for the space program totals at least US$1 billion.

Yang's father was a senior economist with an agriculture company in Huanzhong County. His mother was a school teacher. Both in their seventies, Mr Yang's parents live with their other son and daughter in the city of Huludao, Liaoning Province. Yang's wife, Zhang Yumei, also serves in China's space program. They have an eight-year-old son.

Birth date	1965
Hometown	Suizhong County, Liaoning Province
Education	Bachelor degree, No. 8 Aviation College of the PLA

Background

1983-1987	Joined the PLA and studied at the No. 8 Aviation College of the PLA Air Force
1987-1998	Became a fighter pilot of PLA Air Force
1998-2003	Selected and trained to fly the "Project 921" (later renamed to "Shenzhou") spacecraft
2003-	Selected to become China's first astronaut

Other information

Mr Yang has an older sister and a younger brother. He is married with one son.

Key historic events in China 1900-2004

Year	Events
1911	Wuchang uprising and the Qing dynasty was overthrown
1912	Republic of China was formed in Nanjing with Sun Yat-Sen as President
1912	Kuomintang (Nationalist Party or KMT) founded
1915	Yuan Shikai abolished the national and provincial assemblies and declared himself emperor
1916	Yuan Shikai died
	China thrown into the era of the "warlords" and China was ruled and ravaged by shifting coalitions of competing provincial military leaders
1921	Communist Party of China (CPC) founded
1925	Sun Yat-Sen died
	Chiang Kai-shek seized control of the Kuomintang
1934	CPC forces embarked on the Long March
	Mao Zedong became leader of CPC
1937	Japan invaded China and the Sino-Japanese War broke out
1945	Japan was defeated and the Sino-Japanese War ended
1949	CPC occupied most of the country and Chiang Kai-shek fled to Taiwan
1949	People's Republic of China (PRC) founded
1953	PRC's First 5-year Plan
1954	PRC's first comprehensive Constitution came into effect
1966	The beginning of the Cultural Revolution
1971	PRC was recognised by United Nations as the "only lawful representative of China" to sit in the Security Council
1976	Mao Zedong died
	Cultural revolution ended
1979	Deng Xiaoping became leader of CPC
	PRC-USA Joint Communique on the establishment of diplomatic relations formed
	Economic reforms and China's open door economic policy started
1980	Shenzhen, Zhuhai, Shantou, and Xiamen became China's first four economic special zones
1984	14 more coastal cities were opened to foreign investments
1989	Tiananmen Square incident
	Jiang Zemin appointed the leader of CPC
1990	China's first stock exchange was set up in Shanghai
1992	Market economy introduced
1997	Deng Xiaoping died
	Handover of Hong Kong to China
1999	Handover of Macau to China
2001	China's WTO accession
2002	Hu Jintao became leader of CPC
2003	SARS outbreak
2004	Constitution amended to promote private property rights

sina 新浪
一切由你开始

每个你都如此重要！
一切由你开始